~ The Invention of Argentina ~

The Invention of Argentina

of

Argentina

Nicolas Shumway

University of California Press

Berkeley • Los Angeles • London

University of California Press
Berkeley and Los Angeles, California

University of California Press
London, England

Copyright © 1991 by The Regents of the University of
California
First Paperback Printing 1993

Library of Congress Cataloging-in-Publication Data

Shumway, Nicolas.
    The invention of Argentina / Nicolas Shumway.
      p.   cm.
    Includes bibliographical references and index.
    ISBN 0-520-08284-2
      1. Argentina—History—19th century.   2. Argentina—
Intellectual life—19th century.   3. Intellectuals—
Argentina—Attitudes.   4. Nationalism—Argentina—
History—19th century.   I. Title.
F2843.S47   1991
982'.04—dc20   90-24574
                                        CIP

Printed in the United States of America

1 2 3 4 5 6 7 8 9

The paper used in this publication meets the minimum
requirements of American National Standard for Information
Sciences—Permanence of Paper for Printed Library
Materials, ANSI Z39.48-1984 ∞

To the memory of my father
James Carroll Shumway

Contents

Preface

Borges argues that books write themselves, that however much writers try to choose their subjects, the subject itself eventually dictates its own expression. While in no way equating myself with Borges, I sense that this book's writing confirms his point. Originally, I planned to write an intellectual history of the fifteen-year span bracketed by the coup of 1930—Argentina's first in this century—and the triumph of Juan Domingo Perón in 1945. My goal was to reconstruct the intellectual currents that anticipated Peronism and explain to some degree the extraordinary polarization that has gripped Argentina ever since. I dutifully read nationalists like the Irazusta brothers, Hugo Wast, Carlos Ibarguren, Ramón Doll, and Monsignor Franceschi; populists like Arturo Jauretche and Raúl Scalabrini Ortiz; liberals and cosmopolitans like Eduardo Mallea, Ezequiel Martínez Estrada, Jorge Luis Borges, and Victoria Ocampo. I was particularly interested in how the fierce disagreements among Argentine intellectuals stemmed from radically different concepts of what the Argentine nation was all about: its history, its nature, its role among other nations of the world. But when I began writing, I found that what appeared new in the 1930s was often repeating, reworking, or at least conversing with Argentine thought of earlier times, so much so that my footnotes seemed to grow faster than my text. I eventually bowed to the inevitable and wrote this book—about nineteenth-century Argentina. While I make occasional reference to more recent Argentine thought, the other book, the one specifically about modern Argentina, will have to wait. I console myself thinking that the book I failed to complete might now write itself more easily using this one as a point of departure.

Argentina is widely perceived as a national failure, one of the few countries that has moved from first-world to third-world status in only a few short decades. As recently as the 1920s, no one would have considered Argentina underdeveloped. With an apparently stable government, a highly literate populace, and unequaled prosperity relative to other Latin American nations, Argentina was perceived as one of the world's successful new democracies, equal in many ways to Australia, Canada, and the United States. Yet, despite this early promise, during the last fifty years Argentina has moved from crisis to crisis, sinking into deeper depths of economic turmoil, social disruption, political chaos, militarism, debt, and governmental irresponsibility. Of course there have been bright, hopeful moments, when courageous, committed Argentines have rallied to restore the prosperity and stability of the early twentieth century. But without exception, social unrest, class resentment, and economic uncertainty have thwarted the best plans wrought by the country's brightest people.

What happened? Why is it that a nation blessed with enviable human and natural resources finds it so difficult to reverse this slow and melancholy decline into pettiness and inconsequence? The explanations are numerous, contradictory, incomplete: colonial economic structures, an irresponsible upper class, messianic demagogues like Perón, a reactionary Catholic hierarchy, power-hungry generals, authoritarian traditions, the Communist conspiracy, omnipotent multinationals, meddlesome imperial powers such as Great Britain and the United States.

This book considers another factor in the Argentine equation which is often overlooked in economic, social, and political histories: the peculiarly divisive mind-set created by the country's nineteenth-century intellectuals who first framed the idea of Argentina. This ideological legacy is in some sense a mythology of exclusion rather than a unifying national ideal, a recipe for divisiveness rather than consential pluralism. This failure to create an ideological framework for union helped produce what novelist Ernesto Sábato has called "a society of opposers" as interested in humiliating each other as in developing a viable nation united through consensus and compromise. Although this explanation of Argentina's problems is only one more factor in the complex equation known as Argentina, it deserves analysis and documentation. To this end, this book.

I approach the study of nineteenth-century Argentina's "mythology of exclusion" by breaking it into component parts that I call "guiding fictions." The guiding fictions of nations cannot be proven, and indeed are often fabrications as artificial as literary fictions. Yet they are necessary to give individuals a sense of nation, peoplehood, collective identity, and national purpose. As Edmund S. Morgan argues in his masterful book *Inventing the People:*

The success of government . . . requires the acceptance of fictions, requires the willing suspension of disbelief, requires us to believe that the emperor is clothed even though we can see that he is not. Government requires make-believe. Make believe that the king is divine, make believe that he can do no wrong or make believe that the voice of the people is the voice of God. Make believe that the people *have* a voice or make believe that the representatives of the people *are* the people. Make believe that all men are equal or make believe that they are not. (Morgan, *Inventing the People* 13)

One such fiction that Morgan analyzes at length is the notion of representation. He points out that the federal system of the United States as enshrined in the three branches of government is not in any complete sense "government of the people, by the people and for the people." Rather, evidence suggests that the U.S. government is at best government by competing special interests (including the government itself and its several agencies) who represent no one but themselves. Yet the *guiding fiction* of representative government is both necessary and positive: necessary because the belief that the government represents our interests impels U.S. citizens to consent to state rule with minimal coercion; positive because, through attempts to make reality resemble the guiding fiction of representation, reform is most frequently undertaken (Morgan 14). Other guiding fictions underpinning the United States' sense of national purpose and peoplehood might include *manifest destiny, melting pot,* and *American way of life,* which, although not encoded in official documents, have been just as important as "government for the people, by the people and for the people" in establishing America's collective sense of self, purpose, and community.

This book studies Argentina's early guiding fictions as they emerge in the country's most important writers and thinkers between 1808 and 1880. The cutoff date of 1880 will probably raise eyebrows among those familiar with Argentine history since that year is usually seen as the beginning of the modern Argentine nation, a watershed year separating a period of civil strife, warlordism, and chaos from a period of relative stability, unprecedented growth, and material progress. While it is undeniable that the economic, social, and political achievements of Argentina after 1880 dwarf those of any previous period, I nonetheless believe that the country's guiding fictions and rhetorical paradigms were founded well before 1880, and that these fictions continue to shape and inform the country's actions and concept of self.

Four other methodological considerations deserve mention. First, despite forays into social history, I have kept ideas relevant to the creation of a national self and their interaction with history at the center of discussion. Consequently, certain people may seem more admirable than others simply because their ideas were better. For example, two major thinkers we will study are Domingo Faustino Sarmiento and Juan Bautista Alberdi. Of the two, Sarmiento was certainly the better public servant, particularly in his zealous promotion of public education. As a thinker, however, Sarmiento left a peculiarly divisive ideological legacy, perhaps his least fortunate contribution to the country. In contrast, although Alberdi preferred comment to action and generally refused to dirty his hands with everyday public life, his ideas constantly surprise us with their originality, prescience, and continuing relevance. As a result, in a purely social history Sarmiento would probably appear the better man; here, Alberdi takes the prize.

Second, although the book deals with ideas in nineteenth-century Argentina, it is not a survey of Argentine intellectual history, nor does it examine extensively European antecedents of Argentine thought. Rather, it is a study of Argentina's sense of self as it emerged in the last century.

Third, although I sense that the mind-set and peculiarly Argentine *mentalité* of the last century color to some degree virtually every conversation modern Argentines have about themselves and their country, a detailed analysis of contemporary Argentine thought lies outside the purview of this book.

And finally, since Argentines certainly do not need foreigners to tell them about the history of their country, I have written primarily for an English-speaking audience with little specialized knowledge of Argentina. This choice of audience has prompted the translation of all quotations into English as well as the inclusion of biographical and historical sketches that provide a necessary, albeit schematic, framework for the book's central concerns. Unless otherwise noted, all translations are mine.

The book is organized in the following fashion. Chapter 1 briefly discusses Argentina's colonial heritage and the area's first uncertain steps toward independence. Readers already familiar with Argentine history may prefer starting with Chapter 2, which is devoted to the writings and legacy of Mariano Moreno, the most significant thinker of the Independence period. Chapter 3 studies the work of two early populists, José Artigas, the Uruguayan Independence hero, and Bartolomé Hidalgo, creator of gauchesque literature, a uniquely Argentine and Uruguayan literature whose characters are fashioned after the nomadic country-dwellers of the River Plate pampas. Chapter 4 looks at the blueprint republic of Bernardino Rivadavia which rose and fell in the 1820s. Chapters 5 and 6 are dedicated to the Generation of 1837, a group of writers who polemicized against the popular dictator, Juan Manuel de Rosas, and in the process became the most brilliant generation of intellectuals Argentina has ever produced. Chapter 7 studies a far-ranging debate during the 1850s between Juan Bautista Alberdi and Domingo Faustino Sarmiento, two of the Generation of 1837's most distinguished members whose unified opposition to Rosas quickly dissolved in bitter enmity following Rosas's fall. Chapter 8 discusses the early histories of Bartolomé Mitre, a military general, writer, historian, and politician who contributed greatly to the country's guiding fictions through laying the foundations for an official history. Chapters 9 and 10 study the flowering of a kind of intellectual populism that seriously challenged previously established guiding fictions, thus providing an alternative intellectual tradition to that of the governing elite.

I owe much to many people who have contributed to this book: the editors Scott Mahler, Stanley Holwitz, and Cathy Hertz of the

University of California Press; to Aníbal Sánchez Reulet, who first piqued my interest in Argentina; to colleagues like Sylvia Molloy and Carlos Rosencrantz, who read the entire manuscript and provided invaluable insight; to Leslie Moore, who taught me a great deal about English prose; to historians David Rock and Tulio Halperín Donghi, who contributed many useful comments; to close friends like Robert Mayott and Peter Hawkins, who encouraged me throughout; to Roberto González Echevarría, who goaded me toward finishing the manuscript, partly to avenge his increasing losses in squash; to Yale for allowing me leave time; to the personnel at Sterling Memorial Library, the Biblioteca Nacional Argentina, the Archivo de la Nación in Buenos Aires, and the Biblioteca Pública de La Plata; to countless Argentine friends—Daniel Larriqueta, Héctor Schmerkin, Francisco López Bustos, Josefina Ludmer, Enrique Pezzoni, María Luisa Bastos, Rafael Freda, Ernesto Schóo, Rodolfo Zebrini—who even yet indulge my interest for their country; and finally, to my late father, James Carroll Shumway, to whose memory the book is dedicated.

Chapter One

Prelude to Nationhood

Argentina's path to nationhood begins with Spanish conquest and
colonization. To trace this path, I begin by looking at problems in
nation formation throughout the American continent. Later, I examine specific elements of Argentina's prenational experience as they
set the stage for subsequent developments.

During the late eighteenth to early nineteenth century, no concept engaged the European mind more than the idea of nationhood. With the waning of the Enlightenment and the advent of
Romanticism, notions of universal brotherhood gave way to an up-
surge of nationalist sentiment in which each country affirmed its
ethnic, linguistic, and mythical uniqueness. Folk traditions, peasant life, religious festivals, national histories and heroes, ethnic
idiosyncracies, tribal mythologies, and country landscapes soon per-
meated all the arts, from the historical novels of Sir Walter Scott
and Alexandre Dumas; to the music of Dvorak, Wagner, and
Tchaikovsky; to the paintings of Goya, Turner, and David; to the
poetry of Schiller, Burns, and Becquer. National mythologies were
resurrected when available, created when not, and spread with
evangelical zeal, all with the effect of building a sense of national
belongingness and destiny; these mythologies became the guiding
fictions of nations, guiding fictions that encouraged the French to
feel French; the English, English; and the Germans, German.
When politicians sought to unite people under a common banner
or to legitimate a particular government, appeals to the guiding
fictions of preexisting peoplehood and national destiny proved enor-

2 *Prelude to Nationhood*

mously useful; indeed, without them, the work of men like Bismarck, Gladstone, and Cavour toward national consolidation would have been more difficult and perhaps impossible.

Although a new country, the United States from the outset also had its guiding fictions, particularly in the Puritan dream of establishing a New Jerusalem in the American wilderness. As Ralph Perry, Sacvan Bercovitch, and others have shown, the name of their dream was "America," a name, although intended for an entire continent, which the Puritans took for their own. Even now, common usage the world over employs the names *America* and *Americans* as synonyms for the United States and its citizens, a practice that ignores the fact that all inhabitants of the Western Hemisphere are also Americans living in America. The Puritans defined themselves from the beginning as a nation apart, divinely chosen to exemplary righteousness and prosperity. They viewed themselves as modern Israelites called by God to occupy a promised land; more than a social goal, their work was a holy errand to establish Zion in the New World and be a light unto the iniquitous nations of the Old. The Puritan dream proved a highly adaptable guiding fiction that subsequent generations of Americans transformed into concepts such as manifest destiny and protector of the free world as well as the notion that the United States, more than other nations, should aspire to a higher standard of morality, a standard still invoked by people as diverse as moral majoritarians and civil rights leaders.

Among the Spanish American countries, such guiding fictions for individual nations were harder to come by. Whereas in Europe and to some degree in the United States, myths of peoplehood on which nations could be built were available before the nations themselves were formed, in Spanish America, civil strife following Independence forced nations to emerge in areas that had no guiding fictions for autonomous nationhood. The process of concept preceding political reality found in the United States and much of Europe was in large measure reversed; guiding fictions of national destiny had to be improvised after political independence was already a fact. The Spanish colonies were carefully designed to extend the Spanish Empire, to be culturally, economically, and politically dependent on their mother country. They were not intended to develop a unique and independent sense of nationhood, but to be extensions of Spain, unquestioning in political loyalty, religious faith, and taxes. Moreover, few, if any, of the Spanish American colonists dreamed of a destiny other than that assigned by Spain.

To ensure Spain's hegemony over her American possessions, the Spanish colonies were governed for nearly 300 years by a highly centralized, albeit cumbersome, bureaucracy in which all important political and ecclesiastical positions were held by appointees from the mother country. Although the colonists and their descendants, known as *Creoles* (*criollos*), often disregarded political decrees from above, they seldom questioned the authority of the crown and its appointees on ideological grounds. Their attitude toward the monarchy is well described in the contradictory slogan, *Obedezco mas no cumplo*, "I obey but do not comply," which might also be freely rendered as "I recognize the crown's authority, but on a given issue will do whatever I want." Thus the Creoles could and often did act independently of imperial decrees, but theirs was the liberty of tolerated disobedience in a loosely administered society; it was not the liberty of embryonic nations yearning for independence from the Spanish monarchy.

Because of the rigid social, political, and ideological ties between Spain and her New World colonies, ideas of national uniqueness in Spanish America do not begin emerging until the last years of the eighteenth century, just prior to the independence movements of 1810–1826. Although toponyms like Mexico, Peru, and Chile date from the first years of the conquest, such terms before Independence never connoted a unique national destiny and eventual autonomy as was the case with "America" in the United States. Further, since the independence movement in Spanish America stemmed in large measure from the political collapse of the Spanish monarchy and Napoleon's invasion of the Iberian peninsula in 1808, separation from Spain was in a sense imposed by events from without. Nation formation was further complicated by civil wars in post-Independence Spanish America which eventually broke four viceroyalties into eighteen separate republics. As a result, what had been merely geographic areas of the Spanish Empire suddenly had to understand and define their destiny as autonomous units; they had to create guiding fictions of peoplehood and nationness in order to approach the ideological consensus that underlay stable societies in other parts of the world. Thus were created new countries with new boundaries and freshly minted names like Venezuela, Guatemala, Colombia, Bolivia, and Argentina; no one in those areas a century or even a half-century before Independence dreamed that some day they would be new and distinct nations set apart by a unique destiny. Moreover, in none of those areas did a ready-made myth of national identity unite their inhabitants under a common ideology.

Yet, despite the administrative centralization and the lack of pre-Independence national ideologies, individual areas in Spanish America developed, on a popular level at least, a cultural uniqueness that the ruling classes before and after Independence often failed to appreciate. The Spaniards' goals of cultural and political uniformity were undermined to a remarkable degree by the mysterious, brazenly different, endlessly varied world they dared claim as theirs. From the day Columbus first attempted to understand and describe his discoveries and experiences, the unfamiliar lands interjected themselves into his consciousness and discourse, leaving him transformed and in a sense conquered. He and the conquistadors, missionaries, and settlers who followed him inevitably became partial products of the New World. Nature was the first intrusion into Spain's dream of replicating herself in America. The natural forces of exotic landscapes, tangled jungles, formidable mountains, vast pampas, untold natural wealth, and strange wildlife affected the course of conquest and settlement just as surely as any preconceived notion of empire building.

An even more important intrusion than the land in the Spanish dream of self-replication came from the native Americans, particularly the advanced Indian civilizations of Mexico and Peru. Cultural and sexual intermingling between conquerors and native Americans soon created regional cultural identities distinct from Spain as well as from one another. This blending of native and European cultures was encouraged by the Catholic missionaries, who, rather than totally destroying Indian religion, often tried to transform it by assigning Christian meanings to traditional religious symbols and celebrations—a practice motivated in part by the belief among some missionaries that the Indians were degenerate descendants of the lost tribes of Israel. Because of this cultural mixing, the Creoles soon developed a prenational cultural uniqueness reflected in food, music, dress, dialect, folk traditions, and religious festivals that varied from region to region. Further, given the varying degrees of miscegenation among Spaniards, Africans, and different groups of Indians, each area of the Spanish Empire produced a peculiar racial mix and phenotype, so much so that early in the colonial period Caribbeans were distinguishable from Meso-Americans, and Andeans from inhabitants of the Southern Cone. Even the ruling classes, despite their stubborn claims to racial purity, were more often than not products of some racial blending. *White* and *European* became relative terms, better for maintaining power and keeping family secrets than for describing factual genetic heritage.

With rigid government control on the one hand and fecund popular culture on the other, national, or at least regional, awareness among the Creoles developed in two contrary directions. The ruling classes were groomed in an atmosphere where success and refinement were marked by parroting attitudes received from Spain, in being more Spanish than the Spanish. As a result, high culture in colonial times was in large measure imitative and sterile—with, of course, notable exceptions such as the seventeenth-century Mexican poet Sor Juana Inés de la Cruz. Even after separating from Spain, the Spanish American elite would remain more attuned to the latest fads from Europe than to the popular culture that was uniquely theirs, and regional distinctiveness that could have formed the basis for national identity went largely ignored. With few exceptions, it was not until the twentieth century that Spanish American intellectuals began considering the guiding fictions of national identity, peoplehood, and destiny in terms of their own popular culture.

Where government by the intellectual and citified elite failed, the common people produced their own inchoate systems of government. Region by region among the lower classes, there developed enduring folk traditions, vague but powerful sentiments of class and ethnic solidarity, popular religion and prenational mythologies which created throughout Spanish America a strong sense of peoplehood and localness, or *localismo*. The political reflection of localism was government by a charismatic individual, or *caudillo*, rather than an institution, who somehow embodies cultural folk values. In personalist government, the caudillo becomes a visible symbol of authority and protection who on a smaller scale is not unlike the patriarchal symbols of king and priest with which the popular masses were already familiar. In a choice between abstract theories of government and the caudillo, the masses felt more comfortable with their caudillos, who, however primitive and ruthless their methods, were more sensitive to the fears and desires of the rural masses than the centralist elite. As a result, in the figure of the caudillo, *localism* combined with *personalism*. These two impulses would bedevil elitist approaches to government for decades to come. Indeed, much of the civil strife following Independence can be directly traced to conflicts between localist caudillos and the grand, utopian dreams of the city-dwelling elite.

Because of this unusual disjuncture between derivative high culture and luxuriant, albeit chaotic, popular culture, the Spanish American colonies came to the independence movement of 1810 ideologically ill-prepared for the task of nation-building. The more utopian thinkers of the continent dreamed grandly of establishing a Pan-American state that would encompass the entire continent. More practical people like Simón Bolívar hoped for four or five sizable countries based roughly on the boundaries of the Spanish viceroyalties, as he indicates in his celebrated "Letter to a Jamaican Gentleman" (Bolívar *Obras completas* 1:159–175). Such dreams, however, never materialized: no sooner had the Spanish been defeated than civil wars broke out among the Creoles themselves. Strife among contentious factions in the elite, among rival caudillos, and between opposing provinces engulfed the continent, making institutional government impossible. With no central power, the caudillos were often the only source of order in the embryonic nations, perhaps because their authoritarian, personalist rule embodied folk values while reflecting in miniature the king-centered government of colonial times. But few of the caudillos conceived of nation-building on a grand scale. As a result, Spanish America became increasingly fragmented along both regional and social boundaries. Some of these divisions became permanent: Uruguay and Paraguay separated from Argentina, and what logically would have been one country in Central America became seven. The bickering and threat of anarchy produced a situation in which only strongmen with private armies appeared able to survive. Shortly before dying, Simón Bolívar viewed the mayhem around him and lamented, "We have ploughed the sea."

Faced with the failure of Pan-Americanist visions and the likely possibility of even more splintering, Spanish American thinkers of the mid-nineteenth century devoted much attention to understanding why the first post-Independence governments did not succeed and to creating more realistic plans for the future. That is to say, after the bloody chaos that followed the Wars of Independence, intellectuals throughout the continent set about the crucial task of creating guiding fictions, myths of national identity and peoplehood, that could heal broken countries and perhaps reduce the tendency for further fragmentation.

In the case of Argentina, the country's very name reflects the area's development from colony to country, from imperial territory to nation, for the name *Argentina* had a slow, uncertain evolution, not unlike that of the country itself. In 1514, one year after Balboa discovered the Pacific, Juan Díaz de Solís was commissioned by the Spanish crown to search the coast of South America for a river passage connecting the two oceans. A year later, Solís entered the immense estuary separating what is now Argentina and Uruguay, only to be killed by Indians who, feigning friendship, wooed him and some of his crew to shore. Later explorers, believing that the estuary led to the silver-rich areas of Upper Peru, now Bolivia, renamed it the River of Silver, "El Río de la Plata." From the Spanish word *plata*, meaning silver, comes the English corruption, the River Plate. The name *Argentina* preserves the association with silver in that it derives from *argentum*, the Latin term for silver (Rosenblat, *Argentina, historia de un nombre* 13–18). Popularized in a 1602 poem by Martín del Barco Centenera, the term *Argentina* became an obligatory substitute for *rioplatense* in poetic usage, and acquired a permanent place in patriotic occasional verse in the neoclassic poetry of Vicente López y Planes, famous for his 1807 "El Triunfo Argentino," a celebration of Buenos Aires' victory over a British invasion. Later, in his "Himno Nacional Argentino," the term received some official standing, although it was not until the constitution of 1826, sixteen years after the country rebelled against Spain, that "República Argentina" actually became the official name of the nation (Rosenblat 50–51).

The late emergence of the country's name derives from a simple fact: until Independence, the Argentine was merely an area of the

Spanish Empire, neither a country nor even an idea for a country. Moreover, the Spaniards for 250 years saw no reason to define any of the Southern Cone as a separate political entity, partly because they failed to recognize the area's potential as an autonomous unit. Unlike mineral-rich Mexico and Peru, where the Spaniards built prosperous viceroyalties on the foundations of highly developed Indian civilizations, the Argentine possessed neither gold nor silver, and its mostly nomadic natives preferred exile or death to the virtual serfdom of the Spanish *encomienda*, a neat arrangement by which Indians were forced to work for Spaniards in exchange for European civilization, Christianity, and "protection." The Spanish also failed to appreciate Argentina's greatest resource, the vast pampas that arguably constitute the richest agricultural area in the world. Indeed, had it not been for the Spanish drive to rule and Catholicize the entire continent, much of Argentina might have been forgotten altogether. The term *Argentina*, then, labels a paradox: the country was named for silver, a mineral it did not have while what it had in rich abundance—a huge agricultural potential—passed unrecognized for nearly three centuries.

Given Argentina's perceived lack of promise, early Spanish colonization in the Southern Cone was predictably sporadic and weak. Muddy settlements grew along trade routes established for the transport and refining of Bolivian silver. Since Argentine Indians were less sedentary than those of Mexico and Peru, the colonial pattern of building on preexisting civilizations broke down in most of Argentina. The area produced some tradable goods—livestock, raw cotton, and grain—which were exchanged for imports from Spain, mostly household items, clothing, and weapons. Labor was provided by Indians and a few African slaves bought from the Portuguese. Buenos Aires grew more slowly than did other colonial towns, partly because of a chronic shortage of labor and the distance separating the port settlement from the colonial economic centers in Upper Peru. The distance, however, helped give Buenos Aires a special character in that a large portion of its population was not Spanish but Portuguese (Rock, *Argentina* 4–6, 23–28). Until 1776 the monarchy insisted that Lima, the headquarters of the Viceroyalty of Peru, be the political and economic center of the entire area. Even trade routes between Spain and Buenos Aires had to pass through Lima, following a circuitous path that led over mud-obstructed trails from Buenos Aires through the Andes to Lima to ports on the northern coast of South America and eventually to Spain. The obvious possibility of establishing ports along the Argentine coast was unacceptable to the Spanish and their Buenos Aires intermediaries who were solely interested in maintaining their mercantilist monopoly. Contact between Spain and the colonies was further restricted by the crown's decision to limit trade voyages to the New World to two per year, a choice prompted by the need to ship colonial goods in large armed convoys, or *flotas*, as a defense against raiders like Sir Francis Drake (Gibson, *Spain in America* 102). Funneling everything through Lima was also viewed by Spain's Counter-Reformation hierarchy as a way of limiting the spread of heretical ideas to the colonies.

The commercial potential of Buenos Aires, however, was not lost on traders and smugglers, primarily British and Dutch, who regularly violated Spanish mercantilist law by establishing business contacts with the *porteños*, as people of the port city of Buenos Aires became known. As Germán and Alicia Tjarks have shown, by the late eighteenth century, porteño merchants were selling Bolivian silver, salted meat, cowhide, and handicrafts to non-Spanish traders, making a healthy profit for themselves while evading royal export taxes. Buenos Aires also became an important center of the slave trade as the Portuguese brought in Africans in increasing numbers to meet the labor needs of the growing economy (Rock, *Argentina* 40–49). Because of these contacts, Buenos Aires prospered during the late 1700s and soon took on a European flavor that both titillated and disturbed conservative Spanish appointees and traditionalist Creoles.

Argentina, then, at the end of the colonial period was mostly empty, with an estimated population of some 500,000 in a land as large as the eastern half of the United States. In principle the region was under Spanish rule, but in practice the distances meant little real contact with the Metropolis. In no sense was the area unified by geography, politics, economics, or a particular vision of national destiny. What cities existed were in reality isolated towns and missions connected by poor or nonexistent roads and dreadfully slow land travel. In the west were the small, dusty settlements of Mendoza and San Juan, both in the foothills of the Andes and more closely linked to Chile than to Buenos Aires. To the north were Tucumán, Salta, and Jujuy, culturally closer to the Spanish-Indian cultures of Peru than to the rest of what would later become Argentina. Near the middle was Córdoba, a busy center of political conservatism, scholastic education, and religious fervor. In the northeast were Uruguay and Paraguay, soon to separate from the Argentine. Along the Paraná River, which runs north from the River Plate estuary, in a rich agricultural area commonly called the *Littoral*, were the small settlements of Santa Fe and Paraná. And at the mouth of the great estuary was Buenos Aires, geographically and culturally distant from the rest of Argentina, but destined by its privileged location between the rich pampas and the ocean trade routes to exercise a peculiar hegemony over the interior provinces. Unlike the United States, where easy river travel greatly facilitated contact between coastal and interior cities, Argentine settlements, except those along the Littoral, were connected only by slow overland travel; journeying the some 750 miles between Tucumán and Buenos Aires, for example, took an average of two months. Consequently, Argentine cities and provinces developed in relative isolation, a fact that nourished localist sentiment and loyalties.

Localist sentiment also grew as a result of the colonial political system. Initially, in all of Spanish America there were only two viceroyalties, one headquartered in Mexico City and the other in Lima, Peru. Under each viceroyalty were regional political centers, or *audiencias*, which mediated affairs between the towns and the viceroy. Reporting to the audiencias from each major settlement was the *cabildo*, one of the most enduring political institutions of the colonial period. The cabildos were town councils consisting partially of outside appointees but mostly of *regidores*, or councilors, chosen from native-born or long-term residents deeply rooted in local life. Although Spanish jurists laid out in numbing detail the proper relationships between the crown, the viceroy, the audiencia, and the cabildo, the isolated settlements in the Southern Cone could hardly sustain such organizational complexity. In theory, the cabildos were under the jurisdiction of the audiencia, the viceroy, and eventually the crown; in practice, however, this huge bureaucracy seldom affected the cabildos in outlying areas like the Argentine, and the cabildos became the only real governments, jealously guarding their role as protectors of localist traditions and prerogatives. Since they consisted mainly of wealthy citizens elected by other cabildo members rather than by the general populace, they were not democratic in any strict sense of the term; still, the cabildos undoubtedly understood the concerns of their fellow townspeople to a degree unlikely in an outsider. Moreover, although the cabildos were under the control of the local elites, an old-fashioned noblesse oblige probably made their members more sensitive to the needs of the poor than the dog-eat-dog economics that after Independence would ravish the Argentine interior. Twentieth-century Argentine historians do not agree on the role of the cabildos. "Liberal" historians like José Ingenieros call them "the birthplace of a municipal oligarchical spirit" and the "antithesis" of democracy (Ingenieros, *La evolución de las ideas argentinas* 1:32–33). In contrast, "revisionist" historians, pro-Hispanic nationalists like Julio Irazusta in the main, argue that the cabildos were essentially democratic institutions that predated Enlightenment political theory (Irazusta, *Breve historia* 26–27, 51–54).

Given their localist feelings, the cabildos were early recognized as obstacles to centralized rule. For this reason, during the eighteenth century, the reformist Bourbon kings created an intermediate administrative layer, the *intendencias*, to oversee and limit the power of the cabildos. Again, after the Wars of Independence, the porteño leader, Bernardino Rivadavia, dissolved the cabildos of Buenos Aires and Luján in an attempt to limit local authority. Yet, whether the cabildos existed officially or not, the impulse toward local, autonomist government did not die easily. Without the cabildos, local rule fell into the hands of caudillos, local chieftains and petty dictators who, for all their arbitrariness, enjoyed such loyalty from fellow provincials that Argentine historian José Luis Romero refers to their rule as an "inorganic democracy" (*Las ideas políticas en Argentina* 98–128).

Underpinning the caudillos' rule was another culture, that of the peasants (*campesinos*), or gauchos, which developed in the vast plains and hills separating the settlements of Argentina. The exact nature of Argentina's rural population during colonial times has engendered a raucus, interminable debate between "nationalists" who view the campesinos or gauchos as a repository of authentic Argentine values and "liberals" who see them as untutored masses easily manipulated by demagogues. Both positions (studied in detail in later chapters) overlook the complexity of the rural, lower-

class population. The campesinos consisted of several groups, all
interrelated and all in a state of flux. Some were nomadic, some
were peons in the employ of an estanciero, some were bandits and
smugglers, and many were all of these at one time or another. In its
purest sense, *gaucho* referred to the nomadic, often outlaw inhabitants of the great plains of Argentina, Uruguay, and Brazil. In current usage, *gaucho* usually designates the rural working class in
general.

The gauchos (like the rural population generally) stemmed from
the three ethnic roots: Spanish, Indian, and African. They roamed
freely over the pampas, lived easily off a bountiful land, captured
and rode wild horses, drank abundantly, gambled, smuggled,
robbed, fought, hunted wild cattle, sold cowhide to purchase what
little they needed, ate mostly beef, sang improvised ballads celebrating their heroics and loves, and lived in free unions seldom
consecrated by the sacrament of holy matrimony. In short, they
were superstitious, filthy, unlettered, and happy. While the gauchos left no records of themselves, many colonial chroniclers refer
to them (see Rodríguez Molas, *Historia social del gaucho*, chaps.
1–3). Of these, one of the most entertaining is by Concolorcorvo,
the pseudonym for a Spanish postal inspector, whose description of
the gauchos' "crude and course ways" seems vaguely charged with
envy (Concolorcorvo, "An Unflattering Glimpse of the Gauchos"
57). So attractive were the gauchos' carefree ways that in 1807,
during the British occupation of Buenos Aires, 170 English soldiers
deserted to live among them. Complained General Whitelocke,
"The more the soldiers became acquainted with the plenty the
Country affords and the easy means of acquiring it, the greater . . .
the evil" (cited in Ferns, *Britain and Argentina in the Nineteenth
Century* 57).

Such then was Argentina during the last half of the 1700s: a land
of isolated settlements, autonomist townsmen, nomad gauchos,
relatively docile employees of estancieros, unconquered Indians,
minimal economic and political development—and no sense of national destiny. In this context, the foundations of Argentine nationhood were laid on July 4, 1776, when the Spanish monarch,
Charles III, finally bowed to century-old economic pressures and
created The Viceroyalty of the River Plate with headquarters in
Buenos Aires, which by this time had grown from a swampy settle-

ment lost on the edge of the unending pampas to a city of some 25,000 people and a thriving center of trade—much of it illegal. The throne's primary motive in creating the new viceroyalty was to exert, through a policy ironically named *libre comercio*, or "free trade," greater control on the area's eastward trade, particularly in Bolivian silver bullion that had existed illegally for nearly a half-century. Clever Buenos Aires merchants were quick to establish exclusive contracts with Spanish mercantile monopolies, thus forming the basis for some of Argentina's most enduring private fortunes. In addition to bullion, their primary exports were salted meat and cowhide, a product of prime industrial importance before the discovery of rubber. *Libre comercio* brought relative prosperity to River Plate traders except during periods of disruption provoked by Spain's repeated conflicts with Great Britain (Rock, *Argentina* 66–72).

The new viceroyalty included most of what is now Bolivia, Paraguay, Uruguay, and Argentina, and constituted the first step in establishing a new nation—although no one at the time thought in those terms. The king granted to Buenos Aires the authority to collect customs taxes in the new viceroyalty, a privilege the port city would guard jealously, creating between porteños and provincials the same resentments Buenos Aires had previously felt toward Lima. Distrust of the port city grew as Buenos Aires, reflecting its own localism, increasingly aspired to control the interior. Under the new viceroy, the provincial cabildos were increasingly pressured to follow Buenos Aires, often at the expense of local prerogatives. Moreover, Buenos Aires, through control of customs regulations, interjected itself with growing frequency into the financial affairs of the interior. Faced with Buenos Aires' encroachment on local autonomy and usurpation of profits through the customs tax, provincials came to fear the new hegemony from the porteños; their fears would provide the foundation for nearly fifty years of civil wars beginning soon after the Wars of Independence.

Intellectual life in the new viceroyalty, as in the colonies generally, was severely limited by policy as well as by geographic isolation. In the mostly illiterate society, knowing how to read and write was a marketable skill, so much so that "secretaries" for the caudillos often wielded considerable power. The Church controlled all schools, giving students an authoritarian, scholastic education

that emphasized rote memorization of received truth while attacking or disregarding the empirical and rational epistemologies that
had already caused profound changes in Europe. On an unofficial
level, however, there was more intellectual freedom than popular
notions of Counter-Reformation Catholicism might allow. The
higher officers of the Inquisition did issue edict after edict demand-
ing that incoming books, bookstore stocks, and private libraries be
regularly scrutinized by the Holy Office. Yet, as Irving A. Leonard
reports, the efforts of the inquisitors were frequently honored more
in the breach than in the observance thanks to extensive smuggling
of heretical works, often with the collaboration of lower Inquisition
officials and members of religious communities. Similarly, although
Creole writers were forbidden to write or publish except on noncon-
troversial matters of purely local concern, unapproved editions of
local and foreign works appeared regularly during the colonial period (Leonard, *Baroque Times in Old Mexico* 166–182; *Books of the
Brave* 157–171). After the successful revolutions in the United
States and France, prorevolutionary texts, often written by Spanish
priests, circulated throughout the colonies, despite vigorous attempts at censorship and refutation by conservative clerics (Ruiz-
Guiñazú, *Saavedra* 121–145).

In Argentina intellectual life was even less developed than in
major colonial centers like Mexico City and Lima. In 1776, the year
the new viceroyalty was founded, there were only six primary
schools in Córdoba and four in Buenos Aires, all associated with the
Church. Virtually all women were denied access to schools since
reading and writing were seen in a woman as "items that lead only
to sin or to the temptation to flee from the vigilance of her parents"
(López, *Historia de la República Argentina* 1:243). The two secon-
dary schools in Buenos Aires, El Colegio de San Carlos and El
Colegio del Rey, were staffed mostly by priests limited by both
training and inclination. In the words of Manuel Moreno, who
attended El Colegio de San Carlos in Buenos Aires during the
1780s, the teacher priests all but starved students while imparting
little knowledge worth living. They were, in his words, "intolerant
theologians who spend their time rehashing and defending abstract
questions about the divine nature, angels, etc., while consuming
their lives in discussing opinions of ancient authors who established
extravagant and arbitrary systems about things no one is capable of

knowing." In his view, even those few priests who tried to teach natural sciences were severely limited since "they cannot impart to their disciples what they themselves do not know." He further claims that the monastic teaching orders were much more interested in furthering their material well-being than in educating Creole youngsters (Moreno [Manuel], "Vida," in *Memorias y Autobiografías* 2:16–22).

Despite these limitations on intellectual life, the ideas of the Enlightenment seeped slowly into Argentina. The Bourbon kings, who ruled Spain from 1700 until the Napoleonic invasion in 1808, instituted reforms in Spanish-American society not unlike those of the enlightened despots in France (see Sánchez [Luis], *El pensamiento político*). Foreign thinking in the eighteenth century also influenced a new generation of Spanish rationalists, notably Benito Jerónimo Feijóo, a Benedictine monk, and Gaspar Melchor Jovellanos, a Spanish encyclopedist, whose works were avidly read all through the Hispanic world. In Argentina, the small, literate elite also read Montesquieu, Descartes, Locke, Voltaire, and Rousseau, but as in Spain, enlightened ideas broadened intellectual horizons without provoking outbursts of anticlericalism and subversion (Carbia, *La Revolución de Mayo y la Iglesia* 18–20). Consequently, as Charles Griffin has pointed out, the role of enlightened thought in the independence movement was more one of confirmation than of cause since 300 years of authoritarian rule and scholastic education left an indelible mark on Argentine thinking that would not wash out quickly.

Despite the relative compliance of most Spanish-American intellectuals during the colonial period, in the early 1800s independence from Spain became a popular topic in parlor conversation throughout the colonies and particularly in Buenos Aires, where many porteños had some reason to resent Spain: Creoles were excluded from important positions in both church and government, Charles IV's irresponsibility was an international scandal, and economic restrictions limiting trade with nations other than Spain and the colonies profoundly irritated those porteño merchants not holding contracts with the mercantilist monopolies in Spain. The porteño bourgeoisie was sharply divided between these two groups of "intermediary agents" who benefited from the closed contracts with Spain and those independent merchants who sought trade with other nations. The intermediaries formed a claque of merchants supportive of any government, regardless of ideology, that defended their financial interests; they were forebears of some of Argentina's wealthiest families, including the Anchorenas, whose surname repeatedly surfaces in Argentine history on the side of conservatism and repression. Their opponents included the young Manuel Belgrano, Juan José Castelli, and Pedro de Cerviño, who first locked horns with conservative porteño business interests over the issue of the commercial monopolies that excluded them. Later, inspired largely by the economic doctrines of Adam Smith, members of this second group would become major figures in the Argentine independence movement and "the love and hope for reform" that dominated early Argentine liberalism (López 1:571). In the 1790s there emerged from this group one of the first tracts on economic theory produced in the River Plate: *Nuevo aspecto del comercio del Río de la Plata*, written by Belgrano associate Manuel José de Lavardén. A radical statement against Spanish mercantilism, the tract advocates free trade, privatization of public lands, and the formation of a local merchant marine. It also shows how much the economic thought of Adam Smith and François Quesnay, founder of the French physiocrats and father of the term *laissez-faire*, had influenced the young porteños.

If the liberalism typified by Adam Smith was a major inspiration for Argentine liberals, that inspiration grew in the most unlikely fashion. In 1806, English troops invaded Buenos Aires. Behind the English invasion was more than a desire to add Buenos Aires to the British Commonwealth; since Elizabethan times, the English had done everything possible to break the Spanish trade monopoly, and by 1804, "the subject of how to blow up the Spanish Empire" was discussed at length in the British Cabinet (Ferns 19). Or, as Commodore Sir Home Popham wrote to Viscount Melville in a letter dated October 14, 1804, "The idea of conquering South America is totally out of the question, but the possibility of gaining all its prominent points, alienating it from its present European Connections, fixing on some Military position, and enjoying all its Commercial advantages can be reduced to a fair calculation, if not a certain operation" (letter cited in Ferns 19). The naval officer who first considered the invasion and later transported army troops to Buenos Aires, Popham wanted to liberate Argentina from Spain as a first step toward opening all of South America to English commercial interests.

Popham's aim, however, was obscured by the overconfidence of the army which seriously underestimated porteño resolve and launched an invasion anyway under the command of General William Carr Beresford. The Spanish-born viceroy, Rafael de Sobremonte, fled to Córdoba with the court treasury, leaving the city's defense in the hands of patriot leaders Santiago Liniers and Juan Martín de Pueyrredón. Beresford's efforts were eventually repelled by porteño patriots who, as Manuel Belgrano put it, wanted "either our old master [Spain] or no master at all" (Belgrano, *Autobiografía* 33). Following Beresford's defeat, the British sent reinforcements in 1807 under Lieutenant General Whitelocke, who suffered heavy losses largely due to his own incompetence. Later, after meeting with porteño leaders to arrange a surrender, he became convinced that the whole enterprise was a bad idea from the outset and agreed to evacuate the city, a move that later led to his court-martial (Ferns 38–46). Nonetheless, Belgrano and other porteños not dependent on the Spanish commercial monopoly were much impressed with Whitelocke's evident humanity as well as his promises that England would aid in a rebellion against Spain—what Popham had intended in the first place (Belgrano 33). Indeed, as a result of contacts with Whitelocke and other likeminded Englishmen, many porteño liberals came to view England as an ally in the independence struggle rather than a mercantile nation with commercial ambitions of its own. Owing to such sentiment, Beresford escaped imprisonment.

The English invasions, then, produced paradoxical results. On the one hand, Argentines struggling against a common enemy for the first time sensed their potential as a nation. After the invasions this potential was partially realized as the cabildo, in the Viceroy's absence, assumed all governing power under the direction of Santiago Liniers, who had led the resistance against the English. On the other hand, liberal porteños emerged from the conflict believing that Great Britain, the invader, was somehow a true supporter of republican democracy and "a means of obtaining arms against Spain" (Belgrano 35). The defeat of the occupation also caused the English to change their tactics. In March 1807, Viscount Castlereagh was appointed Secretary of State for War; a pragmatist

who "viewed South America as a matter of British economic interest exclusively and not as a sphere where British political influence
should be exerted," Castlereagh argued that Great Britain should
avoid armed conflict in Spanish America while at the same time
appearing as "auxiliaries and protectors" in political and economic
affairs, a policy that would underlie Anglo-Argentine relations for
the next 126 years (Ferns 48).

Following the English invasions, life in the Argentine would
probably have returned to the slow routine of colonial rule, with talk
of independence confined to polite conversations among Frenchified intellectuals, had not the Spanish court disintegrated in 1808.
That independence resulted largely from the events in Spain and not
just from an autonomous movement in the colonies is borne out in
the writings of at least two of the period's principal players. Manuel
Moreno claims that, although independence from Spain would
probably have come as part of the natural course of history, "most of
America considered its destiny tied to that of that nation which had
conquered her and supplied her with a government and a language.
A great revolution could take place . . . once the ties that held the
empire together were dissolved" (5–6). He later argues that "without the catastrophe in the Mother Country, Buenos Aires would
have remained the same, with little variation" (110). Similarly, Manuel Belgrano contends that after the English invasion, "a year
passed, and without our doing anything towards independence, God
himself presented us with the opportunity in the events of 1808 in
Spain and Bayonne [the city where Charles IV met with Napoleon].
In effect, at that moment ideas about liberty and independence in
America came alive, and Americans began talking openly for the first
time about their rights" (Belgrano 34).

The melodramatic story behind the fall of the Spanish court explains why even the most devout Argentine royalists questioned
Spanish leadership. Although the monarchy had been in serious
decline ever since the death of Charles III in 1778 and was much
weakened by a series of wars with Great Britain, nothing could
match the events of 1808, when Charles IV, the dissolute monarch,
Manuel Godoy, his wife's gigolo and lover, and Ferdinand VII, the
resentful crown prince, got into a bitter fight for supremacy. After
enduring years of intrigue, Charles imprisoned his son Ferdinand on
learning that the crown prince was plotting to depose him. A mob,

feeling that the crown prince was the country's best hope, stormed the palace, forcing the king to abdicate and Godoy to flee. Both Charles and Ferdinand then begged support from Napoleon, whose forces were already in Spain, ostensibly en route to Portugal. After hearing both sides hurl unspeakable insults at each other, Napoleon saw a good political opportunity and appointed Joseph Bonaparte, his dipsomaniac brother, to be emperor of Spain, providing still another incompetent pretender to the throne. The Spanish Cortes, or parliament, refused Joseph's rule and formed a government in exile in Cádiz, the southern port through which most contact with the colonies was funneled. The Cádiz parliament, knowing that revolutionary sentiment was spreading throughout the American colonies, initially tried to include representatives from the Americas, but quickly abandoned that idea on realizing that proportional representative rule would give the colonists a large majority. Approving and then denying representation from the colonies only fed resentment already rampant throughout Spanish America.

Given the events in Spain, the immediate question for most Argentines was not loyalty to the crown, but which crown to be loyal to. The popular Santiago Liniers, swearing loyalty to the crown prince Ferdinand VII, assumed temporarily the duties of viceroy in place of Sobremonte, now discredited because of his cowardly behavior during the English occupation. Ostensibly because of his French origin at a time when anti-Napoleon sympathies were running high and his limited administrative gifts, Liniers was almost immediately attacked by the Spanish community and liberal Creoles, both based in the Buenos Aires cabildo. How groups as opposite as the Spanish-born royalists and the liberals joined forces against the popular Liniers underlines an essential aspect of many Argentine intellectuals during the independence movement: they profoundly distrusted their own masses, a fear prompted no doubt by the terror that followed the French Revolution. On the dangers of populism, the Spanish royalists and Creole liberals could agree.

Under pressure from the Buenos Aires cabildo, the Cádiz government appointed Baltasar Cisneros to replace Liniers as viceroy of the River Plate; contrary to elitist fears, Liniers graciously relinquished his position and retired to private life. His presence in Argentina, however, continued to haunt liberal porteños since he was later executed on the unfounded charge that he was organizing a popular revolt against the independence movement. The real reasons behind Linier's death were as debated by his contemporaries as they are by today's historians. For example, General Tomás Guido, a hero of Argentine independence, writes in his memoirs that the proindependence liberals felt that "The people . . . are not prepared for a violent change in administration. The proletarian masses, who constitute the greatest part of the province [of Buenos Aires], are a kind of cult around General Liniers, in whom they do not see the odious instrument of Spanish absolutism, but the liberator of Buenos Aires, the hero against the [English] invasion" (Guido, *Autobiografía* 1:3–4). Manuel Moreno essentially corroborates Guido's view that Liniers was a dangerous populist allied with every reactionary element in porteño society (74–79, 112–123). No less authoritative, but in total contradiction to Guido's and Moreno's view, is the opinion of Cornelio Saavedra, also an independence hero, who passionately argues in his 1829 memoirs that Liniers was one of the first authentic representatives of the popular classes (Saavedra, *Autobiografía* 1:22–44). Even today, Liniers's significance and the reasons behind his death continue to divide Argentine historians. (Compare, for example, Halperín Donghi, *Politics* 150–238 and Puiggrós, *Los caudillos* 2–81.)

Despite his good intentions, Cisneros was unable to ease the growing tensions between Spaniards and Creoles, liberals and traditionalists, and Buenos Aires and the provinces. When news arrived in Buenos Aires that Napoleon's forces had seized control of Seville, and that the Cádiz government was again on the run, Cisneros called a *cabildo abierto*, or expanded town council meeting, consisting of 225 of the province's principal men, to establish a provisional governing junta, a move that backfired when the Creole-dominated junta refused to elect him president. The Creole leader, Cornelio Saavedra, in one of the most polite revolutionary statements ever, informed the Viceroy that "he who gave Your Excellency your authority no longer exists. Consequently, since you no longer have any authority, you should not depend on the forces under my control to support you" (cited in Ruiz-Guiñazú, *Saavedra* 181). Later, during the debate with the Viceroy and his supporters, Saavedra proclaimed the cabildo as the Viceroyalty's only ruling body "which receives its authority and mandate from the people" (184).

The political process by which the Primera Juunta was formed would be repeated over and over again during the first ten years of independence. The Buenos Aires cabildo was dominated by wealthy porteños, merchants, and landowners, "decent people (*gente decente*)" and not "low-class imitators of the upper class (*la gente de medio pelo*)" as one contemporary wrote in his diary (cited by Sebreli, *Apogeo* 91–92). As representatives primarily of upper-class concerns, the cabildo repeatedly ousted governments that failed to promote business interests, protect the privileges of Buenos Aires, or keep provincial leaders in their place. As a result, the cabildo was a source of both continuity and disruption that managed to keep some kind of government in power while effectively blocking any real accommodation of provincial or lower-class interests (Halperín Donghi, *Politics* 337–345).

From the Buenos Aires cabildo emerged the first Argentine governing body independent of Spain, known in history as *La Primera Junta*. The Junta members gave themselves two main tasks: (1) organize an army to repel the Napoleonic Spanish in the name of Ferdinand, and (2) form a congress with representatives from the different provinces to govern the viceroyalty until order could be restored. On May 25, 1810, porteños of all political stripes swore allegiance to the Primera Junta by assenting to the following oath:

Do you swear before God our Lord and on these Holy Gospels to recognize the Governing Provisional Junta of the River Plate, in name of Don Fernando VII, to defend his august rights, to obey his orders and decrees, to not question directly nor indirectly his authority, and to proclaim his security and respect in public and in private? (*Gaceta de Buenos Aires*, 7 June 1810; Cited in Moreno [Mariano], *Escritos* 233)

Although Argentines consider May 25, 1810, their Day of Independence, this oath can be viewed as a declaration of freedom from Spain only in the context of the confused political events of the time. Swearing allegiance to Ferdinand, who did not occupy the throne, allowed people to reject the incompetent Charles IV and the usurper Joseph Bonaparte while affirming loyalty to the institution of monarchy and thereby not offending Creole and Spanish royalists. Indeed, Saavedra in his memoirs insists that "covering the Junta in the mantle of Ferdinand VII was a farce from the outset, made necessary for political reasons" (53). In short, the oath was more than anything a way of uniting Creoles and Spaniards of all political stripes under one banner; no one objected to swearing allegiance to a nonking.

Since these events occurred in May, the term *Mayo* came to be synonymous in Argentina with independence and a general support of democracy over monarchy; the revolutionary movement, then, is referred to as *Mayo*, and its leaders are called the *Men of Mayo*. The term, however, must be used cautiously since grouping all figures and ideological currents of the revolution under *Mayo* suggests an ideological consensus that never existed. Furthermore, although many provincials sympathized with the May revolution—once they heard of it—Mayo was primarily a Buenos Aires phenomenon in which porteños declared independence from Napoleonic Spain not just for themselves but for all citizens of the Viceroyalty. From Mayo on, then, porteños began a long tradition of confusing Buenos Aires with the entire country. Moreover, with the Primera Junta began a long series of conflicts between porteños and provincial caudillos that frequently ended in bloodshed and civil war. Typical of Buenos Aires localism is Manuel Moreno, who in his biography of his brother Mariano seldom distinguishes between *Buenos Aires* and *the patria*, or fatherland (e.g., 3–4). He paradoxically suggests that while it had been entirely appropriate for all American provinces to rebel against Spain, failure on the part of the provinces to follow Buenos Aires' lead after Independence resulted from "seduction, rebellion and schism" (149). In short, rebellion against Spain was fine, but disagreement with Buenos Aires was another matter. Later, in a flight of wishful thinking characteristic of the porteño elite, he maintains that whenever Buenos Aires sent troops against provincial caudillos the porteños were received by "the people" as brothers since supporters of the caudillos were nothing but "mercenaries" (149–160).

If conflict with the provinces were not enough, the Primera Junta was soon besieged by internal feuding. In structuring the Primera Junta, the Buenos Aires patriots attempted to appoint men who represented several factions within the city's tangled loyalties. Members of the first Junta included Juan José Paso and Mariano Moreno, who had identified closely with the previous cabildo and its anti-Liniers bias, as well as Cornelio Saavedra, a Liniers supporter, who according to his description was chosen as president of the Junta "in order to appease the people" (*Saavedra* 52–53). Although Saavedra's popularity with his troops and the lower classes was indeed a factor in his selection as president, it was also a liability in his dealings with other Junta members who feared he would launch a coup against the government. Despite these fears, the Primera Junta represented a laudable, albeit brief, moment of attempted consensus among Buenos Aires' feuding elites. Nonetheless, as will be seen in the next chapter, from those divisions sprang a prototype of Argentine politics as well as the first significant creator of Argentine guiding fictions: Mariano Moreno.

Chapter Two

Mariano Moreno

I

From Mayo emerged Argentina's first important thinker of national identity, Mariano Moreno, a man who reflects the contradictions of his time as well as those of the country he helped found. As indicated by the 1824 anthology of Argentine poetry, *La Lira Argentina*, the period did not lack for writers, mostly poets, who composed panegyrics to military leaders and their triumphs, replete with classical allusions and imagery. But of the entire generation, Moreno is easily the most original. He has also been assigned a high place in Argentina's pantheon of heroes by liberal historians. Not untypical is the following quotation from an 1845 pamphlet on José Rivera Indarte, written by Bartolomé Mitre, a future general, politician, and historian, whose role as a maker of guiding fictions is studied in a later chapter:

Moreno was at that supreme moment the Michelangelo of the May revolution, who siezed . . . a magnificent block of marble and gave it form and life. Then, before the astonished eyes of the people, he unveiled a statue in which all saw concretized their aspirations for independence and liberty. Firm in his intention and strong in his means, with the work of a few months he destroyed through thought and action the ancient colonial edifice, and laid the foundations of a new society to which he bequeathed its own institutions and essentially democratic ideas. . . . Examples like [Moreno's] are not common in our history, but they have repeated themselves more than once, and they alone have impregnated with their per-

events of May 25, 1810, when Buenos Aires in the name of Ferdinand VII declared independence from the Cádiz government in Spain. Moreno was named Secretary of the Primera Junta, but his principal enemy, Cornelio Saavedra, was appointed President.

Moreno embraced his new position as a man obsessed. He founded and edited a newspaper, the *Gazeta de Buenos Aires*, supervised a census, made plans for a military school and a national library, helped equip troops to fight the royalists, fended off a conspiracy against the Junta, translated and published Rousseau's *Social Contract*, saw that holdovers from the old Viceregal government were exiled, negotiated successful trade agreements with the British, and promoted a constitutional congress. He also made many enemies, the most important one being the Junta president, Cornelio Saavedra, an old-style patriot with broad popular support who, as he reports in his short autobiography, was already suspicious of Moreno and his intellectual coterie for their involvement in the execution of Santiago de Liniers (Saavedra 35–42).

Moreno and Saavedra could not have been more different. Whereas Moreno distrusted provincial leaders, Saavedra went out of his way to bring them into the governing junta, calling the expanded assembly the *junta grande*. He also encouraged provincial autonomists by supporting *juntas provinciales*. In late 1810, Moreno and his followers tried to take control of the Buenos Aires militia, thus depriving Saavedra of his principal support. The militia, however, remained loyal to Saavedra, prompting a frustrated Moreno to resign the Secretariat and sail for England, where he hoped to garner British support for his plans (Rock, *Argentina* 79–83). He died en route of a mysterious fever, which according to dark, unproven rumors may have resulted from poisoning. On learning of his burial at sea, Saavedra reportedly remarked, "They needed that much water to put out that much fire."

Moreno's writings include legal briefs, speeches, newspaper articles, the foreword to his translation of Rousseau's *Social Contract*, decrees, letters, a lengthy defense of free trade with England, and a controversial policy paper, written late in his career, outlining a program for winning the revolution, governing the country, and taking over the rest of South America. His prose reveals at least two Morenos; the first is an heir to the Enlightenment who defends freedom of expression, free trade, common sense, *vox populi*, liberty, equality, and happiness—common fare of any Enlightenment writer and material from which Argentine textbook writers have found much to quote in praise of liberty, reason, and, of course, Moreno. The second Moreno is a frighteningly authoritarian figure reminiscent of Machiavelli, the Grand Inquisitor, and the French Jacobins. On the second Moreno, liberal historians have little to say; indeed, like Mitre, who was quoted at the beginning of this chapter, they usually try to hide Moreno's complex and contradictory nature in a cloud of rhetorical incense as blinding today as when it was written.

Both Morenos are visible in virtually everything he wrote, although the second one becomes predominant in his later works. For example, in an early essay, "Sobre la libertad de escribir" (On the freedom to write), Moreno praises public opinion as a reliable means for debunking untruth and argues that evil is best handled "by giving space and liberty to public writers so they may attack it vigorously and without pity" (Moreno [Mariano], *Escritos* 237). Then in a marvelously contradictory line he affirms that "the people will languish in the most shameful stupor unless they are given the right and liberty to talk about all subjects as long as they do not oppose in any way the holy truths of our august religion and the dictates of the government" (238). In short, anything can be discussed as long as it favors Catholicism and the current government. The problem here is that Moreno, for all his Enlightenment rhetoric, never abandoned the scholastic seminarian's concept of preexisting divine truth waiting to be revealed. Freedom of expression in his view is not a path to new truths by way of shared observation, reason, discussion, and analysis; rather, it is a conduit through which preestablished truth can be passed from the enlightened few to the benighted many. Later in the same essay, he tells us that "truths, like virtue, have within themselves their most irrefutable defense; by discussing and airing them they appear in all their glory and brilliance" (239). That is to say, since truth and all defense of truth exist prior to discussion, true ideas must be accepted in their primitive purity rather than challenged, revised, and challenged again. Moreover, in statements strongly reminiscent of Augustinian concepts of original sin, Moreno argues that resistance to truth derives from selfishness and pride, the great sins of the Fall of Man; in Moreno's words: "Let us once and for all be less partial to our rancid opinions; let us have less love for ourselves; let us make way for the truth and for the introduction of light and enlightenment" (239). All of which begs the question as to who in Moreno's view will determine what is truth in order to impart light and enlightenment to those inferior souls wallowing in self-love and rancid opinions.

One answer to this question is found in a short piece titled "Fundación de *La Gazeta de Buenos Aires*" he wrote for the first issue of the revolutionary junta's official newspaper. Moreno describes the newspaper's fundamental purpose as a conveyor of statements from "enlightened men who support and direct patriotic endeavor and faithfulness." He further affirms that the need for enlightened direction is "never greater than when the clash of opinions could engulf in darkness those principles that only the great talents can make shine in their primitive clarity" (*Escritos* 228). In sum, patriotism must be channeled by an elite of enlightened men who alone can lead the untutored masses to truth and freedom. And how are these enlightened men chosen? By appointment, self-proclamation, birth? These are questions Moreno leaves unanswered. Also interesting is that he again insists that truth is the restatement of primitive values, rather than the discovery of something previously unknown. But where is such truth to be had? Is it the privileged knowledge of a priestly class? Is it the Counter-Reformation's supposed return to primitive Christianity? Is Moreno making an oblique reference to Rousseau's mythical societies where primitive man lived in unsullied purity? Again, Moreno leaves such questions hanging.

Finally, Moreno is manifestly uncomfortable with the fundamental Enlightenment notion that differing opinions can coexist in a pluralist society. In his view, the "clash of opinions" is not a necessary step toward consensus and accommodation, but a real danger that "engulfs in darkness" primitive truth. Again, despite his liberal use of terms popularized by the Enlightenment, the authoritarianism and absolutism of the seminarian are much more evident here than any real appreciation of the pluralist society envisioned by the Enlightenment's best thinkers. His native tongue may have contributed to his failure to understand pluralism. In Spanish, there is no equivalent without paraphrase of the English term *to compromise* wherein the ability of dissenting parties to arrive at a consensus

through give and take is perceived as a positive value. The closest
Spanish equivalents are *ceder, comprometerse,* or *transigir,* each of
which usually suggests surrender of principle rather than princi-
pled surrender.

Not even Rousseau, Moreno's avowed intellectual idol, is spared
Moreno's authoritarianism. In the foreword to his translation of
large portions of the *Social Contract,* Moreno predicts that Rousseau "will be the marvel of all ages" and that making his book
available to Argentines is a necessary part of educating the people
(*Escritos* 379). Earlier in the same essay, he declares that education
is vital in free societies since "if the people are not enlightened . . .
perhaps our fate will be to change tyrants without destroying tyranny" (377). Thus speaks the Enlightenment Moreno. But no
sooner has he praised Rousseau and education than he turns on
both by announcing that "since [Rousseau] had the misfortune of
waxing delirious in religious matters, I am suppressing the chapter
and main passages where he addresses such matters" (381–382),
which in fact he did. Again, scholasticism proved more powerful
than the Enlightenment. For Moreno, even his mentor Rousseau
must be censored when he runs afield of established truth. Despite
Mariano Moreno's attempts to purify Rousseau, at least one cleric,
Juan José María del Patrocinio, strongly condemned Moreno for
propagating the "infernal doctrines [and] pestilential poison" of the
Social Contract (cited in Ruiz-Guiñazú, *Saavedra* 162–163).

Moreno is not, however, just theoretical. Scarcely nine months
after siding with the Spanish in the unseating of Liniers, he
switched political allies by writing a long defense of free trade and a
strong judgment against Spanish mercantilism. The tract is commonly known as the *Representación de los hacendados* owing to the
length of its original name: *Representación a nombre del apode-
rado de los hacendados de las campañas del Río de la Plata dirigida
al excelentísimo Señor Virrey Don Baltasar Hidalgo de Cisneros en
el expediente promovido sobre proporcionar ingresos al erario por
medio de un franco comercio con la nación inglesa* (Representative
Statement of the Legal Agent of the Landowners of the River Plate
Submitted to His Most Excellent Lord Viceroy Don Baltasar
Hidalgo de Cisneros and Constituting a Legal Brief on How to
Provide Income to the Public Treasury by Means of Open Com-

merce with the English Nation). Two items call our attention in this drawn-out title. First, Moreno innocently suggests that the only issue at hand is increasing public income for the strapped Cisneros government. Second, in Hispanic legal proceedings, all documents constituting a particular case are submitted in writing in a brief, or *expediente,* which may include documents from several sources. The repetitiveness and rambling nature of the *Representación* suggests that such was the case in this instance. José Pablo Feinmann goes so far as to theorize that Manuel Belgrano, Alexander Mackinnon, an English businessman, and perhaps even Lord Strangford, British representative in the Court of Brazil, contributed text to the *Representación* (Feinmann, *Filosofía* 22–23). The *Representación* was prompted by the arrival on August 16, 1809 of British trade ships sent to open Buenos Aires to trade, or better stated, to reestablish the commercial contacts that British merchants had enjoyed under Liniers but were now under attack from the pro-Cádiz Cisneros (Ferns 67–70). The action of the Foreign Office was primarily political since British goods were already widely available thanks to a well-developed network of smugglers. In short, the British merchants mostly wanted to challenge the legal monopoly the Cádiz government still claimed over the colonies. The British sweetened their proposal by offering to pay duties on imports to the penniless Cisneros government, thus replicating a similar arrangement worked out with the Portuguese government in exile in Rio. Since Cisneros needed the money but didn't want to offend the Cádiz government, he astutely asked the Spanish consulate for an opinion.

The Spanish Consulate's reply, written by Manuel Gregorio Yañiz, outlined a protectionist position whose major points would become standard fare in later nationalist and populist thinking. Yañiz objects to free trade with the British on two main counts. First, he argues that through increased trade the British will "insert themselves into all affairs of the colony," compromising the authority of local governments. Second, he maintains that while English goods may be cheaper than those produced locally, their ultimate effect would be the ruination of local industry. "It would be foolhardy," he writes, "to pretend that American and English industry are equal. . . . Consequently [in open competition with the English] our factories would be totally ruined and a countless number

of men and women who support themselves manufacturing fabric
and clothing would be reduced to indigence, to such a degree that
wherever one looked all would be desolation and misery" (cited in
Feinmann, 21). Later, Miguel Fernández de Agüero wrote a concur-
ring opinion that underlined even more the need to protect local
industry. Although Yañiz and Agüero were interested primarily in
protecting Spanish trading privileges, their arguments regarding
local industry held considerable truth. Because Spain had never
become an industrial power, the Viceroyalty was largely self-
sufficient in many of the goods England wished for Argentina to
import—clothing, fabric, shoes, furniture, and the like. Moreover,
the economic well-being of much of the interior provinces depended on their ability to manufacture goods for local markets, of
which Buenos Aires was the largest.

To reply to the Consulate, a group of porteño landowners (*los
hacendados*), and pro-British Creole merchants called on Mariano
Moreno to present their point of view as wordsmith and principal
author of the *Representación*. Characterized by his brother Manuel
as a "committed life-long friend of England (Moreno [Manuel] 2:8),
Moreno wasted no time in telling Cisneros—repeatedly—that free
trade with the British would not only bring prosperity to the nation
but that duties on British imports could fill the public purse, now
seriously depleted. He argues that English goods already enter the
country despite "laws and reiterated prohibitions," thus depriving
the treasury of duties it would receive otherwise, and then suggests
that legalizing that trade would not only enrich the government but
also cohere with the "law of necessity" on which all economy is based
(*Escritos* 105–109). He further maintains that increased contact with
Great Britain would expand Argentina's agricultural income while
giving Argentines access to inexpensive, high-quality British manufactures (120–123). Indeed, he asserts that Argentina in some sense
deserves British trade, that people of accomplishment and taste
should not be limited by the shortcomings of local artisans:

A country just beginning to prosper cannot be deprived of [goods] which
flatter good taste and increase consumption. If our artists knew how to
make them as well, they should be preferred. . . . Is it fair to deprive one
of . . . buying a good piece of furniture just because our artesans haven't
committed themselves to make one as good? (217)

How carefully Moreno claims that Argentina's consuming classes deserve the best. And how subtly he affirms that Argentine furniture is not as good as its English counterpart simply because Argentine workers lack commitment. Advertisers and union busters could not have said it better.

In response to the Consulate's statement that imports would ruin local manufacture, Moreno shows complete indifference to the needs of the Interior, an arrogant attitude held by many porteños and one of the principal causes of the country's divisions. Rather, he argues that commerce is much more than manufacture; it is also buying, transporting, selling, repairing, and the like, all of which would grow with increased imports (180–184). While this is true, Moreno does not mention that such activities would for the most part benefit only the porteño merchant class. Moreno further insists that local manufacturers would "acquire by imitation the perfection of their art" by having to compete with the British and ingenuously suggests that, even if British goods were widely available, the provinces would continue to consume local manufactures given the uninformed tastes of provincial peoples (191–192). Moreno's most telling point, however, responds to the Consulate's argument that open trade with the English would lead to loss of local control. Moreno assures us that the English would always "look with respect on the victors" who repelled the British invasion of 1807, and that commerce would be Great Britain's only concern—an argument that overlooked the fact that by their very presence the British were already influencing local politics (193).

The *Representación* can be read in at least two quite different ways. In one sense, it constitutes an unremarkable retelling of the economic wisdom of Smith, Quesnay, and, of course, Gaspar Melchor de Jovellanos, whom Moreno quotes with delight since he was at the time president of the governing board in Cádiz and thereby the Consulate's superior. In this sense, the *Representación* is neither original nor particularly Argentine. In another sense, however, the *Representación* reveals attitudes indicative of Argentina's tragic flaw: Buenos Aires' turn toward Europe and her virtual disinterest in the economic needs of the interior. From the *Representación* onward, duties on imports and exports would go to Buenos Aires; Interior artisans would languish; and when the Interior rightly protested these measures, Buenos Aires would answer with

guns. In this sense, the *Representación* marks the beginning of a
policy to enrich Buenos Aires at the expense of the Interior while
denying the Interior the means for its own growth and progress. As
Juan Bautista Alberdi, one of Argentina's most distinguished thinkers and a man whose writings are considered later in this book,
wrote:

Moreno represents the spirit of the May revolution in the exact sense that
Buenos Aires understands and builds on that revolution: the destruction
and denial . . . of all sovereign authority from both within and without;
domination of Buenos Aires over all the nation, first in the name of Ferdinand VII, and later in the name of the Argentine nation; [and] isolation of
the port [of Buenos Aires] from the rest of the provinces in order to retain
provincial earnings. (*Grandes y pequeños hombres* 93)

This policy provoked sixty years of wars in which thousands would
die. It also created a deep and abiding resentment that persists
even yet.

Near the end of his term as Secretary of the Junta, Moreno,
perhaps commissioned by the Junta, wrote his longest and most
controversial political and economic document, a secret policy paper titled "Operational Plan That the Provisional Government of
the Provinces of the River Plate Should Implement In Order to
Consolidate the Great Work of Our Liberty and Independence."
The Plan was never published during Moreno's lifetime, probably
because, for reasons explored below, it was not intended to circulate widely. Nonetheless, several of his contemporaries apparently
knew of the Plan's existence and, as Ruiz-Guiñazú notes, made
reference to it (*Epifanía* 16). The Plan came to light when a handwritten copy, accompanied by an affidavit affirming that Moreno
wrote the original, was discovered in the General Archive of the
Indies in Seville, Spain around 1890. Norberto Piñero obtained a
copy of this copy and included the Plan in his collection of Moreno's writings (the one used here) of 1895, the first time it was
ever published in Argentina. The Plan immediately caused a stir
since Moreno emerges from its pages as a radical thinker who is not
only intelligent, insightful, and original but also ruthless, bloodthir-
sty, and a little mad. Since this view of Moreno was so different
from that of Official History, liberal historians questioned the Plan's
authenticity from the outset. Although the Plan's authenticity is

now widely accepted, some historians, for reasons explored later, still insist it is apocryphal. In my discussion of the Plan I will first examine its most significant points and then look at the debate regarding its authenticity.

Like an epic poem, the Plan begins with an invocation—not to the Muses but to George Washington: "Where noble and great Washington are your political teachings? Where are the careful rules that provided the plan for your great work? Your principles and rule could guide us, giving us your light towards accomplishing the goals we have set for ourselves" (*Escritos* 456). What Moreno has in mind, however, has more to do with Machiavelli and Robespierre than with Washington. From the beginning he declares that dissidents to the Junta should be ruthlessly suppressed: "Moderation at an inappropriate time is neither sanity nor truth; . . . never in times of revolution has a government followed moderation or tolerance; a man's slightest thought that opposes the new system is a crime because of the influence and obstacles such a thought might cause by its example, and its punishment is unavoidable" (458). To avoid any possibility of doubt concerning the kind of punishment, he adds that "the foundations of a new republic have never been laid except by rigor and punishment mixed with the spilt blood of those members who might oppose its progress" (458–459). Later he again affirms the necessity of violence and murder, saying that "No one should be scandalized by the intention of my words, to cut off heads, spill blood, and sacrifice at all costs, even when they [my words] resemble the customs of cannibals and savages. . . . No decrepit state or province can regenerate itself nor cut out its corruption without spilling rivers of blood" (467).

Should anyone question his authority, Moreno claims to be God's instrument: "I placed myself in the hands of Providence so that God could guide my knowledge regarding our most just and holy cause" (464). So much for reason; in a crunch, Moreno waxes prophetic. Moreover, potential dissidents are advised that "the teachings developed in this Plan are, on my honor, not just the only practical ones, but the best and the most admirable inasmuch as they lead to effort and eventual triumph in the battle we are waging" (465). He concludes the introduction affirming that once the Constitution, at this time still unwritten, "protects the legitimate enjoyment of true liberty, allowing no abuses, then the American

State will solve the real and great problems of the Social Contract"
(468). In short, Moreno embraces the contradictory position of
establishing peace through terror, democracy through repression,
freedom through coercion.

What is the source of Moreno's fascination with terror? Liberal
Argentine historians, ever in search of European roots, have in the
main attributed it to his "Jacobinism." Chief in this regard is José
Ingenieros, a brilliant writer whose two-volume study, first published in 1918, *Evolución de las ideas argentinas*, continues to be a
useful work, despite the pronounced biases of its author. As Juan
Pablo Feinmann points out (*Filosofía* 49), Ingenieros takes special
delight in casting the entire revolutionary period in Argentina as a
replay of the French Revolution. In this scheme, the Morenistas
become the Jacobins, the Saavedristas are the *feuillants*, and the
Primera Junta is the Directory (Ingenieros 1:99–110, 127–135).

While Moreno's similarity to Robespierre and the French Ja-
cobinists cannot be denied, his rhetoric is decidedly of another origin: the Crusades, the Inquisition, and the Counter-Reformation. At
no point is Moreno's proximity to the most regressive elements of
Catholic history more apparent than in the passages just cited. By
violence and bloodshed—whether of a Holy War or the divinely
sanctioned state of which Moreno claims to be prophet—the land is
by blood cleansed of iniquity, enemies are killed, and the revolution
is accomplished. Then, by uttering the right words, in a Constitution
rather than a decree of absolution, the state of innocence found in
the primitive Social Contract is reinstituted. The elimination of
"enemies" was in fact a major activity of the Primera Junta until
Cornelio Saavedra began questioning the wisdom of assuming guilt
on the basis of anonymous charges (Saavedra 58–60). Not pleased by
this call to sanity, Moreno merely renewed his efforts to discredit the
Junta president.

To identify enemies, Moreno recommends establishing a secret
police force: "In the capital and in all towns, the government
should retain spies, to be recruited not according to talent or circumstance, but by their manifest devotion to the cause" (473).
Once these spies are in place, they should denounce all enemies of
the government, real or merely suspected. Furthermore, in Moreno's view, a spy's every testimony should be taken seriously: "The
slightest suspicion denounced by a patriot against any individual

who appears to have the character of an enemy should be heard and acted upon . . . so that the denouncer will not lose the zeal of his calling" (475–476). This echoes his earlier advice that "with [enemies] the government should follow a most cruel and bloody policy . . . the slightest semi-proof of acts, words, etc. against the cause should receive capital punishment" (472–473).

Fear of enemies also leads Moreno to recommend that the state operate in absolute secrecy. To this end he counsels that the government "be silent and reserved with the public, even the healthy part of the people, so that our enemies will not understand anything about our operations." He further advises that "the quantity of *Gazetas* [the Junta's newspaper] to be printed be very small, so that . . . it will circulate less, both within and beyond our provinces and thereby be less likely to cause the government problems in which our enemies repeat and contradict our positions" (477). Later, this man who once praised the free exchange of ideas proclaims that no newspapers critical of the government be allowed to circulate (477). Secrecy also motivates an extreme suspicion of foreigners who in his view should be exiled to the Malvinas (Falkland) Islands, the cold, uninhabited Argentine Patagonia or "some other place considered convenient" if they "have not shown proof of their adherence to the cause" (499).

The Plan also discusses economic policy, but in terms decidedly different from those of the *Representación* studied earlier; indeed, the meddlesome government envisioned in the Plan has almost nothing in common with the invisible hand glorified in the *Representación*. Moreno's new economic order as seen in the Plan is capsulized in a phrase that anticipates Bentham's hedonic calculus. "The best government," he affirms, "is . . . the one that makes the greatest number of its inhabitants happy." From this he argues that "gigantic fortunes of a few individuals . . . are not only pernicious but work towards the ruination of civil society" (519). Therefore, he recommends that the State initiate an aggressive policy of wealth redistribution, from the rich to the poor. The first to lose their property would be the "enemies" (498–499) followed by all those who in the State's view own too much: "Let five or six thousand grow unhappy so that the advantages [of prosperity] can fall on eighty or a hundred thousand inhabitants" (521). Yet, since he is also concerned that wealth so bestowed might corrupt its recipients, he quickly adds

that the State should, just like a good shepherd, ever keep the
people from "idleness and direct them towards virtue" (522). Moreno's disdain for the rich may have been justified by the actions of
traders like Tomás de Anchorena and Juan Pedro Aguirre, who ex-
torted vast amounts of money from the revolutionary movement
through usury and huge profits (Sebreli, *Apogeo* 97–101).

His economic plan also includes the creation of a State commission to supervise all sales, prevent the concentration of wealth, stop
the export of goods needed at home, and control all imports, especially of those products that "like a corrupting vice, represent excessive and sterile luxury" (523). Moreno particularly wants a self-
sufficient nation "with no need to seek abroad what it needs for the
preservation of its inhabitants" (522–528). Yet Moreno recognizes
that foreign trade is necessary even if it means Argentina must
"suffer some extortion," an apparent reference to foreign profits
(508–509). Nonetheless, Moreno recommends caution, particularly
with England, which in Moreno's view is "the most conniving of all
nations" (532). Moreno's balanced this suspicion of Great Britain
with a peculiar admiration; England may be the most conniving of
nations, but it was also the nation Moreno most wanted as a trading
and political ally. Moreover, when forced to resign, he immediately
embarked for England to seek support for his views.

Every bit as far-reaching as Moreno's economic proposals are his
ambitious foreign policy recommendations. What begins with a
feasible plan for putting down a localist rebellion in Uruguay ends
up as a grand strategy for freeing all of South America from Spanish
and Portuguese domination, dismembering Brazil, and dividing
the conquered territories between Argentina and Great Britain
(535–551). Moreno's methods for accomplishing this ambitious
agenda are nothing short of Machiavellian. He confesses freely that
promoting Mayo in the name of Ferdinand was a sham perpetrated
to unite Creoles of all persuasions against Spain and thereby to
initiate the liberation of all of South America and its subsequent
division between Moreno's state and the British. To this end, he
recommends dirty tricks (false letters, misinformation, and the like)
to sow discord, divide loyalties, spread popular rebellion, and foment civil wars in Uruguay and Brazil. Once the target lands are
engulfed in civil strife, he advocates similar tactics to sow enmity
between England and Portugal. After civil strife has rendered the

coveted territories ripe for the picking and the English have pushed the Portuguese out of the picture, he urges the Buenos Aires Junta to enter "secret treaties with England" to divide up the conquered territories (535); he is convinced that the inhabitants of both Uruguay and Brazil will greet the Argentine and English invaders with open arms once they understood "the happiness, liberty, equality and benevolence of the new system" (540), a fantasy just as loony as his apparent belief that the English would willingly share territorial booty with a "State" that at the time had no name, no boundaries, no permanent government, no institutional army, no navy, no infrastructure, and no established economic base.

What to make of the Moreno's Plan? At first blush, it appears so totally disassociated from reality that decorous folk dismiss it altogether, without ever taking it seriously. Another and potentially more misleading way to dismiss the Plan is by asking the wrong questions: Was Moreno paranoid in discussing "enemies"? No doubt about it. Did he suffer delusions of grandeur? Obviously. Did he urge bloodshed, terrorism, and intrigue? Most certainly. Yet, to determine the real significance of the Plan, a better question than these might be, "Does the Plan identify or foreshadow any currents in Argentina's emerging guiding fictions that must be taken seriously, despite their extreme nature?" Viewed in this light, the Plan is perhaps the most significant document of Mayo.

As a maker of national mythologies, Moreno transmitted to Argentine discourse a concept of political evil still observable in many of Argentina's ongoing guiding fictions. These guiding fictions rest in some sense on Moreno's sense of evil that, following traditional Christian teachings, he defines as the absence of good. Evil for Moreno is anything that is less good than it could be. As such, evil is defeated by denying it space in the good. Moreno's sense of evil allows no middle ground, no area where "good" and "evil" blend with "possible" and "ambiguous." Given this definition, it is only logical that Moreno would define an enemy as any person who is less than utterly committed to the cause—as defined by Moreno. His world is populated by patriots who agree with him and traitors who do not. Since evil can be combatted solely by allowing it no space in the good, Moreno sees only one way to deal with enemies: eliminate them through death or exile, an idea that opens the door to the most vicious kind of repression. Interestingly, Moreno couches his terrorism in a peculiarly apologetic tone, wherein he recognizes that civilized people do not advocate spying on citizens, shooting people for the mere possibility of treason, cutting off heads, and irrigating the soil in blood. But his is ultimately an apology for violence that, however deplorable, he considers inevitable for the country to be saved. In short, evil and its incarnation in "enemies" must be excised by radical surgery in order to restore the body politic to health.

The survival of such guiding fictions in contemporary Argentina can be seen in several twentieth-century movements, some relatively innocuous and others quite deadly. In the first group is the peculiar usage of the word *intransigente* as a positive value. One of Argentina's most important political leaders in this century was Hipólito Yrigoyen, a populist who first succeeded in making universal suffrage a reality. Although I readily confess considerable admiration for Yrigoyen, I remain puzzled and disconcerted by his penchant for defining himself and his positions as "intransigent," that is to say, so right, so pure, so orthodox that compromise was beyond question. Even today, long after Yrigoyen's death, the term *intransigente* in Argentine politics connotes principle, morality, and uncompromising defense of truth; in all of this, of course, are echoes of Moreno's self-righteousness, wherein compromise becomes sellout, and consensus becomes collaboration with enemies.

Yrigoyen's intransigence, however, was hardly the most pernicious legacy of Moreno's sense of political evil. Moreno's notion that a progressive state could be attained only by eliminating enemies was also a necessary guiding fiction behind the "Dirty War" waged by the 1976–1983 military government against some real and many fictitious subversives. Quite simply, the military felt that the political situation in the mid-1970s had become so dangerous that only a policy of extermination, no matter how tenuous the evidence against its victims, could solve the country's problems; the Plan suggests that Moreno would have approved at every step.

Moreno also anticipated Argentina's sense of state, which in modern times has meant the constant intervention of the government in labor and commerce, making Argentina's the most overgoverned, overregulated economy in the capitalist world. While stopping short of a genuine socialism, governmental tampering with the economy has produced such a morass of regulations, industrial

subsidies, job protection, labor rights, price supports, artificial exchange rates, state industries, and the like as to effectively paralyze
the economy. The justification for such repeated intervention resonates Moreno's desire to domesticate capitalism in the name of
forced equality.

Given the extremist positions espoused in the Plan and the very
different view of Moreno the Plan forces on today's readers, some
of Moreno's liberal defenders have understandably tried to call the
Plan apocryphal. Indeed, the controversy surrounding the Plan's
authenticity is almost as interesting as the Plan itself. When the
Piñero anthology appeared in 1895, Paul Groussac, a dyspetic
French-born scholar living in Buenos Aires who made a grand
career of denigrating most things Argentine, devoted an entire
issue of *La Biblioteca*, a magazine he edited, to debunking the Plan
as the work of someone who "if not a mystifier or madman, had an
evil soul married to the intelligence of an imbecil" (Groussac, "El
Plan de Moreno" 145). Although Piñero responded ably to
Groussac's invective, the latter's view remained popular among
Argentine liberals who refused to believe that Moreno could have
written such a thing. Some twenty-five years later, Groussac's criticism of the Plan was taken up by Ricardo Levene, author of a four-
volume work on Moreno, who apparently refused to accept the
Plan as authentic, largely because its contents totally contradict the
image of Moreno he tries to present—that of a high-strung patriot
who, while given to excesses, was nonetheless firmly committed to
Enlightenment principles. Levene later published a calligraphic
analysis of the handwritten copy and thereby determined that it
was written by an exiled Uruguayan named Andrés Alvarez—
which in fact proved nothing since the copy had never pretended
to be anything but a copy; identifying the copyist hardly disproved
Moreno's authorship.

More frightening than the liberals who rejected the Plan on the
basis of allegedly flimsy evidence are those Argentines who view
the Plan with approval. The best of these is nationalist historian
Enrique Ruiz-Guiñazú, who, in 250 pages of well-documented arguments, shows that Groussac's and Levene's objections cannot
stand close scrutiny and that the Plan coheres point by point with
other of Moreno's writings whose authorship is unquestionable.
While conceding some corruption in the copy found in Seville,

Ruiz-Guiñazú demonstrates that Moreno's contemporaries and later historians were aware of *a* Plan's existence similar, albeit not identical, to the surviving version (Ruiz-Guiñazu, *Epifanía* 181–331). Later, in the 1960s and 1970s, third-world leftists resuscitated the Plan as a way of giving authority to their support of violent revolution, forced redistribution of wealth, and an isolationist antiimperialism. Principal among this group is Rodolfo Puiggrós, perhaps Argentina's leading Marxist historian.

Moreno's place in Argentine history is difficult to assess. His radical attitudes early distanced him from less extreme elements in the Junta and were naturally anathema to conservative oligarchs. His name, however, remains before the public eye thanks to schoolbook histories that invariably portray him as an enlightened hero, a view whose survival demonstrates that few read him anymore in his entirety. Yet, whatever the intrinsic merit of his work or the distortions of Official History, Moreno is useful as a paradigm of the contradictory attitudes that run throughout Argentine thought. On the one hand, he used the rhetoric of liberty to advocate a reign of terror; he preached free expression while personally supporting censorship; he appropriated a hegemonic role for Buenos Aires while occasionally giving lip service to notions of provincial equality; he advocated a representative constitutional congress and then tried to exclude provincial leaders he disagreed with; he spoke grandly of popular sovereignty but favored rule by a small "enlightened" minority; he assumed a superiority for Argentina in Latin America that even now renders his country one of the least popular in inter-American relations; he supported the concept of a paternalistic, isolationist, and interventive state that still saps the country's economic potential. Yet, on the other hand—and this point cannot be overemphasized—Moreno was the principal conduit of the greatest ideals of Western political thought. He introduced into Argentine discourse concepts of universal equality, freedom of expression and dissent, individual liberty, representative government, institutional rule under law. And even though Moreno betrayed those goals, the vocabulary he introduced into Argentine thought became the frame within which all governments would be judged, the necessary point of departure for every attempt to reform and improve the patria. In short, during his life, Moreno's influence was early checked by his extremism, intransigence, and untimely death. But as a precursor of guiding fictions still very alive in his country, he is a man of unusual transcendence.

After Moreno's departure, the Junta disintegrated into internal rivalries. From these rivalries emerged two major currents: *Morenismo,* named after Don Mariano, and *Saavedrismo,* named after his archrival Cornelio Saavedra, the Junta president. Morenismo soon gave birth to the Unitarian party, which as its name suggests favored a strong centralist government controled by porteño elites. Similarly, Saavedrismo quickly evolved into an opposing party called *Federalist,* which favored provincial autonomy and tended to be more populist. Although in principle, the Federalists were committed to provincial autonomy and the Unitarians to centralism, in practice, personal and economic rivalries blurred ideological distinctions between Federalism and Unitarianism to such a degree that Federalists from Buenos Aires eventually became as ruthlessly centralist as the most doctrinaire Unitarians. Much can be learned about the Unitarian–Federalist conflict by studying each party's antecedents, namely, Morenismo and Saavedrismo.

Despite its namesake, Morenismo was more the creation of Moreno's followers than of Moreno himself. These followers, a small group of young porteño intellectuals, doggedly kept his memory alive, largely through a club called the *Sociedad Patriótica* whose meetings were dedicated to political discussions, oratory and literary readings, all with a liberal bent (Ibarguren, *Las sociedades* 60–75). Chief among Moreno's supporters was Ignacio Núñez, who criticized Saavedra as a man "who sounds like a president [but] appears good only at speaking up for business interests" (cited in Ruiz-Guiñazú, *Saavedra* 386). Like Moreno, he was even more critical of the provincial deputies who in his view were "a vulgar lot bereft of knowledge and experience in even the most common public matters." In Núñez's view, the provincials had been "removed too suddenly from their ranchos and hick towns" and were "confused men, good only for domestic, financial, and municipal concerns" (*Saavedra* 386–387). That is to say, weighty matters like political organization, independence, and foreign relations should be left to the educated elite from Buenos Aires.

The haughtiness of the Morenistas contrasts sharply with the attitude of Saavedra and the Saavedristas. In his memoirs, Saavedra claims that his followers were more authentically American than the high-born, intellectually pretentious Morenistas, and he ridicules Moreno for his involvement with the Spanish-dominated cabildo during the Liniers affair (*Saavedra* 38–39). A man of good instincts rather than well articulated ideas, Saavedra attempted to give equal representation to the provincials, but from the arrogant young Morenistas he received only disdain. Included among Saavedra's supporters, however, was another group who would later discredit him, namely, conservative porteño businessmen who, already resentful for having lost their commercial contacts with Spain, feared the radicalism and questionable religious orthodoxy of the Morenistas. The Saavedra faction, then, was much less homogenous than the Morenistas. It was in sum an odd, even contradictory mix of popular sentiment, concern for the provinces, and old-line, pro-Spanish, pro-Catholic conservatism—a configuration that would characterize Federalism throughout its history.

The factionalism represented by *saavedrismo* and *morenismo* presaged the most difficult problem of Argentine nationhood: an enduring rupture in the body politic that the country's most imaginative leaders have never been able to heal. In a sense, Argentine society from the first days of independence appeared to be built on a seismic fault. No Argentine institution has withstood the fault's unpredictable, violent movements, and its existence underlies much of the country's perpetual instability.

On one side of the fault were the Morenista elite, youthful dreamers who wanted to make their country a showplace of Western civilization. In politics they supported a strong unified government centered in Buenos Aires, a position that later identified them as Unitarians. Although they sympathized with some kinds of protectionism, they generally favored a liberal free-trade policy, especially with the British, their enemies of a few years earlier. They came from the upper classes who lived off their rents and educated their children in Europe. They lived looking northward reading French and English authors, and believing, like José Arcadio Buendía of García Márquez's *One Hundred Years of Solitude*, that Culture had to be imported. And they were ashamed of the backward Argentine provinces with their caudillo leaders and illiterate, mixed-blood gauchos. Of course, as students of European thought, they spoke grandly of the eventual formation of a democratic republic and gave lip service to Enlightenment notions of universal equality and brotherhood. But theirs was a peculiarly antidemocratic democracy whose leaders were more philosopher princes than representatives drawn from the people.

On the other side of the fault was the motley opposition to Morenismo, sometimes Saavedristas, sometimes Criollistas, who distrusted the porteño intellectual elite and often felt more comfortable with the personalist government centered in a king, dictator, or caudillo than with an institutional government easily dominated by those educated in the ways of Europe. The provincial Criollistas feared porteño hegemony and generally supported provincial autonomy, a position that later identified them as Federalists. Moreover, they maintained a paternalistic interest in the lower classes, feared foreign political and economic involvements, and sympathized with provincial concerns. Juan Bautista Alberdi, one of nineteenth-century Argentina's most able thinkers, summarized the difference in the following words: "Saavedra's party was the truly national party, since he wanted that all the nation be involved in the government. Moreno's government was localist, since he wanted that all authority be centered in the capital city, not in the nation" (Alberdi, *Grandes y pequeños hombres* 99). In sum, Alberdi's words signal the most damning aspect of Argentine liberalism: it was never truly "liberal" if we understand liberalism to include representative, participatory democracy.

The resulting conflicts between *saavedristas* and *morenistas*, conservatives and liberals, protectionists and free-traders, provincials and porteños, populists and elitists, nationalists and cosmopolitans, personalists and institutionalists, Federalists and Unitarians, in odd ways still haunts the country. Of course the names and the configuration of alliances on both sides of the fault would change according to the times. Moreover, the schism was not always drawn along class lines since the wealthy changed their political loyalties according to commercial interests. As Halperín Donghi shows in his remarkable *Politics, Economics and Society in Argentina in the Revolutionary Period*, porteño landowners were alternately liberal or protectionist, cosmopolitan or nationalist, depending which side was best for business at a given time (383–391).

In the twentieth century, a cosmopolitan elite, nourished by the landed oligarchy and centered in Buenos Aires, would take the place of the Morenistas; they would pay lip service to democracy and go through the motions of democratic pluralism, yet beneath the show their enduring suspicion of the lower classes would lead them repeatedly to support an authoritarianism occasionally as brutal and duplicitous as anything recommended by Moreno. On the other side of the fault, industrial workers and immigrants would supplant the provincial gauchos in populist movements. Messianic leaders like Juan Domingo Perón and his wife Eva Duarte would replace the personalist caudillos. Protectionist economic policies and an insular worldview would reflect the localism of a century earlier. Fascists and third-world communists would become the new paternalists. Yet in all these changes there is a peculiar, déjà vu quality so pronounced that it would appear that Argentina is not one country, but two, both enormously suspicious of the other yet destined to share the same homeland.

Chapter Three

Populism, Federalism, and the Gauchesque

Although the first Creole rebellions occurred in 1810, Spanish forces remained on South American soil until 1824. During this fourteen-year span, Creole leaders spent much of their time seeking the troops, arms, funding, physical strength, and moral energy to repel their powerful former masters. Argentina (if I may be allowed to use a term that did not acquire official sanction until 1826) played a major role in the events that liberated South America. Argentine heroes like José de San Martín, Juan Lavalle, and Martín Güemes not only fought for Argentina's freedom but also helped free Chile, Peru, Bolivia, and Ecuador from colonial rule.

Concurrent with the struggle for independence was an effort among River Plate intellectuals to justify the wars according to fresh mythologies of a new people and a new nation. The Morenistas reflected one aspect of this effort in their support of a peculiarly doctrinaire democracy in which a small group of enlightened men would govern—for the people, perhaps, but certainly not by the people. The guiding fictions underpinning the Morenistas' claim to power asserted their innate intellectual superiority over their detractors and their greater familiarity with modern (European) ideas. As mentioned earlier, the centralist, elitist notions of government favored by the Morenistas would eventually produce the Unitarian party. Opposition to the Unitarians coalesced in the Federalist party, which, as its name indicates, wanted greater autonomy for each of the provinces. Although porteño and provincial

47

Federalism shared a name, they differed on several key points. For porteño Federalists, autonomy meant preserving the port city's income from tariffs on imports and exports; moreover, porteño Federalists tended to be more conservative, more Catholic, more Hispanic. For the interior and Littoral provinces, Federalism meant resisting attempts to concentrate power in the port city and, at its best, defending the rights of the poor and the low-born. While not identical, both Federalisms generated guiding fictions to justify their claim to power, some of which for lack of a better term I call *populist*.

I confess to being uncomfortable with the term *populism* since it invokes images of demagoguery, anti-intellectualism, and mob rule, especially in modern Argentina, where populism is often an alternate term for Peronism. Nonetheless, I persist in its use since a narrowly defined populism can greatly aid our discussion of nineteenth-century Argentina. The term as I use it refers to three main concepts. First is the notion of radical democracy in which all elements of society, regardless of race, class, and provenance, participate equally. Radical democracy does not stop at the voting booth; it also includes concepts of equal access to education and to the sources of wealth (land in Argentina's case). A second characteristic of nineteenth-century Argentine populism is the federalist ideal that saw the provinces as primarily autonomous entities involved with each other only through mutual consent; such federalism grew in direct opposition to the centralist ambitions of the Unitarians. And finally, much Argentine populism, both past and present, is imbued with a nativist impulse that would try to define Argentina in terms of its popular culture, particularly the culture of the gauchos and lower classes. Argentine nativism grew as a counterbalance to the Europeanized ways of the Morenistas and the Unitarians.

In studying the roots of Argentine populism, we will examine the work of two men, one a politician-thinker and the other a poet. The politican was José Artigas (1764–1850), a Uruguayan caudillo who was the first in the River Plate area to clearly articulate notions of federalism and radical democracy. For nearly a decade, Artigas successfully withstood Buenos Aires' designs on his province, and became for a time the dominant political figure in Uruguay and the Littoral. The second man studied in this chapter is Bartolomé

Hidalgo (1788–1822), also a Uruguayan, who fought under Artigas and was no doubt familiar with the caudillo's ideas. Hidalgo is best known as the inventor of gauchesque poetry, also called the *género gauchesco* or simply the *gauchesque*. Although Hidalgo borrowed heavily from centuries-old literary traditions of portraying popular-type characters in colloquial dialect, he was the first to present concrete images of the River Plate gaucho in literature, as well as the first to use that image for frankly political purposes, many of which cohere with Artigas's notions of radical democracy. He also deserves credit for first promoting the gaucho as a national type, a popular figure with mythical overtones who in some sense embodies the real Argentina.

Lest anyone wonder why two Uruguayans are the focus of this chapter, it should be remembered that Uruguay, or the *banda oriental* (the eastern shore) as it was known, formed part of the River Plate viceroyalty in colonial times, and that until the 1820s, it continued seeing itself as merely one more province of the United Provinces. Uruguay's independence in large measure resulted from external forces, particularly from Brazil and Great Britain, rather than from domestic separatism. In the decade following Independence, Artigas and Hidalgo, just as much as the porteños, viewed themselves as citizens of the United Provinces of the River Plate. Moreover, neither they nor many of their Uruguayan contemporaries aspired to separate nationhood.

Following Moreno's death, Argentina entered one of the most difficult and confusing periods of her history, comparable in some sense to what would have happened in the United States if the Revolutionary War, the War of 1812, the collapse of the Confederation, the Civil War, and the French-Indian War had all occurred at once. Danger loomed everywhere. Spanish armies could at any moment move to reclaim the colonies; smoldering political tensions threatened to erupt in civil war; provincial caudillos chafed against porteño pretensions; Upper Peru (what is now Bolivia) and Paraguay talked of permanent separation from Buenos Aires; and Brazil, wanting to safeguard river shipping from its southwestern provinces, claimed the *banda oriental* for itself. The situation was not helped by the chronic instability of the porteño governments that were dissolved and reconstituted under different names several times. Despite the political instability, however, most Argentines, porteños and provincials alike, were united in pursuing three major goals: to maintain the viceroyalty boundaries, to expel the Spanish not just from the viceroyalty but from the entire continent, and to select a form of government everyone could live with. None of these goals was reached initially.

Their first goal, that of maintaining the viceroyalty, proved impossible. On May 14, 1811, Paraguay became the first territory of the viceroyalty to declare its autonomy. Buenos Aires immediately sent troops under General Manuel Belgrano to bring the errant province back into the viceregal fold. Having no good reason to submit to the Buenos Aires government, the Paraguayans defeated . the porteño army, forcing Belgrano to sign a treaty recognizing their province's autonomy. All Belgrano got for his efforts was a tepid agreement from Asunción that "the province of Paraguay should remain subject to the government of Buenos Aires in the same fashion as all the other United Provinces"—a statement of some irony since the nature of that union would dominate River Plate politics for the next seventy years (Busaniche, *Historia* 325–326). Behind Paraguay's intentions, however, lay a frankly separatist sentiment that would shortly become manifest in the beginning of the isolationist dictatorship of *El Supremo*, the legendary Dr. José Gaspar Rodríguez Francia.

Initially, the independence struggle met with as little success as attempts to keep Paraguay in the union. Patriot forces during 1810–1811 met repeated defeat in the northern provinces at the hands of the royalists. The porteño leader in these frustrated campaigns, Juan José Castelli, a radical member of the original junta and friend of Moreno's, exacerbated the crisis by alienating local elites in the nothern provinces on issues of Indian labor and taxation (Rock, *Argentina* 82–83). The struggle for independence began turning in Argentina's favor when in 1813 the government appointed General José de San Martín, a twenty-year veteran of the Spanish army, to head the patriot troops. Owing to the discipline and professionalism San Martín brought to the rebel forces, from 1814 on, Argentina's war for independence met with increasing success. Argentine armies, which included patrician porteños as well as gauchos under caudillo generals, drove the Spanish not only from Argentina but also from Chile, Bolivia, and Peru. With limited supplies, the Creole troops fought heroically on some of the most challenging terrain in the world. One particularly daring exploit was San Martín's surprise attack on loyalist troops in Chile after crossing the Andes mountains; in twenty-one days and with soldiers, horses, and cannons, he covered 300 miles of terrain that included heights in excess of 13,000 feet—a feat no less remarkable than the epochal mountain crossings of Hannibal and Napoleon. So surprised were the Chilean royalists that they never regained their equilibrium. In 1822, San Martín and Simón Bolívar met in Guayaquil, Ecuador, after which San Martín inexplicably entered voluntary exile in Europe. His reasons for abandoning Argentina at such a crucial point in its development remain one of the great mysteries of Latin American history. Perhaps in his encounter with the brilliant but ambitious Bolívar, he glimpsed how aspiring men would turn the military success of independence into political disaster; perhaps his distaste for politics and news of political strife in Buenos Aires convinced him that as a soldier rather than a politician he had no future in Argentina. Whatever his reasons, with his departure, Argentina lost one of the most selfless, patriotic leaders ever to cross her stage.

Notwithstanding the hardships of San Martín and his allies, expelling the Spanish proved simple compared to the task of building a new nation consisting of all the remaining provinces under institutional government. The country's two emerging political parties, Unitarian and Federalist, embraced opposing concepts of government. Frenchified porteños, in the main Unitarians inspired by Moreno, supported a peculiarly exclusivist democracy controlled by enlightened men like themselves. After the abortive campaigns in the north, Saavedra, who sympathized with federalist concerns, lost credibility and in September 1811 was replaced by a three-man pro-Unitarian government, known as the *Triumvirate*. The most visible member of the Triumvirate was Bernardino Rivadavia, a devout liberal, pro-porteño, and occasional monarchist, discussed in detail in the next chapter.

The Triumvirate quickly dissolved the cumbersome albeit representative bodies through which Saavedra had governed, the *junta grande* and the *juntas provinciales*. As if fighting the Spanish were not enough, they also launched a protracted campaign against the Federalist caudillo José Artigas in the Banda Oriental and his allies,

Francisco Ramírez and Estanislao López in the northeastern provinces of Entre Ríos and Santa Fe. On November 11, 1811, the Triumvirate, under the inspiration of Rivadavia, issued a peremptory document titled *Statute of the Supreme Government of the United Provinces of the River Plate in Name of Ferdinand VII*, proclaiming the need to "constrain popular arbitrariness" and impose "the rule of law" until provincial representatives could "establish a permanent constitution" (Busaniche 323–324). In short, the Buenos Aires Triumvirate sought to maintain exactly the same control over the provinces that the port city enjoyed during colonial times as capital of the viceroyalty. Of course, no province had in any way delegated such authority to the porteño government, and the authority of Ferdinand VII, whom Buenos Aires claimed to represent, was at this point not universally accepted. The porteño invocation of Ferdinand VII reflected the porteños' continuing interest in establishing a constitutional monarchy in the River Plate. In a way, such sentiment merely reflected ongoing debates in Europe, where the English system seemed infinitely preferable to the disorder of France; lurking behind the Unitarians' interest in monarchy, however, was their desire to concentrate power in the city and limit the authority of the provinces.

To maintain some appearance of representative government, however, the Triumvirate hastily organized a general assembly that supposedly represented the interior, although most of its members were porteños. When certain members of even this carefully chosen body expressed provincial concerns, the Triumvirate ordered its police force to dissolve the assembly altogether, thus ending even the pretense of democratic rule and further exacerbating provincial suspicion of Buenos Aires (Rock, *Argentina* 85–88). Although tracing the labyrinthine political developments of the next several years lies outside the scope of this book, these early clashes between the centralist, elitist Unitarians and the autonomist, often populist Federalists would become paradigmatic for understanding the intellectual disagreements underlying Argentina's guiding fictions.

The chief spokesman for the Federalist cause was José Artigas. Artigas breaks almost every stereotype of the caudillos that pro-Unitarian (i.e., liberal) historians have tried to foist on their readers. Rather than an untutored, primitive tribal chieftain surrounded by hordes of semisavage gauchos, he was acquainted with basic tenets of democratic political thinking and a great admirer of the United States revolution. He also left thousands of documents to be collected in the *Archivo Artigas,* an enormous publishing effort which since 1950 has published twenty volumes and still remains incomplete. Reportedly, Artigas dictated many of his statements, which might explain their rambling structure and curious diction (Luna, *Los caudillos* 59). Nonetheless, his works often reflect careful thought, and frequently display concepts more progressive and more original than those entombed in the well-crafted prose of his Unitarian enemies. He also had the courage to follow the premises of democracy to their ultimate conclusions and came up with ideas that strike even comtemporary readers as radical. Not without basis, he has become a *cause célèbre* of leftist historians like Lucía Sala de Touron and Oscar H. Bruschera ever anxious to claim American roots.

Artigas was forty-seven years old when the porteños declared independence from Napoleonic Spain in May 1810. For twenty years he had served in a national police force charged with protecting Uruguay's western flank from incursions of Indians and Portuguese soldiers. News of the May 25th rebellion in Buenos Aires sparked similar sentiments in the Banda Oriental. In March 1811, Artigas visited Buenos Aires and offered his services to the Junta. He was appointed lieutenant colonel in the patriot army and returned to Uruguay to fight the royalist forces headquartered in Montevideo. Artigas quickly mobilized the Uruguayan countryside against the Spanish forces; his success in raising a popular army clearly showed his ability as a leader of the masses. After several important victories in the countryside, Artigas's forces began marching on Montevideo. He was later joined by troops from Buenos Aires. And then occurred one of the most puzzling developments of Uruguay's independence movement: the Buenos Aires Triumvirate, under inspiration of its principal member, Bernardino Rivadavia, signed an agreement with the Spaniards returning to Spanish rule all of the Banda Oriental and part of Entre Ríos!

The man most affected by this outrageous arrangement was José Artigas, who by this time was unquestionably the most popular man in Uruguay. Why did the porteño government consent to such an agreement? It has been suggested that Rivadavia felt the Spanish could best resist the Portuguese invaders who now occupied part of western Uruguay, and that by accepting Spanish rule on the other side of the estuary, Buenos Aires could concentrate on the wars in the north. Neither of these explanations makes sense, since both would allow the Spanish a permanent hold on American territory, and there was no reason to think the Spanish would not eventually move against Buenos Aires. A more probable explanation was Buenos Aires' fear that the enormously popular Artigas was spinning out of control and that his large army consisting of mixed-blood gauchos and country folk constituted a form of "popular arbitrariness" that the Triumvirate had deplored earlier. As things turned out, Buenos Aires' attempts to play the Spanish against the Portuguese (if that is really what the Triumvirate had in mind) was a complete failure. The Portuguese continued strengthening their hold on Uruguayan territory while the Spanish fortified themselves in Montevideo. Rivadavia's concession did, however, have a devastating effect on Artigas and his army. Caught between the Portuguese and the Spanish with no hope of aid from Buenos Aires, he led some 16,000 Orientales to the western shore of the Uruguay River where they tried to regroup as a viable army. Artigas thus recognized that he had three deadly enemies: the Spanish in Montevideo, the Portuguese in Brazil, and the Unitarians in Buenos Aires (Busaniche 325–326).

On October 8, 1812 a new Triumvirate assumed power in Buenos Aires. Although the new government remained faithful to Unitarian pretense by proclaiming itself the "depository of superior authority in the United Provinces," it did have the good sense to repudiate the Rivadavian agreement with the Spanish and to send General Manuel de Sarratea to Uruguay to assault the Spanish stronghold in Montevideo. Sarratea was also instructed to bring the popular Artigas under control. A member of the first Triumvirate, the autocratic Sarratea managed to offend Artigas at every turn until eventually open warfare broke out between them. Finally, Sarratea's second-in-command, José Rondeau, sided with Artigas and sent Sarratea packing. With the irksome Unitarian out of the way, Artigas and Rondeau marched together against Montevideo (Busaniche 329–331).

In the meantime, the General Constitutional Assembly first planned in 1810 finally convened in Buenos Aires in January 1813.

Several interior provinces instructed their delegates to approve only a Federalist constitution, but none of the delegations carried instructions as extensive as those of the Orientales. These instructions resulted from one of the most remarkable meetings of the period. On April 4, 1813, under Artigas's leadership, delegates from several Uruguayan towns met in a provincial congress to decide whether the Banda Oriental should participate in the General Constitutional Assembly. After a moving speech by Artigas, in which he insisted that "my authority emanates only from you," the provincial congress decided to send delegates to Buenos Aires ("Oración inaugural," April 4, 1813, *Documentos* 95).

In a later meeting, the provincial representatives under Artigas's direction drafted a position paper to be submitted to the national congress in Buenos Aires (Artigas, "Instrucciones que se dieron a los diputados de la Provincia Oriental," April 13, 1813, *Documentos* 99–101). The first article of this remarkable document insists that the United Provinces demand "absolute independence" and the dissolution of "all obligation of fealty to the Spanish crown, the Bourbon family and the state of Spain." Artigas had learned his lesson well: as long as porteños like Rivadavia could lay claim to being the exclusive representatives of Ferdinand VII, the provincial governments were in danger. Article 2 asserts that "no other system will be allowed but that of a confederation by mutual pact of all the provinces that make up our state." Here Artigas sought to replace Buenos Aires' claims to central authority with a genuine federation of equal provinces, thus avoiding the kinds of abuses he and his consituency had suffered at the hands of the first Triumvirate. Article 14 insists that the Uruguayan port cities of Maldonado and Colonia be allowed free commerce and their own customs office, and "that no tarrif or tax be placed on articles exported from one province to another, nor that any preference be given for the regulation of commerce or income to the ports of one province over those of another, nor should ships en route from one province to another be forced to enter, drop anchor, or pay taxes in another." Just as Article 2 tried to limit Buenos Aires' political authority, Article 14 sought to curb the port city's economic power. From the beginnings of the independence movement and throughout much of the last century, Buenos Aires tried to maintain the same control over imports, exports, customs revenues, and interprovince trade that the city had enjoyed as head of the viceroyalty. Such control not only kept the provinces on a short leash; it also provided the porteño government with its major source of income. Artigas understandably found such privileges unacceptable. Article 16 affirms that each province "has the right to sanction the general constitution formed by the Consitutional Assembly." Artigas rightly suspected that the porteños would try to impose a constitution on the provinces without proper ratification—as indeed they did, once in 1819 and again in 1827. And finally, Article 19 maintains "that it is necessary and indispensable that the place of government of the United Provinces be outside of Buenos Aires." By this time, no Uruguayan trusted Buenos Aires.

As it turned out, the Uruguayan position paper was not even considered. As soon as the Uruguayan delegates arrived in Buenos Aires, they learned that the Constitutional Assembly had decided not to admit them owing to a legislative sleight-of-hand of the Unitarian porteño, Carlos María de Alvear. A new assembly was called, but this time the Buenos Aires government instructed Rondeau to make sure that no *artiguista* attend. At this point, relations between Artigas and Rondeau had deteriorated to such a degree that this final insult came as no surprise. Artigas then made one of the most controversial decisions of his life: in January 1814 he abandoned Rondeau, who still had not managed to oust the Spaniards from Montevideo, and regrouped his troops along the Uruguay River. He evidently saw no reason to fight for a government that denied him a place in it. The Buenos Aires government, now called the *Directorate* and under the direction of Gervasio Antonio de Posadas, accused him of treason and offered 6,000 pesos for his capture, dead or alive. On learning of Artigas's latest feud with Buenos Aires, the Spanish royalists in Montevideo offered the disillusioned caudillo the rank of general and a considerable sum of money. He refused. As historian Félix Luna points out, Artigas disagreed with Buenos Aires, but did not abandon his commitment to the United Provinces (*Los caudillos* 44–46).

Artigas quickly renewed contact with his caudillo allies in the Littoral provinces, and soon became the dominant political figure on both sides of the Uruguay River. His fame as a spokesman for Federalism also brought him in contact with leaders from the western and northern provinces, much to Buenos Aires' dismay. Posadas sent several armed expeditions against Artigas, but all were defeated. Faced with the prospect of a united Federalist front across Argentina's northeastern edge, Posadas finally negotiated a peace treaty with Artigas ("Convenio suscrito por José Artigas con los delegados del Director Supremo," April 23, 1814, *Documentos* 130–131). Although neither side put much faith in the treaty, its terms are remarkable for their moderation. The first article specifies that Posadas would retract his statement that Artigas was a traitor and issue a decree restoring "the reputation and honor of Citizen José Artigas." Artigas's concern for clearing his name indicates how much he valued his standing as an honorable citizen of the United Provinces, even in Buenos Aires. The treaty further specifies that Entre Ríos and Uruguay will be independent "and not bothered in any way." But Artigas carefully specifies that "this independence is not national independence; consequently, it should not be considered sufficient to separate great masses of people from others, nor should it interfere with the general goals of the revolution." In sum, Artigas was an autonomist, not a separatist; he never quit hoping for a confederation of equal provinces. The remaining articles of the treaty commit Buenos Aires to continuing its support of the siege against the Spanish at Montevideo (i.e., no more agreements like Rivadavia's) and then specifies that, once the siege was over, the porteño troops would return directly to Buenos Aires— and, by implication, not attack Artigas.

Of course, it didn't turn out this way. Montevideo finally fell to American forces on June 23, 1814, and just as Artigas had feared, the porteño troops promptly turned on him. The man who claimed the victory over Montevideo was Carlos María de Alvear, the porteño politician who prevented the Uruguayan delegation from participating in the constituent congress of a year earlier. Alvear attacked Artigas from the east, and Posadas sent troops from the south, but Artigas and his gaucho soldiers proved more than a match for the porteños. Faced with this military failure, and the capture of Montevideo by the Artiguistas, Posadas resigned and was replaced by Alvear, who again sent troops against the Artiguistas, but again the porteños were defeated. Following Artigas's latest victories over the porteños, the Spanish again contacted Artigas, this time by way of General Joaquín de la Pezuela, who in name of the Lima Viceroy sent Artigas a letter offering him the rank of general and aid in his battles

against "the caprices of the mindless people of Buenos Aires" if only
he would join the royalist cause. Artigas' reply again shows his loyalty to an independent, federated Argentina: "I am not for sale, nor
do I want any greater reward for my work than to see my country free
of Spanish control" ("Contestación de Artigas a Pezuela," July 28,
1814, *Documentos* 126–127).

By mid-1815, Artigas was at the height of his influence. Having
proclaimed Uruguay, Entre Ríos, Corrientes, and Santa Fe to be
the League of Free Peoples of the Littoral and himself, their Protector, he was the de facto ruler of the area. Although there is little
doubt but that Artigas the Protector would have won an election,
he did not arrive at his position through any institutional mechanism, a fact that has led critics to see him as merely one more
populist dictator, in embryo if not in fact. And it is true that Artigas
showed that dictator's affinity for grand decrees and high-sounding
pronouncements. The context of his decrees also suggest an odd
governance structure in which towns in the area elected cabildos,
or town councils, which in turn received apparently binding instructions from the Protector. His ideas, however, hardly support
the notion that he aspired to dictatorship. He encouraged local
cabildos to elect their officials through popular elections and to
discuss issues in town meetings. Moreover, in June 1815 he convened the Congreso de Oriente as a first step toward producing a
federalist constitution of some sort. Unfortunately, the Protector's
political fortunes went sour before a constitution could be written,
so we really don't know what role he would have played in an
institutional government. Nonetheless, during what remained of
1815 and the first months of 1816, he produced several documents
that address themes fundamental to Argentine populism: protectionism in foreign commerce; economic as well as civic democracy;
the political and economic inclusion of mixed-bloods, Africans, and
Indians; and a pro-American, nativist impulse that occasionally borders on xenophobia.

The debate between protectionists and free traders, as we saw in
the last chapter, already had a good airing in Yañiz's statement and
Moreno's response. Although Yañiz, as spokesman for the Spanish
Consulate, addressed the need to protect local industry, his real
interest was preserving the Spanish trade monopoly. Artigas, as son
and representative of the countryside, also defended protectionism

but from a much different perspective. On August 12, 1815, Artigas issued a statement to the Montevideo Cabildo directing that English traders be allowed into Uruguayan ports, provided they respect local law and not trade with Buenos Aires until conflicts with the porteño government could be resolved. He further argues that "the English must recognize that they are the beneficiaries [of our trade] and should therefore never try to interfere in our affairs" ("Fragmentos," *Documentos* 147). On September 9, 1815, he issued a rather detailed list of tariffs against imports clearly indicating his hopes of protecting local industry while increasing exports ("Reglamento Provisional," *Documentos* 148–149). In a later trade agreement of August 2, 1817, the English were specifically prohibited from any business activity not directly involved with ocean shipping ("Tratado de Comercio," *Documentos* 151–152). Unlike his counterparts in Buenos Aires, Artigas did not want foreign merchants and investors getting involved in the domestic economy.

Just as important as protectionism in Artigas's economic thinking were his plans for economic democracy through land distribution. The Spanish crown rewarded the early conquistadores and religious orders with large land grants that anticipated today's *latifundia*, the concentration of land in the hands of a few. Artigas realized that no democracy could function in a society of many peons and few *patrones*. He therefore repeatedly sought to break up large haciendas in order to give land to his humble followers. On September 10, 1815, he decreed that the provincial governor of the Provincia Oriental "be authorized to distribute lands" ("Reglamento Provisorio," *Documentos* 159–160). For this purpose, the Protector directed the governor and his staff to "review all available land in his jurisdiction as well as the most worthy beneficiaries of this grace, with the premise that the most unfortunate will be the most privileged. Therefore, free Negroes, *zambos* [Indian-African mix] of this same class, Indians, and poor Creoles, all shall be graced with some kind of *estancia* [ranch], if with their labor and manliness they work toward their happiness and that of their province" (160). Fearing that wealthy people might then buy land that had been distributed to "the most unfortunate" Artigas further ordained that "the beneficiaries cannot transfer ownership nor sell these kinds of estancias, nor contract against said properties any kind of debt." Recognizing, however, that without credit of some sort, the new landowners could not build up their flocks, he further mandated that available cattle also be distributed to "the most unfortunate" (162).

And from where would such land and cattle come? On one occasion Artigas directed the Montevideo cabildo to order all hacendados to make an inventory of their lands to determine which were underutilized. Where idle lands were found, he decreed that "the most illustrious governing cabildo should threaten [the hacendados] with the punishment that their lands will be transferred to the hands of workers [*brazos útiles*] who with their labor will increase . . . the prosperity of the country" ("Instrucciones sobre extrañamiento de los españoles," August 4, 1815, *Documentos* 155). Another source would be outright expropriation of lands and cattle owned by "Europeans and bad Americans" who did not support the revolution. Artigas does, however, allow the children of "Europeans and bad Americans" to receive "enough land for them to support themselves in the future; all other lands are available, provided [the original owners] had too much land in the first place" (161).

Lest this sound too much like a benign dictatorship, it should also be pointed out that Artigas sought full political participation for the lower classes. Nowhere is this more apparent than in his concern for the Indians. Unlucky in both love and marriage, Artigas adopted a Guaraní Indian as his son whom he called Andrés Artigas. He later placed Andrés in charge of the province of Misiones. In planning the Congreso de Oriente, which took place in Arroyo de la China, beginning in June 1815, Artigas asked his son in a letter dated March 13, 1815, to have "each town send an Indian representative to Arroyo de la China. You should allow each community full liberty to elect their [representatives] and to make sure that their representatives are good men with ability to accomplish what is needed" (*Documentos* 137). In a similar letter dated May 3, 1815, to José de Silva, Governor of Corrientes, Artigas wrote:

My desire is that the Indians in their communities govern themselves, so they can tend to their interests as we tend to ours. Thus they will experience a practical happiness and escape from that state of annihilation to which misfortune has subjected them. Let us remember that they have the principal right and that it would be a shameful degradation for us to keep them in the shameful exclusion that until now they have suffered because they were Indians. (*Documentos* 164)

Artigas also tried to bring Indians into the greater society through colonization. As a later writer would note, one of the River Plate's primary problems was underpopulation. To remedy this situation, Artigas offered lands, tools, and starter herds to entire communities of Indians to attract them to Uruguay's fertile hills. Had Buenos Aires and Brazil allowed him to continue these experiments in colonization, the history of the River Plate Indians, most of whom were exterminated, would have been quite different.

It is particularly remarkable that Artigas spoke of including the Indians in the revolutionary society at all. Perhaps the greatest tragedy of Independence was what it did to the Indians. The Spanish colonial rulers had created a legal system to protect Indian communities and properties. While these laws were frequently abused, they did give the Indians legal status and legal recourse, however imperfect. In contrast, the post-Independence societies abandoned colonial legal and economic structures in favor of new theories of private property and free trade. In so doing, they unleashed forces of greed and rapacity that led to the annihilation of virtually all River Plate Indians. As we will see in future chapters, these policies of extermination were supported by guiding fictions that denied the Indians a place in the emerging community. It is in this context that Artigas's attempts to include the Indians as part and parcel of "the people" are most remarkable. He tried to create a guiding fiction in which the people were not merely an excuse for clever men like the Morenistas who claimed power in the name of an abstract people no one ever saw. Artigas's people were real and visible; they included the low-born, the Africans, the zambos, the gauchos, and the Indians. Could this be the "popular arbitrariness" that so upset Unitarian Buenos Aires? Perhaps what most frightened the Unitarians about the Protector was his naive belief that government by the people should include everyone.

Well, almost everyone. Artigas made an exception when it came to the Spanish high-born, or Europeans as he called them. And these he singled out for a peculiar kind of persecution. First, as discussed earlier, he directed underlings to confiscate the lands of wealthy Spaniards in order to redistribute them to the poor. Second, as he wrote to Governor de Silva, he tried to exclude all Spaniards from public office:

It is not right that any European (with no exception of persons) remain in any job, particularly in positions . . . of public administration. I further warn you that if there are any [Europeans] in the army, they should be removed and Americans should be put in their place. (*Documentos* 165)

Later in a directive dated January 9, 1816, to the head of the cabildo of Montevideo on how to organize local governments and choose representatives to the provincial congress, he specifies, "All who have voice and voting rights should be Americans; if not, they will be excluded" (*Documentos* 171). Yet significantly, in another directive to Montevideo, dated August 4, 1815, Artigas tempers his nativism with a willingness to accept Europeans of low birth. For example, after directing that all Europeans be imprisoned lest they use "their influence and power" against the revolution, he specifies that "your lordship spare from this punishment the pitiable [*infelices*] craftsmen and workers who can help develop the country" (*Documentos* 155). It would therefore seem that Artigas's attitude toward Europeans was based more on class resentment than on xenophobia; he saw in European craftsmen and workers natural allies to the revolutionary cause against Spanish appointees and aristocrats.

Underlying much of the above is Artigas's willingness to suspend all concepts of class divisions in the New World and see "American" as a single category. Indians, Creoles, Africans, campesinos—all in his scheme of things are referred to as "American." And as Americans they can vote, hold office, own property, establish commercial contacts among themselves, and do so with priority over all foreigners. In a personal history of the Uruguayan rebellion against Spain, Artigas specifies that the Orientales were inspired by "the Americans of Buenos Aires" as if to say that the porteños rebelled because they were Americans, not because they read Rousseau or took offense at Napoleon's invasion of Spain ("José Artigas a la Junta Gubernativa del Paraguay," December 7, 1811, *Documentos* 58). Similarly, when he writes General Ambrosio Carranza in October 1811, Artigas speaks of "the honor, the humanity, the grand cause that constitutes the passion of all Americans" as though the category of "American" somehow predated the revolution and American identity was something waiting to be discovered rather than created (Artigas, *Citas a Artigas* 128). It is precisely this guiding fiction of America that allowed him to see all natives of American soil as a single mythical group, members of a future nation, all deserving of the same rights; similarly, this concept of America permitted him to classify his enemies as people whose notions of hierarchy led them to deny what Artigas sensed as the essential unity of a mythical America, an America already present as a collective sentiment and soon to be realized as a dynamic new nation.

Artigas, however, was not destined to play a role in that new nation. Perhaps overconfident with the triumphs of 1815 and 1816, Artigas failed to recognize how powerful a reorganized Buenos Aires could be. From his Congreso de Oriente, Artigas sent a delegation to Buenos Aires to try to sell again his notion of federation. Buenos Aires answered with a drastic proposal urging Artigas to form a separate nation of Uruguay (which the porteños knew he wouldn't accept) or send a delegation to a new Constitutional convention, to be held in Tucumán, with no strings attached. And here Artigas committed a serious tactical error by insisting that the provinces under his control—la Banda Oriental, Entre Ríos, Corrientes, and Santa Fe—would participate only if certain guarantees were made in advance, a condition Buenos Aires could not meet. As a result, the Artiguistas boycotted the convention and thus failed to participate in one of the most important historical developments of the period. Other interior provinces sent delegates, many of whom were Federalists still willing to discuss differences with their enemies (Luna, *Los caudillos* 49–50).

The Congreso de Tucumán accomplished a great deal. First, the deputies completed the work of Mayo and finally declared on July 9, 1816, total independence from Spain without giving lip service to the deposed Spanish monarch, Ferdinand VII. The Congreso's decision was made easier by Ferdinand himself, who now occupied the Spanish throne and was rapidly proving as reactionary and intolerant a monarch as his worst forebears. To underline their commitment to preserving the integrity of the former Viceroyalty, they took as their name The United Provinces of the River Plate and adopted a blue and white flag whose design is attributed, probably erroneously, to Belgrano himself (Rosencrantz, *La ban-*

dera de la patria 194–201). As its final act, the Congreso de
Tucumán appointed as Supreme Director of the United Provinces
Juan Martín de Pueyrredón with instructions to establish a government in Buenos Aires whose primary responsibilities would be
foreign relations, the war against Spain, and the creation of a constitution. The most divisive issue of all—Buenos Aires' relationship
with the Interior—was thus set aside until the actual drafting of a
constitution. Because of his intransigence, Artigas was excluded
from these and future deliberations.

The new Supreme Director, Pueyrredón, was an astute politician who had distinguished himself a decade earlier in leading
porteño forces against the British occupation. A gifted administrator, Pueyrredón garnered political and financial support for San
Martín's continuing military efforts—no small accomplishment
given the government's limited resources. He was also a determined enemy of Federalism and its chief exponent, José Artigas.
In his struggle against the Federalists, Pueyrredón was helped
enormously by a second Portuguese invasion of Uruguay in June
1816. Artigas was no match for the professional Portuguese troops,
and in January 1817, Montevideo fell to the Portuguese, who then
directed their attention to driving Artigas out of Uruguayan territory. Artigas immediately appealed to Buenos Aires for help, but
Pueyrredón was only too happy to let the Portuguese destroy
Artigas and his "barbarian democracy." Pueyrredón also feared
that opposing the Portuguese might provoke Portugal into siding
with Spain against the independence struggle. Artigas vehemently
denounced Pueyrredón's inaction, saying that "even a Portuguese
ruler would not behave so criminally" as to abandon a compatriot
to a common enemy (letter to Pueyrredón, November 13, 1817,
Documentos 177). Artigas also turned to his sometime allies Francisco Ramírez and Estanislao López in Entre Ríos and Santa Fe,
but he soon learned that their allegiance to him waned as his
power diminished before the relentless Portuguese.

In the meantime, with the collaboration of a committee repre-
senting several provinces, Pueyrredón in 1819 presented a constitution to all the provinces for ratification. The new constitution called
for a strong executive, or Supreme Director, to be elected by congress rather than by popular vote. Congress, in turn, would consist
of a lower house of popularly elected provincial representatives

whose numbers would vary according to the population of each province, a provision that greatly favored Buenos Aires. Although the senate was originally intended to correct this imbalance by having the same number of senators from each province, the final version of the constitution specified that new senators would be selected, not by popular election, but by standing senators who would choose new members from a list of nominees submitted by the provincial legislatures. The constitution also left open the possibility of a constitutional monarchy. The obvious porteño bias of these measures met immediate opposition in the interior. To impose the constitution, Pueyrredón sent troops into Santa Fe, where they were repelled by López's gauchos. López and Ramírez then joined forces and begin marching toward Buenos Aires. Faced with mounting opposition both in the provinces and at home, Pueyrredón resigned in 1819, allegedly for reasons of poor health (Rock, *Argentina* 92–93).

His successor was Artigas's erstwhile companion in arms, José Rondeau, to whom Artigas sent yet another entreaty for aid against the Portuguese, urging him in a letter dated July 18, 1819, to recognize that "Our union is the best shield against any kind of coalition [between Spain and Portugal]. . . . Let us begin with the enemy before us, and the Spanish campaign will find, in the defeat of the Portuguese, a foretaste of their own defeat" (*Documentos* 187). Rondeau, however, proved just as unwilling as Pueyrredón to legitimize Artigas by helping him fight the Portuguese. Moreover, he had his hands full with the impending invasion of Buenos Aires by López and Ramírez. By late 1819, Artigas sensed that defeat was at hand, and instructed his oldest son in the caring of his stepbrothers and the family servants. After a major defeat on January 22, 1820, Artigas fled Uruguayan territory, perhaps hoping to regroup his forces as he had before.

In the meantime, Rondeau met the armies of López and Ramírez in Cepeda, not far from Buenos Aires. The porteños were defeated, leading Juan Manuel Beruti to write in his *Memorias curiosas* that the patria was "filled with parties and destined to be the victim of the low-born mob, which is armed, insolent and desirous of striking down the decent people (*gente decente*), ruining them and making them equal to their own vileness and misery" (cited in Haleprín Donghi, *Politics* 333). On February 23, 1820, the provincial leaders

forced Buenos Aires to sign an agreement known as the Treaty of
Pilar, which in some sense was a triumph for Artiguismo that did not
include Artigas. It declared the provinces autonomous and provided
that a new federal congress be formed to determine the role of the
central government. Article 10 of the treaty specifies that a copy of
the treaty be sent to Artigas "so that he can establish the relations
that might behoove the interests of the province under his command, whose incorporation with the federation would be considered
a happy occurence" ("Pacto celebrado en la capilla del Pilar," *Documentos* 192). Whether intended or not, these words contained a
cruel irony, for Artigas at that moment had no province under his
command and was facing imminent defeat at the hands of the Portuguese. Moreover, the treaty failed to include what Artigas most
wanted from Buenos Aires and the other provinces: a declaration of
war against Portugal to retake the Banda Oriental. Not only was such
a declaration lacking; in some sense the treaty made Ramírez and
López de facto allies of Buenos Aires. So incensed was Artigas at
Ramírez's perceived betrayal of Uruguayan interests that hostilities
soon broke out between the two caudillos. Wanted by the Portuguese in Uruguay and pursued by Ramírez in Entre Ríos, Artigas
finally fled to Paraguay in September 1820, where he lived the last
thirty years of his life in exile (Rock, *Argentina* 92–93).

Of all the provincial caudillos, Artigas is the most remembered.
His survival in history stems from the odd irony that Uruguayans
consider him their founding father, thus proclaiming him the independence hero of a nation whose independence from the United
Provinces he opposed. Politics aside, Artigas enters the pantheon
of River Plate leaders as the first to articulate basic notions of
Argentine populism. Artigas saw himself as a Federalist, and, indeed, he defended the interests of the provinces with vigor and
courage. His federalism, however, included much more than the
simple notion of equal provinces in a loosely bonded confederation,
for Artigas's thinking was also imbued with a lower-class consciousness that loudly claimed a place for workers, Indians, Africans,
zambos, and the low-born, coupled with a powerful resentment of
upper-class privilege and pretension. Artigas was also the first major political leader to recognize the dangers free trade posed for
South America's fledgling industries, and particularly for the interior provinces that would be most adversely affected by Buenos

Aires's aspirations to become a great importer. And finally, he was one of the first to claim "America" as a mythical patrimony that defined this continent as a land destined to be more than a derivation from Europe. The cultural colonization seen in the Morenistas' devotion to European ideas made no sense to Artigas. Yet, as is often the case with populists, Artigas had no clear idea of how to institutionalize his political sentiments. His was a politics of feelings and actions, not of institutions and law. Moreover, his rule through decree and his suppression of detractors feeds the suspicion that, had his government lasted longer, he may have proved more personalist dictator than institutionalist democrat. In sum, for both good and for evil, he embodied antiliberal, protectionist, populist, nativist, and personalist guiding fictions that still define elements of the Argentine nation.

The populist guiding fictions underlying Artigas's Federalism are not, however, found only in statements by the caudillos; indeed, their primary mode of conservation and transmission may be through an odd, peculiarly River Plate literature called the *género gauchesco,* or the literature of the gauchesque, which emerges in Argentine letters concurrently with Artigas's rise and fall in the late 1810s. It is generally conceded that the creator of the gauchesque is Bartolomé Hidalgo, an Orientale who fought under Artigas and later settled in Buenos Aires, and whose poetry, like Artigas's pronouncements, claims a place for the rural poor in the revolutionary society. Hidalgo, however, goes an important step beyond Artigas in articulating a populist point of view: whereas Artigas confined his statements to the abstract, Hidalgo gave populism a human face and a human voice. What in Artigas were primarily theories, in Hidalgo become the archetypal gaucho, an image that is both the Argentine peasant of the late 1810s and also the mythical repository of the authentic Argentine spirit. As Josefina Ludmer (to whom my interpretation owes a great deal) points out, Hidalgo announces "a new social signifier, the patriot gaucho" (Ludmer, *El género gauchesco: Un tratado sobre la patria* 27). My interpretation of Hidalgo, however, differs from that of other admirable critics—Henríquez Ureña, Sánchez Reulet, and Caillet-Bois, for example—in that I argue that he was the first Argentine writer of any importance to enunciate populist guiding fictions to counterbalance the doctrines of exclusion that characterized antifederalist thought. Moreover, I suggest that his ideological significance equals and perhaps outweighs his literary import. In making this point, I do not deny his importance as the creator of gauchesque forms; I do, however, feel that excessive preoccupation with the formal aspects of his poetry has led many to miss the importance of his political position. Nothing in our study of Argentine guiding fictions holds greater importance than Hidalgo's populism as seen in the gauchesque, its origins, its ongoing significance, and the often unfriendly debate it continues to provoke.

But first a word about gauchesque literature generally. In matters of form, gauchesque literature usually consists of first-person narratives written in a language filled with ruralisms of varying degrees of authenticity, local color, type characters, and forced imagery that purportedly reflect lower-class rural life and speech. The linguistic and formal aspects of the gauchesque were destined to live a long life; virtually every generation of Argentine writers after Hidalgo has contributed something to gauchesque literature. The masterpieces of the genre, *The Gaucho Martín Fierro* and its sequel, *The Return of Martín Fierro,* by José Hernández (both of which are studied in detail in a later chapter) appeared in the 1870s, and in this century, Ricardo Güiraldes published a popular gauchesque novel, *Don Segundo Sombra,* in 1922. Even today's writers occasionally try their hand at the gauchesque.

Although all gauchesque literature shows similarities in its use of language, it developed along two quite different, if not opposing, ideological lines. Much of the best-known gauchesque literature after Hidalgo aspires to little beyond entertaining upper-class audiences with parodies of gaucho speech and rural backwardness, not unlike blackface routines that caricatured blacks in North American vaudeville theater. Such literature has been seen as merely entertaining by some as well as profoundly antipopular by others. Opposing this current is the populist gauchesque of which Hidalgo is the first example. Populist gauchesque literature sought to affirm a place in the country's guiding fictions for the common folk, the rural poor, the mixed-bloods, the nonelite. In this endeavor, Hidalgo identifies the gaucho not only as one more kind of Argentine but also as the authentic Argentine, the true symbol of an emerging nation. Moreover, Hidalgo makes his case for the gaucho using a kind of studied folksiness that when combined with his political point of view can only be called populist.

The peculiarity of gauchesque literature begins with the term *gaucho.* In his authoritative book *El gaucho,* the Uruguayan scholar Fernando O. Assunçao outlines and documents no fewer than thirty-eight theories concerning the possible origins of the term, ranging from the Gallic *gauche,* suggesting outlaw, to the South American slang term *guacho,* perhaps of Indian origin, meaning orphan (Assunçao, 383–520). River Plate intellectuals continue arguing over the "true" meaning of the term in a polemic that apparently will not accept the idea that words have and acquire new, even contradictory, meanings according to how, when, where, and by whom they are used.

The contemporary debate ranges between two extremes. On one side are purists who claim that *gaucho* originally meant vagabond, delinquent, or outcast, and that no self-respecting *campesino* (peasant) would consent to being called a gaucho. The purists further argue that attempts to romanticize the gaucho as a national type are in fact glorifications of banditry and lawlessness. Most typical of this school is Emilio A. Coni's well-researched but mean-spirited book, *El Gaucho: Argentina, Brasil, Uruguay.* On the opposing side are the romanticizers who use the word to label the authentic Argentine spirit, marked by common sense and generosity. In Argentina, to say that someone is *muy gaucho* suggests the person is helpful, accommodating, and endowed with good people sense—a typical *criollo.* Similarly, a *gauchada* or gaucho-like action, is understood as a special favor, a generous act of one friend to another.

The romanticizers can trace their use of the word to the early days of independence when royalists called the anti-Spanish revolutionaries *gauchos,* that is to say, bandits and criminals. So incensed at this usage was General Martín Güemes, caudillo of Salta, sometime ally of Artigas, and an important revolutionary leader, that he turned the term into a rallying cry, saying that if his soldiers were gauchos, *gaucho* must mean a patriot rebel fighting against unjust, autocratic rule. Some independence writers were fully aware of this transformation; as early as March 22, 1817, *La Gazeta de Buenos Aires* declared that "the title of gaucho, which used to provoke an unfavorable image of the person to which it was applied, has now become a glorious term by virtue of the many great deeds of the honorable workers and estancieros from Salta" (cited in Ludmer 27 fn. 5). Also on the side of the romanticizers is the gauchesque poetry of writers like Bartolomé Hidalgo, who used the image of the gaucho to symbolize the anti-Spanish revolutionary and in some sense the authentic American. Typical of this viewpoint in this century is Ricardo E. Rodríguez Molas's 1968 study, *Historia social del gaucho*. The term underwent further change in the 1840s when Domingo F. Sarmiento, an important writer discussed later, insisted on calling the soldiers of Facundo Quiroga gauchos; since these were men from the western provinces, far from the pampas where "real" gauchos lived, the term in Sarmiento's hands became roughly synonymous with country-dwelling nomads whom he viewed as natural supporters of *caudillismo* and thereby an obstacle to progress. The term *gaucho* acquired particular significance in this century when nationalist and populist writers, following Hidalgo's lead, made the gaucho the symbol of the authentic Argentina, which supposedly had been violated, betrayed, and pillaged by a rapacious, pro-European, anti-Argentine upper class and its foreign allies.

Owing to these radically different opinions, it is now virtually impossible to discuss the meaning of *gaucho* without taking sides in this bitter, often unpleasant debate. I therefore use the term with caution and in its most denotative sense: to refer to the country-dwelling poor, mixed-bloods in the main, whose lives were linked to the land. At the same time, I document in subsequent pages the transformation of the term into a nationalist rallying cry that in this century has made *gaucho* synonymous with *authentic Argentine*. In this regard the term labels one of Argentina's principal guiding fictions.

Just as problematic as the "true" meaning of the word *gaucho* is a parallel problem concerning the origin of gauchesque literature. There are two contradictory theories regarding the birth of the gauchesque. The first holds that gauchesque literature was merely an outgrowth of the popular poetry of the rural lower classes. However attractive this idea, it cannot be proved. Although many observers noted the existence of gaucho folk poetry, mostly song lyrics, prior to 1810, none of it was recorded. Decades later when some popular verse was transcribed, it consisted of ballads and love songs totally devoid of the folksy language and images associated with the gauchesque. The second theory concerning the origin of gauchesque literature holds that it was developed by educated men for whom it was a literary conceit just as artificial as any other. As Jorge Luis Borges points out, "The country troubadors never versify in a deliberately plebian language using images taken from rural life; making art is, for the popular classes, a serious, even solemn matter" (Borges, "El 'Martín Fierro,' " *Obras completas en colaboración* 515). More to the point, in a well-placed critique of the literary nationalism of the Peronist years, Borges wrote:

To my understanding there is a fundamental difference between the poetry of the gauchos and gauchesque poetry. . . . Popular poets, from rural areas as well as from poor city neighborhoods, poetize on general subjects: the trials of love and absence, the pain of love, always using a general lexicon; in contrast, the gauchesque poets cultivate a deliberately popular style that would never be used by a popular poet. I do not mean that the language used by popular poets is proper Spanish; I merely mean that if they make errors, such errors are the product of their ignorance. In contrast, the gauchesque poets always search for native words, a profusion of local color. . . . As a result, [gauchesque literature] is a literary genre as artificial as any other. (*Obras completas* 268)

Although Borges's intention was to depoliticize the gauchesque for which Argentine nationalists were making quite extravagant claims, there is no question but that the difference he establishes between the gauchesque and the authentically popular is fundamentally true. Borges's statement further implies, however, that the folksy language of gauchesque poetry somehow makes it less than "a serious, even solemn, matter." Nothing could be further from the truth—as Borges himself concedes in other contexts. Indeed, some of the most sublime moments in Spanish American literature are found in the gauchesque.

Since the género gauchesco is not then merely popular poetry transcribed, what is it, or better said, what specifically did Hidalgo bring to literature that justifies calling him the "father of the gauchesque"? In the words of the Dominican critic Pedro Henríquez Ureña, Hidalgo's creation was both modest and revolutionary (Henríquez Ureña, *Las corrientes literarias* 115). It was modest because verse, usually satirical, using popular characters and popular speech was common throughout the entire Hispanic world during the late eighteenth century, and particularly in the short ballads and skits (*cielitos* and *sainetes*) of the River Plate (Sánchez Reulet, "La 'Poesía Gauchesca' " 286–287). It was revolutionary because it placed such forms at the service of a specific political intention. In short, what had been burlesque and parodic became in Hidalgo's gauchesque a means of instructing the gauchos in their civic duties while using those same gauchos as a legitimizing symbol of an emerging nation—a symbol of undeniably populist connotations.

Each concern—didacticism and legitimization—is evident throughout Hidalgo's "modest" inventions. Borrowing from the balladlike *cielitos*, he created a new poetic voice in which a gaucho *payador* (troubador) addresses political subjects. For example, in "Un gaucho de la guardia del monte contesta al manifiesto de Fernando VII," one of his *cielitos*, an unnamed gaucho responds to a manifesto from the once deposed and now rethroned King Ferdinand VII, who claimed control of the River Plate—an act that prompted Argentina's definitive break from Spain in the Congreso de Tucumán of 1816. In response, Hidalgo's *payador* tells the king "to keep his trashy piece of paper / and light a light for Independence" (*Antología de la poesía gauchesca* 75)." Punctuating his ballad with the rhythmic refrain "*Cielito, cielo que sí*" ("Little heaven, heaven indeed"), the *payador* affirms:

> Cielito, cielo que sí,
> I tell you, Fernando:
> Accept us as free men
> And stop raising so much hell.

> Cielito, cielo que sí,
> keep your chocolate;
> we're pure-blooded Indians over here
> and drink only *mate*.

> And if you don't like it
> send over one of your frilly expeditions;
> but when your soldiers retreat to the woods,
> don't say it was because we betrayed you.
> (*Antología de la poesía gauchesca* 77–79)

Although Hidalgo's adolescent irreverence holds undeniable charm, most striking in these verses is their unabashed populism. Not only in the forced colloquialisms of the language do we see an attempt to identify independence with the gaucho; the very notion that the Spanish should keep their hot chocolate and leave Argentines to their *mate*, a bitter tea popular among the pampa Indians and their gaucho cousins, underlines the point that the common people were sufficient to win independence, that the low-born "the pure-blooded Indian" would make short work of the king's frilly armies, that the lower classes somehow embody the true spirit of the new nation.

And for whom were these lines intended? Surely not for the king, to whom they are addressed, and just as surely not for Hidalgo's contemporaries who, like Moreno, considered themselves intellectual descendants of Europe's most enlightened. The educated did not need to be told that "This business about the divine right of kings / is a lot of nonsense" (*Antología* 77). Nor did they need to hear

> Cielito, cielo que sí,
> In America, kings are not needed
> to govern other men
> but beneficial laws.
>
> What the King wants
> are his gold and silver mines . . .
>
> But the times have ended
> when rational beings
> died like animals
> in the bottom of those mines.
>
> Cielo, I swear by a whore,
> that the Kings of Spain had their nerve.
> They Christianized us by force
> And then walked off with our money.
> (*Antología* 78–79)

The intended audience was quite clearly the gauchos themselves, who, although they had fought for independence, now needed to be incorporated into a new civil structure. And it is here that we see the frankly populist emphasis of Hidalgo's thought. Prior to Hidalgo, no writer of any importance addressed the notion of offering the gauchos a niche in the emerging nation. Indeed, Beruti and the Morenistas stubbornly insisted that Independence was purely a product of enlightened men and must be protected from the "low-born mob" if it was to retain its purity. Consequently, Hidalgo's importance in Argentine intellectual history is much more than literary. While he undoubtedly deserves a high place in Argentine letters for his creation of the *género gauchesco,* just as remarkable were his populist intuitions that led him to address the issue of social pluralism at a time when the intellectual elite were fortifying the buttresses against all but themselves. Although no intellectual match for his better-educated contemporaries, Hidalgo must be given credit for better political intuitions, intuitions close to those articulated by his former military leader, José Artigas. Indeed, much of the civil strife that would engulf Argentina for the next fifty years might have been avoided had the self-styled aristocrats of Buenos Aires been as sensitive to the lower-class aspirations reflected in the modest revolution of this first gauchesque poet.

Just as Hidalgo turned the ballad-like *cielitos* to a political purpose, he later transformed the *sainete,* a popular theatrical form, into a vehicle for political instruction, commentary, and protest. In his hands, the *sainete* became the patriotic *diálogo* in which one gaucho, slightly more learned than most, instructs another on subjects ranging from the history of the Revolución de Mayo to Enlightment concepts of citizenship—much like what we saw in the verses cited earlier. But there is in the diálogos a note of protest against other Argentines not found in the cielitos. The emerging social order of the early 1820s had little use for former gaucho soldiers, nor were the high ideas of the Congreso de Tucumán reflected in the increasing strife between Buenos Aires and the provinces. The gauchos were in large measure the first victims of this failed idealism, and Hidalgo's diálogos reflect their disillusionment. Says Jacinto Chano, the "educated" gaucho of Hidalgo's "Diálogo patriótico interesante," to his good-natured interlocutor, Ramón Contreras:

> Contreras, from the very beginning [of the revolution],
> things went badly:
> people began putting one
> province over the others,
> as if all were not warmed
> by the same sun.

People started distrusting
each other, and all of a sudden,
dissension won the field.
And when we let down our guard,
that same dissension did us in.

(Antología 83)

These verses indicate that the failure of the independence movement for Hidalgo was not a failure of will or law or economics.
Rather, it was the failure of the few to include the many, as though
"all were not warmed by the same sun." Hidalgo found this failure
initially in the inability of the provinces to make good on the promise of Tucumán, to forge a united Argentina of equal provinces
according to the federalist ideal. But he quickly adds that the political failure was also a moral failure, a betrayal of principle, and a
retreat from the revolution itself. While the political failure may be
understood solely in political terms, Hidalgo emphasizes that the
underlying problem is individual: that some individuals saw themselves as better than others and therefore above the law to which
they gave lip service:

Why should some think
they are better than others? . . .
There is only one law,
and she gives her protection
to all who respect her.
Whoever the law offended,
should now have things set right;
this is what God demands.
Whatever justice requests,
and reason claims;
without asking whether the offender is porteño,
salteño [from Salta] or puntano [from San Luis]
or if he's the wrong color.
The law is the same against all crime
and doesn't distinguish between
brooks and lakes
nor between rich and poor.
For the law, a poncho [a gaucho cape]
is as good as a waistcoat and trousers.

(Antología 84)

Here the *payador* clearly laments that the independence won largely by gaucho sacrifice was now benefiting only the wealthy. What had started out, at least in the gauchos' mind, as a struggle for equality under the law, regardless of wealth or provenance, was now corrupted by wealthy porteños seeking to enrich themselves further while forcing their will on everyone else. But even more important is Hidalgo's deliberate focus on issues of unequal income, race, and place of origin, for it is here that we see the undeniable populist emphasis of his thought. In his schema, under the rule of law all races and classes are equal. Income (rich and poor, poncho and waistcoat), color, and provenance simply do not figure in his concept of ideal law. Now while it is true that the educated liberals of Buenos Aires, particularly the Morenistas, talked grandly of the rule of law, they quickly backtracked when confronted with notions of giving provincials, darker races, and gauchos standing equal to their own. Hidalgo is most significant precisely because, like Artigas, he takes the opposite tack. He speaks not only of equality under the law but also of the specific issues—race, income, and place of origin—that his more sophisticated compatriots addressed only as items to be postponed. Like Artigas, Hidalgo took the words of the Enlightenment at face value, assuming positions later to be identified as unabashedly populist. And also like Artigas, Hidalgo feared he was destined to be ignored:

> But my talk is in vain;
> until I see that crimes are
> punished without considering
> the criminal's status,
> I swear we won't be free
> until my horse starts talking.
> (*Antología* 84)

Here Hidalgo clearly distances himself from Beruti's fear of mob-rule. For Hidalgo, the most fearsome threat to the independence movement is not mob-rule but its opposite: the privilege of living above the law that social rank bequeaths to the few at the expense of the many.

Yet, while Hidalgo attacks visible attempts to exclude the gaucho, his rhetoric transcends the visible and imbues the gaucho with mythical qualities. Just as the term *American* in Artigas's pronouncements suggests a new nation and a mythical destiny, Hidalgo's gaucho does more than represent a deprived social class: he also reflects the spirit of an adolescent nation that arrogantly defies European pretense and asserts a new identity. Nowhere is this usage of the term *gaucho* clearer than in the following passage from "Nuevo diálogo patriótico" in which Contreras describes to Chano one of Ferdinand's attempts to regain a foothold in the River Plate. Chano begins the dialogue with a question regarding a rumor that King Ferdinand "anxiously requests through his deputies / to be recognized here / swearing he was by his constitution." Contreras replies:

> That rumor's been floating around for several days,
> they weren't just fooling you;
> the deputies came
> and from their ship they sent
> a stack of official papers (*papelería*)
> in name of King Fernando.
> With sleepy-eyed innocence they came . . .
> the damn furriners [*la pu . . . maturrangos*]!
> But, friend, our Junta
> let them know what's what right away
> and sent them an answer
> prettier than San Bernardo.
> Ah, yes, gaucho lawyers
> on cigarette paper!
> Seeing they weren't getting anywhere,
> and that [the Junta] had won the match
> the deputies hoisted anchor
> and, turning their ship around,
> they ran off without saying goodbye.
> May two hundred devils go with them!
>
> (*Antología* 92)

Most striking in this passage is the phrase *gaucho lawyers* (*gauchos escribanistas*) who rejected the overtures of the king. Just as the term *American* for Artigas suggested a mystical unity and preexisting identity, *gaucho* in Hidalgo's usage refers to a unified spirit in which even lawyers can be gauchos. Also, in appropriating a term that previously suggested lower class or delinquent, he suggests that the new national identity would be determined not by its upper class but by the mixed-blood, low-born campesino. The name of the gaucho thus labels and defines a national spirit that is both new and preexisting. The gaucho for Hidalgo is the authentic American whose political intentions cohere with the purity of the new country and are thereby true. He saw the low-born and socially marginal as people already of worth, the real Argentines in some sense, and the inescapable identity of the country. He therefore sought to teach the gaucho principles of citizenship and civic responsibility, not as a precondition for inclusion as the Morenistas might have said, but as people already part of the mainstream, full-fledged citizens of the new nation whose right to education and full acceptance is beyond debate. Moreover, Hidalgo's position is unabashedly populist. The odd phrase, "gaucho lawyers on cigarette paper" underlies the commonness of the revolutionary movement; whereas the king sent a mound of official documents, the gaucho lawyers replied on scraps of paper that were the common property of all. Given the exalted nature of their rebellion, they had no need of fine paper; theirs was a rebellion of substance and principle, not of form. Hidalgo's literary creation was perhaps a modest revolution; his ideological position, however, was truly radical, and certainly one of the most progressive of Argentina's first decade of nationhood.

Had Hidalgo's "modest revolution" not found resonance in the Argentine spirit, gauchesque poetry would probably have been lost like so many other patriotic verses written during the independence struggle. The *género gauchesco* survived, however, largely because Argentine writers continued finding the gauchesque an important, perhaps even essential, medium for political discussion. How better, they apparently thought, to claim popular support for an idea than to articulate that idea in what passed for popular language? One of Hidalgo's first imitators was Fray Francisco de Paula Castañeda, a vociferous priest who during the 1820s often promoted his peculiar blend of populism, federalism, and Catholic orthodoxy in gauchesque verse (Rivera, *La primitiva literatura gauchesca* 51–53). Similar in intention was Luis Pérez, a populist poet who supported the federalist dictatorship of Juan Manuel de Rosas (more on Rosas in later chapters). Ironically, Pérez's success in promoting Rosas's version of federalism in the gauchesque medium provoked Unitarians to do the same—but with opposing political intentions (Rivera 58–60; Sánchez Reulet 291). Chief among the Unitarian gauchesque writers was Hilario Ascasubi, who between 1830 and 1850 waged a tireless campaign against Rosas, frequently in gauchesque verse. But Ascasubi never endows his gauchos with the symbolic worth seen in Hidalgo's characters; rather than being the real Argentines and undefiled patriots of Hidalgo's poetry, Ascasubi's gauchos exist either as tedious mouthpieces of Unitarian politics, or as bumpkins whose backwardness entertains the enlightened elite. Another writer who continued in this "blackface" version of the gauchesque is Estanislao del Campo, whose chief work, *Fausto*, written in 1866, offers an undeniably entertaining portrait of one gaucho who, having just witnessed a performance of Gounod's *Faust*, tries to retell the story to a fellow gaucho.

Thus the *género gauchesco* after Hidalgo became a divided tradition; like the Mayo revolution that early split between populist Saavedristas and elitist Morenistas, the gauchesque seemed destined to serve two contrary traditions. Hidalgo created the genre and identified one of those traditions: that of populist advocacy for the excluded and low-born. The greatest work of the gauchesque, *El gaucho Martín Fierro* of 1872, studied at length in a later chapter, continues this populist tradition. The other current in the gauchesque takes its form from Hidalgo but eschews his politics. Its goal was to entertain upper-class audiences with the antics of the supposedly ignorant but happy country folk—and occasionally get in a few digs at federalism in the process. Even criticism about the gauchesque reflects this peculiar division. In this century, the origin, purpose, function, and ongoing importance of the gauchesque continue to provoke an often unfriendly, always inconclusive debate that in itself is an important paradigm of Argentine identity.

By 1820 the fault underlying Argentine society and history was clearly visible. (It could be argued that it had been visible on the first day that Moreno disagreed with Saavedra.) On one side of the fault were the liberals, mostly the Unitarians of Buenos Aires, who lived facing Europe, and were anxious to import the latest, most modern ideas from abroad, to wrench their embryonic nation into modernity whatever the cost, and to make it a showplace of European civilization. In their scheme, Buenos Aires would serve as exemplar and tutor of the provinces and perhaps for all of Latin

America. On the other side of the fault were Federalists, provincial caudillos, and populists of several stripes. Although their dream for Argentina was less clear and less articulate than that of their liberal enemies, they sought a more inclusive polity where there was a place for the campesino, the Indian, the mixed-bloods, and the gauchos. Some of them, like Artigas, also recognized that political rights without property meant nothing. Both sides of this divided society were initially united in wanting to expel the Spanish. Once that task was accomplished, however, they would direct their enmity against each other, plunging their country into sixty years of civil strife and bloodshed. Both sides developed guiding fictions to define and support their point of view. As we will see in subsequent chapters, these fictions, and the conflict they reflect, would evolve independently of one another, bequeathing to the modern Argentine nation an ideological divide that in odd ways still thwarts consensus and stability.

Chapter Four

The Rivadavians

The Rivadavians were a group of porteño Unitarians loosely organized around Bernardino Rivadavia, a Morenista whom we first saw as secretary of the Triumvirate government of 1811. During the 1820s he led a short-lived government that foreshadowed virtually every significant attitude of Argentina's liberal and educated classes. The Rivadavians were not in power long enough to make long-lasting structural changes in the country. Nonetheless, Rivadavia left a blueprint for social institutions, cultural aspirations, and governing style that still holds a major place in the guiding fictions of Argentine liberalism. Indeed, no element of society—the military, education, literature, music, art, jurisprudence, medicine, politics, economic policy, the Church—was left untouched by Rivadavia's administrative vision. Most praiseworthy in the Rivadavians' legacy were their cultural and educational aspirations. Less admirable was the unabashed elitism of their politics. And least admirable were their economic policies, which indebted the nation, concentrated power in the hands of a landed oligarchy, and allowed Great Britain to stifle real economic development just as surely as colonial Spain had ever done. The events leading to the Rivadavians' rise to power, their work toward organizing the country, their attitudes toward other Argentines and Latin Americans, their defeat and exile—to these subjects this chapter is addressed.

The Rivadavian experience begins in the chaotic year of 1820. The confederation plans articulated in the Congreso de Tucumán barely four years earlier were in shambles. The Argentine interior was virtually controlled by the caudillos and their gaucho armies. Enormous contention gripped the Buenos Aires cabildo, pitting Unitarians against Federalists, centralists against autonomists, conservatives against liberals, and "Jacobin" anticlerics against the Church. After months of near anarchy, the Buenos Aires cabildo selected General Martín Rodríguez as governor, a post he held for four years. Tomás de Iriarte, a contemporary who left several volumes of extraordinary memoirs, considered Martín Rodríguez "a vulgar man, a smart gaucho [who] selected well his advisors and then let himself be governed" (Iriarte, *Memorias* 3:20). Whatever the truth of Iriarte's characterization, Martín Rodríguez proved a good choice. Moreover, as a Federalist committed to including Unitarians in his government, he started off on a conciliatory note seldom sounded in Argentine politics. He also inherited the perennial responsibility of forming a constitutional congress to draft yet another constitution that might be ratified by all the provinces. The contemporary press often refers to this committee as the national congress, although it had no legislative authority. A more titular than real leader, Rodríguez relied heavily on Bernardino Rivadavia, his Minister of Government and Foreign Affairs, who initiated a series of reforms that in large measure served as the blueprint for liberal aspirations well into the twentieth century. Indeed, although he did not head the Buenos Aires government until 1826, Rivadavia so overshadows Martín Rodríguez that the governor is usually mentioned as a footnote to his minister.

A stubby, unattractive man, Rivadavia entered politics just after the fall of the Primera Junta in 1810. Beginning in 1814, he traveled extensively in Europe and represented several Argentine governments in matters that ranged from finding a suitable crown prince to govern Argentina, to beginning but never finishing a translation of Bentham's *Théorie des peines et des récompenses* (Piccirrilli, *Rivadavia y su tiempo* 2:11–27). In Europe, he grew to admire the English political system, became enamored of Jeremy Bentham's utilitarianism, exchanged letters with the English thinker (Piccirrilli 427–444), and acquired the high tastes and pretensions of a French dandy. In 1821 he was called back from Europe to serve as Rodríguez's Minister of Government and Foreign affairs; in 1825, under Rodríguez's successor, General Las Heras, he went on another short mission to England, and in 1826 the national congress elected him president of the United Provinces, a position he held until forced out of office in 1827. Although supposedly committed to forming a democratic republic, Rivadavia early showed a strong antipopular bias as well as a weakness for decrees formulated only in consultation with his own private principles. Between 1821 and 1827, he is the dominant presence in porteño political, cultural, and intellectual life, a period labeled by sympathetic Argentine historians, *La feliz experiencia*, or "The Happy Experience."

The Happy Experience resulted from the apt confluence of four ingredients necessary for High Culture: prosperity, a nascent upper class with time on its hands, peace, and a fascination with the ways of European aristocrats. Prosperity by 1820 was already a fact of porteño life thanks largely to Europe's insatiable appetite for cowhide and salted meat. Moreover, within the province, city merchants acquired more and more land while landowners were increasingly involved in city businesses; from this union between the landowning and merchant classes emerged the Argentine oligarchy whose last names would dominate much of Argentine history (Sebreli, *Apogeo* 111–142). Peace resulted from a temporary lull in the war with Brazil (the Portuguese now held Montevideo) and the Treaty of Pilar, which for a short time allowed porteños a respite from trying to force the reluctant provinces into submitting to Buenos Aires. Also in Buenos Aires' interest were new hostilities between the caudillos Ramírez and López. Ramírez aspired to become the new Artigas. López resisted and eventually in 1821 defeated and executed the hapless Ramírez. Ramírez's defeat weakened the Federalist alliance to such a degree that Buenos Aires not only discarded the Treaty of Pilar but again blockaded the Paraná River as a means of controlling commerce in the interior. However much the provinces resented these measures, their own divisiveness rendered impossible any united resistance to Buenos Aires. In the meantime, Buenos Aires increased contact with European travelers, traders, and scientists. Both Humboldt and Darwin spent time in the Argentine. Through foreign travel, children of the emerging oligarchy became increasingly conversant with the ways of Europe, often to the point of feeling less at home in Argentina than abroad.

The catalyst for fusing these ingredients of peace, prosperity, and High Culture into The Happy Experience was Bernardino Rivadavia. With immense energy Rivadavia set about organizing a

new society that he dreamed would become a showplace of Western Civilization, an exemplum of European culture in the Americas, Paris in the Pampas. His dream for Argentina still informs
Argentine liberalism, and no map of the country's guiding fictions
is complete without him. Yet oddly, he left no important writings
beyond obligatory letters, pro forma statements, and government
documents. As his chief biographer, Ricardo Piccirrilli, puts it:
"The duties of the pen never gave [Rivadavia] the slightest sense of
even a minute pleasure" (Piccirrilli 2:16). His work and memory are
his text.

One of Rivadavia's first reforms sought to demilitarize the province of Buenos Aires, a necessary move in view of the thousands of
unemployed officers and poor recruits who, no longer needed to
fight either the Spanish or the temporarily disassociated provinces,
were considered a potentially dangerous political force. To render
that force impotent, both military and government personnel were
forced into retirement. Moreover, as Minister of Finance Manuel
José García explains it, the pensions were deliberately stingy to
encourage "men accustomed to a fixed salary" to cease "place-
seeking" and "rely on their own industry" (cited in Halperín
Donghi, *Politics* 350). One former military leader who felt cheated
by the pensions was former president and independence hero
Cornelio Saavedra, who in his memoirs recalls bitterly how it was
only his wife's inheritance that kept the family afloat (Saavedra,
"Autobiografía" 1:82–85). In a decree of September 7, 1821, unemployed men, many of them former gaucho soldiers, were defined as
"delinquents addicted to mendicancy" and were either sent to jail
or forced to labor on public projects (cited in Halperín Donghi
350). At the same time, despite an apparent labor shortage in the
burgeoning economy, the government placed ceilings on wages
paid common laborers, many of them returning soldiers, to ensure
"their dependence on daily labor" (cited in Halperín Donghi 351).
Evidently, the Rodríguez government's alleged commitment to liberal orthodoxy stopped short of letting wages seek their own level;
indeed, employers caught paying more than government allow-
ances were subject to stiff fines. Under Rivadavian liberalism, the
working-class peons "had to improve their lot, using [whatever]
instruments the economy provided" (Halperín Donghi 352). This
was a significant departure from the paternalistic, protective con-

cern for the poor exhibited by the Church-influenced colonial governments in their better moments and by the caudillos like Artigas. Indeed, given the Rivadavians' attitudes toward the working class, it is no wonder that workers preferred the caudillos.

In addition to the military reform, The Happy Experience is the history of several remarkable institutions, all modeled after what Rivadavia had seen in Europe. First among these was the University of Buenos Aires, founded in 1821 with Father Antonio Sáenz, a liberal priest who had been active in politics since 1806, as the first rector. The university was divided into six schools, or *facultades*, consisting of preparatory studies, exact science, medicine, law, sacred sciences, and elementary education. To staff the university, Rivadavia imported scholars from Europe, particularly England, charged with teaching mathematics and science, subjects much neglected in the scholastic education of previous generations. Also imported was a chemistry laboratory complete with an Englishman to run it. Since the university was intended primarily for the Province of Buenos Aires, in 1823 Rivadavia founded the *Colegio de Ciencias Morales* expressly for provincial youngsters who were selected by examination and granted full scholarships. The Colegio brought together for the first time a group of teenagers who fourteen years later would form the Generation of 1837, arguably the most distinguished group of intellectuals in Argentine history and the subject of the next two chapters. Distinguished men who studied in the Colegio include Miguel Cané, essayist and novelist; Juan María Gutiérrez, critic and novelist; Esteban Echeverría, a poet and essayist who will be discussed extensively in the next chapter; Juan Bautista Alberdi, an essayist of unusual perception and clarity who contributed enormously to Argentina's first effective constitution, also to be discussed in later chapters; and Vicente Fidel López, author of the now classic *Historia de la República Argentina*. The story of the Colegio was later described by one of its students, Juan María Gutiérrez, in *Origen y desarrollo de la enseñanza pública superior en Buenos Aires*.

Rivadavia did not stop with the Colegio. Concerned that not all young Argentines could attend school in Buenos Aires, he sent bright proteño youths to teach in the interior in an outreach program that in the backward province of San Juan helped shape the early life of Domingo Faustino Sarmiento, a future president and writer whose importance as a creator of guiding fictions will become readily apparent in later chapters.

Three major differences separated the schools founded by the Rivadavians from their colonial precursors. First, although some of his teachers were priests, his schools were not under the control of the monastic orders traditionally charged with education. Second, following the lead of the English utilitarians he so admired, Rivadavia insisted that young Argentines learn a practical skill with emphasis on mathematics and the physical sciences. And finally, the Colegio's announcement of the free scholarships assured parents that "in all state schools all systems of humiliating the young through cruel corrections are forbidden" and that students "will not find hangmen masquerading as teachers, but rather, concerned teachers who are also friends and counselors" (cited in Piccirrilli 41). Despite this avowed consideration for students, one of the Colegio's most distinguished graduates, Juan Bautista Alberdi, wrote in his autobiography that he initially found the discipline intolerable, so much so that his older brother, seeing his "sufferings," removed him from the Colegio for a year (*Escritos póstumos* 15:274). He later returned, going on to become his generation's most distinguished political thinker.

With the government's emphasis on education, Rivadavia's Buenos Aires became a city of readers and discussers. Literary soirees dedicated to the most recent trends from Europe sprang up throughout the city, one of which Vicente Fidel López described as follows:

At times the soiree members surrounded Don Tomás de Luca, a well-informed reader, to hear what he had to say about the latest tract by Mr. Pradt in favor of America and against Spain. . . . At other times he spoke about Benjamin Constant or Bentham, in favor of liberty and representative government. Or Mr. Bompland, with his blue tailcoat, white tie and yellow vest, after placing his umbrella in a corner . . . would find himself surrounded by people anxious to hear from this celebrated founder of the study of natural history in our country. Every night he enchanted his listeners by describing some new useful and valuable herb he had discovered in his morning outings. His most charming lessons would be followed by another from another wise man, Mr. Lozier, who spoke on recreative physics and experiments in slight-of-hand movements. . . . In addition to such attractive activities, or better said, because of them, Mr.

de Luca's soiree would conclude with the declamation of dramatic and literary selections which were most in vogue at the time, and were presented with exquisite and applauded taste, reflecting the most accredited and delicious fashion of European literary salons. (*Historia* 9:39)

What most calls our attention here is López's portrayal of a society obsessed with bringing Argentina up to date, with maintaining an intellectual and artistic level in this outpost of Western culture on a par with that of Europe. Underlying the soirees was an apparent belief in culture as a product to be imported.

In 1822, the literary salons led Rivadavia to support the creation of The Literary Society of Buenos Aires, a quasigovernmental organization foreshadowed by the Morenista Patriotic Society and the Society for Good Taste in Theater of several years earlier. Organized under the direction of Julián Segundo de Agüero, a liberal porteño priest, the Society was composed first of twelve and later of twenty-four members. The goal of the Society, as indicated by its first communiqué, was "to give foreign nations a knowledge of the state of the Country and its progress, to spread enlightenment, [and] to organize opinion" (cited in Piccirrilli 57). In short, the Society gave itself the mission of civilizing the Pampas while informing other nations that civilization had indeed taken root in the Argentine. To meet these goals, on January 22, 1822, the Society took over the foundering *El Argos de Buenos Aires,* increasing its publication from twice a month to twice a week. Under the Society's direction, *El Argos* continued publication until December 3, 1825, when, for reasons the editors keep hidden, the government of Juan Gregorio de las Heras, Rodríguez's successor, no longer allowed the paper to be printed on government presses (*El Argos,* 3 Dec. 1825, 421).

El Argos, which means vigilant person in Spanish, serves as an early prototype for liberal porteño journalism generally: urbane, internationally focused, austere without being unstylish, informed, unabashedly supportive of intellectual elitism, unwavering in its loyalty to liberal causes, disdainful of popular classes and culture, and excruciatingly tasteful. Indeed, I cannot read *El Argos* without thinking of Victoria Ocampo's *Sur,* a literary journal that began publication in 1931, which as John King states in his superb history of the magazine, "perceived its role as that of the civilising minority in the literary and ideological 'chaos of the pampa' " (King, *Sur* 56). King's description of *Sur* could just as easily be applied to the Literary Society's *El Argos* of 1822.

Every issue of *El Argos* included an extensive survey of world and Latin American news, local politics, and the emerging High Culture of Buenos Aires. Given the distances information had to travel, the international news was usually three or four months late, and, despite attempts to attract foreign correspondents, often consisted of material gleaned from Latin American, English, French, and Spanish newspapers. In addition, although The United Provinces of the River Plate were at this time united in name only, *El Argos* earnestly printed news from all areas of the interior, thus promoting the fiction that, despite political disunion, Argentina was unified in spirit.

Such interest in the provinces notwithstanding, *El Argos* never lost its porteño localism. For example, in a column celebrating the thirteenth anniversary of the May Revolution, an anonymous writer asks: "What was South America before Buenos Aires raised its daring face on that day, making its voice resonate as eloquent thunder? A mass of slaves condemned to groan under the whip of their Overlord. And what is Buenos Aires today? A heroic nation of free men . . . that has humilliated those who previously humiliated her" (28 May 1823, 178). So much for the provincial caudillos like Güemes and Artigas, who also contributed enormously to expelling the Spanish. In another rite of self-congratulation, *El Argos* reported that "Buenos Aires enjoys a great reputation [in England] . . . because of the institutions that have been created in the last five years [and] the principles of liberty and enlightenment that these institutions have spread. . . . These circumstances have improved the reputation of our country to such a degree that we can now glory in having deserved the high consideration of the freest most powerful nation in Europe" (3 Aug. 1825, 261). But not content to glory in its own good fortune, the editors of *El Argos* in the next issue write that, having received the ultimate validation in the London press, "we should now turn our consideration to the current state of the provinces and the necessity they feel in every way, each one of them, to promote their particular prosperity using the same means that we have identified in the Province of Buenos Aires" (5 Aug. 1825, 265). The fiction reflected in these words of

Buenos Aires as exemplar, civilizer, and preceptor of the continent survives in porteño hauteur just as surely as it continues to offend Argentine provincials and Latin Americans of other nations.

Case in point: in September 1825, several representatives from Upper Peru, now Bolivia, met in La Plata, now Sucre, to make official their desire to form a separate state independent of Buenos Aires. The Bolivian declaration was more ritual than real since Buenos Aires, preoccupied with the Portuguese in the Banda Oriental, Indian wars, and unending internal conflicts, had offered little opposition to Bolivia's independence. Nonetheless, *El Argos* editors could not resist the temptation to advise their neighbor on the true path to liberty:

It is perhaps true that whatever opinion in this regard that comes out of Buenos Aires will cause other people to accuse her of desiring to dominate, a charge often brought against us. But whatever reasons may exist to explain this [charge], which has always been unjustified, these reasons cannot exist once those liberal principles have been proclaimed and adopted upon which are founded our social institutions. . . . To deny some the fruits of civilization because their enjoyment is not yet available to others or to hold back some provinces by tying them to the slowness of others is to impede the establishment of good laws. We are not embarrassed to affirm that such is the case regarding the United Provinces and Upper Peru; sufficient proof is found in considering that the former have lived fifteen years in the enthusiasm of liberty and enlightenment, whereas the later have been dominated by the most irrational despotism. (14 Sept. 1825, 315)

Three points warrant attention here. First, for the editors and by extension for many porteño liberals, charges of porteño hegemony are unfounded; rather, they result from the fact that the accusers live in a primitive state devoid of the social institutions that elevate Buenos Aires above her neighbors. Second, Buenos Aires decided not to protest the independence of Upper Peru since "tying some provinces to the slowness of others" would merely impede Argentina's own progress; in sum, why bother with Bolivia when such a backward place would merely slow Buenos Aires down. And finally, the rightness of the United Provinces' chosen path is visible in that they "have lived fifteen years in the enthusiasm of liberty and enlightenment." This arrogant statement ignores fifteen years of feuding caudillos, civil war, fragmentation, and porteño coups and countercoups. Needless to say, Buenos Aires' enthusiasm for itself did not prevent the Bolivians from seceding.

The *El Argos* editors also strove to correct "barbarism" wherever they found it, most often in popular culture. For example, the Carnaval celebration preceding Lent was deplored as a time when "the most distinguished people stoop to behavior that must be called barbarous . . . showing every sign of having lost their reason; and sometimes we see them associating with the grossest sort of plebians. . . . We therefore hope that the refined people in Buenos Aires will show by their example how such diversions, which must be considered holdovers of barbarism, can be replaced . by other kinds of pleasure marked by the good taste, order and sensitivity which must characterize a people now embarked on the great work of civilization" (9 Feb. 1822, 28). A week later, after Carnaval was over, the same good editors lamented that their counsel had gone unheeded and that Carnaval had "called into question our level of civilization in the eyes of foreigners." Particularly offensive was the practice of injecting water into empty eggshells that were then thrown at unsuspecting victims "regardless of their dress or character." The piece closes lamenting that "despite all we say, our hopes have been shattered, and we must painfully conclude that there are yet among us many profane people unable to enter the temple of good taste" (13 Feb. 1822, 36). As we will see in the next chapter, the editors' terms for describing the conflict— barbarism versus civilization—would become one of the great rallying cries of Argentine liberalism. Later writers, particularly Domingo F. Sarmiento, would popularize the terms, but he did not invent them. They were already in Argentine political discourse at least as early as the Rivadavians.

The Literary Society also founded a magazine, *La Abeja Argentina* (The Argentine Bee), to be "dedicated to political, scientific and industrial affairs and also to contain selected translations, recent discoveries among civilized peoples, national weather information, details on the constitution of years and seasons, a resumé of monthly illnesses, and a summary of improvements in the Province [of Buenos Aires]" (*Actas de la Sociedad*, cited in Piccirrilli 64). A typical issue includes a windy manifesto on political rights in Brazil, a meditation on the nature of authority with numerous quotations from Enlightenment writers, a poetic discourse on the relationship between science and art, again with extensive reference to European thinkers, a chemistry lesson "as taught in London by the celebrated Sir Humphrey Davy," and a report on recent illnesses in the Province (*La Abeja* 15 Sept. 1822). *La Abeja* survived only a few months, partly because of insufficient funds, poor circulation, and disagreements between the editors and the Literary Society. Indeed, on one occasion Nuñez complained that "two or three editions of *La Abeja* had been published without proper revision and approval by the Society" as if to suggest that the Literary Society maintained veto power over whatever the editors did (cited in Piccirrilli 64). The conflict between the Literary Society and *La Abeja* may also have been political since the magazine's editor was Manuel Moreno, brother of Mariano whose increasingly Federalist sympathies placed him at odds with the Rivadavians. But even despite these local conflicts, *La Abeja* clearly demarcated the same cultural pardigms apparent among the Rivadavians generally: Europe and more Europe.

Since the University and the Colegio admitted only male students, Rivadavia also organized *La Sociedad de Beneficencia* (The Beneficent Society), which was staffed exclusively by women and charged with "the supervision and inspection of girls' schools, the House of Expositions, the House of Public and Private Births, the Women's Hospital, the School for Girl Orphans and all other public establishments founded for the good of individuals of their sex" (cited in Piccirrilli 49). With belated approval of the new organization, *El Argos* entoned, "When all the results of the [Beneficent Society] are felt, women will concern themselves with more serious tastes, and more authentic pleasures, while at the same time ceasing to be frivolous (we speak of women in general) and becoming more congenial" (15 March 1823, 88). Education for women, however, had to include appropriate training in "feminine" arts as the telling title of one of the Society's publications indicates: *Manual for Primary Schools for Girls, or an Outline for Mutual Education Applied to Reading, Writing, Arithmetic, and Sewing* (Piccirrilli 51). In addition to overseeing female education, the Society was charged with preparing text materials for all Argentine schools, most of them translations of French and English textbooks, or "scientific catechisms" as they were called, which covered more traditional subjects such as chemistry and geography. Despite its charitable and educational intentions, the Society soon became an enduring social club whose activites were obligatory for any woman with upper-class aspirations.

In addition to his literary and educational interests, Rivadavia lent considerable support to creating a national theater. Reviews in *El Argos*, however, indicate that theater under the Rivadavians consisted mostly of melodramatic or comical works translated from English and French; local works were evidently not encouraged. Believing that theater had potentially larger audiences than other media, Rivadavia wrote a letter to the Literary Society on December 6, 1822 requesting a proposal to form "a school to teach the principles of declamation, to produce capable teachers, able to present themselves on stage with all the perfection that a cultured and enlightened people deserve" (cited in Piccirrilli 65). The Society took up the Minister's request in its next meeting, drafting a "Proposal for the Erection and Budget of Expenses for a School of Acting and Declamation," an unusually short document that merely states that qualified teachers should be contracted to train "young men and women of noble appearance and harmonious voices who can also read and write." The list of expenses contains no actual figures, but specifies that a teacher should be employed, that a small theater be built, and that "plaster statues, or pictures or engravings of celebrated writers and actors performing interesting scenes" be provided (cited in Piccirrilli 66–67).

The drama school was only one of the Rivadavians' attempts to transport theater, culture, and good taste to the Pampas. Several theater groups flourished with his support, and from 1823 on, theater notices appear regularly in *El Argos*. As early as 1825 porteño audiences attended productions of Shakespeare's *Othello* and the Rossini operas *Cenerentola* and *The Barber of Seville*. Moreover, as if to demonstrate porteño cosmopolitan aspirations, *El Argos* editorialized that "although singing in our national language would no doubt increase public interest in theater, we, as individuals are completely satisfied by Italian, and we disapprove of attempts which have been made to render in Spanish arias and duets heard [originally] in that musical language" (10 July 1824, 256). Although bringing European works to Buenos Aires received priority, Rivadavia also made money available for publishing both translated and national literature, including one of the first anthologies of Argentine verse, *Colección de Poesías Patriotas*. Given the primitive printing facilities available in Buenos Aires, several government-supported publications were prepared in Buenos Aires but actually printed in Paris, including the pioneer collection of poetry, *La Lira Argentina* of 1824.

Typical of what the Rivadavians considered good taste was the neoclassic poetry of Juan Cruz Varela. Easily the most significant poet of his generation, Varela, like his contemporaries, wrote mostly patriotic verse and love poetry strongly punctuated by classical allusions and imagery. Lauding San Martín's and González Balcarce's victory over the Spanish at the River Maipú on August 5, 1818, Varela wrote:

> Beloved of Calliope, sons of Phoebus,
> Nurtured on the heights of Parnasus,
> Forgive me for daring to interrupt
> The elevated notes of your song.
>   Surely I should not
>   Tune my humble lyre;
>   But who on this day
> Could resist the burning that inflames my breast?
> I see two heroes; their unique renown
> Ignites with enthusiasm the sacred flame,
> And I feel myself inspired by Apollo.
>
> (Varela, *Poesías* 57)

What follows is an eight-page miniepic written in the same grand mode detailing the Creole victory. The themes are Argentine, but the forms are those of a previous century. As Argentine critic Ricardo Rojas observes, "Varela's political ideals were liberal and subversive, but his literary forms were conservative and colonial in their exoticism and their dogmatic adherence to principles taught by colonial teachers. Between the authoritarian principle of divine right and the authoritarian principle of classical rhetoric, there was no difference other than the field in which they were applied" (Rojas, "Noticia preliminar" 14).

If we view Varela's poetry only in the context of neoclassicism, Rojas's criticism seems unfair since his appeal to classical models could be seen merely as the literary fashion of his time. Indeed, we need look no further than Virgil's imitation of Homer to realize that creative imitation can produce great art. Rojas's point, however, takes on greater meaning if we see Varela's theoretical premises as indicative of a mind-set that viewed culture as an import and in so doing denigrated its own national uniqueness. In short, Varela imitated neoclassic poetry just as his coreligionists imitated European conventions in everything else. Moreover, his was an imitation, like that of the Rivadavians generally, that often excluded rather than enhanced his own country. .

An employee of the government and active member of the Literary Society, Varela was a strong supporter of Rivadavia's reforms. Indeed, for proof of Varela's loyalty to Rivadavia and of his ability to versify on any subject, one need look no farther than his "Profecía de la grandeza de Buenos Aires" ("Prophecy of the Grandeur of Buenos Aires"), a panegyrical defense of Rivadavia's proposed water system that all but suggests that Columbus discovered America so Buenos Aires could have pressurized water (*Poesías* 156–162). With Rivadavia's coming to power, however, Varela's writing changes directions. The classical allusions that had merely framed his patriotic and amorous verse became his subjects to such a degree that Varela ends up writing two lengthy, involved tragedies, *Dido* and *Argia*, both based on classical texts and strongly reminiscent of Corneille. Moreover, unlike his patriotic verse, neither play has much to do with Argentina.

A dramatization of the fourth book of Virgil's *Aeneid*, *Dido* offers a particularly good view of officially received art during The Happy Experience since it was first presented in Rivadavia's home, published with government backing on August 24, 1823, and repeatedly extolled in the government's official newspaper, *El Argos* (23 Aug. 1823, 282). Thematically, the play departs not at all from Virgil's story, while structurally it rigidly observes Aristotle's unities, reducing the characters to mere narrators of important events—all of which happen off stage before the curtain rises *comme il faut.* Following the first production (which was in fact little more than a dramatized reading), an anonymous reviewer gushed in *El Argos*, "The author, carried away in poetic inspiration, spreads profusely tender and sublime thoughts . . . [while] subjecting his work to the rigid censor of an enlightened society." The production's leading actor is extolled for declaiming "with that truly tragic cadence and tone of

voice that distinguish the French theater." The reviewer goes on to
praise Varela "for the brilliant career with which he initiates our
national theater" (30 June 1823, 253). National theater based on
Virgil and patterned after Corneille? No wonder modern nationalist
critics like Rojas consider Varela a symptom of cultural colonialism.

After another presentation of Varela's *Dido, El Argos* published a
second review in which the play is praised as a work in which "only
art occupies the ultimate place" and therefore "must be viewed as a
model of art and talent." The second review also makes explicit the
connection between Varela and the neoclassic French playwright
Corneille, who preceded Varela by more than a century (6 Sept.
1823, 297–298). Varela's *Dido* is again in the news in a later edition
of *El Argos* wherein the anonymous reviewer, in a rarefied debate
that surely would have honored the court of Louis XIV, discusses
Varela's own explanations of the play's structure, Aristotelian theories of drama, and Virgil's real intentions (27 Sept. 1823, 322).

The critical premises underlying the play and the reviews—the
rigid censorship of "good taste" found in an enlightened society, the
esthete notion of art as something pure and unconnected to reality,
the rightness of neoclassical artistic formulae, the French classical
theater as an object to be imitated—partly explain why the Rivadavians and their intellectual descendants, for all their artistic aspirations and activity, produced only pale derivations of European literature and society: their sense of "good taste" encouraged imitation
rather than genuine creativity. Good art, good government, right
thoughts, and correct behavior were predetermined according to
formulas no less rigid than the received truths of scholasticism. Like
Mariano Moreno, who masked an inflexible authoritarianism behind
the vocabluary of the Enlightenment, the Rivadavians grandly sang
of independence, progress, and cultural renovation while tena-
ciously holding to outmoded artistic and intellectual forms. Their
fear of the new, the unproven, or the non-European effectively
checked the creation of anything authentically Argentine. Indeed,
glorifying the often sterile derivations of neoclassicism as the beginnings of a national theater suggests an odd desire among the cultural
elite to be old before their time—an attitude garishly out of place in a
nation supposedly feeling the first stirrings of adolescence. In addition, the carefully orchestrated critical success of Varela's plays underlines just how far removed the cultural baronate in Buenos Aires

was from the popular traditions of their own country—and from the remarkable achievements of Bartolomé Hidalgo's gauchesque of only a few years previous.

The *El Argos* editors' disdain for popular traditions was again underlined in a review of Rossini's *The Barber of Seville* where the comic actors are praised for their tasteful work. The review ends, however, with "One hopes that our comic theater group will take advantage of these scenes in order to learn how to represent comic action without giving in to the ridiculousness and vulgarity of the *sainetes*" (12 Oct. 1825, 354). The *sainetes* were a popular theater form with roots in early Spanish national theater, much appreciated by porteño lower classes, and, as we saw in the last chapter, a probable source of inspiration for Hidalgo's *diálogos*. Argentine literature is best when its writers abandon European models—or modify and parody them as Borges did; unfortunately, the pale derivations of European literature written by the Rivadavians engendered many children, just as pale and just as unconvincing as Varela's contrived dramas.

The Literary Society and its offspring were widely imitated in the creation of other professional and academic organizations, usually by a flourish of Rivadavia's pen. Among these was the Academy of Medicine, decreed to exist on April 16, 1822, whose duties would include training and certifying of doctors and pharmacists, maintaining public health, and appointing medical personnel to different areas in the Province of Buenos Aires (*El Argos* 20 April 1822, 112). Also in 1822, an Italian expatriate named Virgilio Rabaglio founded the Academy of Music, "in order to promote in this country an art which is today one of the joys of all cultured nations" (*El Argos* 12 June 1822, 172). Several months later on October 1, 1822, Rabaglio's first students performed at an inaugural concert attended by both Governor Rodríguez and Rivadavia. The concert included an original composition titled "The Glory of Buenos Aires," which in the words of an ecstatic reviewer in *El Argos* "moved and elevated the souls of all present." The unnamed reviewer further informs us that on hearing the music "all hearts fluttered with that innocent and pure pleasure that we so often need during the painful moments of life. From all we saw and heard in this lovely new affair, beautified by Argentine women, we believe that the School of Music will increase the civilization and

culture of the American family" (2 Oct. 1822, 304). Again, Buenos
Aires is seen as the conduit of culture for the entire continent.

A year later Rivadavia supervised the creation of the Academy of
Theoretical and Practical Jurisprudence, sometimes called The
Academy of Legislation, which with mixed metaphors he praised as
a means of "perfecting institutions by following the path of enlightenment as the only fountain of public prosperity" (cited in Piccirrilli
75). Soon thereafter Rivadavia oversaw the founding of the Public
Museum of Buenos Aires dedicated "to the sons of the patria" as a
"repository of all historical and artistic objects related to general
knowledge and to all celebrated men born on her soil" (Piccirrilli
80).

No less extensive but unfortunately more lasting than the
Rivadavians' cultural innovations were their economic policies,
which, although conceived as reforms, ended up being a recipe for
perennial indebtedness and consequent surrender of national sovereignty. Argentina's current debt problems have frequently been in
the news since the late 1970s. What is less well known is that the
pattern of indebtedness underlying the current situation was well
established in the mid-1820s under the Rivadavians. With Manuel
José García as Minister of Finance, the government borrowed heavily from the British to finance new projects in the Province and to
pay off war debts, some outstanding since the first years following
Independence. These loans were tendered, often at usurious rates,
using land and futures on cattle products as collateral. In one particularly notorious loan, contracted through the Baring Brothers of
London, the porteño government received credit for only 570,000
pounds sterling in exchange for a debt of 1,000,000 pounds (Ferns
103). To make matters worse, most of the money earmarked for
Argentina actually remained in England in the form of credits toward purchasing English manufactures and to pay commissions to
brokers and intermediaries, thereby benefiting Argentine investment minimally (Rock, *Argentina* 99–100). According to some cal-
culations, final payment in the loan principal was not made until
1906. During the intervening near-century, the British banks,
through continual refinancing, received the original amount of the
loan several times over (Scalabrini Ortiz, *Política británica* 79–97).
In this century, Argentina's early and continual indebtedness to

Great Britain as a mechanism supporting British exploitation and control in Argentina has been a major theme in antiimperialist writings of both the left and right.

In 1825, to make official the economic relationship Great Britain had already established with Argentina, Woodbine Parish, British Consul-General in Buenos Aires, Under Secretary of State George Canning, and Manuel José García signed the Anglo-Argentine Treaty of Friendship, Commerce, and Navigation. Its chief provisions were that Great Britain would recognize Argentine sovereignty and independence (a ticklish issue given England's resentment at losing its own American colonies), that both British and Argentine citizens living in the other's country would enjoy the rights accorded all foreigners, and that subjects of both countries would be allowed free access to the trade of the other (*El Argos* 26 Feb. 1825, 70–71). The treaty was, in short, "an effort to create a free-market relationship between an industrial community and a raw-material-producing community. In this relationship the role of the state was reduced to that of guaranteeing the operation of an automatic market mechanism" (Ferns 113). The Treaty also indicated a naive willingness on the part of its Argentine negotiators to accept economic theory from England as objective and scientific rather than self-serving and profit-motivated. Interestingly, one of the few successful attempts under Rivadavia to erect trade barriers in the Argentine was a prohibition against importing grain passed by the provincial legislature on November 29, 1824. The new law was roundly condemned in *El Argos* as "opposed to the most sane economic principles and . . . contrary to the spirit of all the laws and institutions . . . which have given us credibility abroad . . . and will surely begin a hateful race for privileges and prohibitions which will both ruin and discredit us" (10 Aug. 1825, 432). Even in economic matters, the Rivadavians were fully in thrall to European ways.[1]

1. By point of contrast, the United States followed a significantly different policy. Although dependent on British capital and technology, the United States in the last century erected high tariff barriers to protect its early industries, which at the time were in no condition to compete with British manufacturing. Tariffs were in place in the United States as early as 1789 and increased in 1816 specifically to protect cotton, woolen, and iron manufactures. Despite repeated objections from Southern politicians that tariff policy favored Northern industrialists, the tariffs survived with only minor modifications until 1934 when Cordell Hull, Democratic

Superficially a model of laissez-faire economic theory, the Anglo-Argentine Treaty reflected attitudes that boded ill for Argentina's future—and of course were at radical variance with the protectionist sentiments articulated by Artigas and other spokesmen of the interior. The Treaty was in effect a way of opening to free trade a pond in which Great Britain was far and away the biggest fish; because of England's uncontested economic strength, free trade ultimately meant free reign for English capitalists and their porteño collaborators, regardless of the whole country's best interest. By abolishing import barriers and opening the country to nearly unlimited foreign investment and trade, the Rivadavians devastated local manufacturing, guaranteed that most manufactured goods from that point forward would be imported, and limited the country's economic future to one of provider of agricultural goods and raw materials to an industrial power. Moreover, by agreeing to ship only on English ships or ships constructed in Argentina (this in a country with minimal industrial capacity), Argentina effectively renounced ever having its own shipping industry. There is, then, in the Treaty a certain irony: while explicitly disavowing mercantilism, it ensured that England, owing to its greater power over all possible competitors, would maintain an essentially mercantilist relationship with Buenos Aires. As observed by John Murray Forbes, head of the United States mission in Buenos Aires between 1820 and 1831, "The Treaty's supposed reciprocity is a cruel mockery of the absolute lack of resources in these provinces and a guarantee that Argentina will never develop its own maritime shipping industry" (Forbes, *Once años en Buenos Aires* 345).

In addition to its economic ramifications, the Anglo-Argentine Treaty had major social consequences in that it effectively concentrated power in the hands of Great Britain's most important ally: the already powerful porteño oligarchs whose wealth came from their lands and their ability to serve British commercial interests. By assuming only the role of an abundant provider of agricultural goods, the Rivadavians ensured that real power would remain with

---

Secretary of State under Franklin D. Roosevelt, secured passage of the Reciprocal Trade Agreements Act. Although Hull's main argument held that trade barriers threatened world peace, he was also aware that protecting the United States' highly developed economy was at that point no longer necessary.

the landed and commercial bourgeoisie, a fact that would seriously limit access to power for anyone born outside the oligarchy's privileged circles, and foment the class resentment that in this century has rendered the country all but ungovernable.

Other moves by the Rivadavians further tied the Argentine economy to Great Britain. English economic "advisors" were invited to sit on policy-making boards, empowered to contract government loans, emit national currency, and regulate foreign commerce and investment. Such positions of power were, of course, used to England's advantage, so much so that during its earliest years Argentina became a loan-dependent, capital-dependent country—a position that has repeatedly compromised the nation's ability to control its own affairs, just as it does today. The entry into Argentina of British commercial power and its consequent political influence during the Rivadavian years was so overwhelming that Forbes complained that the British were "an enormous foreign presence in control of the government which it can either support or oust whenever it pleases" (Forbes 352).

Parallel to the economic reform, and perhaps even more devastating in its long-term implications, was Rivadavia's land reform. In 1824, he promulgated a formula based on the Roman principle of emphyteusis by which corporations or individuals could lease public lands from the government for a period of twenty years, paying a minimal annual rent. Although meant to spread the wealth and create an immigrant class of middle-class farmers, Rivadavia's rentals went mostly to the already wealthy (Sebreli, *Apogeo* 130–134). By 1830, under Rivadavia's distribution policies, 538 individuals or corporations had received 20,000,000 acres, an average of 37,175 acres each. Moreover, one man received 880,000 acres, and another, 735,000. Intended to be merely rentals subject to periodic review, these grants after Rivadavia's demise eventually became personal property, increasing the wealth of the emerging oligarchy, while guaranteeing that there would be less good land available for future immigrants (Herring, *A History of Latin America* 624–625). Rivadavia's land-distribution policies, emulated a half-century later by other liberal governments, also greatly concentrated wealth in Buenos Aires and along the Littoral, where the best lands lay. As Díaz Alejandro points out, nature itself appeared to militate against an equitable distribution of power and wealth in Argentina. Unlike in the United States, where the discovery of richer farmland in the Great Plains and California forced the Northeast to industrialize, the best lands in Argentina were distributed first, thus ensuring that the country's first oligarchical families would remain its richest and most powerful. Decades later, as territory was wrested from the Indians, the same families would continue acquiring more and more land (Díaz Alejandro, *Essays on the Economic History of the Argentine Republic* 35–40; 151–159).

In politics, the Rodríguez government under Rivadavia's prompting set about gathering power to itself. Since the 1810 revolution, the Buenos Aires cabildo, which for the most part was dominated by conservative porteño business interests, had been the prime mechanism for forming successive governments—and then ousting them when they ran afoul of localist interests. Or, in the words of one contemporary observer, the cabildo "secretly promoted rebellions in order to keep real power in its own hands" (Iriarte 3:31). To avoid such interference, the Rodríguez government abolished the cabildo in both Buenos Aires and Luján. Although well motivated, dissolving the cabildos raised a red flag to conservative porteño oligarchs, the already suspicious provincial caudillos, and the masses for whom the cabildo in Iriarte's words "was the most immediate authority. . . . It was the head, the father, and its children worshiped it, respected it, and rendered it voluntary allegiance, an exalted devotion" (Iriarte 3:31–32; see also Sebreli, *Apogeo* 135–136). Although the cabildos were clearly a relic from colonial times, they were functioning political bodies, always representative of at least some segments of the society and in some cases, as in Artigas's Banda Oriental, remarkably democratic. In retrospect, it may have been wiser to try incorporating the cabildos into a new administrative system rather than to abolish them altogether. But Rivadavia had seen truth in the political organization of England and France, and those European models did not include cabildos. In the meantime, Rivadavia organized a provincial legislature that later included some popularly elected officials. Ostensibly a body to check executive powers, the legislature was initially little more than a debating society that routinely rubber-stamped Rivadavia's decrees.

Much more inflammatory than the abolition of the cabildo were Rivadavia's ecclesiastical reforms, which, although mild in com-

parison to French anticlericalism, helped isolate the Rivadavians
from both the conservative oligarchs and the popular classes. Although conservative priests were understandably disturbed by the
anticlerical currents in enlightened thought that inevitably reso-
nated among Argentine liberals, the church Rivadavia sought to
reform was hardly a bastion of antirevolutionary traditionalism.
During the 1700s, enlightened ideas entered Spanish America
often through the clergy, occasionally in defiance of official disapproval. Further, liberals like Moreno learned about Voltaire and
Rousseau from priests at the Catholic University of Chuquisaca,
and some clerics were major players in the independence struggle. Under Spanish pressure Pope Pius VII excommunicated some
liberal priests, but enough remained to provide a liberal presence
in the priesthood (Frizzi de Longoni, *Rivadavia y la reforma
eclesiástica* 10–22; 37–39). No Jacobin religion hater, Rivadavia
himself fit in well with the liberal clergy. He included priests at
all levels in his administration, instituted school prayers in Latin,
and urged underlings to cease "promoting practices contrary to
religion" (Carbia, *Revolución* 91–92).

   Ideology aside, Argentine ecclesiastics had other reasons to support independence. As with most sectors of colonial society, the
Church was dominated by Spanish appointees who fanned resentment by confining Creole clerics to lower ecclesiastical positions.
As a result, twenty-two priests participated in the *cabildo abierto* of
May 25, 1810, that declared Argentina's independence, and clerics
were major players in the ongoing revolution, supporting not only
independence but also national patronage by which ecclesiastical
appointments were made in Argentina rather than in Rome or
Madrid (Carbia, *Revolución* 22–33, 78–81). National patronage endured partly because, under Spanish pressure, the Vatican kept the
bishop's chair in Buenos Aires vacant between 1812 and 1830
(Carbia, *Revolución* 78–88). The Argentine Church further declared its own independence from Spain, and to a degree from
Rome, by changing prayers to favor national, rather than colonial,
causes (Carbia, *Revolución* 54). Strong support among clergy for
liberal causes continued well into the 1820s; indeed, some of
Rivadavia's strongest allies were clerics, including Antonio Sáenz,
the first rector of the University of Buenos Aires.

   Why, then, did Rivadavia get into so much trouble with the

Church? The answer is relatively simple: he made an issue of the Church's extensive involvement in material matters, which was at once the Church's most vulnerable and embarrassing weakness. Since colonial times, the real economic muscle of the Church rested primarily in the hands of monastic orders that over the years acquired enormous assets ranging from land to small factories. Moreover, social services, including schools, hospitals, asylums, and orphanages, were the exclusive province of the religious communities, which often competed with one another for wealth, prestige, influence, and new members. Tied to parent orders in Europe, the Argentine monastics followed their own law to such a degree that even the nonmonastic, "lay" hierarchy often resented their independence. The power of the monastic communities had long been under attack by Argentine liberals; in the second issue of *El Argos de Buenos Aires,* for example, an anonymous writer fantasizes that someday curious travelers will look on the ruins of monasteries as "monuments to the ever-changing whims of mankind" (19 May 1821, 10). Like most of his fellow liberals, Rivadavia saw three items in the Church's economic and social organization: inefficiency, anachronism, and petrification. In his mind, the social institutions of the Church belonged under the direction of a modern state. His reforms, then, were directed toward the socioeconomic Church and had little, if anything, to do with doctrine.

His first moves were to abolish the ecclesiastical *fueros,* which allowed monastics their own courts and a sizable income from the State, to confiscate the properties of orders that in his view were merely sitting on wealth rather than serving society, and to centralize all religious activity under the diocesan prelate as a way of breaking up the fiefdoms of individual orders (Frizzi de Longoni 61–75). One of the first communities affected by Rivadavia's reform was El Convento de la Merced, which was reportedly "serving only the needs of the priests" and not of the public in general (*El Argos* 1 March 1823, 72). In a long decree published in *El Argos,* the acting bishop of Buenos Aires seconded Rivadavia's attempts to place Church finances under one head while returning monks and nuns to their original vows of mendicancy (8 March, 1823, 79–80). To ensure that viable religious communities survived while not getting too powerful, Rivadavia also decreed that no community could have fewer than sixteen members nor more than thirty, and that novitiates be at least twenty-five years old. To allow monastics greater freedom, he guaranteed pensions for priests left without support from their orders and organized a clerical senate consisting of representatives from several orders to assist the bishop in running the diocese (Carbia, *Revolución* 105–107). In the meantime, he formed state institutions like the Beneficent Society, the College of Moral Science, and the University of Buenos Aires to oversee education, thus depriving the Church of its best contact with the young. By placing control of Church affairs primarily in the hands of secular rather than monastic priests, Rivadavia opened the door for nuns and monks alike to assume a role in the Church outside their orders, a choice many evidently made (Carbia, *Revolución* 108–113).

The ecclesiastical reform, although widely supported by progressive priests like Antonio Sáenz, Deán Funés, and Mariano Zavaleta, provoked cries of outrage among conservatives. Chief among these were two Franciscans, Cayetano Rodríguez, and Francisco de Paula Castañeda, who published fiery diatribes against the Rivadavian "infidels" (Frizzi de Longoni 81–87). So incensed was Fray Castañeda that he composed several now famous parodies of Church litanies to express his disapproval of Rivadavia. Examples:

> From Mr. Fishnose—libera nos Domine.
> From the diluvian frog—libera nos Domine.
> From the drunken ombu tree—libera nos Domine.
> From Mr. Rifle Tongue—libera nos Domine.
> From the Anglo-Gallic monster—libera nos Domine.
> From the Destroyer of the Earth—libera nos Domine.
> From Him who fights the Pope—libera nos Domine.
> From Rivadavia—libera nos Domine.
> From Bernardino Rivadavia—libera nos Domine.
> Kyrie eleison—To God Our Father, we pray.

Under Castañeda's pen, the Apostles Creed became:

I believe in God Almighty, creator and preserver of Bernardino Rivadavia, and in Jesus Christ, redeemer of Rivadavia, who is currently suffering death and passion in Buenos Aires under the power of Rivadavia. I believe in the Holy Ghost whose light seeks Rivadavia. I believe in the communion of Saints whose communion has passed Rivadavia by. I believe in the forgiveness of sins which Rivadavia will never receive as long as he denies the resurrection of the flesh and the life everlasting. Amen. (Cited in Piccirrilli 293–294)[2]

Aside from the tasteless references to Rivadavia's appearance, Castañeda's parodies contain two significant accusations: heterodoxy and elitism. The heterodoxy charge is easily refuted since nothing in the reform touches on doctrine. The charge of elitism, however, presages one of the most enduring currents of antiliberal feeling in Argentina, as effective today as it was 150 years ago: that progress according to liberal models was English or French, and therefore anti-Argentine.[3] More significant criticism came from the papal nuncio in Chile (as an expression of official disapproval for the revolution, the pope at the time had no representative in Buenos Aires), who argued that the Church as a divine organization was not subject to civil law. Two of Buenos Aires' most distinguished priests, Deán Funes and Mariano Zavaleta, came to Rivadavia's defense, but against the emotion-laden arguments of the reaction, there was no defense.

Rivadavia's enemies immediately jumped on the religious issue to destabilize the porteño government and sow discord between Rivadavia and the already distrustful provincial caudillos (Frizzi de

2. Castañeda's hatred for Rivadavia knew no bounds. On one occasion, he sent a letter to Governor Martín Rodríguez claiming that a mysterious stranger had informed him of a plot Rivadavia was allegedly planning against the governor. Both stranger and conspiracy were products of Castañeda's imagination, designed to sow discord between the governor and his best minister (Piccirrilli 295–296). Castañeda was also a great Yankee baiter. In a letter to John Quincy Adams, American diplomat John Murray Forbes writes, "I have already mentioned the maliciousness to which some inhabitants of this city resort to cast shadows on our national and personal character. The poison of all these disaffected people has been gathered and spread to the public in the writings of a Franciscan Friar named Castañeda . . . a man whose audacity is matched only by his wickedness" (Forbes 69).

3. These arguments remain standard fare among Argentina's right-wing nationalists. As an indication of their durability, see Federico Ibarguren's *Nuestra tradición histórica* (297–309), where he praises the fanatical Castañeda as an authentic Argentine voice; and later (345–365), where he argues that the primary motive behind the caudillos' anti-Unitarian feelings were religious. Ibarguren feels that Argentina's true heritage is pre-Enlightenment, Counter-Reformation Catholicism, to which the country must return to fill its destiny. Hardly an isolated fanatic with an axe to grind, Mr. Ibarguren under the first government of Juan Domingo Perón taught at the University of La Plata, arguably Argentina's foremost university, and headed the Argentine History division at the University of El Salvador in Buenos Aires during the 1976–1981 military regime.

Longoni 93–112). Mobs led by disgruntled priests raged through the streets of Buenos Aires and Luján (*El Argos* 22 March 1823, 97). In response to the disorder, Rivadavia sent a strong letter of protest to the acting Bishop of Buenos Aires, Mariano Zavaleta, complaining that "civilization, religion, fatherland, and morality have not received a decorous reception among those who call themselves earthly pastors; [these priests] have taken the gospel in name, but have rejected its precepts." Bishop Zaveleta supported Rivadavia's position, arguing for "the reform of those abuses and habits which degrade our Holy Religion" (*El Argos* 29 March 1823, 107–109). Of course, since Zavaleta was an appointee of the civil government and not of the Pope, his support did little to tame the rebellious clerics. In the meantime, when news of the ecclesiastical reform hit the provinces, it was only days before Juan Facundo Quiroga, caudillo of the distant province of La Rioja, coined one of the most effective slogans of the anti-Unitarian, Federalist reaction: *Religión o muerte* "Religion or Death." The passions stirred by the ecclesiastical reform would smolder for several years before finally exploding in support of the reactionary government of Juan Manuel de Rosas, the dictator who would eventually succeed the Rivadavians.

Rivadavia's last years in power were unpleasant for both him and his countrymen. Martín Rodríguez stepped down from the governorship in 1824 and was replaced by Juan Gregorio de las Heras. Rivadavia first continued as minister under the new governor, but was later sent on a diplomatic mission to garner British support for Argentina in the Brazilian-Argentine war over Uruguay. Since Great Britain was at this point playing Argentina and Brazil against each other, Rivadavia returned empty-handed, wounded by the cool reception he received from the British he so admired. Back in Buenos Aires, he found that The Happy Experience was rapidly unraveling, primarily because of mounting discontent among landowning Federalists like Rosas and the Anchorenas. Although never supporters of Rivadavia, these conservative oligarchs had tolerated his liberalism as long as it gave them more land and better trade agreements with England. But as the Rivadavians tried to turn words into policy, the conservatives, much like the Buenos Aires cabildo of ten years earlier, began plotting against the government. Hoping Rivadavia could restore confidence in the Unitarian government, his supporters in the congressional convention named him president of the entire country, an act that clearly exceeded their authority and further irritated the Interior. As "president," he seemed to press even harder to alienate his detractors.

Impatient and doctrinaire as always, he and his Unitarian party presented to the nation a new constitution that tried to resolve the perpetual conflict between Buenos Aires and the provinces by declaring the port city a federal rather than provincial capital whose income would be shared equally by all Argentines. Although a good idea, his plan met devastating opposition from Buenos Aires Federalists, including Juan Manuel de Rosas and his wealthy cousins, the Anchorena clan, who had no desire to share the Buenos Aires customs earnings. Following the United States model, the new constitution also provided for a bicameral legislature in which one body would give equal representation to each province. But again, the conservative oligarchs wanted no part of it. Authority and subordination were their principles of government, and not the accommodation and compromise of representative rule. Despite such widespread opposition, the Unitarians proclaimed the constitution the law of the land, an arrogant move that further undermined Rivadavia's support. In the meantime, Rivadavia endorsed a controversial plan to attract European immigrants to the Argentine. Again, the conservative oligarchs were horrified at the twin prospect of sharing Argentine land with immigrants and of seeing their Catholic traditions diluted by foreign infidels.

The final blow to Rivadavia's presidency came when his envoy to Brazil, Manuel José García, overstepped his authority and signed a treaty that effectively gave Brazil control of the Banda Oriental. News of the treaty arrived in Buenos Aires just about the time that nine provincial legislatures withdrew their support from Rivadavia. Hoping to rally support with a show of patriotism, Rivadavia sent a message to congress disavowing García's treaty. And then, with a touch of drama, in July 1827 he also submitted his resignation, thinking that the legislature would never let him go in a moment of national crisis. Crisis or not, his enemies jumped at the chance to get rid of him, and forty-eight of fifty legislators voted to accept his resignation. After several unseemly attempts to regain power, Rivadavia eventually emigrated to Spain, where he died in poverty and exile. Controversial even in death, he was remembered by his followers as the prime mover behind the short-lived Happy Experience, and vituperated by his detractors as an *europeizante* (Europeanizing), anti-Argentine heretic.

Argentine historians are sharply divided in their evaluations of Rivadavia and the Rivadavians. Liberal historians, who often reflect a porteño, pro-European bias, see Rivadavia as the first architect of modern Argentine society, a man who failed only because the blueprint he drew was too progressive for the times. In contrast, nationalist historians of both the left and right consider him the first large-scale *vendepatria*, or country-seller, who created an elegant mechanism by which Great Britain could exploit the Argentine in the name of free trade. Right-wing nationalists go on to argue that he betrayed Argentina's Spanish and Catholic past and in so doing vitiated whatever real identity the country could ever have.

There is ample ground for both praise and condemnation. On the positive side, no one more than Rivadavia so completely gave himself to the service of his country. As a member of the first Triumvirate that ruled after the Primera Junta, as a diplomat under several governments between 1814 and 1820, as minister under Martín Rodríguez, and finally as president, Rivadavia served with energy and dedication. Moreover, his dream of recreating Europe in the Southern Cone became a powerful guiding fiction that still informs the hopes of many Argentines for their country. The specifics of his programs, however, often showed good intentions without good sense.

What, for example, can we make of the Rivadavian cultural effort? It would surely be mean-spirited not to admire the aspirations and energy of those Rivadavian porteños who founded newspapers, magazines, schools, universities, theaters, drama institutes, museums, tail-coated literary societies, music conservatories, academies of science and jurisprudence, a women's beneficent society, boarding schools for provincial youngsters, and just about every other institutional sign of European High Culture. All this they did in less than three years in a largely illiterate city of 55,000 inhabitants lost between empty pampas on one side and the Atlantic Ocean on the other. Nonetheless, it is only slightly mean-spirited to point out that the Rivadavians were in some sense actors in an elaborate play who aspired to little more than establishing a repository and conduit for European culture. Unlike Artigas, they never allowed their country the dream of a unique destiny that might surpass Europe. Further, the Rivadavians were early seduced by appearances, apparently feeling that recreating Paris in the Pampas was merely a matter of decree and imitation. Where there was no substance, they sculpted a façade. Their literary societies produced no memorable literature, and their academies of science, except for imported experts, predated their scientists. Moreover, from The Happy Experience comes not one insightful essay, poem, or play on Argentina. In short, the Rivadavians pretended to live in a country that never existed while aspiring to rule the real Argentina, which they never understood. The Happy Experience in some sense was little more than theater, complete with empty sets and actors who tried to sound European.

This failure of the Rivadavians stemmed largely from their condescending indifference toward the popular, largely provincial, culture that legitimated in some degree the gauchos, the mixed-blood lower classes, the caudillos, the cabildos, and the colonial church. Imaginative policies seeking ways to incorporate these social groups and de facto institutions into modern systems of government were never considered, much less attempted. The gauchos and lower classes were ignored altogether—except when recruits were needed. The caudillos were denounced as barbarians to be eliminated, rather than natural leaders to be included in some kind of institutional government. And the cabildos in Luján and Buenos Aires, quasi-democratic organizations with two centuries of proven effectiveness, were decreed out of existence simply because they had no place in the trendy governmental theories the Rivadavians consulted. Rivadavia's problems with the Church reflected the same dogmatic political naiveté; however desirable the ecclesiastical reforms in principle, it was surely foolish to not court the good will of the Church and the deeply pious masses. Had Rivadavia known his people better, he certainly would have treated the religious issue more gingerly. To be sure, the ecclesiastical reforms were less extreme than the attacks on the caudillos and the cabildos; indeed, had the caudillo populists not felt so pressed on other fronts, the religious reforms would probably have encountered less resistance. Still, Rivadavia's moves against existing political and religious institutions repeatedly revealed a naive faith in the power of enlightened decrees and little comprehension of what was actually possible in the country he sought to rule. Indeed, in listening only to themselves, the porteño liberals were every bit as localist as the localists they denounced. Had the Rivadavians been more attuned to the sentiments of populists like Artigas and Hidalgo and less inclined to impose lofty theories from abroad, The Happy Experience might have been a lasting experience rather than the Golden Age dream so embellished by sympathetic historians.

The problems caused by Rivadavia's cultural, political, and ecclesiastical reforms pale, however, when compared with the insidious legacy left by his economic policies. Land distribution under Rivadavia concentrated huge tracts of Argentina's best resource in the hands of a select few, thus denying future generations access to any real economic and political power. Moreover, by using the country's enormous economic potential as collateral, the Rivadavians contracted Argentina's first large foreign debt, thus beginning the country's chronic dependence on foreign capital despite the huge personal fortunes amassed by the landed oligarchy. Indeed, the ease with which García and Rivadavia obtained foreign loans for government expenses established a pattern by which wealthy Argentines could avoid taxes and spend their considerable fortunes on foreign investments and sterile luxuries while contributing little to capital formation within the country—a pattern as alive today as it was 150 years ago. Argentina remains a capital-dependent country that is paradoxically a major exporter of capital. Finally, by allowing Great Britain nearly untrammeled access to all facets of the Argentine economy, from trade and investment to banking and monetary policy, the Rivadavians created an unholy alliance between the landed and commercial porteño bourgeoisie and their English overlords. Although Great Britain has largely been replaced by the United States and Japan, the uncontrolled presence of foreign economic interests in Argentina continues to undermine the country's control of its own affairs.

With Rivadavia's departure, doctrinaire democratic idealism in Argentina ended—at least for a while. His most positive contribution to the nation was his dream of creating a European state in the southern hemisphere, a dream that for a few short years engaged the imagination of an entire city. Nonetheless, the redoubtable memorialist Tomás de Iriarte, contemporary and sometime admirer of Rivadavia, summed up Don Bernardino's contribution as follows:

He lacked the patience to let his [decrees] soak in; he had no respect for time nor customs and even less for popular concerns. The people were not ready to see so much light all at once. . . . Rivadavia believed that it was enough to issue a decree. For this reason, his most intelligent ideas came to nothing. They were impractical. The people did not have adequate preparation for the new system he wanted to establish. His was a single-minded obsession with decrees. (3:31),

Juan Bautista Alberdi, the most impressive intellectual of the next generation and an acerbic critic of porteño pretense, summarizes The Happy Experience as follows:

Rivadavia left only scaffolding. His localist creations in Buenos Aires, in isolation from the nation, were intended to prepare the land for the building of national government. [Those who glorify him] take lodging in the scaffolding, covering it with tarps. Now they call this sort of country tent a definitive building. (*Grandes y pequeños hombres* 25)

Despite such criticism, The Happy Experience survives in the memory of Argentine liberals as a few years of peace, when Utopias could be had for the dreaming. As such, it would remain the prototype of liberal aspirations for years to come. The dark side of The Happy Experience was its legacy of indebtedness, concentration of wealth, exclusivity, antipopular sentiment, and cultural dependency. These, too, would circumscribe the efforts of future Argentines to build a viable, inclusive society.

Chapter Five

The Generation of 1837,
Part One

The Generation of '37 was a group of impassioned young men, mostly in their twenties and early thirties, who in 1837 organized a Literary Society as part of an ongoing critique of their country that would eventually produce some of Argentina's most durable guiding fictions. Despite the century and a half that separates us from their first writings, the Generation of '37 arguably remains Argentina's most distinguished group of intellectuals. The Men of '37 assigned themselves two major intellectual tasks: to identify without idealization the problems confronting their country, and to devise a program that would make Argentina a modern nation. In describing their country's problems, they created what has become an unfortunate genre in Argentine letters: the explanation of failure. We can easily understand why failure obsessed them. During their formative years, all members of the Generation of '37 witnessed the failure of the several provinces to unite in a single unit, the failure of porteño liberals to provide inclusive leadership, the failure of the masses to elect responsible officials, and the failure of high-sounding European theories to realize a constitutional alternative to the rule of the caudillos. It is therefore not surprising that explaining those failures, with a mercilessness that borders on self-defeating negativism, characterizes the Generation. As for their second task, to create a new program to correct Argentina's inadequacies, they borrowed heavily from their European contemporaries, often to the point of repeating the Rivadavian error of believing too much in the redemptive power of new theories from Europe and North America, proper words, and well-crafted decrees.

The story of the Men of '37 cannot begin with them, however, since their intellectual development and group identity are paradoxically linked to the reign of their political enemy and ideological bête noire, Juan Manuel de Rosas, the dictator who dominated Argentine politics from 1829 to 1852. While Rosas was in power, the Men of '37 were forced to consider how their country produced such a dictatorship and why the lofty ambitions of the Rivadavians came to such a devastating end. Since it is only against the backdrop of Rosas's dictatorship that the Generation of '37 can be fully appreciated, this chapter considers the rise, nature, and importance of *rosismo*, and then studies the early theories the Men of '37 offered to explain their country's ills.

Following Rivadavia's resignation, the Province of Buenos Aires seemed headed for a period at least as bad as the terrible year of 1820. Gone were the facile culture and easy prosperity of The Happy Experience when gentility could be decreed and credit was available for the asking. And gone was the relative political peace that allowed Governor Martín Rodríguez to work amicably with both Federalists and Unitarians. Unitarian promises had come to naught, and Federalism was on the rise. As the Unitarians saw their political hold weaken, a new nastiness crept into civil discourse. In his *Memorias*, Tomás de Iriarte describes the polarization of the two parties in the following terms:

The [Unitarian] party was considered aristocratic while the [Federalist] party was the popular one. Among the Unitarians there was greater talent, more men with new ideas, a greater affinity for the theories and spirit of the times, more brilliance and eloquence; the Unitarians also . . . lived more stylishly. But they were dominated by a disagreeable spirit—that of exclusivism; and their liberal doctrines contrasted sharply with their pronounced and obnoxious intolerance. From every pore they exuded a pigheaded pride, an extreme fatuousness incompatible with true knowledge. Their airs of insulting condescension had rendered them totally unpopular . . . among the common classes, and even among the majority of the middle class. They were mannered men with imitative customs, whose parody of Europe offended local values and habits. . . . [The Federalists] were, with few exceptions, pure Creoles, stuck in the routine of the

Old School. . . . For them everything else smelled of foreignness, which for many amounted to an apostasy from the duties of an outmoded nationalism. (4:74–75)

On August 12, 1828, the provincial legislature, now dominated by Federalists, elected Manuel Dorrego as governor of the Province of Buenos Aires, much to the horror of the Unitarians, who considered him a crazed rabble-rouser opposed to the ways of Europe. According to Iriarte, the Unitarian press did everything possible to provoke Dorrego, "calling him a mulatto and exhausting the Dictionary of Improprieties to exasperate him" (4:70–71). Dorrego, however, who in years past had earned a reputation for hot-headedness, surprised everyone by carefully staying within his legal prerogatives. He further showed good political sense by retaining Manuel José García, Rivadavia's Minister of Finance and chief negotiator with Brazil, and by appointing Manuel Moreno, Mariano's brother, to Rivadavia's old position as Minister of Government. Although a Federalist who had opposed the Rivadavian constitution, Moreno possessed intellectual credentials beyond reproach, even among Unitarians. Dorrego also cultivated the conservative estancieros by offering a cabinet post to Tomás Manuel de Anchorena (which he rejected) and making Juan Manuel de Rosas commander of the southern militia (Iriarte 4:72–74). The American ambassador at the time, John Murray Forbes, wryly describes Dorrego's conversion to pragmatism (i.e., side with the wealthy and the British, but shelve the Rivadavian constitution) in these terms:

The governor, Colonel Dorrego, who always distinguished himself by his virulent hostility towards the English . . . has undergone a complete change in his political sentiments. The Harlequin of this new farce is Manuel José García, who despite unanimous popular disapproval, has managed to gain the most complete control over the new government. The first indication of this extraordinary transformation was the appointment of Manuel Moreno as Minister of Government . . . who is known publicly for his devotion to the cause of the English and his great friendship with Lord Ponsonby and Mr. Parish. (Forbes 473–474)

Not only did Dorrego cozy up to the landowners and the British; with considerable success, he set about mending fences with the provincial caudillos and building a popular political base in the Province of Buenos Aires, culminating in his landslide victory in the provincial elections of May 1828. His victory, however, greatly alarmed porteño Unitarians, who loudly attributed Dorrego's success to election fraud. Faced with the the possibility of never regaining power from this popular Federalist, the Unitarians chose a "solution" that has become tragically familiar in this century: in the name of democracy and constitutionalism, they staged a coup against an elected government.

Their opportunity came when Dorrego, through his minister García, signed on September 5, 1828, an agreement with Brazil that made Uruguay an independent nation. While the terms of this treaty were considerably better than those first accepted by García under Rivadavia's presidency, hard-line Unitarians were not satisfied. Particularly upset was General Juan Galo Lavalle, a firebrand soldier and Independence hero who was at the time head of porteño troops in Uruguay. On hearing the news of the treaty, he regrouped his soldiers and marched toward Buenos Aires. Although warned of an imminent coup, Dorrego badly underestimated the Unitarians' hunger for power. According to British consul Woodbine Parish in a letter to the Earl of Aberdeen, dated December 2, 1828, Dorrego refused to believe that "friends of order" like the Unitarians would rebel against his entirely legitimate government, freely elected by the Province of Buenos Aires and supported by a majority of the provincial legislatures (cited in Ferns 196–197).

On December 1, 1828, Lavalle pronounced against the unprepared Dorrego government. With Lavalle's rebellion, the porteño Unitarians immediately forgot their fine words about institutional, democratic rule and flocked to support Lavalle in his coup against Dorrego. Significantly, when faced with Dorrego's popularity, the Unitarians did not seek an institutional solution to the charges of fraud, say, a court ruling or a recall election; instead, they reached for the gun. The two armies met at Navarro on November 9, 1828, where Lavalle's battle-seasoned troops easily routed the tiny Federalist militia, forcing Dorrego to flee for his life. Later, Dorrego was captured in flight by one of his own officers and turned over to Lavalle.

In the meantime, Lavalle, in a rigged election, became governor of the Province of Buenos Aires, a job for which he proved singularly inept. One of his first moves was to dissolve the Federalist-dominated provincial legislature. Then, fearful of Dorrego's continuing popularity, he committed one of the most tragic errors in Argentine history: on December 18, 1828, following the counsel of his Unitarian advisors and perhaps of Rivadavia himself, Lavalle had Dorrego killed without trial (Iriarte 4:129–131). As if ousting a legally constituted government and installing a fraudulent one were not enough, the Unitarians were now associated with a political assassination. Moreover, with Dorrego's execution, they lost all credibility in their claim to the moral high ground that supposedly separated them from the caudillos—a point not lost on Federalist apologist Pedro de Angelis, who chides the Unitarians for condemning "the cruel assassination of the illustrious Governor Dorrego" while extolling "his assassins with such zeal" (cited in Lynch, *Argentine Dictator* 196–197). After Dorrego's assassination, lawlessness and violence characterized the Unitarians as much the "barbarous" caudillos they deplored.

The Unitarians' reasons for supporting Dorrego's murder can be comprehended only in terms of their flawed perception of Federalism. For the Unitarians, Federalism was not an opposition movement to be accommodated within a pluralistic, democratic framework. Rather, it was pure demagoguery, "populist arbitrariness," the product of a few charismatic individuals who beguiled the savage masses and obstructed enlightenment. Given this opinion, the Unitarians apparently felt that Federalism would disappear only if a few key men like Dorrego were eliminated. Of course it didn't work, but the idea that progress and enlightened government would result if the right people were killed has haunted Argentine history from Mariano Moreno right down to the present. Dorrego's death also silenced the most sensible voices in Federalism, and cued the entrance of the party's most reactionary elements, namely, Juan Manuel de Rosas and the Anchorenas.

With the shock of Dorrego's murder, Federalist opposition coalesced around Rosas, who, with his gaucho militia and in league with the troops of Estanislao López of Santa Fe, prepared for war against Lavalle. Faced with widespread desertion among his own troops and the likely possibility of a Federalist victory, Lavalle decided to strike a truce with Rosas's forces and to call new elections, which produced a three-month caretaker government under General Juan José Viamonte. In the meantime, Rivadavia fled the country, never to play an important role in Argentine politics again. Shortly thereafter, the cries for revenge from Dorrego's friends also caused Lavalle to lose his taste for politics and beat a quick retreat to the newly independent Uruguay.

After Lavalle's fall, anarchy again threatened Buenos Aires, but this time there was a new savior. In Juan Manuel de Rosas, the Province of Buenos Aires now had its own caudillo, a man proven in battle, idolized by the urban poor and the rural gauchos, firmly linked to conservative landowners, and apparently capable of restoring order by dint of his powerful personality. A handsome man with piercing blue eyes, not only did Rosas mesmerize Buenos Aires and eventually the entire country; his nature and significance in Argentine history continue to fuel an often unfriendly debate among Argentine historians (see Kroeber, "Rosas and the Revision of Argentine History" and Navarro Gerassi, *Los nacionalistas* 131–145). The largely Federalist provincial legislature, which had been dissolved by Lavalle, was reconstituted on December 1, 1829, and after five days of debate, it appointed Rosas, only thirty-five years old, as the new governor. But more important than Rosas's election were the terms under which he was appointed. As proposed by his cousin, Tomás Manuel de Anchorena, reactionary oligarch par excellence, Rosas was given extraordinary powers, or *facultades extraordinarias*, which with legislative sanction made him a virtual dictator for the next three years (Lynch 42–47).

In his first term as governor, Rosas, not wanting to frighten his enemies too much, used his powers judiciously. He protected property, "liberated" more land from the Indians, fortified anti-Indian defenses, kept porteño–provincial disputes at a low temperature, and managed to bring some semblance of fiscal responsibility to the debt-ridden government. All but the most doctrinaire Unitarians were impressed with him, even the British. Of course, order had its price. Except for continued land distribution for the rich and increased commercial contact with the British, Rosas effectively annulled Rivadavia's reforms; he restricted the press, neglected education, supported the conservative clergy, strengthened the army, and muzzled critics. But lest anyone accuse him of authoritarian ambitions, right on schedule, on November 19, 1832, he returned his *facultades extraordinarias* to the legislature and went back to his estancia. A grateful legislature accepted the resignation, thanking him for bringing the province to "the happy state of living in tranquillity under the authority of the laws" (cited in Lynch 49).

Following Rosas's resignation, disorder again engulfed Buenos Aires, convincing many porteños that without Rosas there was no law and order. After two administrations failed in rapid succession, the legislature voted on June 27, 1834, to reappoint Rosas to the governorship. But not liking the terms of the offer, he declined. Finally, after considerable pressuring from his chief supporters, the landed bourgeoisie, he agreed to accept the post—but only if the legislature allowed him the "fullest of public authority" (*la suma del poder público*). On March 7, 1835, the legislature gave him what he wanted, and he became governor for the second time. Thus began the Rosas dictatorship, not by force or coup, but by the consent of the legislature and the acquiescence of a society exhausted by war and anarchy (Lynch 49). While never officially more than Governor of the Province of Buenos Aires, Rosas dominated the country's politics for the next seventeen years.

Until his fall in 1852, Rosas retained power without the niceties of elections. To be sure, for public relations purposes, he routinely sent his resignation to his hand-picked congress; and just as routinely the legislature rejected the resignation, begging him to continue as govenor (Lynch 165–166). Yet, despite these staged elections, even his best-known critic, Domingo Faustino Sarmiento, confesses "out of respect for historical truth [that] there was never a government more popular, more desired nor more supported by public opinion" (Sarmiento, *Vida de Juan Facundo Quiroga* 130). Rosas's most important constituency were conservative estancieros like himself who gave little thought to political theory as long as the Indians continued yielding up land and the market for cowhide and salted meat remained strong. To this group Rosas stayed loyal, even if it meant crossing political boundaries. As he wrote to Felipe Arana, "I believed it important to accustom the people always to regard with respect the upper classes of the country, even those whose opinions differ from the prevailing ones. This is the reason why all my punishments were reserved for the scoundrels and rebels, for the whole pack of officials and ambitious leaders, whom I have always been convinced should be punished with severity and without indulgence" (cited in Lynch 99–100). Still, Rosas also enjoyed the support of the poor, seduced by his carefully cultivated political persona that was at once imperial, populist, and paternalistic. Rosas could ride and talk like a gaucho, but he also knew how to affect the airs of royalty (Lynch 108–119). In more ways than one he presaged the rule of another populist presidency: that of Juan Domingo and Eva Perón, who in this century dressed like aristocrats while affirming solidarity with the poor.

No one would call Rosas an intellectual; indeed, his only point of academic pride was apparently his near-perfect orthography. He was, however, considerably influenced by his well-educated and reactionary cousin, Tomás Manuel de Anchorena ("a man of rancid and anti-social ideas" according to Iriarte [4:72]) who was well versed in the thought of Edward Burke, Joseph de Maistre, Gaspar Real de Curbán, and other critics of the French Revolution and popular sovereignty (Sebreli, *Apogeo* 72–73). Self-proclaimed as "The Restorer of Laws," Rosas signified in large measure a return to colonial practices. Rosas himself said as much in an oft-reprinted speech he first gave on May 25, 1836, in celebration of the May Revolution: "Our revolution [Mayo] was not a rebellion to replace legitimately constituted authority, but an attempt to fill the void left when that authority vanished, leaving the nation without leadership." He goes on to affirm that Mayo was primarily a "heroic act of loyalty and fidelity to the Spanish nation and its unlucky monarch" and not "a disguised rebellion" against the authority principle itself (cited in Gandía, "Estudio preliminar" 12–13). Rosas on another occasion argued that the postrevolutionary period "was not a time of quiet and tranquillity like those that preceded the May Revolution" precisely because antiauthoritarian currents among liberals had perverted the true nature of Mayo (Gandía 15). In an interview he stated succinctly, "For me the ideal of happy government would be a paternal autocracy" (cited in Lynch 304). His kindly view of "paternal autocracy" no doubt contributed to his restoring full privileges to the Church (Ramos Mejía, *Rosas y su tiempo* 200–203). In return for favors received from the Rosas government, Bishop Medrano of Buenos Aires, in a pastoral letter dated September 7, 1837, instructed his priests to exhort the faithful to support the Federalist system "without which we would be victims of the blackest passions and would see blood flow from our very brothers" (cited in Mayer, *Alberdi y su tiempo* 154–155).

In sum, although Rosas enjoyed great popularity, he was in no sense a real populist. The theories of inclusion, protectionism, and nativism enunciated by Artigas and Hidalgo repelled him just as much as the Frenchified liberalism of the Unitarians. Rosas thus disclosed the other face—the antipopular face—of Argentine federalism: an aristocratic notion of authority and privilege that might provide for the poor out of a paternalistic impulse, but in no way would include the low-born as equal citizens in a pluralistic government. His was a restoration of the hierachical society of the Spanish monarchs. Or, as Sarmiento puts it, "Rosas invented nothing; his only talent consists of plagiarizing his forebears" (*Facundo* 37). What Sarmiento and most of his generation failed to see, however, was that Rosas was not a caudillo like any other. Whereas Rosas was aristocratic, paternalistic, and reactionary, other caudillos, like Güemes and Artigas, had been populist and progressive. Although known as a Federalist, Rosas gave only lip service to ideas of equally federated provinces and real democracy. Indeed, his regime hardened Buenos Aires' grip on the interior more than any of his Unitarian predecessors had done. Nonetheless, his government is still known in Argentine history as the Federation, although in practice his brand of federalism differed markedly from that of the best provincial caudillos.

The Rosas who returned to power in 1835 quickly interjected himself into every aspect of Argentine society. Careful to attend to outward symbols of power, he forced the citizens to wear the red Federalist insignia, and his picture appeared in all public places, even beside church altars. Elaborate public ceremonies, arms displays, forced rallies, costume balls in which the Unitarian color blue was proscribed, and military processions became the order of the day, particularly as "the military, merchants, officials and others competed to show their loyalty to Rosas" (Lynch 165). More sinister was Rosas's increasing use of terror and violence to impose his will. One of his first acts was the execution without trial of three alleged conspirators in the Plaza del Retiro on May 29, 1835. From that point forward, Rosas's enemies, real and imagined, were increasingly imprisoned, tortured, murdered, or driven into exile by the *mazorca*, a band of spies and thugs supervised personally by Rosas and in some sense a forerunner of this century's paramilitary death squads (Lynch 201–246). Publications were censored, and porteño newspapers became tedious apologizers for the regime.

Despite its backwardness and cruelty, Rosas's government was not without accomplishments. The economy grew significantly under his rule (Scobie, *Argentina* 102–104). Following Rivadavia's emphyteusis formula, new lands were liberated, usually ending up in the hands of the already land-rich oligarchs (Lynch 51–59). Rosas skillfully negotiated with British creditors, making sure loan repayments did not inhibit his ability to pay his own soldiers and civil servants and thereby maintain their loyalty (Ferns 218–224). Indeed, Rosas got on quite well with the British. As the American agent William A. Harris wrote to Daniel Webster in a letter dated September 20, 1850:

One of the most unaccountable and strange peculiarities of the Governor, and as a necessary consequence also, of all the principal men of note in this country, is the extraordinary partiality, admiration, and preference for the English government, and the English men, upon also all occasions and under all circumstances. I characterize this partiality and preference as *unaccountable* and *strange*, in view of the arrogant and selfish policy, and the meddlesome and sinister influences, which the British government and people have always endeavoured to exercise in these countries. (Cited in Lynch 293)

Rosas's only major conflict with the British came from refusing to respect the treaty Dorrego signed with Brazil granting Uruguay its independence. In league with the conservative Uruguayan rebel Manuel Oribe, Rosas repeatedly tried to get Uruguay back under Buenos Aires' control, much to the irritation of Uruguay's trading partners—Brazil, France, and England. At one point the French and British, alarmed at Rosas's interference with their Uruguayan trade, blockaded the Buenos Aires port completely. Rosas weathered the blockade, however, and in 1850 signed treaties with both France and England. Today, pro-Rosas historians make much of his attempts to recapture the lost province of Uruguay and his successful resistance of the Anglo-French blockade (e.g. Ibarguren [Carlos], *Rosas* 414–417; Irazusta [Julio], *Breve historia* 126–136). Even San Martín, from his deathbed in Paris in 1850, directed that his saber be given to Juan Manuel de Rosas for "the firmness with which he has sustained the republic's honor against . . . the foreigners who sought to humiliate her" (cited in Herring 638). Another of Rosas's accomplishments, however, was surely one he never intended: his reactionary rule stimulated the development of Argentina's first important generation of intellectuals, the Generation of 1837.

I will examine the Generation of '37 in two stages. I will begin with an important essay by Juan Bautista Alberdi entitled *Fragmento preliminar al estudio del derecho* (Preliminary fragment to the study of law), and then examine key ideas as they developed in the writings of the entire generation. This organization is justified by the fact that the *Fragmento* was written before the Generation actually coalesced as such. Moreover, the *Fragmento* contains ideas quite different from those of the Generation as a whole; indeed, even Alberdi temporarily abandoned certain concepts of the *Fragmento*, as we shall see later, not to take them up again until nearly twenty years later.

Despite the modesty of its title—both fragmentary and preliminary—the *Fragmento* was the most significant essay on Argentine identity to appear since Moreno's writings of nearly two decades earlier. Published in the early part of 1837, the *Fragmento* shows unusual independence in understanding the Rosas phenomenon and the caudillos in general. Alberdi came naturally by his sympathy for the caudillos. A native of the northern province of Tucumán, he was the protegé of Alejandro Heredia, caudillo of Tucumán, and a Rosas ally. In 1834 Heredia wrote a letter to Facundo Quiroga, caudillo of La Rioja who at the time was living in Buenos Aires, asking that Quiroga provide Alberdi with funds for a year of study in the United States. According to Alberdi, Quiroga graciously made the funds available. It is not clear why the trip did not take place as planned (Mayer, *Alberdi* 112–114). Only months later, in February 1835, Quiroga was assassinated while returning to Buenos Aires. In March of that same year Rosas was elected governor and endowed with *facultades extraordinarias*.

Despite rumors implicating Rosas in Quiroga's assassination, Alberdi's portrayal of the dictator in *Fragmento* is surprisingly conciliatory. He arrives at this position, however, through arguments Rosas would never have comprehended; perhaps for this reason the dictator failed to engage this young thinker who might have brought intelligence and respectability to his reactionary rule. Admitting his debt to Savigny, Alberdi opens the *Fragmento* arguing that organic law (*derecho*) is more than "a collection of written laws." Rather it is "the very constitution of a society, the ineluctable order in which the individuals comprising [that society] develop" (Alberdi, *Obras completas* [*OC*] 1:103–104). Consequently, the only government possible in a given society must spring from that society, and not from theories imposed from above since "the juridical component of a people develops in inevitable parallelism to the economic, religious, artistic, and philosophical components of that people" (104). "Knowing written laws (*leyes*)," Alberdi continues, "is not the same as knowing organic law (*derecho*), because written laws are merely the imperfect and frequently distorted image of organic law which lives in lively harmony with the social organism" (105). Using these premises, Alberdi affirms that a viable nation can be formed only in concordance with that organic law that springs from the people themselves. "A nation is not a nation," he argues, "except by the profound and reflective awareness of those elements that comprise it. Only at that moment [of awareness] is a nation civilized; prior to that moment it had been instinctive, spontaneous, developing without knowing itself, without knowing where, how or why" (111). From here he turns specifically to the case of Argentina, arguing that "we should cleanse our spirit of all false colors, of all borrowed clothing, of all imitation, of all servility. Let us govern ourselves, think, write and proceed in all things, not through imitation of any other people on earth, no matter that people's prestige, but exclusively according to the demands of the general laws of the human spirit and the individual laws of our national condition." He further argues that the success of the United States sprang from its ability to "adopt from the beginning institutions appropriate to the natural circumstances of a national spirit (*un ser nacional*)" (112). As Alberdi admits, his ideas in this regard are informed by Lerminier and Savigny; he could also have mentioned Hegel. More striking in my view, however, is the affinity of his thinking to that of Artigas and Hidalgo, who, although far from Alberdi's intellectual equals, also postulated notions of an American or gaucho spirit, a preexisting national soul that alone could form the basis of a viable nationhood. Moreover, like Alberdi, these early populists also distrusted excessive reliance on foreign models.

Using these ideas as a point of departure, Alberdi develops an astonishing apology for Rosas. Referring to the Argentina of 1837, he writes:

Our current mission, then, is the study and peaceful development of the American spirit, under the most appropriate and adequate form. We must suppose that the great and powerful person who now directs our public destiny also possesses a sturdy intuition of these truths, as witnessed by his profound, instinctive antipathy to exotic theories. Devoid of the concerns of a narrow science which he never studied, and thanks to his spontaneous intelligence, he is clearly aware of . . . the impotence, ineffectiveness, and pointlessness of the means of government previously practiced in our country: that such imported means of government, devoid of all national originality, could have no application in a society whose normal conditions of existence differed totally from those societies in which such exotic ideas originated, and that, as a result, a system of our own was for us indispensable. (116–117)

Alberdi thus attributes the failure of the Unitarians and Rivadavians to their love of exotic theories of government, of "narrow science" that had nothing to do with Argentina. But more important, at this point in his life he considered Rosas a man of "spontaneous intelligence" who intuited the needs of the Argentine nation, and whose existence in power had to be seen as an expression of the national spirit to be accommodated and not deplored simply because such a caudillo did not figure in fine theoretical systems from abroad. He further argues that his generation is called to support the caudillo, to develop whatever in Rosas was distinctly Argentine and thereby essential to national development:

What the great magistrate has tried to practice in politics, Argentine youth is now called to attempt in art, philosophy, industry, and sociability: that is to say, the youth are called to study the laws and the forms of the development of all elements of our American existence, without plagiarism, without imitation, and only in the intimate and profound study of our people and our things. (117)

While recognizing that Rosas was hardly a representative leader in any institutional sense, Alberdi nonetheless saw him as a bona fide spokesman for *el pueblo*. Moreover, Alberdi specifically defines the term *people* in its broadest sense: "Here we do not understand the term people to mean the thinking class or the property-owning class alone; rather [we understand] it to mean universality, majority, the multitudes, the *plebe*. We understand the term as did Aristotle, Montesquieu, Rousseau, Volney, Moses and Jesus Christ" (125). In fact, Aristotle with his notions of natural slaves and Rousseau with his condescending attitudes toward women did not mean "universality." Alberdi, however, much unlike other Argentine liberals, most certainly did.

But more than a natural leader of the entire *pueblo*, Rosas in Alberdi's view was a necessary transition from civil war to stable democracy. "Nations, like men," he writes, "do not have wings; they make their journeys on foot, step by step. . . . It is therefore necessary to arrive at our democracy according to the law of gradual development to which all creation is subordinated; and of course to accept the fact that our current democracy must be imperfect" (126). In sum, Alberdi counsels his generation to support Rosas as a stable leader whose very stability will allow Argentina to evolve organically toward greater and greater democracy. Moreover, he sees Rosas as a natural leader whose existence must be accepted as a necessary step toward the "adulthood of nations." He further suggests that any attempt to bystep or eliminate Rosas would merely result in the chaos that besieged the country since its beginnings in 1810.

While Alberdi showed remarkable insight regarding the caudillo phenomenon, he underestimated Rosas's malevolence. Indeed, less than two years later he fled Rosas's Buenos Aires for Montevideo, and joined other Argentine expatriots in a protracted struggle to unseat the dictator. Nonetheless, his *Fragmento* stands alone in the period as a thoughtful work that tried to understand *caudillismo* as something other than a barbarism to be eliminated whatever the cost. During the years of struggle, Alberdi became closely identified with the Generation of '37, to such a degree that his best-known work, *Bases y puntos de partida* (see Alberdi, *Las "Bases" de Alberdi*), which we will consider later in this chapter, is arguably the major text of the time. Yet the ideas found in *Fragmento*, as we shall see, emerge again in Alberdi's later work. For the time being, however, for the years 1837–1852, the major task at hand was to unseat Rosas. In this endeavor Alberdi joined others of the Generation of '37 in formulating the ideas considered below.

The name, the "Generation of '37," comes from a literary salon organized in May 1837 in a Buenos Aires bookstore by "youths impassioned in their love of beauty and liberty [who] met to read, discuss and converse" (Gutiérrez, "Noticias biográficas" 46). Founded several months after Alberdi published his *Fragmento*, the Association was modeled after and inspired by the youthful revolutionary societies that had sprung up all over Europe (Echeverría, *Dogma socialista* 169–174), and became known as *La asociación de la joven generación argentina* or *La asociación de mayo;* the latter refers to the Argentine independence movement of May 1810. The choice of the term *Mayo* was more than an attempt at validation through appeal to prior authority. It was also an ideological goal based on the notion that the errors of previous generations could be erased, and a New Argentina could rise from the ruins of Rosas's tyranny, just as Mayo had cast off the yoke of colonial rule.

But unlike the insurgents of 1810, the Men of '37 showed greater trust in ideas as a necessary point of departure for reforming Argentina. Theirs was a generation of writers who apparently felt that progress lay in the right words, the right beliefs, and the right constitution. Their slogan, emblazoned in bold letters above their meeting room, came from St. Paul: *Abnegemus ergo opera tenebrarum et induamur arma lucis:* "Let us therefore cast off the works of darkness, and let us put on the armour of light" (Romans 13:12). Unfortunately, as Alberdi notes in *Mi vida privada*, "The arms of light were not in fashion under the government of the time" (*Escritos póstumos* [*EP*] 15:297).

The importance of words for the Generation was underlined in the Association's first meeting by Esteban Echeverría, the group's founder. In his "Discurso de introducción" he argues that Argentine history since Independence was divided into two periods: "The first, the greatest and most glorious page of our history, belonged to the sword. But that period was followed by the truly heroic age of our own social action . . . [in which] is inaugurated the forum of intelligence, where rigorous and profound reason proclaims a new era: a new dawn from the same sun, the adult and reflective age of our *patria*" (*OC* 1:99). The term *science* applied to social governance reveals Echeverría's link to the French thinkers, Saint-Simon and Victor Cousin, for whom government could supposedly be just as scientific as Newton's laws of motion. Echeverría later makes explicit his connections to French social theorists (106).

What was needed in Echeverría's view were new ideas for a New Argentina; "not vague, erroneous, incomplete ideas that produce moral anarchy, which is a thousand times worse than physical anarchy, but systematic ideas, full of the knowledge of social science" (103). The New Generation, then, must find the genius and ability to enlighten the people. And what sort of person might typify that genius? "He will drink from the fountains of European civilization, he will study our history, he will examine with a penetrating eye the depths of our society, and, enriched by all the treasures of study and reflection, he will . . . bequeath a legacy of works that will enlighten and ennoble the patria" (107). Underlying Echeverría's prescription for Argentina is an extraordinary faith in ideas. By the right words, Argentina would be saved.

To enlighten the people, the Salon first founded a weekly magazine, *La Moda*, which managed to publish twenty-three issues between November 1837 and April 1838 before Rosas shut it down. Under the heading of "Long Live the Federation," the first issue of *La Moda* announced its goal: to report on fashion, poetry, art, literature, music, and dance from both Europe and Buenos Aires. True to its prospectus, the first issue contains commentary on French furniture, hats (gray was in, black was out), men's trousers (no buttons, please), and a short musical composition by Alberdi (*La Moda* 18 Nov. 1837, 1–5). Subsequent issues included original poems and information on Rossini operas and French novels. Like the Unitarian newspaper *El Argos de Buenos Aires* of some fifteen years earlier, *La Moda* appears most concerned with bringing European culture to the Argentine. Unlike *El Argos*, however, it contains no explicit political commentary except for an occasional obligatory accolade for Rosas and Federalism. Indeed, to avoid problems with the dictator, *La Moda* carefully supported the regime's policies, no matter how mindless. For example, in the 18 November 1837 issue, Rosas's decree that all citizens wear the red Federalist insignia is defended, ironically perhaps, in the following terms: "When a political idea adopts a color as its symbol, and that idea is elevated above all others, the color that symbolizes it soon becomes fashionable in the hands of public spirit. . . . For us, such is the color red, emblem of the Federative idea: it is both a political color and a color of fashion"

(2 December 1837, 4). Thus the young men of *La Moda* claim that whatever is done in the name of "public spirit" and the "Federative" idea is also fashionable. Of course they didn't really believe such a thing, but maintaining a public image of loyalty, however absurd, was a demand of the times.

In like manner, virtually every item in *La Moda* seems hampered at some level by the writers' underlying fear of offending the regime. Typical is a short article by Alberdi titled "Urbane Rules for a Visit":

I teach what I have seen, what is used, and what is accepted as beautiful among people known to be cultured.

To make a visit, it is not necessary to know the hour; let watchmen and school teachers worry about the hour. It is more *romantic* and *fashionable* [*sic*] to let yourself be carried in the arms of a sweet distraction, to change if possible like Byron or M. Fox the night into day or the day into night. Make your visit even if it is two in the afternoon; that is what is done in Paris and London. (2 Dec. 1837, 1)

The cultivated pointlessness of this kind of writing attempted to deflect the danger members of the Association faced from Rosas, who had already imprisoned, killed, or driven into exile several of their friends. It might also be argued that Alberdi was merely imitating the slice-of-life sketches of his confessed model, Spanish writer Mariano José de Larra. Larra's articles, however, were often satirical or politically motivated, despite their light touch. Given the repression of the times, Alberdi could imitate Larra's lightness, but little else. The ruse of lighthearted frivolity, however, did not convince all; one of the magazine's few editorials states, "We would like to see many people convinced that *La Moda* is nothing more than a frivolous paper for amusement." The anonymous writer also assures readers that "*La Moda* is not a hostile plot against current customs of Buenos Aires, as some have apparently believed" (17 March 1838).

If frivolity was their public pose, in private the members of the Association were deadly serious. Among their first acts was drafting fifteen "Symbolic words"—Association, Progress, Fraternity, Equality, Liberty, and the like—followed by hortative explanations written in a high-sounding style with echoes of Biblical wrath: "The selfish and evil will gain their reward: the judgement of posterity awaits them" (Echeverría, *Dogma* 171). Although the salon members took pains initially not to offend Rosas, he soon closed it down and began persecuting its members who, after meeting clandestinely for a several months, finally fled the country in fear of their lives (Palacios, *Esteban Echeverría* 475–477). By 1841, most of the Generation of 1837 was living in exile, either in Chile or Uruguay. Although linked by name to the year 1837, they wrote their chief works in exile long after that year.

Before pursuing their ideas further, I should introduce in a more systematic fashion the Generation's chief members and their works. Principal among the salon's organizers was Esteban Echeverría, an intense young poet recently returned from France, where he had become thoroughly imbued with Romantic sentiment and the social theories of Saint-Simon (Ingenieros, *Los iniciadores* 113–119; Korn, *Influencias filosóficas* 152–162). Beloved as a poet, Echeverría is also known for two long essays, *Dogma socialista* of 1837 and *Ojeada retrospectiva sobre el movimiento intelectual en el Plata desde el año '37* of 1845, a personal memoir of the Generation. Also of prime importance was Juan Bautista Alberdi, whose *Fragmento preliminar* was discussed earlier. Among his voluminous writings, the most read and remembered is *Bases y puntos de partida para la organización política de la República Argentina* of 1852, a text closely linked to the Generation of '37, but not necessarily representative of Alberdi's earlier and later thought. *Bases* served as a major source of inspiration for much of Argentina's civil code as well as for the Constitution of 1853. This constitution, with minor changes, would remain in force until it was replaced by Perón in 1949; after Perón's fall, an amended version of the 1853 constitution was reinstituted and continues to be the supreme law of the land. Other significant members of the literary salon were Miguel Cané, a journalist and novelist; Vicente Fidel López, a sometime novelist who later became a highly visible historian; and Juan María Gutiérrez, a novelist, critic, and chronicler of the generation.

Two important members of the Generation of 1837, although not part of the Buenos Aires literary salon, later became closely associated with its former members when all were in exile. The first was José Mármol, a novelist and poet best known for his devastating anti-Rosas novel *Amalia*, published serially in 1851 and in its complete form in 1855 (Ghiano, "Prólogo" xliii–xliv; Lichtblau, *Argentine*

Novel 43). A political maverick, he was exiled by Rosas in 1841, despite rumors that he was a Rosas sympathizer. Ironically, he got along no better with governments that succeeded Rosas (Ghiano xiii, xvii). The second member of the Generation not associated with the porteño group initially was Domingo Faustino Sarmiento, perhaps the most important figure of his time. A poor youth from the intellectually barren province of San Juan, Sarmiento followed the activities of the literary salon as closely as possible and actually tried to organize a similar group in San Juan. Several years later, when they were all in exile, he established personal, albeit often polemical, contacts with members of the then defunct literary salon.

Of the entire generation, Sarmiento had the most successful public career. He went on two diplomatic missions to the United States for Chile, his expatriate homeland. After returning to Argentina, he founded literally dozens of public schools staffed by young teachers, mostly women, freshly graduated from normal schools also established by Sarmiento. In politics, he served as Minister of Education, Ambassador to the United States, and President of the country. Yet he still found time to write works collected in fifty-two volumes. It was perhaps as a writer that he was most influential, leaving two or three texts that remain basic to understanding how Argentines view their country. Foremost among these is *Civilización y barbarie: Vida de Juan Facundo Quiroga* of 1845, usually referred to as *Facundo*.

As writers, the Men of '37 evidence a problem common to Spanish American writers even in this century: their work often exhibits an unfinished quality, a quality the Mexican critic Alfonso Reyes has compared to bread pulled from the oven too soon. Men of action living in a chaotic society, they viewed their writings as part of a larger political process and not ends in themselves to be perfectly sculpted and polished. Conscious of the problem, Sarmiento often declared that "Things have to be done. Well or poorly, they have to be done. (*Las cosas hay que hacerlas. Bien o mal, hay que hacerlas.*)" Similarly, Alberdi laments that his works are "books of action, written rapidly." But he defends them as "works written to meet their time," which, like wheat, must be sown in the proper season to be ready for the harvest (cited by Mayer, "Prólogo" 165).

Despite its mostly Unitarian sympathies, the Generation of '37 distinguished itself from the old-guard Unitarians in various ways. First, although they were thorough readers of European thinkers (Locke, Bentham, Mill, Spencer, Saint-Simon, Fourier, Comte, Lamennais, Leroux, Lerminier, Hegel, Savigny), the Men of '37 tried to be more cautious than their Rivadavian forebears in applying European theories to Argentine problems. In his *Ojeada retrospectiva* of 1846, Echeverría asserts that a peculiar Argentine vice is "searching for the new, . . . while forgetting the familiar." He later argues that "European books and speculative theories often lead to confusion and prevent good seeds from taking root . . . by maintaining restless spirits in a state of sterile and perpetual strife" (Echeverría, *Ojeada retrospectiva* 116). Earlier in the *Dogma socialista*, he wrote that "every people has its own life and its own intelligence. . . . A people that enslaves its intelligence to the intelligence of another people, is stupid and sacrilegious" since such attitudes violate natural (divine) law" (169). Alberdi also affirmed the need for intellectual independence in his opening address of the Salon's first meeting: "To continue the life begun in Mayo, is not to do what is done in France or the United States, but what the double law of our age and soil demands of us. To seek development is to acquire one's own civilization, however imperfect, and not to copy foreign civilizations, no matter how advanced. Every people should be of its own age and its own soil. Every people should be itself" (Alberdi, *OC* 1:264). Similarly, Sarmiento, despite his admiration for Rivadavia, twits the porteño Unitarians for blindly imitating European fashions. "Voltaire discredited Christianity, and Buenos Aires did the same. Montesquieu established three powers of government; we had three powers, too. Benjamin Constant and Bentham disputed the authority of the Executive; he was born without authority here. Buenos Aires confessed and believed everything educated people in Europe confessed and believed" (Sarmiento, *Facundo* 66–67). Nevertheless, despite such statements, the Men of '37, as will be seen further on, manifested a similar enthrallment to European ideas and North American models, not unlike that of the Unitarians. Their brave words proclaiming independence from foreign thought were not enough to break the conditioning of 300 years of colonialism: just as for the Morenistas and the Rivadavians, new ideas and social models

for the Generation of '37 came from abroad, despite their protestations to the contrary.

A second area where the Generation of '37 tried to break with
their intellectual fathers, again with mixed success, was in attempting to end the bloody factionalism between the centralist Unitarians
and the autonomist Federalists that had repeatedly threatened national integrity. The Unitarians in Echeverría's view were "a defeated minority with good inclinations but without . . . socialist understanding, and rather disagreeable because of their proud,
exclusivist and supremacist attitudes" (*Ojeada* 83). The term *socialist,* as Echeverría uses it here—in line with Saint-Simon, whom he
greatly admired—appears to mean something akin to "social conscience" or "social awareness" in which the good of society is the
primary determiner of policy. No reference to a particular economic
order is intended. In contrast to the Unitarians' goal, the purpose of
the new generation was, according to Echeverría, "to unitarize the
Federalists and federalize the Unitarians. . . . through creating
ideas that would reconcile all opinions and all interests in a vast and
fraternal embrace" (*Ojeada* 86–87). Unfortunately, at other times he
undermined such sweet inclusiveness by holding that Federalism
was a system "supported by the popular masses and the genuine
expression of their semi-barbarous instincts" (Echeverría, *Dogma*
83). Like Moreno, Echeverría could sound inclusive, but theirs was
an inclusiveness that allowed no place for the uncultured.

Similarly, Alberdi argues that the sterile disputes between Unitarians and Federalists "lead public opinion in our Republic to
abandon all exclusive systems." The New Argentina they aspired to
create must have a "mixed government which embraces and recon-
ciles the freedom of each Province and the Nation as a whole," free
of "vain ambitions for exclusive power" (*Bases* 290). Although
Alberdi accepts the Federalist–Unitarian rift as genuine, he frequently suggests, as seen above, that a more basic division in Argentine society lay between Buenos Aires and the Provinces. This is a
recurrent theme in Alberdi's thought and, as documented in later
chapters, would constitute a major area of contention between him
and Sarmiento in later years.

In explaining Argentina's difficulties, the thinking of the Generation of '37 ranges between two poles. On one extreme is Sarmiento,

impassioned, romantic, brash, and often more poetic than practical, a fact evidenced by the opening lines of *Facundo:*

Terrible shadow of Facundo! I now conjure you up, so that, by shaking the blood-stained dust that covers your ashes, you will arise to explain to us the secret life and internal convulsions that claw at the entrails of a noble people! You possess the secret. Reveal it to us!

On the other extreme is Alberdi, lucid, analytical, and not infrequently peeved at Sarmiento's maddeningly quotable exaggerations. Although Alberdi and Sarmiento agreed on many theoretical points, their personal antipathy for each other is now the stuff of legend. Moreover, as will be seen in later chapters, after Rosas's fall when they no longer shared a common enemy, Alberdi and Sarmiento became bitter and abiding enemies.

In an odd sense, democracy was both the problem and the solution for the thinkers of 1837. On the one hand, they subscribed in principle to notions of institutional representative government; on the other, they deeply distrusted the will of the people since the masses were solidly behind Rosas and the traditional authoritarianism he represented. Without the active support of the masses, Rosas could never have retained power as long as he did. The mission of the Men of '37 then is a mission of paradox. They must discredit the masses and the "inorganic democracy" represented by caudillo rule while at the same time reorganizing Argentine society in the name of the masses and laying the foundation for institutional democracy once the masses are ready for it. To reach this paradoxical goal, they lauched a sustained attack against what they perceived as the sources of Rosas's power: the land, the Spanish tradition, and the mixed-blood poor consisting of gauchos, domestic servants, and common laborers.

Regarding the land, the Men of '37 saw the Argentine pampas as a beast to be tamed. In an argument influenced by Montesquieu's ideas on the relationship between national character and nature in *De l'Espirit des Lois*, Sarmiento found in the Argentine land a primary source of the country's problems. He writes that "the evil that afflicts the Argentine Republic is its vast emptiness" (*Facundo* 11). It is a land where death and uncertainty reign supreme, where mysteri-

ous electrical forces excite the human imagination and the land itself
militates against European civilization. Like the Romantics he read,
Sarmiento is fascinated by the horrific power of electrical storms
when "a fearful and overwhelming power forces the soul back upon
itself, and makes it feel its nothingness in the midst of a raging
nature; and makes it sense the presence of God himself in the terrible magnificence of his works" (*Facundo* 22). But Sarmiento's is a
fascination that does not rejoice; in his view the mysterious force of
the pampas, untempered by forests or cities, is the force of barbarism. Rather than a lost mother to return to, nature must be over-
come if Argentina and her peoples are ever to be civilized.
Sarmiento repeatedly laments that even Buenos Aires, despite the
European façade carefully sculpted by the Rivadavians, had accepted the barbaric rule of Rosas because "the spirit of the
Pampa . . . breathed on her" (13). The caudillos, in Sarmiento's
mind, were the incarnation of the "Spirit of the Pampa" and Rosas a
barbarian birthed "from the deep womb of the Argentine earth" (10).
The cause of his generation was not, then, merely a fight against a
particular politician, but a monumental struggle that pitted the
forces of civilization against the powers of barbarism; Civilization or
Barbarism are the choices Sarmiento offers us, and to a degree those
terms became the rallying cry of the entire Generation.

Yet the obvious choice Sarmiento dictates of civilization over
barbarism masks a complex ambivalence much studied by literary
scholars like Noé Jitrik, Beatriz Sarlo, and Carlos Alonso. While
Sarmiento, the liberal progressive, wants to eradicate all vestiges of
"barbarism," Sarmiento, the romantic poet, finds the gaucho attractive, as indicated by his beautiful portrayals of gaucho types, customs, songs, and poetry (*Facundo* 21–34). He is similarly drawn to
the titanic personality of the caudillo, the primitive hero who defies
and transcends human law. Although undeniable on a literary
level, such ambivalence all but disappeared in Sarmiento's public
life, where he consistently sought to eradicate gaucho and Indian
life (by extermination if necessary), exclude dissenters, and force
survivors into his vision of civilization: a modern, Europeanized
Argentina.

Sarmiento's portrayal of the land as a source of barbarism also
identified and perhaps initiated a durable tradition in Argentine
letters: a tendency to attribute Argentina's problems to natural

causes rather than human error—a concept guaranteed to deflect
accusations of blame. That the country's failure derived from an
inherent organic weakness would continue to comfort disillusioned
intellectuals for generations to come. Sarmiento's negative determinism would find, for example, a strong echo in one of the most influential books of this century: Ezequiel Martínez Estrada's *Radiografía
de la pampa* published in 1933, which argues that Argentina, like a
sick person with an endemic illness, cannot avoid failure.

Alberdi had little patience for Sarmiento's polarities and even
less for his romantic obsession with the land as evil determiner of
the Argentine spirit. In clear refutation to Sarmiento's famous
duality of Civilization and Barbarism, Alberdi argues that the only
real division in Argentine society is between the "man of the
coast" or littoral man, and the "man of the interior" or meridional
man, a point that underlines his principal concern with relations
between Buenos Aires and the provinces (*Bases* 243). Alberdi also
disputes Sarmiento's notion of the land as a source of barbarism.
"The patria," he writes, "is not soil. We have had soil for three
centuries but a patria only since 1810." Fixing the beginning of
Argentina with a precise date suggests that Alberdi, more perhaps
than any of his contemporaries, believed nation-building to be the
result of human will rather than historical and material circumstances, although, as will be seen further on, in other contexts he
subscribed to a quasihistoricist, evolutionary view of history in
which superior cultures, which were not necessarily tied to a
particular land, inevitably replaced inferior ones. In Alberdi's
view it is through ideas (the right words), work, effort, and institutions that modern nations are built and not through the elusive
purposes of nature (*Bases* 248). Even Echeverría, romantic poet
por excelencia, chides Sarmiento for his rigidity and wishes he
had spent more time formulating a "policy for the future" instead
of a questionable explanation of the past (*Ojeada* 122). They nonetheless agreed with Sarmiento's prescriptions for subjugating the
land—through railroads, better river transportation, new sea-
ports, private ownership of land, and foreign investment.

This program for taming the land repeated commonplaces of
European economic liberalism, much as Mariano Moreno had done
in his famous *Representación de los hacendados* of three decades
earlier. Sarmiento, however, takes notions of laissez-faire capital-

ism beyond a desire for prosperity. Private property, in his view, was also a necessary step toward eradicating the nomadic life of the gauchos and Indians. Echoing his deterministic notion that environment decides lifestyle, Sarmiento maintains that Argentina's gauchos and Indians resemble Middle-Eastern Bedouins because land distribution in both areas permitted people to live in similar ways. Indeed, although in 1845, when he wrote *Facundo,* he had never seen either the pampas or the Middle East, he insists that life in the Argentine plains showed a "certain Asiatic cast that never ceases to be well pronounced" (*Facundo* 14). He later developed this idea at great length after finally visiting North Africa and observing Bedouin cultures firsthand; he further decided that France, in "civilizing" the Bedouins, faced problems similar to those of Argentina in "civilizing" the gauchos and Indians (*Viajes por Europa, Africa y Estados Unidos* 2:78–103). In sum, for Sarmiento and his generation, capitalist development would not only bring prosperity to the pampas; it would also end the "barbarism" of the pampa's natural inhabitants.

In addition to agreeing that subjugating the land was essential to progress, the Men of '37 were in almost total accord about the alleged deficiencies of Spain, their cultural parent. The Oedipal drama in which Spain's Argentine children seek to purge Spanish influence assumes many faces. Anti-Spanish sentiment understandably characterized much of the Argentine independence movement. Yet even after winning political freedom from Spain, Argentine liberals continued deprecating Spain. Tomás de Iriarte, for example, the prolific diary-keeper who observed nearly a half-century of Argentine history, wrote not long after 1820 that the collapse of the 1816 confederation was caused by the "plebianism" of "a people educated by Spain" (*Memorias* 3:19). Anti-Spanish sentiment became even more virulent among the Men of '37, symbolized by a striking tendency, still common in modern Argentina, to exclude Spain whenever the term *Europe* is invoked. *Europe* in Argentina came to mean northern Europe, the source of modern (non-Spanish) culture.

The impulse behind this peculiar usage is well seen in the Men of '37. Echeverría, for example, argues that Spain left Argentina a tradition "that denies analysis and choice; in a word, the suicide of reason" (*Dogma* 191). He later deplores "the rancid Spanish enlightenment, which with its books and its concerns sowed such bad seed in American soil" (*Ojeada* 121). Similarly, Sarmiento laments that Argentina had not been colonized by a more "civilized" country that would have left Argentina a better legacy than "the Inquisition and Spanish absolutism." Spain for Sarmiento is the "backward daughter of Europe," a country cursed with paradox where democratic impulses are crushed by popular despots and enlightened religion must regularly submit to Counter-Reformation fanaticism. In Sarmiento's view, from Spain comes "the Spanish American peoples' lack of ability in political and industrial matters which keeps them in constant turmoil, like a ship churning in the ocean, with no port or rest in sight" (*Facundo* 2).

Sarmiento's accusations against Spain were reinforced in 1847, when he first visted the Iberian Peninsula, two years after finishing *Facundo*. With an arrogance that still puts off modern readers, Sarmiento announces that he visited Spain with the "holy purpose of placing Spain on trial" in order to "justify an accusation" he, Sarmiento, "as a recognized prosecutor" had already made "before the tribunal of American opinion" (*Viajes* 2:8). Since Spanish culture in 1847 was at the low point of its history, Sarmiento quickly found plenty to support the accusations already recorded in *Facundo*. In his view, whatever had been great and noble in Spain was now dead. In the intellectual realm, only translations offered the discerning reader anything substantial since Spanish writers merely clothed their vacuity in "antiquated phrases and worn, moth-eaten words." Similarly, her historians regularly gave themselves over to "the national bad taste" of violating historical fact in order "to pretend that theirs is an important country" (2:45–46). And on a popular level, Sarmiento finds Spaniards incredibly ignorant of the world beyond their borders: "For the Spaniard, there are in the world only Frenchmen and Englishmen. He may believe in the existence of Russians; Germans, on the other hand, are more problematic. And of course Swedes and Danes are myths, fables, inventions of writers" (2:44).

In equally vivid terms, Sarmiento derides Spanish government. General Narváez, caretaker ruler for the degenerate Isabel II, whose adulteries titillated all of Europe, is seen as representative of caudillismo, just like the hated Rosas. What had been the glory of Spain, Sarmiento finds symbolized in El Escorial, the palace, museum, and monastery built by Phillip II and allegedly Spain's great-

est architectural triumph. El Escorial is in Sarmiento's view "a still
fresh cadaver, which stinks and inspires disgust," symbolic of a
country that, with the death of Phillip II in 1598, also began to die,
slowly sinking into the sterility of militarism and monasticism
(2:49). Yet, as in *Facundo*, although Sarmiento is repelled by Spanish government, culture, and intellectual life, he finds an ambivalent pleasure in her quaint folk traditions and in the violent spectacle of the bull fight that he considers at once perversely attractive
as well as symbolic of "a corrupting government" that entertains the
abject masses while giving vent to their worst instincts (2:25–37).
In short, Sarmiento's trip to Spain merely confirmed what he already believed: Spain was the cradle of barbarism, a parent to be
cast off and replaced. Sarmiento's argument that Argentina's Spanish heritage is a source of barbarism echoes his criticism of the land;
both arguments appeal to preexisting conditions to explain failure.
This implicit determinism is also a built-in excuse for overlooking
human error, since failure can always be blamed on the barbarism
of the land and the inadequacy of Argentina's Spanish past.

Although Alberdi, like Sarmiento and Echeverría, also condemns Spain's "stultifying piety" and lack of industrial capacity
(*Bases* 236), he adds to the debate a different perspective on
Spain's errors. As has been noted, Alberdi's faith in the positive
results of informed human action distanced him from the naive
historicist belief that human progress emerges inevitably from all
historical movement; nonetheless, central to his thinking is the
notion that Spanish America is the result of an organic expansion
in which superior civilizations inevitably replace weaker ones.
Spain participated in this natural historical process by conquering
the "primitive" Indian civilizations and implanting European culture in Spanish America. Alberdi goes on to say, however, that
Spain ceased being nature's tool (and in a sense ceased being part
of Europe) when she tried to close Spanish America to the superior ways of France and England, thus violating the law of cultural
expansion (*Bases* 155–158.)[1] This anti-Spanish bias among Argen-

1. Alberdi's notion of cultural distension echoes ideas widely discussed in
Europe at the time. In Alberdi's "Lectura en el Salón," (*OC* 1:103), he mentions
that the literary salon read Lerminier's "Introduction a la science de l'histoire,"
published in the widely disseminated *Revue des deux mondes* 3 (1833): 308. By
1852, when *Bases* was published, Alberdi could also have been familiar with the

tine intellectuals was never seriously challenged until the twentieth century when, as Marysa Navarro Gerassi has shown, Argentine writers like Ricardo Rojas, Enrique Larreta, Manuel Gálvez,
and Carlos Ibarguren, in what would become known as the
hispanidad movement, would seek to vindicate Argentina's Spanish heritage (107–128).

Ironically, much of the anti-Spanish current among nineteenth-
century Argentine intellectuals was inspired by the Spanish writer
Mariano José de Larra (1809–1837), who wrote devastating cri-
tiques on Spanish culture under the pseudonym Fígaro. Alberdi so
admired Larra that he signed some of his own articles in *La Moda*
with the diminuitive "Figarillo," explaining that "I call myself
Figarillo . . . because I am the son of Fígaro, . . . [I am] his product, and his imitation to such a degree that if there had been no
Fígaro, there would be no Figarillo. [I am] the posthumous work of
Larra" (*La Moda* 16 Dec. 1837, 1). Seconding Alberdi's enthusiasm, Sarmiento called Larra "the Cervantes of the regenerated
Spain" (*El mercurio* 19 Feb. 1842).

In addition to berating their Spanish heritage, the Men of '37
were in almost universal agreement regarding the inadequacy of
Argentina's ethnic groups, or "races" as they were called. The term
race during most of the nineteenth century, as Nancy Stepan points
out in her book *The Idea of Race in Science,* referred to any perceived ethnic group, from Europeans to Spaniards to Indians to
mixed-blood gauchos (170–189). Following the received racial theories of his time, Sarmiento writes:

A homogenous whole has resulted from the fusion of the [Spanish, African, and Indian] races. It is typified by love of idleness and incapacity for
industry, except when education and the demands of a social position
succeed in spurring it out of its customary crawl. To a great extent, this
unfortunate outcome results from the incorporation of the native tribes
through the process of colonization. The American aborigines live in idleness, and show themselves incapable, even under compulsion, of hard

"dinamique social" arguments of Auguste Comte, whose *Sistéme de philosophie
positive* was published in Paris between 1830 and 1842. Given his semihistoricist
orientation, it is also possible that he was conversant with the basic premises of
Herbert Spencer's *Social Statics* (London, 1851), one of the first attempts to apply
Lamarckian concepts of biological evolution to the development of societies, a
kind of social Darwinism before Darwin.

and prolonged labor. From this came the idea of introducing Negroes into America, which has produced such fatal results. But the Spanish race has not shown itself more energetic than the aborigines, when it has been left to its own instincts in the wilds of America. (*Facundo* 15)

Sarmiento also makes explicit the supposed connection between race and political failure by deriding the mixed-blood supporters of Rosas as *lomos negros* or "black backs" (*Facundo* 130) and even suggests that Rosas's political success was attributable largely to a "zealous spy network" of black servants from "a savage race" placed "in the breast of every Buenos Aires family" (141).

A later member of the Generation, José Mármol in his landmark anti-Rosas novel *Amalia* of 1851 also speaks of the fear Unitarians had of their own servants, blacks and mulattos in the main, who generally supported Rosas. In one particularly telling episode, Eduardo advises Amalia to fire all her servants from Buenos Aires since "[Under Rosas] the doors have been opened to them to threaten families and fortune under the miserable authority of the lowborn and the *mazorca* [Rosas's secret police]" (18). In a similar episode, a maid betrays to the *mazorca* her employer who is trying to escape to Uruguay (48).

Sarmiento returned to this racialist explanation of Argentina's failure in his last major work, *Conflictos y armonías de las razas en América*, a rambling treatise that according to some consists of notes intended to be a book Sarmiento never finished. Finished in 1883 when Sarmiento was seventy-two years old, *Conflictos* is a sad book that Sarmiento himself called "a *Facundo* grown old" (cited in Bunkley, *The Life of Sarmiento* 503). In *Conflictos*, Sarmiento argues that despite an enlightened constitution, a democracy of sorts, prosperity, modern transportation, schools, academies, universities, and all the trappings of progress, Argentine society in 1883, although better-dressed and more genteel than under Rosas, was still plagued by corruption, personalism, and a general disregard for institutional rule. He explains this failure as the result of racial inadequacy. An ambitious attempt to rewrite much of world history from a racialist perspective, *Conflictos* provides detailed analyses of English success and Spanish failure in colonization. In each case Sarmiento suggests that the failure of democracy in Spanish America can be explained only by taking into account the inadequacy of

Latin peoples, particularly when combined with the "barbaric" Indians, to govern themselves. According to Sarmiento, every Latin American leader he considers "barbaric"—Rosas, Paraguay's Dr. Francia, and Uruguay's Artigas, for example—resulted from the fatal mix of Latin and Indian blood (*OC* 37:284–313). In one of his last articles, "El constitucionalismo en la América del Sur," published posthumously and perhaps intended as the beginning of a second volume of *Conflictos*, Sarmiento writes that of all Christian peoples only "the Latin races in America have been unable for more than seventy years to organize a lasting, effective government" (*OC* 38:273). Argentina, he concludes, is better off than other Spanish American countries because it has more white people. In contrast, a country like Ecuador "has a million inhabitants, of whom only 100,000 are white. Result: three military strongmen make up nearly all of her history" (38:282–283).

All the Men of '37 agreed essentially with Sarmiento regarding race. Mármol, with uncharacteristic succinctness, defines Rosas's supporters as "a people ignorant by education, vengeful by race, and impulsive by climate" (*Amalia* 44). Even Alberdi, who usually avoids the racialist caricatures found in Sarmiento, regrets Argentina's mixed-race origins. For Alberdi there is no America worthy of the word other than the Europeanized one:

The South American republics are the product and living testimony of Europe's presence in America. . . . All that is civilization on our soil is European. America itself is a European discovery. . . . Those of us who call ourselves American are nothing more than Europeans born in America; our skull, blood, color—everything is from [Europe]. . . . Who among us would not prefer a thousand times over to see his daughter marry an English shoeman rather than an Araucanian prince? In America everything that is not European is barbaric: there is no division other than this one: Indian which is synonymous with savage, and European which means those of us born in America, who speak Spanish and believe in Jesus Christ. (*Bases* 239–241)

Nor does Alberdi accept the notion that substantial changes can be wrought among the mixed-blooded poor through education. "Take one of our ragamuffins, or gauchos, or half-breeds—the essential ingredients of our popular masses—through all the transformations of the best educational system, and in a hundred years you will not

make of him an English laborer" (252). Also in *Bases,* Alberdi argues
that "it is utopistic to think that we can establish a representative
republic . . . without profoundly altering and modifying the dough
or paste of which our Hispanic-American people is formed" (405). As
shown in later chapters, Alberdi subsequently modified his opinions
of Argentina's mixed races considerably; but as indicators of a genera-
tional view, his words are self-explanatory. It was Echeverría, however, who wrote the Generation's most effective statement on
race—not in an essay but in one of the first and best short stories in
Spanish American literature, "El matadero" (The slaughterhouse),
written probably in 1838.

The plot of "El matadero" is simple enough. Owing to a shortage .
of beef, Rosas's followers are beginning to doubt their leader's
ability to provide for the nation. An announcement that several
steers will be slaughtered on a given day brings Buenos Aires'
lower classes en masse to the slaughterhouse. Echeverría describes
in stomach-turning detail how the cattle are killed and dismem-
bered by filthy, blood-drenched men; how people fight over different parts of the animals, including brains and entrails; and how the
accidental death of a child provokes no compassion from the meat-
hungry crowd. But the climax of the story involves a cultured youth
who happens by the slaughterhouse while failing to wear the man-
datory pro-Rosas insignia. Obviously a Unitarian and symbol of the
civilized Argentina Rosas suppressed, he is seized by the mob and
forced off his horse. Things quickly get out of hand as the mob
threatens to strip and beat the youth, who, rather than suffer such
indignation, dies of noble rage, as a "torrent of blood spouted,
bubbling from [his] mouth and nose" (Echeverría, "The Slaughterhouse," in *Borzoi Anthology* 1:222).

The obvious equations in "El matadero" of the slaughterhouse
as Rosas's Argentina and the butchers as Rosas's henchmen could
become tedious if the ideological problem involved were not so
unusual. Recognizing that Rosas remained in power by virtue of
broad support among Argentina's lower classes, Echeverría sets
out not merely to write another diatribe against Rosas, but to
discredit the masses themselves, who, in his view, are the real
reason behind Rosas's power. Echeverría accomplishes his goal of
defaming the masses by recording in horrifying detail their behavior and by repeatedly calling attention to their race. For example,

the offal collectors are "black and mulatto women . . . whose ugliness matched that of the harpies" (214). Later we read that "two black women were dragging along the entrails of an animal. A mulatto woman carrying a heap of entrails slipped in a pool of blood and fell lengthwise under her coveted booty. Farther on, huddled together in a long line, four hundred black women unwound heaps of intestines" (215). Such references to race occur throughout. Echeverría's intention to discredit the Rosistas is further realized by vivid portrayals of their barbaric behavior— fighting over a bull's testicles, using foul language, cowardly bullying an innocent Englishman, and finally brutally killing the Unitarian youth. Lest there remain doubt concerning his intention, he concludes his story with "Those were the days when the butchers of the slaughterhouse were apostles who propagated by dint of whip and poniard Rosas's Federation, and it was not difficult to imagine what sort of Federation issued from their heads and knives. . . . From the foregoing episode, it can be clearly seen that the headquarters of the Federation were located in the slaughterhouse" (222). Such are the words of a writer who in other contexts speaks piously of reconciling Federalists and Unitarians. Whatever admiration Echeverría's skill as a narrator may inspire, there can be little question concerning the antipopular intention behind his story. Since Rosas retained power through the support of the masses, criticizing him was not enough; the masses themselves had to be denigrated and debased. Few documents in Argentine history better reflect the odd mixture of fear and hostility upper-class Argentines felt toward their own lower classes than Echeverría's "The Slaughterhouse."[2]

2. Echeverría's story inspired a fascinating imitation in this century. During Perón's first presidency (1946–1955), Jorge Luis Borges and Adolfo Bioy Casares, under the pseudonym of Bustos Domeq, wrote a story titled "Fiesta del monstruo" or "Monsterfest." The central character is a worker describing his participation in a pro-Perón demonstration in the Plaza de Mayo. Using the most vicious terms imaginable, Borges and Bioy describe the Peronists as deformed, vulgar, stupid, ugly, flat-footed, flat-nosed, overweight—in sum, genetic throwbacks unworthy of respect much less voting rights. As the mob lunges toward the Plaza de Mayo, they find a Jew whom they brutally murder. The story ends in the Plaza as Perón, the smiling monster, begins his harangue. Echeverría, Borges, and Bioy Casares, despite the century separating them, faced a similar dilemma: how to support democracy in theory while discrediting the majority's enthrallment to a Rosas or Perón. Their solution is to portray Argentina's lower classes in the most brutal,

But why the focus on race? Of all possible explanations of failure or prescriptions for success, why did race occupy such a prominent place in the thinking of the Men of '37? The easiest explanation would hold that the Argentines were merely repeating prejudices common in Europe, where the notion of inherent inferiority of darker peoples had been popular for nearly two centuries. While the influence of European racism on Argentine thinkers is undeniable, the rise of racial prejudice in Europe points to an additional explanation. The denigration of black Africans in European thought, according to Nancy Stepan, was relatively uncommon prior to the slave trade. With the institutionalization of slavery, however, the alleged inferiority of black Africans gained widespread credence precisely because racism provided an ideology for the subjugation of blacks (*Race in Science* xxi–xxiii). In short, racism grew popular in order to justify the exploitation of a particular group. In the case of Argentina, these arguments suggest that at some level the Generation of '37 was building a prior ideological framework for a political system that would exclude, persecute, dispossess, and often kill the "racially inferior" gauchos, Indians, and mixed-bloods—just as the Morenistas had a generation earlier. And in fact, this is exactly what happened. The process of slowly wresting land from the Indians that had begun in colonial times increased sharply in mid-nineteenth-century Argentina, particularly after liberal Argentines like Sarmiento came to power in the 1860s. In the Argentine equivalent of the United States' "Winning of the West," the liberal governments embarked on a land-grab campaign, known in Argentina as "The Conquest of the Desert," which displaced or killed thousands of Indians and gauchos, thereby making their homelands available to white settlers and land speculators. Later, through a cleverly exclusive electoral system, those same groups were effectively kept out of the political process. Using the racial stereotyping of the Generation of '37, the ideological justification for such actions was readily available.

The Men of '37, then, attributed their country's ills to three

---

denigrating, and ultimately dismissive fashion possible. Thus Echeverría, Bioy Casares, and Borges illustrate the paradox of Argentine liberalism in both the previous and present centuries: while theoretically prodemocracy, they are profoundly antipopular and in no sense egalitarian.

great causes: the land, the Spanish tradition, and race. But in addition to explaining failure, the Men of '37 had to prescribe remedies for their troubled land. The next chapter studies how they planned to make their dreams for Argentina a reality.

Chapter Six

The Generation of 1837,
Part Two

As seen in the previous chapter, the Men of '37 imaginatively and vigorously diagnosed their country's problems. But identifying the illness was only half their mission; also necessary was a prescription for improvement and health, a new formulation of governing principles and guiding fictions to put Argentina on the road to progress. They argued that progress was not simply the result of Hegelian historical movement, that progress had to be won by conscious struggle against the forces of superstition, reactionary Hispanic cultural patterns, race, and inherited privilege. None of them believed their struggle would be won in their generation; rather, they sought to provide an ideological framework, "to found beliefs" as Halperín Donghi puts it, which would enable future governments to build toward prosperity and democracy under constitutional rule (*El pensamiento de Echeverría* 26).

What, then, was the solution for a population "cursed" by Spanish tradition and racial inadequacy? In a word, immigration. Rivadavia had already advocated immigration as a solution for Argentina's problems, and Alberdi mentioned it in his *Fragmento preliminar al estudio del derecho* of 1835 (*OC* 1:123). But no one supported immigration more vigorously than did Sarmiento in the final pages of *Facundo*, where he declares that "the principal ingredient towards order and ethics in the Argentine Republic is immigration from Europe" (159). Some eighteen months after finishing

Facundo, Sarmiento visited Germany, where his experiences confirmed the desirability of bringing northern Europeans to Argentina. Borrowing from German romantics, he claims that "the German race" is historically migrant, that it began in India, moved to northern Europe in Roman times, and was in the nineteenth century moving yet again to the United States of America, "driven by racial instinct more than by necessity" (*Viajes* 2:232). He argues for an official policy to attract Germans to South American shores, proposing that South American governments subsidize travel, settlement, tools, seed, and land acquisition for newcomers. He further recommends that information and emigration offices be established in Germany to make such measures known to people who otherwise would go to North America (2:231–236). A year later, during his first visit to the United States, Sarmiento was amazed that some North Americans viewed immigrants as "an element of barbarism [because] they come from Europe's most needy classes, are usually ignorant, and are never schooled in the republican ways of their [new] land" (*Viajes* 3:83). He nonetheless marvels at the process through which immigrants to the United States are assimilated, primarily through religion and public education, into a culture that despite the influx of immigrants, remained in his view basically Puritan.

Alberdi also supported European immigration as a sure solution to Argentina's ills. In *Bases* he writes:

Each European who comes to our shores brings more civilization in his habits, which will later be passed on to our inhabitants, than many books of philosophy. We understand poorly what can't be seen and touched. A hard-working man is the most edifying catechism.

Do we want to sow and cultivate in America English liberty, French culture, and the diligence of men from Europe and the United States? Let us bring living pieces of these qualities . . . and let us plant them here. (250)

From this thinking derives Alberdi's most celebrated aphorism: *gobernar es poblar;* "to govern is to populate." It is not, he tells us, through education or "many books of philosophy" that Argentina will be changed, but by bringing "living pieces" of northern European culture to be planted in the Argentine soil and thereby change the country's ethnic makeup. But in order for those living pieces to take root, Alberdi insists that they be planted in a nourishing environment—meaning that Argentina must change its laws on land acquisition, civil rights, and religion.

Of these, religion was potentially the most inflammatory. Remembering the problems Rivadavia had with the Catholic hierarchy, the Men of '37 tried to finesse the religious question by strongly affirming their faith in God while promoting freedom of religion and secular education as "enlightened" religion. In the "Symbolic Words" of the *Asociación de Mayo*, Echeverría, with frequent references to Christian scripture, defends at length "natural religion" (humanity's primordial impulse to believe in a higher power) and "positive religion" (religion supported by historical fact). He further argues that "the best of all positive religions is Christianity, because it is nothing other than the revelation of humanity's moral instincts. The Gospel is God's law because it is the moral law of conscience and reason" (*Dogma* 175). He scolds pro-Rosas priests for allowing themselves to become "docile and most useful instruments of tyranny and backwardness," and he hopes that in the future the clergy "will understand its mission, and stop meddling in politics" (*Ojeada* 99–100).

Religious education was (and remains) a particularly thorny problem. Alberdi, nonetheless, minces no words about the role of the clergy in education: "Let priests educate themselves, but do not put them in charge of training our lawyers and statesmen, businessmen, shippers and generals. . . . [The clergy] could never give our youth the business and industrial instincts that should distinguish the South American man" nor the sense of "entrepreneurship that will make of our youth Spanish American Yankees." Moreover, Alberdi felt not only that the clergy should be kept out of the classroom but also that humanistic education, which in his view was a holdover from Catholic scholasticism, should be replaced with practical studies in physics and engineering, and that "English as the language of liberty and order" should replace Latin. "How else," he asks, "can we receive the example and civilizing influence of the Anglo-Saxon race without a generalized competence in its language?" (*Bases* 234–235). Without these reforms he predicts that Argentine schools and universities will continue to be "nothing more than factories of charlatanism, idleness, demagoguery, and diplomaed pretension (*pretensión titulada*)" (233).

Yet none of the Men of '37 wanted to rid Argentina of religion. Echeverría chides Argentine intellectuals, the Rivadavians in particular, for their indifference, if not hostility, toward religion. "In our proud self-sufficience, we discarded religion, the most powerful mechanism available for moralizing and civilizing our masses. . . . If you take religion away from our people, what do you leave in its place? . . . What moral authority will morality have in [the people's eyes] without the divine seal of religious sanction?" (*Ojeada* 97). More to the point, Alberdi writes:

Respect the altar of every belief. Spanish America, limited to Catholicism to the exclusion of any other religion, resembles a solitary and silent convent of nuns. . . . To exclude different religions in South America is to exclude the English, the Germans, the Swiss, the North Americans, which is to say the very people this continent most needs. To bring them without their religion is to bring them without the agent that makes them what they are. (*Bases* 258–259)

Later, in an unconvincing nod to Rome, he declares that opposing freedom of worship is an "insult to that noble church so capable of associating itself with all human progress" (259).

In this elaborate attempt to grant religious freedom to Protestant immigrants without offending Rome, Alberdi and Echeverría reveal their real agenda: to use religion as a tool toward building their vision of Argentina. Nowhere do they indicate real belief. As Halperín Donghi says of Echeverría's relationship to Christianity, "The entire path of Echeverría's thinking remains punctuated by ideological residuals, signs that have been emptied of all meaning. . . . Religious sentiment has no place whatsoever in his deepest concerns" (*El pensamiento de Echeverría* 85–86). What the Men of '37 wanted was a docile church that would give up claims to exclusive authority and truth in order to assume a subservient role in shaping positivist Argentina. That the Generation of '37 believed the church would peacefully accept such a role suggests considerable naiveté, supported by the very arrogance toward religion that they denounced in the Unitarians. Rather than include the Church in a productive dialogue, they prefer dictating religious norms in the name of Echeverría's "enlightened gospel" and Alberdi's call to noble sentiment. The Argentine hierarchy resisted such attempts on their prerogatives, particularly with regard to religious education. The Church lost many skirmishes with the reformers of '37 and their intellectual offspring, but would remain a potent force in Argentine society, invariably on the side of tradition. Even today, Argentine Church leaders are arguably the most conservative, if not reactionary, in Latin America.

The Men of '37 realized that their immigration plans, economic schemes, and prescriptions of religious liberty smacked of utopianism and failed to address the question of what to do in the meantime. Given the Generation's attitudes toward their own people, what kind of government could fill the gap until, in Echeverría's words, "the people become a people" (*Ojeada* 106)?

Universal suffrage and numerically representative government were out of the question. Remembering Rosas's popularity and the interminable electoral feuds between Buenos Aires and the Provinces, Echeverría writes, "Universal suffrage bequeathed everything it could: the suicide of the people by its own hand, and the legitimization of Despotism" (*Ojeada* 104). Rather than allow all people immediate access to government, he recommends they be "taken through a series of gradual progressive steps" until they reach "the perfection of institutional democracy" (106). To accomplish this goal, real power must first be left in the hands of a natural elite, "the natural hierarchy of intelligence, virtue, capacity and proven merit" (*Dogma* 173). Echeverría further argues that:

The sovereignty of the people can only reside in the *reason of the people*, and only the most sensible and rational portion of the social community is called to the exercise of reason. The ignorant portion remains under the tutelage and guardianship of laws formulated according to the uniform consensus of the rational people. Democracy, then, is not the absolute despotism of the masses, nor of the majority; it is the rule of reason. (*Dogma* 201)

In a notable departure from the almost populist sentiment expressed in his *Fragmento preliminar*, Alberdi is no less emphatic when he calls universal suffrage universal ignorance. "Suffrage of the multitude where the multitude is incapable of it . . . can produce no other practical result than placing the country's government in the hands of . . . those who are best at getting votes through coercion or trickery. . . . Any country governed by the ignorant multitude . . . unfailingly has at its head tricksters and masters of intrigue" ("América," *EP* 7:344, 375).

It thus becomes apparent that democracy for the Generation of 37, as for the Morenistas before them, was defined as a government for the people but not by the people. That the new government would not include the "people" in any universal sense was made explicit by Sarmiento: "When we say people, we understand noteworthy, active, intelligent people; a governing class. We are decent people, belonging to a patrician class. For that reason, in our legislature one should not see gauchos, negros, nor poor people. We are decent people; that is to say, patriotic people" (cited in Paoli, *Sarmiento* 175). Like the Morenistas, the Rivadavians, and Beruti and his *gente decente*, the Men of '37 sought an exclusivist democracy. Far from the radical democracy of Hidalgo and Artigas, their concern for the people bore an odd resemblance to the paternalistic, autocratic rule of Rosas.

The question of popular suffrage forced the Men of '37 to explain the government Argentina already had: that of the caudillo who, more than a symbol, was also a man of flesh and bone, supported perhaps by a majority although no formal elections were ever held. No one describes the caudillo phenomenon better than Sarmiento. The caudillo, he writes, is "the mirror which reflects in colossal proportions the beliefs, the necessities, the concerns and customs of a nation of a given moment in history" (*Facundo* 6). He is a predetermined enemy of progress, the natural man sprung from the depths of the savage American soil, and heir to the medieval Spanish tradition (18). His rise to power is "destined, inevitable, natural and logical" (4).

Sarmiento's most enduring explanation of the caudillo's power postulates a mystical bond between the masses and their leader in which the caudillo mysteriously reflects the unarticulated will of the masses (130)—an argument also used later to support populist strongmen as diverse as Mussolini, Hitler, Perón, and Castro.[1] It

1. For example, Raúl Scalabrini Ortiz, who later became a Peronist apologist, claims that only a caudillo in tune with the "feelings" or *pálpitos* of the people can govern Argentina, that "men who are only intelligent will always fail in public

has been suggested that Sarmiento's fascination with the caudillo merely reflects his century's interest in the hero figure, the titanic individual who forces his personal imprint on history, a well-known theme popularized by Hegel and later taken up by men as diverse as Beethoven, Stendhal, Wagner, and Arnold. Hegel's hero, however, is quite unlike Sarmiento's caudillo. In *The Philosophy of History*, Hegel insists that the great men of history stand out because their "own particular aims involve those large issues which are the will of the World-Spirit." Yet their personal greatness is more apparent than real since they "appear to draw the impulse of their life from themselves" but in fact are merely reflections of the World-Spirit (30). Although Sarmiento's interest in the caudillo figure occasionally belies a romantic fascination with Hegel's hero, he inverts Hegel's terms. In Sarmiento, the caudillo reflects not the World-Spirit, which is the force of history and progress, but the popular spirit, which is the force of barbarism. Rather than be allowed to follow its course, the caudillo's rule must be forcibly supplanted by the rule of reason. However much Sarmiento flirts with Romantic irrationalism, ultimately the vision he and his generation wish to impose on Argentina is rational and positivistic in which people are not necessarily pawns manipulated by unseen historical movements, but rational beings capable of making the world over according to their essentially positivistic vision.

In contrast to this rational view of the world, the caudillo is the voice of nonreason. He may reflect the unarticulated popular will, but all authority is centered in his person. In Sarmiento's opinion, he rules by decree, not persuasion. Since the slavish obedience of his underlings is sufficient to validate his authority, force to ensure such obedience becomes the only necessary form of government. Justice under the caudillo is administered "without formalities of discussion" since determining decisions by discussion, instead of by decree, places authority outside the person of the caudillo

---

service" (*Scalabrini Ortiz, El hombre que está solo y espera* 79–80). Similarly, Ernesto "Che" Guevara assures us in *El socialismo y el hombre en Cuba* that Fidel Castro has "earned the trust of [the people] through a faithful interpretation of [their] desires, their aspirations, and the sincere struggle to see promises fulfilled. . . . The exemplary human being has an invisible umbilical cord that links him to the society around him" (105–107). Sarmiento said it first, but with no sign of approval.

(*Facundo* 130). His government is the creation of his arrogant will. "The State is a *tabula rasa* on which he writes something new and original. . . . He will give birth . . . to his ideal republic with no awareness of timeworn traditions, concerns of the period, . . . individual rights and existing institutions. . . . Everything is new, the work of his genius" (131–132). By overlooking the evident irony of these words, it is easy to see how the romantic hero—the man greater than nature, the titanic figure who, like God, creates from nothing—influenced Sarmiento's description of the caudillo. Indeed, in ways Sarmiento emulated the caudillo he so hated. For example, Sarmiento condemns caudillismo as a government "without forms and without debate"; no better description could be found for much of Sarmiento's writing. Rather than using carefully constructed arguments based on verifiable evidence, Sarmiento often resorts to passionate declamation based on no evidence beyond his personal authority. In short, he writes by decree, a fact that prompted Alberdi to call him "a *caudillo* of the pen" (cited in Bunkley 356). In Sarmiento's best books—*Recuerdos de provincia, La vida de Dominguito*—such bombast is happily absent. Yet despite Sarmiento's romantic fascination in the caudillo titan, he spent his life condemning caudillismo. The caudillo for Sarmiento is the incarnation of evil who must be exorcised if Argentina is to become civilized.

Like Sarmiento, Alberdi recognized that the caudillo was somehow indigenous to Argentina. As we saw in his *Fragmento preliminar,* Alberdi was initially interested in using Rosas as a step toward a modern republic. Alberdi quickly lost hope in Rosas, but without abandoning his belief that the recurring figure of the caudillo was visible evidence of a peculiarly Argentine fact of life: the need for a strong executive. This need, he felt, explained the attempts of several distinguished Argentines of previous generations, including General José de San Martín, Argentina's chief leader in the Wars of Independence, to establish a monarchy as the most effective means of giving the country the stability necessary for survival. "Give to the executive all the power possible," Alberdi wrote. "But give it to him by means of a constitution. This kind of executive power constitutes the dominant need in constitutional law at this time in South America. The attempts at monarchy, [and] the tendency . . . towards dictatorship are the best proof of the need we speak of" (*Bases* 352). He approvingly quotes Simón Bolívar: "The new states of formerly Spanish America need kings under the name of presidents" (229). Primarily because of Alberdi's support of a strong executive, the Constitution of 1853, which in the main resembles that of the United States, contains an important distinction: the executive can "intervene" in almost any aspect of Argentine life that in his judgment threatens the integrity of the nation. This power to "intervene" has been used, often with self-serving arbitrariness, for everything from canceling the results of provincial elections to closing universities.[2]

Taming caudillismo through a strong executive was not the Generation's only prescription for their ailing nation. They also devoted considerable attention to defining an economic policy for the Argentina they dreamed of. Principal in this respect was Alberdi, who had read well the laissez-faire economists of his time. To prepare

2. Articles 5 and 6 of the Argentine constitution, although similar to Article IV, Section 4 of the Constitution of the United States, allow the Argentine executive broader powers in defining and handling domestic crises. The United States Constitution reads as follows: "The United States shall guarantee to every State in this Union a Republican form of government, and shall protect each of them against invasion, and, on application of the Legislature, or of the Executive (when the Legislature cannot be convened) against domestic violence." The corresponding articles in the Argentine Constitution of 1853, written largely under Alberdi's inspiration, state that "Each province in this Federation shall adopt its own constitution to be framed upon the republican representative plan, in agreement with the principles, declarations, and guarantees of the national constitution in order to assure the administration of justice, municipal government and free primary education. Provincial constitutions shall be reviewed by Congress before being adopted. Upon these conditions, the federal government shall guarantee to each province the enjoyment and exercise of its institutions." Article 6, which establishes the executive power of intervention, reads that "The federal government shall have the right to intervene, with or without the request of provincial legislatures or governors, in the territory of any province only when necessary to reestablish public order threatened by sedition, or to protect national security under threat of attack or foreign danger." Attempts to determine what constitutes "sedition" and "national security" have accomplished little toward restraining heavy-handed executives. In some cases, for example, provinces have been "intervened" merely because a political rival won an election. Further, since the executive is under no obligation to request approval for intervening from Congress, most interventions have been by executive decree. For a lawyerly discussion on the differences between the two constitutions, see Alexander W. Weddell, "A Comparison of the Executive and Judicial Powers under the Constitutions of Argentina and the United States."

for the immigratory wave that he hopes to attract he writes that "the best ways to bring Europe to . . . our continent on a large enough scale [and] to accomplish significant change in few years are the railroads, free river travel and commercial freedom. Europe comes to these distant regions on wings of commerce and industry, searching for the richness of our continent. Wealth, like population and culture, is impossible where the means of communciation are cumbersome, inadequate or costly" (*Bases* 261). Yet, since Argentina was an undeveloped country, rich in natural resources but poor in capital and technology, identifying necessary projects was not enough; fundamental questions concerning investment money and know-how also had to be answered.

The solution most often suggested to remedy Argentina's capital and technological shortfall was, not surprisingly, Europe. Just as European immigrants would supposedly solve Argentina's demographic problems, European investment and expertise were viewed as the best way to build the country's infrastructure. Using arguments strongly reminiscent of Moreno's *Representación de los hacendados,* Alberdi recommends abolishing all protective tariffs and opening the country wide to foreign investment, loans, and business parternships (*Bases* 181, 425). When faced with the objection that Washington had advised in his Farewell Address that American nations should avoid foreign entanglements, he answers "Everything has changed in this period. Copying a system which was good at a time and for a country unlike ours will only lead us to ignorance and poverty" (181). He further insists that "Friendly commercial agreements are the honorable way to place South American civilization under the protectorate of world civilization." And to anyone fearing that a foreign power might invest only for its own and not Argentina's good, Alberdi answers "Deal with all nations . . . give all of them the same guarantees so some will check the aspirations of others" (257). He later recommends, just as Rivadavia did before him, that railroads and other projects necessary for progress be paid for with foreign loans. "It is childish to think our own income is sufficient for such expenses. Invert the usual order of things; start with expenses and then you will have income. . . . In the meantime, protect all private businesses for the construction of the railroads. Smother them with advantages, privileges and every imaginable favor. . . . Is our capital insufficient for [building railroads]? Then let

foreign capital do it" (264–256).[3] Similar advice is given regarding
the development of river navigation and ports. With foreign capital
and foreign immigrants, everything is possible. "Open your doors
wide," Alberdi wrote, "to the majestic entrance of the world" (*Bases*
272).

We have seen in some detail how the Men of '37 viewed their
country's problems mostly in terms of land, race, and tradition.
Further, we have discussed how their solutions generally involved
some sort of appeal to Europe and the United States, through
imitation, immigration, investment, or imported technology. But
what overriding mission did they sense was theirs? What was Argentina's destiny among the nations of the world?

In an unfortunate sense, it would appear that their mission was
less one of creation than of re-creation. Their goal was to re-create
European civilization in America and to a lesser degree repeat the
success of the United States. This was to be accomplished by literally
bringing to Argentina "living pieces" of those societies in the form of
immigrants and by imitating their institutions. Although Sarmiento,
Echeverría, and Alberdi chided the Unitarians for their slavish imita-

3. Alberdi's enthusiasm for foreign capital and foreign involvement, like
Rivadavia's, would harvest bitter fruit. For reasons that have never been clear,
Argentina, despite enviable prosperity and immense personal fortunes, has always
been capital-dependent and thereby beholding to loaner nations in ways that
seriously compromise the country's ability to run its own affairs. The railroads
were in fact built by British capital and remained in British hands until Perón
nationalized them in 1948, at considerable and unnecessary expense. The British-
owned railroads, although modern and efficient for their time, were, however, a
mixed blessing. In addition to overcharging and price-fixing, abuses like those that
made the Robber Barons infamous in the United States, the British owners built
the railroads primarily to bring goods from the interior to exporters (also British-
controlled) in Buenos Aires rather than to develop internal markets in Argentina.
In this fashion, the rail system, in unregulated British hands, did more to ensure
Buenos Aires' dominance over the economy than any porteño chauvinist could
have hoped. Moreover, through astute hiring practices and an occasional well-
placed bribe, the British owners and their Argentine partners effectively checked
all attempts to reform the system. The question of economic dependence brought
through foreign loans and investment smoldered for decades, becoming a hot
issue in the 1930s with the publication of Rodolfo Irazusta and Julio Irazusta's *La
Argentina y el imperialismo británico: Los eslabones de una cadena 1806–1833*
and Raúl Scalabrini Ortiz's *Historia de los ferrocarriles argentinos.* Although
initially associated with nationalist politics, both books are now staples of the antiimperialist left and right.

tion of Europe, in large measure, they fell into the same trap. Their admiration of European ways was just too great for it to be otherwise. Alberdi at one point, for example, affirms with all apparent earnestness that "the Englishman is the most perfect of all men" and that the United States is "the model of the universe" (*Bases* 271–272). Echeverría proclaims that "Europe has been for centuries the center of civilization and human progress" (*Dogma* 169). And in *Facundo,* Sarmiento justifies his opinions and observations through a continual appeal to an authority called Europe—a place that at that time he knew only through books. Like José Arcadio Buendía in García Márquez's *One Hundred Years of Solitude,* the Men of '37 apparently believed that civilization and culture had to be imported from the North since the autochthonous people and traditions—Spanish, Indian, and African—were enemies of "progress." In a sense, then, the Generation of '37 merely reformulated what had been the overriding goal of their Spanish ancestors who conquered and settled Argentina in the first place: to extend Europe. That Europe to the Men of '37 was positivist France, Germany, and England rather than Counter-Reformation Spain is a significant difference; but the basic impulse to impose a particular vision of Europe on the American wilderness typifies the Spanish conquest as well as the Generation of '37.

Nationalist thinkers in this century, men like Arturo Jauretche, have suggested that the goal of re-creating Europe was unduly modest, that it undercut the creative energy Argentina needed to establish a vigorous, sovereign nation (Jaureteche, *El medio pelo* 81–101). In fairness to the Men of '37, it must be pointed out that, in theory at least, they disavowed the slavish imitation of Europe and the United States, of which they are accused by twentieth-century nationalists, both in themselves and in their Unitarian forebears. For example, Echeverría, in his poem "El regreso," composed in 1830 shortly after his return to Argentina from Europe, writes

> Confused by your vast face,
>   Degraded Europe, I have seen
>   Nothing but luxury and weakness
>   And little that elevates the soul;
>   Roses cover
>   The wealth and pleasure
>   While the oppressive bonds
>   Of vile iron oppress your progeny.

He later praises the Argentine insurgents of 1810 who "With rare courage / Defeated fanaticism and oppression" thus freeing an entire hemisphere from a "long and degrading captivity" (*OC* 736–737).

Sarmiento showed similar ambivalence toward Europe and the United States during his first trip beyond the borders of Argentina and Chile. France was his biggest disappointment. On arriving in Le Havre in 1846, a year after finishing *Facundo*, he was shocked at the money-grubbing behavior of the French poor: "Ah, Europe! Sad mixture of greatness and poverty, of knowledge and stupidity, sublime and filthy receptacle of everything that elevates and degrades mankind, kings and lackeys, monuments and flophouses, opulence and savagery" (*Viajes* 1:146). Horrified at the inefficiency and petty corruption of the French bureaucrats, he at one point referred to them as "two-legged beasts" (1:176). Particularly galling were the ignorance and disinterest French policy-makers showed toward Latin America (1:173–175). An afternoon in the French Chamber of Deputies convinced him that the government was little more than a "mob of accomplices" and prompted him to write a stormy, now amusing, list of recommendations by which France could redeem itself (1:180–188). Although he never ceased admiring France as the cultural capital of the world, he left the country convinced that Argentina should seek its models elsewhere. Italy, like France, captivated him with its beauty and its sense of past, but again he found little in either Italians or contemporary Italy that could contribute to building the New Argentina.

Switzerland and Germany were a different story. He writes, "I was sad and disillusioned before entering Switzerland by the misery and backwardness of most nations. In Spain I had seen in both Castilles and La Mancha, a ferocious people, ragged and hardened in ignorance and laziness; the Arabs in Africa were fanatical to the point of self-destruction, and the Italians in Naples showed me the lowest degree below zero to which human dignity can descend. Of what worth are the monuments of Italy if after contemplating them one's eyes fall on a beggarly people with outstretched hands! . . . Switzerland, on the other hand, has renewed my love and respect for people; I bless in this country the republic that knows so well what enobles mankind" (2:220–221). In Germany, he found even more to praise, beginning with the Prussian public education system that had in his view reached "the beautiful ideal to which other peoples merely aspire" (2:227). Later, in marked contrast to his suspicion of the popular vote in Argentina, he declares that "Prussia, thanks to her intelligent system of education, is more prepared than even France for political life; universal suffrage would not be an exaggeration where the use of reason has been cultivated in all social classes" (2:229).

The last leg of Sarmiento's voyage brought him to the United States, where he visited New York, Boston, and Washington and traveled through the upper Midwest and down the Ohio and Mississippi rivers. Sarmiento records that he left the United States "sad, thoughtful, pleased and humbled; half of my illusions broken or tattered while others struggle with my powers of reason to decorate again that imaginary panorama where we always keep ideas we have not seen, just as we give appearance and voice to a friend we know only through letters" (*Viajes* 3:7). Yet despite these initial disclaimers, Sarmiento's travel journal indicates that his impressions of American resources, river and rail transportation, government, education, technology, industry, people, and immigration policies were overwhelmingly favorable, that the country impressed him as "the highest point of civilization thus far attained by the most noble part of the human species" (3:9). He even endorsed the United States' expansionist war against Mexico, arguing that once Canada and Mexico are under the Stars and Stripes, "the union of free men will begin at the North Pole and end, for lack of more land, at the Isthmus of Panama" (3:14)—an attitude that thoroughly distances him from most Latin Americans, who, like Emerson, Lincoln, and Thoreau, recognized the United States's war with Mexico for what it was: an outrageous land grab by which Mexico lost half its territory.

Sarmiento's most sustained use of the United States as reference model for Argentina is his *Argirópolis*, a short book written in 1850, which, while attacking Rosas, outlines a program for a post-Rosas Argentina. Dedicated to Juan José de Urquiza, the progressive caudillo of Entre Ríos who would eventually unseat Rosas (and probably never read Sarmiento's book), *Argirópolis* rehashes themes already found in *Facundo:* the need for unregulated river navigation, free trade, better schools, immigration, institutional government, and the like. But *Argirópolis* also argues that Argentina was destined to be The United States of South America, and should include Uruguay and Paraguay—a fanciful notion that had contributed to not a few wars (*OC* 13:31–37). He further holds that the capital city, like Washington D.C., should be moved from Buenos Aires to a more central location. Sarmiento chose the Island of Martín García, a small, mosquito-infested islet situated at the joining point of the Paraná and Uruguay rivers. Sarmiento had never been there, but since Martín García was near the geographic center of his imaginary country, it looked good on the map. Again, this proposal is justified through constant reference to the United States (*OC* 42–53). *Argirópolis*, in Bunkley's words, is "typical of Sarmiento's thought. It was a blueprint conceived wholly in the abstract. It was an intellectual ideal that was far removed from reality" (322). *Argirópolis* also shows the degree to which Sarmiento believed that Argentina's most exalted destiny was to become a mirror image of the United States on the other extreme of the hemisphere.

Thus it was that although Echeverría, Alberdi, and Sarmiento found plenty to criticize in Europe and the United States, when it came time to give substance to their protestations of independence from European and North American culture, none of the Men of '37 recognized much in Argentina that could be defined as positive and unique. Indeed, the uniqueness of America, glorified in the Americanism of Artigas and Hidalgo's gaucho, was in their minds an obstacle to progress. Nor did they envision any special mission or potential unique to their country; transplanting Europe and imitating the United States were good enough. Consequently, it is hardly surprising that in devising a framework for their New Argentina, they repeatedly failed to break away from foreign models and create institutions peculiar to Argentina. Among the Men of '37 and their cultural descendants, as with their Morenista and Rivadavian forebears, imitation of European and North American culture continued to be the hallmark of refinement. Rather than forge a new identity unencumbered by European guides, the Generation of '37 and their intellectual progeny in large measure merely substituted one cultural tutelage for another; what had been Spain was now France, England, and the United States. Moreover, Argentine letters in the main would continue this worshipful stance toward Europe even up to the present. Nowhere in Argentine thought do we find anything like the insolent, adolescent arrogance towards Europe that typifies Mark Twain's *Innocents Abroad, The Prince and the Pauper,* and *A Connecticut Yankee in King Arthur's Court.* For Mark Twain, appearing European meant pretentious. For educated Argentines, it meant *culto.*

The Generation's reverence toward northern Europe and the United States contrasts sharply with their facile dismissal of Spain. Spain, for the Men of '37, was the cradle of barbarism, the backward daughter of Europe, the poor relation to be avoided at all costs. Such a matricidal attitude could hardly build national self-confidence. Indeed, one of the most important intellectual currents of this century, the *hispanidad* movement that begins in the early 1900s and figures prominently in the rise of Peronism, was specifically targeted against the anti-Spanish bias of nineteenth-century liberals.

Yet while the Men of '37 looked to Europe and North America for cultural models, they apparently felt, like Mariano Moreno and the Rivadavians before them, that the rest of Latin America should learn from Argentina. Sarmiento in *Argirópolis* argues that Argentina is destined to lead Latin America, if for no other reason than by virtue of its greater European population. Even Alberdi, usually more sensible in these matters, was caught up in the jingoism that proclaimed Argentina the natural leader of South America. In a pamphlet written in 1847 to commemorate the Revolución de Mayo titled *La República Argentina 37 años después de su Revolución de Mayo*, he wrote:

The Argentine Republic has not one man, one event, one defeat, one victory, one discovery, one detail in its life as a nation for which it need feel ashamed. . . . In every period the Argentine Republic appears at the head of this America's evolution. Both for good and for bad, her initiative capacity is the same: when they don't copy our liberators, they imitate our tyrants. In revolution, the Plan of Moreno spreads throughout the continent. In war, San Martín shows Bolívar the road to Ayacucho. Rivadavia gives [this] America its plan for progressive change and improvement. (*OC* 3:222–223)

Alberdi even praises Rosas for unifying the country, "an evil and a cure," and suggests that such a dictator could help other Latin American states in their retarded evolution. But he quickly adds that Rosas's greatness, however mixed, is not his own, but that of

Argentina, "which from the first days of this century never left
center stage, either in her men or her acts" (3:226). Alberdi compromises his praise of Argentina, however, by attributing her greatness to her imitativeness: "As the closest to Europe, Argentina first
received the influence of progressive ideas. . . . [It is] the future
for the States less close to the transatlantic well-spring of American
progress; their future is the past of the River Plate States" (3:233).
In this sense Argentina sought to be a guide for Latin America, but
not as a force destined to change the world, discard the tired ways
of Europe, and create a new Jerusalem from which all peoples
would seek light and knowledge. No, Alberdi in 1847, like the
Rivadavians, believes Latin America should follow Argentina because Argentina is such a successful imitation.

In the Generation's avowed intention to imitate and re-create
foreign models, there lies a profound irony, for their own writings
constitute a remarkable testimony to Argentine (and Latin American) creativity—a creativity that defies European literary and intellectual models at every turn. There is no better example of this
than Sarmiento's *Facundo*. Gallons of ink have been spent trying to
decide whether *Facundo* should be catalogued under history, sociology, biography, essay, or some other neat category invented for
European letters. Too inaccurate and undocumented for history,
too intuitive for sociology, too fictive for biography, and too historical, biographical, and sociological for essay, *Facundo* establishes its
own genre. Nor is labeling the book's ideological orientation any
easier: critics, including some of Sarmiento's own generation, still
debate whether *Facundo* is fundamentally a romantic work. Although some elements of the work reflect the romantic impulse,
particularly in the author's preference for impassioned prose and
personal intuition over supportable fact, *Facundo* is in other ways
specifically antiromantic: it finds in the land a source of evil, it
distrusts rather than glorifies popular tradition, it converts strongmen into tyrants rather than heroes, and it is specifically international rather than national in its aspirations. In short, like much
Latin American literature, which from the colonial chronicles onward has stubbornly insisted on its own definitions, *Facundo* demands a new understanding of what constitutes literariness. As a
work of literature, *Facundo*, much the same as the mixed-blood
peoples its author deplored, gathers like a prism the variegated

hues of European influence and New World freshness into a work of enormous originality. In short, *Facundo* would be inconceivable without taking into large account Sarmiento's peculiar genius and the constant intrusion of the New World that eschews representational modes developed in Europe. What irony that a text of such implicit newness in the realm of literary discourse should explicitly denigrate autochthonous Argentina while in essence preaching an imitative submission to foreign cultural templates.

But more than original, *Facundo* is prophetic, for it anticipates the most distinctive aspects of contemporary Latin American fiction: as in García Márquez's *Cien años de soledad*, *Facundo* overwhelms the reader with a dizzying abundance of detail through which the author paints in broad strokes a portrait of an entire people; as in Carpentier's *Los pasos perdidos* and *El siglo de las luces*, *Facundo* describes synchronic time frames that coexist in the primitive life of the pampas, the colonial scholasticism of Córdoba, and the ever-trendy pretensions of Buenos Aires, which regularly calls itself the Paris of South America; as in José Eustasio Rivera's *La vorágine* and Juan Rulfo's *Pedro Páramo*, *Facundo* evokes the corrupting and ineluctable presence of untamed nature; as in García Márquez's *El otoño del patriarca*, Carlos Fuentes's *La muerte de Artemio Cruz*, Miguel Angel Asturias's *El señor presidente*, and Augusto Roa Bastos's *Yo el supremo*, *Facundo* explores the psychology of both caudillos and their followers—as Roberto González Echevarría perceptively analyzes in his article "The Dictatorship of Rhetoric/The Rhetoric of Dictatorship: Carpentier, García Márquez, and Roa Bastos." Today's nationalists who denounce Sarmiento as a facile imitator, in thrall to foreign paradigms, read him too literally and fail to notice the remarkable contradictions between Sarmiento's avowed sociopolitical intentions and the book he actually wrote: where Sarmiento preaches imitation in economics and government, he writes a book defiant of foreign models; where he explicitly wants Argentina to be like the most progressive countries of his time, his book departs significantly from the romantic impulse of his contemporaries; where *Facundo* is today regularly denounced by nationalists as the work of an Argentine sepoy, it foreshadows the most original aspects of contemporary Latin American fiction. While we can ignore neither Sarmiento's intention nor the effect his writing might have on literal readers, *Facundo* remains a work of astounding and prophetic creativity. Yet for all its originality, there is no escaping an unhappy fact: the Men of '37 were ultimately more concerned with re-creating Europe in the Southern Cone than in developing a new country that would blend the best of the Old and New Worlds.

Most of the Men of '37 would not live to see their ideas put into practice. Nonetheless, their understanding of their country's problems and their proposals to solve those problems became and remain guiding fictions of Argentine liberalism. From the 1860s on, and especially during Argentina's boom years of 1880–1915, liberal governments followed with essential sameness the program first enunciated by the Men of '37: domination by an *europeizante*, enlightened elite based in Buenos Aires; elaborate attempts to build a European-like society in the Argentine; a seemingly democratic government that in fact limited debate to the elite, through fraud if necessary; laissez-faire economics confined mostly to people whose prior wealth and position allowed them access to the economic order; spectacular material progress fueled by foreign investment, debt, and a consequent surrender of national sovereignty; and continued disdain for the rural and urban poor reflected in elaborate attempts to "improve" the ethnic mix by infusions of immigrants from northern Europe.

History's judgment of the Generation of '37 is mixed. Until the revisionist historians who became prominent in the 1930s, it appeared that the Men of '37 would occupy an undisputed place of honor in the Argentine pantheon of national heroes, partly because the first Argentine histories were in fact written by men associated with the generation, Bartolomé Mitre and Vicente Fidel López being the best-known. These histories later formed the basis of school textbooks that successfully preached to young Argentines the glories of the country's liberal forebears. In this century, however, the antiliberal, and anticolonial nationalist sentiment of both the right and left have systematically sought to discredit the Men of '37, with Sarmiento being a prime target. The anti-Sarmiento fervor in some circles became so foolish that in 1978 the government of the isolated province of Neuquén actually forbade the reading of Sarmiento in the public schools.

Only the most blindly biased could deny that in the Men of '37 there is much to praise. With inexhaustible energy they and their ideological successors diagnosed the "barbarism" of their country, prescribed solutions, and did their best to hammer Argentina into the "civilized" country they dreamed of. To combat the barbarism of empty spaces, they used gauchos to fight Indians, thus freeing up vast tracts of land that were then parceled out, fenced with barbed wire, and distributed partly to settlers but mostly to high bidders from Buenos Aires. To combat the barbarism of distance, they brought in foreign, mostly British, investors and engineers to criss-cross the country with telegraph lines and build the most extensive railroad system in Latin America. To combat the barbarism of popu-list caudillos they instituted electoral politics that allowed debate and free elections among the elite, while "intervening" whenever "populist arbitrariness" threatened to disrupt their plans. To combat the barbarism of ignorance they constructed literally hundreds of public schools staffed by freshly minted normal-school graduates who would give Argentina the highest literacy rate in Latin America. Indeed, those who criticize Sarmiento today probably learned to do so in schools he founded. To combat the barbarism of race, they instituted polices that eventually attracted millions of immigrants to Argentine shores—although most of the newcomers were Italian and Spanish rather than Swiss and German. To combat the barba-rism of poverty they greatly expanded the economy by cultivating vast tracts of virgin land with wheat and sorghum while opening their doors to unfettered trade and investment, mostly from Great Britain. Although the chief beneficiaries of their economic policies were landowners, merchants, traders, lawyers—and of course the British—common laborers also reached a standard of living higher than that of their counterparts in the rest of Latin America. To combat the barbarism of populist armies, they founded military academies to professionalize the armed forces.

The practical success of these programs is the subject of much debate, most of which lies outside the limits of this study. More central to our purposes is the ideological legacy left by Argentina's early liberals, much of which now appears unfortunate. Foremost in this regard is the relative modesty of their overriding goal, of their chief guiding fiction: to bring Europe to the Southern Cone. Rather than create something new, to build a new Jerusalem and be a light unto the nations, they merely sought to re-create Europe and North America in the Argentine, to be a light unto the rest of Latin America, not as a new idea but as a successful derivation. Perhaps three centuries as a colony with eyes only toward Europe made such thinking inescapable. But the effect has been to stifle inventiveness while rewarding imitation, and probably accounts for the peculiarly mirrorlike quality of much Argentine high culture, particularly in Buenos Aires. Even some of the most original aspects of Argentine culture—folklore, tangos, Borges's understated subversions of Western literary assumptions and cognitive systems—gained wide recognition in Argentina only after first receiving validation in Europe.

No less damaging than the Generation's explicit recommendations to establish Europe in America, often at the expense of a useful sense of national purpose, is a current in their writing that might be described as an underlying metaphor of national illness, or the notion that the country is so sick that only drastic cures can work, be they the violent surgery of eradicating portions of the society—Indians, gauchos, or "subversives"—or the insertion of healthy tissue in the form of foreign immigrants. Such thinking probably underlies the predisposition throughout modern Argentine history to accept radical changes, from military repression to democracy to messianic populism, as necessary, even natural ways of solving problems. It has also made the Argentine economy the most experimented with and manipulated in the world—with disastrous results. Whatever wind of economic doctrine blows from London, Chicago, or Paris finds an immediate and willing laboratory in Argentina.

Corollary to the metaphor of illness is the metaphor of endemic incurability. When the Generation of '37 explains failure in terms of the Spanish tradition, the land, and the racial mix, they suggest that illness is an inescapable result of past, place, and ethnicity. If incurability is endemic, there are no solutions and no one is really accountable for what goes wrong. Representatives of such thinking abound among liberal Argentine thinkers. In 1885, for example, Eugenio Cambaceres published *En la sangre*, a novel based on social Darwinist notions of ethnic inadequacy as they explain Argentina's problems. In 1899, Dr. José María Ramos Mejía, sometimes called the "father of Argentine psychiatry," published a supposedly scientific broadside against the nation's character titled

The Argentine Masses: A Study in Collective Psychology that postulates that Argentina's native and immigrant lower classes combine to make *guarangos,* a term meaning vulgar, common, uncultured, and—for Ramos Mejía—unimprovable (see Salessi, "La intuición del rumbo" 69–71). In this century, the most important practitioner of the metaphor of endemic incurability is the still influential Ezequiel Martínez Estrada, who in 1933 published *X-Ray of the Pampa (Radiografía de la pampa)* in which he develops anew Sarmiento's sense that endemic flaws in the land, cultural heritage, and ethnicities predestine Argentina to failure. People in the street express the same sentiment with the ubiquitous *Este país ya no tiene arreglo* (This country is beyond solution).

Finally, the embittered polarity of the Generation's rhetoric, particularly in Sarmiento's unyielding dualities, left an unserviceable framework for debate that allows neither middle ground nor compromise. The Men of '37 described their country in terms of binary oppositions: Spain versus Europe, country versus city, Spanish absolutism versus European reason, dark races versus white races, Counter-Reformation Catholicism versus enlightened Christianity, meridional man versus littoral man, scholastic education versus technical education, and—the one that became a slogan— Barbarism versus Civilization. Although the Generation made pious noises about reconciliation, their sense of productive compromise was undoubtedly undermined by their hatred of Rosas and his lower-class supporters, a fact that inevitably militated against inclusive rhetoric. When one side is so right and the other so wrong, compromise and inclusion become synonymous with surrender and sin. Even Alberdi, the most conciliatory of the group, frequently falls into a rhetoric that divides rather than synthesizes, implying that solutions come from excluding one part in favor of the other. The Men of '37 described division. In a real sense, division continues to be their most pervasive and least fortunate patrimony.

Chapter Seven

Alberdi and Sarmiento:
The Widening Breach

While Rosas was in power, the Men of '37 were united in common cause against the porteño dictator. With his fall, this union in opposition disappeared. The most important manifestation of the ideological breakup is a debate between Sarmiento and Alberdi that touches on issues of fundamental importance in Argentina's guiding fictions. Since the debate rises from the political events of the time, this chapter looks at the dictator's downfall, the first post-Rosas governments, and then at the details of the Sarmiento–Alberdi polemic.

In 1849 Rosas seemed firmly in control. The Buenos Aires provincial legislature had just reappointed him governor following another staged resignation, the French and the British gave him grudging respect for withstanding their blockade and maintaining order in a disorderly country, the Unitarian exiles' conspiracies to unseat him had come to naught, and the provincial caudillos appeared well in hand. Three internal problems, however, militated against a happy denouement to the Rosas story. First, Rosas, now fifty-five, was apparently bored by maintaining the discipline and intrigue that sustained his power. Second, petty corruption, favoritism, and nepotism were getting out of hand even by Rosas's standards. And third, he faced the perennial problem of all personalist governments: who would succeed him. Without Rosas there would be no *rosismo*. His children showed little interest in politics, and since Rosas had systematically eliminated talented underlings in order to suppress potential rivals, there was no heir apparent within the government. Always a master of the grand gesture, Rosas strove to keep up a vigorous appearance by renewing his claims to Uruguay and Paraguay. But these measures accomplished little since even his supporters were tired of the expense and forced conscription of war.

In addition to the decay within *rosismo*, the years 1849–1850 saw new stirrings toward autonomy in the interior as provincial Federalists admitted that Rosas's alleged Federalism merely masked porteño hegemony. The first cracks in the Rosist edifice became visible when Angel Vicente Peñaloza, caudillo of La Rioja, and Justo José de Urquiza, caudillo of prosperous Entre Ríos, added to their ritual support of Rosas's reelection a call for national reorganization under constitutional government—concepts Rosas rightly viewed as antithetical to his personalist rule. Resentment toward the Buenos Aires' customs monopoly was also resurfacing, particularly in the Littoral, an area potentially as wealthy as Buenos Aires. At the same time, new industries in sheep raising and wool exports had attracted Basque, Gallician, and Irish immigrants who, unlike the estancieros and Creole lower classes, felt no automatic loyalty toward Rosas (Scobie, *La lucha* 19).

Provincial resentment, however, was not enough to unseat the dictator. The necessary additional push came in October 1850 when Brazil, tired of Rosas's meddling in Uruguay and his refusal to allow free navigation on the Paraná River, broke with Buenos Aires and formed an alliance with Paraguay. In Entre Ríos, Urquiza, encouraged by Brazil's action, surprised everyone by refusing to renew his compact with Rosas and entering into an agreement with Brazil and Uruguay. He further rebelled against Rosas by collaborating with Brazil in unseating the pro-Rosas government of Uruguay. Urquiza's defection was a major blow to Rosas, for not only was the Entre Ríos caudillo the most powerful and respected of the provincial leaders; he also commanded a large army that ironically had been equipped mostly by Rosas himself as a hedge against Unitarian exiles in Uruguay. Knowing that conflict with Rosas was inevitable, Urquiza expanded his army until it reached 24,000 men, including 10,000 of his regular soldiers and another 14,000 volunteers from other provinces, Buenos Aires, Brazil, and the exile community in Uruguay. It was the largest army ever assembled on South American soil.

Unitarian intellectuals, including Sarmiento, could hardly wait to join Urquiza's campaign. But theirs was an uneasy alliance since, in the Unitarians' view, Urquiza had collaborated too long with Rosas and was too closely identified with other caudillos to be trusted. Sarmiento in particular got on badly with the Entre Ríos caudillo. Already irritated that Urquiza had not made *Agirópolis* the New Argentina's official blueprint, Sarmiento was further upset when Urquiza appointed him official chronicler of the campaign rather than a military officer. Even though Sarmiento had no military experience, he felt his journalistic campaign against Rosas entitled him to greater glory in the military struggle against the dictator.

The opposing armies of Rosas and Urquiza met at Caseros, near Buenos Aires, on February 3, 1852. Although it would have made more military sense for Rosas to engage Urquiza's forces farther from the city, low morale among his men made him reluctant to send underlings where he couldn't watch them. Urquiza's troops, helped by Brazilian soldiers, defeated Rosas's men in less than half a day. Fearing for his life, Rosas wrote a hasty resignation for the House of Representatives, disguised himself as a gaucho soldier, and fled to the home of the British chargé d'affaires, naval Captain Robert Gore. From there, he and his family were transferred to the *HMS Conflict* for their journey into exile. Rosas settled in England on a small farm near Southampton where he spent his old age in isolation and self-pity. Some Rosistas, particularly among the popular classes, remained loyal to him, but most of his wealthy supporters, including first-cousin Nicolás de Anchorena, quickly made peace with their new rulers, demonstrating again that money, not principle, was their major concern (Sebreli, *Apogeo* 203–206). Ironically, Urquiza became Rosas's chief defender in Argentina. Not only did he try (and fail) to protect Rosas's property against confiscation; he also sent the exiled Rosas money to live on (Lynch 341–343).

Urquiza also surprised his detractors by turning out to be a sensible political pragmatist committed to maintaining order while unifying the country under constitutional rule. Although some Rosistas were executed and others were driven into exile, Urquiza managed to stem the tide of terrorism that could have engulfed the country, and sent his best soldiers to help porteño police prevent looting (Scobie, *La lucha* 23). Moreover, knowing that no national government could succeed without the cooperation of the Federalist provincial governors and caudillos, he carefully identified with the notion of equal rights for the provinces and let it be known that under his rule there would be no purges. In short, what he offered was a real federalism to replace the porteño counterfeit that had been Rosismo.

These compromises did not sit well with many Unitarians, including Sarmiento, who wanted to make a clean sweep of all Rosas collaborators. Already unhappy with Urquiza's refusal to give him a major role in the new government, Sarmiento was further incensed that Urquiza and his followers continued to wear the red Federalist insignia. Eventually, Sarmiento submitted a self-righteous resignation to Urquiza, upbraiding him for dissipating "all the glory that for a moment you had gathered about your name" (*OC* 14:59). With wounded vanity in tow, he then embarked for Brazil in late February 1852, where he immediately began campaigning against "the new Rosas." It was also during this exile that Sarmiento's presidential ambitions took shape. Without a trace of modesty, he instructed confidant and supporter, John Posse: "Present me always as the champion of the provinces in Buenos Aires. Present me as the provincial who is accepted in Buenos Aires as well as in the provinces, the only Argentine name accepted and esteemed by all: by the Chilean government, by the Brazilian government, by the provinces, by Buenos Aires, by the army, by the Federalists, by the Unitarians—as the founder of the policy of the fusion of parties as a result of all my writings" (cited in Bunkley 346). From this strategy came Sarmiento's political motto for himself: "Provincial in Buenos Aires; porteño in the provinces" which also became the title of an embarrassingly self-serving book he wrote several years later (*OC* vol. 16). After a short stay in Río de Janeiro, Sarmiento left Brazil for Santiago de Chile to continue fighting against "the new Rosas."

For Urquiza, providing some semblance of orderly government was infinitely more urgent than smoothing Sarmiento's ruffled feathers. To allay porteño fears that he was a provincial barbarian intent on imposing gaucho rule on the cultured capital, he took as his motto "Neither Victors nor Vanquished," and proclaimed a general amnesty with "fraternity and union of all parties" (cited in Bosch, *Urquiza y su tiempo* 227). He later appointed an interim provincial government that, faithful to his goal of reconciliation, included Valentín Alsina, whom historian James R. Scobie calls a "member of the old-line Rivadavian school which supported Buenos Aires supremacy at any cost" (*La lucha* 28). To resolve the even bigger problem of writing a national constitution, Urquiza appointed a committee of porteño, provincial, Federalist, and Unitarian leaders to draft ground rules for a constitutional convention and provide for an interim national government. From this committee came the Pact of San Nicolás of May 31, 1852, which stipulated that a convention consisting of two representatives from each province would write a national constitution to be ratified later by the provincial legislatures, that the city of Buenos Aires would be the Federal Capital of all Argentina and not just of the Province of Buenos Aires, that customs revenues from the city's port would thereby be part of the federal rather than provincial treasury, and that Urquiza would have full powers for maintaining order until a constitutional government could be established—measures very similar to those sought by Rivadavia in 1826 and recommended later by Sarmiento in *Argirópolis* (Bosch 248–250; Mayer, *Alberdi y su tiempo* 412– 413). In Scobie's words, "The Pact was not a threat of dictatorship, but a necessary step towards ensuring order during the process of national organization" (*La lucha* 47).

Despite the Pact's reasonableness, intransigent porteños refused to accept it. Leading them was Bartolomé Mitre, a new man in Argentine politics, a historian and major creator of Argentina's guiding fictions (the subject of the next chapter). From his seat in the provincial House of Representatives and through his newly acquired newspaper, *Los Debates*, Mitre launched a vociferous campaign against the Pact of San Nicolás, arguing that it gave Urquiza "dictatorial, irresponsible, despotic and arbitrary powers" and "sought to dispossess us of our treasure" (cited in Mayer, *Alberdi y su tiempo* 411, 427). In fact, Urquiza encouraged congressional debate and freedom of the press. Although at one point, exhausted by porteño wrangling, he disbanded the provincial congress and called new elections, not once did he waver in his support of democratic, constitutional rule. Although this was hardly the behavior of a despot, Mitre's attacks grew increasingly vehement, appealing to the porteño exclusivist spirit that had always resisted sharing power and customs revenues.

Sensible porteño leaders like Juan María Gutiérrez and Vicente Fidel López argued valiantly in favor of the pact. López, in particular, stood against the majority of his fellow provincial legislators, saying:

I understand very well how much support can be found among us for those who seek to flatter provincial passion and local jealousy; but gentlemen, for that very reason I rise against them. I want no good other than that of the Nation . . . I love as much as anyone the people of Buenos Aires, where I was born! But at the same time I raise my voice to say that my homeland is the Argentine Republic and not Buenos Aires. (Cited in Chiaramonte' *Liberalismo y Nacionalismo* 122–123)

Despite such efforts, less than three weeks after the Pact was completed, the Province of Buenos Aires, under Mitre's leadership, rejected it. Most porteños, regardless of political persuasion, quickly closed ranks behind him, including liberal Unitarians returned from exile and Rosas henchmen like Nicolás de Anchorena. On September 11, 1852, porteño rebels, under the direction of Mitre and Valentín Alsina, marched against Urquiza. The rebellion succeeded, for the time being at least, not because of porteño military might, but because Urquiza, still hoping to woo the wayward province into a government of national unity, refused to crush it (Bosch 267–270). Urquiza's voluntary withdrawal, however, did not keep Mitre from editorializing with misleading eloquence in the newspaper *El Nacional:*

Reinstated in the full enjoyment of her provincial sovereignty and with her trampled rights now revindicated, the Province of Buenos Aires has risen up, with sword in hand, willing to repel all aggression, support all movements in favor of liberty, and combat all tyranny, accept all cooperation, and concur with all forces after the triumph of the grand work of National Organization. (*El Nacional* 21 Sept. 1852, 62)

These grand words had little to do with the facts. Buenos Aires' "triumph" sprang primarily from Urquiza's desire to avoid bloodshed. Urquiza still believed that, by setting a good example, he could win the stubborn porteños to his side. In this he was mistaken. With Urquiza's withdrawal, Buenos Aires was again a nation apart. The autonomist Alsina was named governor of the province and Mitre became his minister of government and foreign affairs, thus confirming Mitre's statement that the porteños would "concur with all forces" only after they had organized the nation on their own terms.

Despite Buenos Aires' secession, Urquiza convened a constituent congress in Santa Fe in late 1852. In his opening words, Urquiza declared, "Out of love for the people of Buenos Aires, I grieve over their absence from this meeting. But their absence does not mean permanent estrangement. . . . Geography, history and old covenants bind Buenos Aires to the nation. Buenos Aires cannot live without her sister provinces, nor can her sisters live without her. There is room on the Argentine flag for more than fourteen stars, but no one of them can eclipse the others" (cited in Gandía, *Historia* 659–660). The constitution was completed in May 1853, under the considerable inspiration of Alberdi's *Bases y puntos de partida,* although Alberdi, still in Chile, wrote not a word of it. Ratified by all the provinces except Buenos Aires, the constitution immediately became the law of the land. Urquiza was elected the first constitutional president, and the federal capital was placed temporarily in Paraná, the capital of Entre Ríos.

Urquiza tried valiantly to organize a progressive society from Paraná. He upstaged the porteño government by obtaining the official recognition of England, France, and the United States, and established an alternative port to Buenos Aires in Rosario, a city that remains the country's second most important trade center. He began an ambitious program to improve transportation in the interior, founded a public school system, and tried to imitate some of Buenos Aires' cultural institutions. In addition, he sent Alberdi to the United States and Europe as his ambassador-at-large to shore up foreign support and appeal for much needed foreign credits. But economics militated against his programs, and the Paraná government sank deeper and deeper into debt. Without the revenues of Argentina's wealthiest province, it soon became apparent that no government could succeed. Moreover, lacking funds to give the central government credibility, provincial leaders were occasionally tempted by the nonstop campaign of the porteño government to woo them away from Urquiza (Scobie, *La lucha* 63–75).

In contrast, Buenos Aires embarked on a period of construction reminiscent of the Rivadavian period, complete with schools, theaters, libraries, and literary societies. The Buenos Aires government also appointed Mariano Balcarce, San Martín's son-in-law, as ambassador to Europe, where in his quest for legitimacy he frequently crossed paths with Alberdi. But most importantly, with its already developed agriculture and control of the country's principal port and customs revenues, the Province of Buenos Aires did not lack for money. Consequently, despite setbacks in international relations, it soon became apparent that Buenos Aires could live more easily without the provinces than vice versa. Moreover, Buenos Aires never relaxed its claims and conspiracies against the Paraná government. As Mitre editorialized in *El Nacional*, despite the fact that thirteen of fourteen provinces supported Urquiza, Buenos Aires still had the "right to act as the national rectoress" (cited in Scobie, *La Lucha* 126). Moreover, in its provincial constitution, ratified in 1854, Buenos Aires arrogated to itself authority over the national congress, holding that "Buenos Aires is a state with the full control of its domestic and foreign sovereignty, as long as said state does not expressly delegate that sovereignty to a federal government" (cited in Scobie, *La Lucha* 127). With policies like these, it is hardly surprising that reconciliation between Buenos Aires and the provinces would be possible only on Buenos Aires' terms.

The period 1852–1854 was, then, decisively important in Argentine history. It saw Rosas's defeat, Urquiza's rise to prominence, the Pact of San Nicolás, Buenos Aires' secession from the Republic, Urquiza's constitutional convention of the thirteen other provinces, and the establishment of two federal governments, one in Paraná and one in Buenos Aires, both with claims on the rest of the country. It was also an important year in Argentina's intellectual evolution. In Chile, Sarmiento and Alberdi engaged in a public debate concerning issues of transcendental importance in the nation's concept of self, while in Buenos Aires, Mitre established himself as a major political thinker and polemicist. In the remainder of this chapter the Alberdi–Sarmiento debate is discussed; in the next chapter, Mitre and the invention of Argentine history.

The Alberdi–Sarmiento conflict began in mid-1852, just after Sarmiento returned to Chile, where Alberdi had remained during the Urquiza campaign against Rosas. Aware of Alberdi's influence,

Sarmiento felt duty-bound to keep the taciturn man from Tucumán from joining the Urquiza government. Although Alberdi fought with other members of the Generation of '37 in their struggle against Rosas, purist Unitarians had always suspected him of being soft on caudillismo. Many remembered the famous *Fragmento* he wrote in 1837, studied here in chapter 5, in which he argued that Rosas was destined to play a historical role in the development of an organic Argentina, that the dictator for all his defects represented a necessary transition between an unformed, primitive nation and a modern democratic republic. Again in 1847, in a famous pamphlet titled *La República Argentina 37 años despúes de su Revolución de Mayo*, Alberdi argued that Rosas and the caudillos were factors not to be excluded from the Argentine equation (*OC* 3:229–242). Rosas had reportedly so liked this pamphlet that he invited Alberdi to return to Argentina and work with the regime— an invitation Alberdi declined (Lynch 307). Still, although suspicious of these flirtations with caudillismo, Sarmiento deemed it crucial to gain Alberdi's support for the porteños. Alberdi and Sarmiento had never gotten on well, but prior to the Urquiza– Mitre conflict their disagreements had been more academic than practical. This time, however, there were real political stakes involved. The most serious was a secessionist porteñō government in need of ideological legitimization.

To convince Alberdi, Sarmiento first tried honey, praising his introverted contemporary's newly published *Bases* as "the Argentine Decalogue"; Alberdi responded by sending copies of his book to Urquiza's constituent congress. With Sarmiento at an estancia in Yungay and Alberdi in Valparaíso, the two corresponded frequently. Sarmiento tried to turn Alberdi against Urquiza while Alberdi recommended practicality and patience in hopes of keeping Sarmiento's famed ego and temper in check. The open break began on August 16, 1852, when Alberdi and several pro-Urquiza friends formed El Club Constitucional de Valparaíso, a discussion group of exiled Argentines who used the organization to make their support of Urquiza official. Knowing of Sarmiento's hostility toward Urquiza, not to mention his polemical and grandstanding ways, the club further resolved to not invite him to join (Mayer, *Alberdi y su tiempo* 433– 437). News of Alberdi's club and Mitre's revolt against Urquiza of September 11 reached Sarmiento at about the same time. Furious with Alberdi, Sarmiento quickly organized his own club, El Club de Santiago, to support Buenos Aires and the Mitristas. Its members were for the most part aging porteño exiles too weak to return to Buenos Aires. In a letter dated November 14, 1852, to Félix Frías, Alberdi referred to Sarmiento's club as an organization of "respectable mummies" (cited by Mayer, *Alberdi y su tiempo* 439). Blind with fury, Sarmiento scribbled off three pamphlets: an open letter to Urquiza titled "Carta de Yungay" (Letter from Yungay) of October 13, 1852; a lengthy newspaper piece evaluating the Pact of San Nicolás, dated October 26, and a tract exalting the contribution of men from San Juan—Sarmiento's native province—to the building of Argentina. Although first published in Chilean newspapers, the pamphlets were targeted for one particular reader: Juan Bautista Alberdi.

The "Carta de Yungay" displays Sarmiento at his haughty and insulting worst. To suggest that Urquiza was just a small-time caudillo rather than a national leader, Sarmiento addresses the letter to the "General from Entre Ríos" followed by a quotation from *Facundo* with which Sarmiento often defended himself when accused of intolerance: "Among Rosas's supporters, among the very mazorqueros, beneath the surface of their criminal behavior, there are virtues that some day might be rewarded." Having thus assured Urquiza that he might have some redeeming qualities, Sarmiento negates any conciliatory intention by asking, "How can one deny that your previous public life will require the indulgence of history?" (*OC* 15:23). Sarmiento apparently considered such writing conciliatory. What continues is one false accusation after another. He accuses Urquiza of packing the government with his "domestic help" (24), this despite Urquiza's attempts to include Unitarians, Federalists, and representatives from all the provinces including Buenos Aires in the constitutional convention. Sarmiento repeatedly chides Urquiza for not heeding the counsel of "patriotic publicists" who could have helped him avoid error (25). In particular, Sarmiento tells Urquiza he should have listened to the author of *Argirópolis*—who just happened to be Sarmiento himself (47–49). Sarmiento concludes by calling Urquiza "a lost man, with no possible rehabilitation" and then assures him that his only motive in writing the "Carta de Yungay" was "to tell the entire truth, without shortcuts, the truth one speaks when God in heaven is our witness." A more likely motive appears a sentence later when he laments that owing to events in Argentina "I have been forced to renounce my future," followed by a threat to take out Chilean citizenship permanently unless Urquiza heeded his advice (51–52). It is doubtful Urquiza would have viewed such a move with disfavor. The other two pamphlets, *Convención de San Nicolás de los Arroyos* (The pact of San Nicolás de los Arroyos) and *San Juan, sus hombres y sus acciones en la regeneración argentina* (San Juan, her men and their actions in the regeneration of Argentina) add little to the "Carta de Yungay." The first merely repeats the porteño position that the most populous province should have a proportional number of representatives—which would have effectively given . Buenos Aires control of the convention. The second attacks the Santa Fe constituent convention on several grounds, the overriding one being that Argentina's best men, of whom Sarmiento considered himself one, were not part of it.

Sarmiento's most direct attempt to engage Alberdi in a debate and his nastiest attack on Urquiza is a book titled *Campaña en el ejército grande de Sud América* (Campaign in the Great Army of South America) published in several versions in late 1852.[1] Written in a hurry, *Campaña* is ostensibly a history of Urquiza's campaign against Rosas. In fact, however, it is a confused narrative drawn from three main sources. The first source is the official war bulletins (*boletines*) Sarmiento published for distribution to the soldiers as he traveled with the campaign. A second source are his personal letters and diary in which he recorded his private disapproval of Urquiza—often in clear contradiction to the sycophantic boletines he was publishing officially. And finally *Campaña* includes new material added in Chile consisting mostly of unrelenting attacks on Urquiza. With characteristic pugnacity, Sarmiento dedicates the book to Alberdi while also suggesting that armchair

1. The exact date of publication is difficult to determine since different portions of the book were published within weeks of each other in Río de Janeiro, Santiago de Chile, and Buenos Aires. The first part appeared in Río in 1852 shortly after the campaign was over. Additional sections appeared almost simultaneously in newspapers in Santiago de Chile and Buenos Aires during December of the same year. The volume in the *Obras completas* includes letters and articles pertinent to the period which did not appear in the 1852 newspaper versions. As a result, not only is the date of publication impossible to ascertain; there is no "original" text.

Mariano Moreno, secretary of the Primera Junta, 1810–1811, essayist and prominent liberal. (Attributed to H. Clemente, Museo Colonial e Histórico Enrique Udaondo)

Cornelio Saavedra, president of the Primera Junta, 1810–1811.
(Painted by B. Marcel, Museo Histórico Nacional)

Bernardino Rivadavia, president of the republic, 1826–1827.
(Archivo Gráfico de la nación)

Four lithographs, gauchos roping cattle and ostriches.

(Lithographs published by the American Bank Note Company, New York, 1869)

Esteban Echeverría, poet, essayist and primary inspiration of the Generation of '37. (Portrait by Carlos E. Pellegrini, 1831, Museo Nacional de Bellas Artes)

Coronel Manuel Dorrego, governor of the Province of Buenos Aires, 1827–1828; executed by order of General Lavalle. (Anonymous, c. 1828, Museo Histórico Nacional)

Country scene: A Stop at the Pulpería, Pulperías were country stores and gathering places. (Painted by Prilidiano Pueyrredón, Museo Nacional de Bellas Artes)

*View of Buenos Aires, c. 1832. (painted by Ricardo Adams, Museo His-
tórico Nacional)*

Juan Manuel de Rosas, governor of the Province of Buenos Aires and leading politician in the country, 1829–1852. (Portrait attributed to Arturo Onslow, Museo Colonial e Histórico Enrique Udaondo)

General Estanislao López, caudillo of the Providence of Santa Fe, 1818–1838; enemy of Rivadavia and ally of Rosas. (Lithograph by Carlos E. Pellegrini, Buenos Aires, 1830)

Juan Bautista Alberdi as a
young man.

Juan Bautista Alberdi, taken at
the time of the Paraguayan War.
(Photograph from the 1860's,
Archivo Witcomb)

Domingo Faustino Sarmiento, depicted with the presidential sash; president, 1868–1874. (Archivo Nacional de la Nación)

General Justo José de Urquiza, caudillo of Entre Ríos who ousted Rosas; president of the confederation, 1853–1859. (Lithograph, c. 1841)

Dominguito Sarmiento, Sarmiento's only son. Killed in the Paraguayan War. (Painted by Processa Sarmiento de Leloir, Museo Histórico Sarmiento)

Bartolomé Mitre, first elected President of the entire country, 1862–1868. (Archivo Gráfico de la Nación)

Bartolomé Mitre, picture corresponding to the late 1870's or early 1880's when Mitre published his famous biographies. (Archivo Gráfico de la Nación)

Olegario V. Andrade, poet and essayist famous for his defense of the provinces against Buenos Aires. (Archivo Gráfico de la Nación)

Carlos Guido y Spano, poet and essayist, famous for his attacks on porteño pretense. (Archivo Gráfico de la Nación)

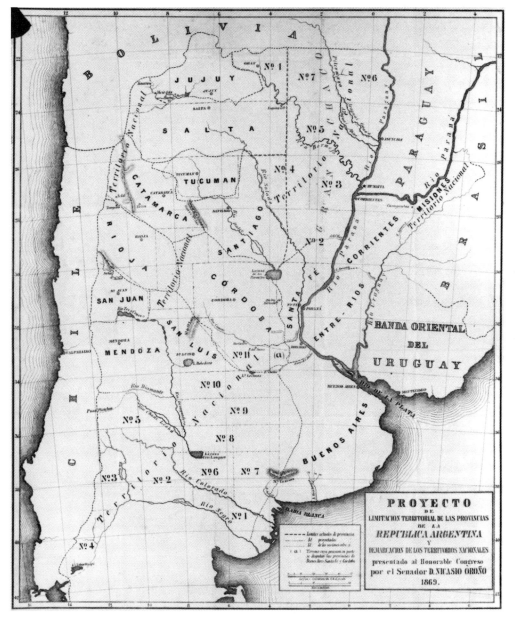

Map of Argentina, 1869, one of the first maps commissioned by the national government. (Yale Map Collection)

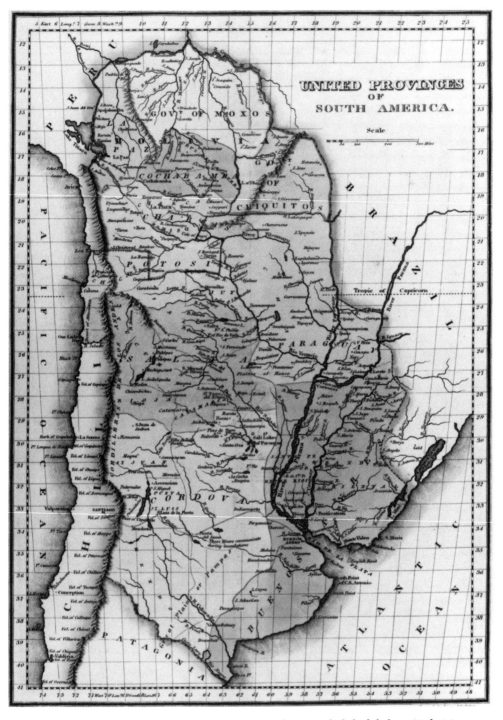

Map of Argentina, 1822, drawn by J. Finlaysen of Philadelphia. (Yale Map Collection)

warriors (like Alberdi) should defer to the opinion of better-informed people (like Sarmiento) who actually participated in the campaign (*OC* 14:78–81). Ostensibly a history of Urquiza's triumph over Rosas, the book is in fact a savage attack on the Entre Ríos caudillo, motivated primarily by Sarmiento's resentment at being excluded from power. These motives become clear in the final chapter, where he writes that "with this narration, I have tried to demonstrate . . . the necessity of again rising up against General Urquiza. I have tried particularly to dissipate the perverse criticisms that poorly informed men in favor of Urquiza are now gathering against Buenos Aires" (353).

To accomplish these ends, Sarmiento presents Urquiza as "a man with no qualities whatever, neither good nor bad . . . with no sign of astuteness, energy or subtlety" (125). Later, he is portrayed as "a poor country bumpkin with no education" whose grand army is little more than "a mass uprising of country hicks" (221). Indeed, Sarmiento repeatedly makes light of the gauchos in Urquiza's army, "people in dirty country clothes, with no idea of military organization, who couldn't string two words together in their proper order" (221). When not attacking Urquiza and ridiculing his followers, Sarmiento loses no opportunity to flatter himself and his contribution to Rosas's downfall. Indeed, Sarmiento's exaltation of self makes the work primarily autobiographical. The following passage is representative:

Travelling at my own expense with my own weapons and horses, like the Spanish captains of old; leaving behind family and fortune, in quest of a free and civilized patria, I sailed along the Atlantic and the Pacific, journeyed up the majestic Uruguay and the fecund Paraná rivers; crossing the Argentine provinces of Entre Ríos and Santa Fe; visiting the capital cities of Montevideo and Buenos Aires, struggling on land and sea; travelling, fighting, and withstanding fatigue and enjoying deep emotion; pondering what my eyes saw and what my ears heard; thinking and writing and living the feverish enthusiasm of struggle. (*OC* 14:63–64)

According to Sarmiento, his glory as a writer rivaled that of Urquiza. "[Since] I was a well-known writer," he remarks, not at all in passing, "it was not unusual for as many people to gather around me as gathered around the General" (247). Urquiza at one point became so exasperated with Sarmiento's attempts to upstage everyone else that he wrote him a curt reminder that "the presses have been shouting in Chile and other places for many years [but] until now Juan Manuel de Rosas has not been frightened" (cited in Bunkley 339).

Particularly revelatory of Sarmiento's enthusiasm for himself is his account of the only extensive interview between Sarmiento and Urquiza during the campaign. By his own admission, Sarmiento met with Urquiza on only three occasions, a fact that undermines his claims to special knowledge regarding the Entre Ríos caudillo. Of this particular encounter Sarmiento writes, "I began to detail to [Urquiza] the practical object of my visit, to be sure, to instruct him on the state of the provinces, the opinion of the people, the abilities and nature of the governors, my work begun in Chile, and everything else bearing on the questions of the moment" (126). And from whence came this knowledge of the provinces, the people (whom Sarmiento ridiculed as ignorant and dirty), the governors, and everything else bearing on the questions of the moment? Certainly not from personal contact with Argentina since Sarmiento had just returned from a ten-year exile, much of it spent in Europe, Africa, and the United States. Understandably defensive, Urquiza tried to show that he was not an empty-headed rube waiting to be "instructed" by an odd-looking man he hardly knew. After all, Urquiza successfully governed Argentina's most prosperous province after Buenos Aires, led the largest army in South American history, headed a coalition of all provincial leaders, expected to overthrow Rosas (at the time of this interview), and was remarkably well read for a man who, like Sarmiento, had little formal education. "What most surprised me in the general," continues Sarmiento, "is that, after that simple narration of facts with which I introduced myself, he never showed any desire to hear my opinion on anything. And when, with a modesty I do not have, with feigned deference, with circumlocutions which I never used when talking to Cobden, Thiers, Guizot, Montt or the Emperor of Brazil, I wanted to express an idea, he cut me off in mid-sentence" (127). At this point Sarmiento probably missed Rosas; at least the dictator had taken him seriously.

Given Sarmiento's limited contact with campaign leadership, external appearances are his major ground for criticism. And predictably, his primary objection to Urquiza is that he didn't do things as Europeans would have. He didn't organize his army according to French military textbooks (228). He didn't ride and wave like an Englishman during his triumphal ride through Buenos Aires (267). And worst of all he didn't know how to dress. Not only did Urquiza fail to wear a European uniform (247–248), he allowed his followers to wear a gaucho's poncho and *chiripá* (a baggy peasant trouser) while marching under the red Federalist flag rather than the light-blue banner of the Unitarians (268–273). Urquiza's insistence on using the red Federalist insignia was probably motivated by a desire to maintain support from the Federalist provincial governors, who, although tired of Rosas, were understandably wary of porteño Unitarians, particularly those returning from exile. Nonetheless, the disproportionate attention given the matter by both Sarmiento and Urquiza seems a little silly.

Sarmiento, of course, describes himself as the exemplar of culture, called to set standards of European ways and exquisite taste. He bedecked himself in a brand-new military uniform from Europe that must have looked quite odd in the steamy pampas of Argentina's summer, and in his military tent he maintained "the most refined epicurism" (214). And for diversion he loved telling gauchos, who had all but grown up on horses, that the English and French were better horsemen (222).

Unreliable as history, libelous in its treatment of Urquiza, and disjointed in its narration, *Campaña* shows the worst aspects of Sarmiento's complex personality. His ambition, his shameless self-promotion, his astonishing gift for dropping names, his disdain for the popular classes, his enthrallment to Europe and the United States, his creative ways with fact, his inability to recognize another's talent—all invite a harsh judgment on its author who in other contexts was a most admirable man. And yet, *Campaña* is still an enjoyable book. Even when libeling everyone else while promoting himself, Sarmiento remains a superb stylist whose narrative sense and occasional insight make for good reading. The book also provoked another response: It brought Alberdi into a debate that would resurrect certain Argentine guiding fictions that had lain dormant since Artigas and Hidalgo. Moreover, the debate forced Alberdi to reevaluate some of the assumptions of his *Bases* and embrace positions that would define his thought for the rest of his life.

Alberdi's best-known response to *Campaña* came in the form of four lengthy open letters written in January and February of 1853 and addressed to Sarmiento. Titled "Cartas sobre la prensa y la política militante de la República Argentia" (Letters on journalism and militant politics in the Argentine Republic), the letters are better known as the *Cartas quillotanas*, since they were written at Alberdi's temporary home in Quillota, Chile. The *Cartas quillotanas* signal a significant turn in Alberdi's thinking, away from the elitism of the Generation of '37 and toward attitudes that are nationalistic, proprovincial, and at times even populist. It is therefore possible to view the *Cartas* as a return to concerns Alberdi first enunciated in the *Fragmento* of 1837 where he takes a much more practical view of Rosas. The *Cartas* can also be seen as a continuation of the proprovincial, inclusivist sentiment found in Artigas's improvised decrees and Hidalgo's homely gauchesque poetry. In sum, although Alberdi was too world-wise to embrace the facile populism of Saavedra, Artigas, and Hidalgo, in the *Cartas* he reconnects with a nationalistic, populist tradition that had been present in the River Plate at least since Saavedra organized his *junta grande* in 1810. Moreover, the Alberdi seen in the *Cartas* is much more typical of positions he supported throughout most of his life. What this means is that Alberdi's best-known book, *Bases*, is actually his least representative.

In the *Cartas*, Alberdi identifies a new enemy: Argentine liberalism as reflected in the old-time Unitarians and the Mitre porteño group. "I am a conservative in both Chile and Argentina," he affirms; "there through my actions and here through my sympathies" (*OC* 4:79–80). What Alberdi means with the term "conservative" becomes clear in subsequent passages where he reproaches the liberals' proclivity for rapid change and their intolerance of things traditionally Argentine. He particularly criticizes Sarmiento's and Mitre's inflammatory rhetoric—not because he disagrees with their avowed principles but because they use those principles to mask personal ambition. In lucid, detached prose, so unlike Sarmiento's bombast, Alberdi finds in Argentine liberalism two destablizing forces: "the journalism of combat and the silence of war; [these] are the arms which the liberal party used in 1827, and their result was the rise of Rosas and his twenty years of despotism" (4:11). The reference, of course, is to the Rivadavians who through journalism destabilized the Dorrego government and through war silenced detractors, ousted a constitutional government, and murdered Dorrego, thus paving the way for Rosas to impose the order of dictatorship. Alberdi further points out that liberal wars were in fact "wars of extermination against the nature (*modo de ser*) of our pastoral classes and their natural representatives [the caudillos]" (4:12). Here in prose that resonates with the populism of Artigas and Hidalgo of nearly four decades earlier, Alberdi not only suggests that the gauchos and their ways are a necessary part of Argentine identity but also argues that "their natural representatives" be given a role in the emerging constitutional system.

These ideas would grow full-size in essays written during the 1860s, some of which appear in *Grandes y pequeños hombres del Plata,* a useful posthumous collection of Alberdi's work published in 1912. In these later essays, Alberdi contends that the caudillo represents "the will of the popular masses, the choice of the people." Caudillismo is in his words a "badly organized democracy" and thereby better than the antipopular "democracy of the intelligentsia" that makes room for only the Europeanized, porteño elite (*Grandes y pequeños* 197–198). In his new appreciation of the gauchos and their caudillos, Alberdi signals an important departure from the racist condemnation of the mixed-blood natives and cries for immigration that he preached in *Bases.* Moreover, his acceptance of the caudillos helps explain his support of Urquiza, who was both a smart gaucho and a caudillo.

Alberdi's vindication of the gauchos and their caudillos also extends to practical politics. He condemns the exclusivist haughtiness of the Unitarians, arguing that their concern for ideological purity and ethnic perfection merely postponed the political organization of the country:

In other times it was deemed a crime for Rosas to delay organizing the country until he could get rid of the "Unitarians." Now his enemies imitate his example, postponing the constitutional organization of the country until the "caudillos" are eliminated. . . . We should establish as a theorem: any delay in writing the Constitution is a crime against the Patria, a betrayal of the republic. With caudillos, with Unitarians, with Federalists, with every kind of person that shapes and lives in our sad Republic, we should proceed to its organization, excluding not even the bad people, because they also form part of the family. If you exclude them, you ex-

clude everyone, including yourselves. All exclusion is division and anarchy. You may say it is impossible to have perfect liberty with bad people.
Remember that imperfect liberty is the only kind available in view of the
possibilities of the country. If we try to annihilate part of our population
because it is incapable of constitutional order, tomorrow you will say it is
better to destroy the entire population and replace it with foreigners,
accustomed to living in order and liberty. Such a principle will then lead
you to suppress the entire Spanish, Colonial, and Argentine Nation . . .
and replace it by force with an Anglo-Republican Argentine Nation, the
only kind that will never have caudillismo. . . . But if you want to build
the . . . patria you have, and not the one you wish you had, you must
accept the principle of 'imperfect liberty.' . . . The day you believe it
proper to destroy and suppress the gaucho because he doesn't think as
you do, you write your own death sentence and revive the system of
Rosas. (*OC Cartas* 16–17)

This remarkable passage is much more than a call to pluralism.
Recognizing that Argentina is inherently different from the foreign
models Europeanists like Sarmiento sought to impose on her,
Alberdi argues that Argentina's unique population (the gauchos),
government (the caudillos), and heritage (colonial Spain) were the
only possible points of departure from which to build a country.
These arguments explicitly reject the facile and exclusivist Europeanism of the Morenistas, the Rivadavians, and Sarmiento who, in
Alberdi's words, "preach Europeanism while making of it a weapon
against the caudillos" and the masses they represent (*OC* 4:21).
Moreover, Alberdi in this instance comes closer to Artigas and
Hidalgo than to the Rivadavian teachers he studied with as a teenager. His position in the *Cartas* also differs markedly from that of the
Literary Salon thinkers, including the younger Alberdi himself, who
through immigration would have brought "living pieces" of foreign
cultures to replace the local population and thereby eliminate the
popular base of caudillismo. In practical terms, Alberdi's arguments
meant supporting the enlightened caudillo Urquiza, collaborating
with the provincial governors, many of them caudillos, and respect-
ing the Hispanic traditions of the popular classes. Moreover, by
defending the gauchos, the caudillos, and the Spanish tradition,
Alberdi foreshadows populist sentiments that repeatedly surface in
Argentine history in the form of pro-Hispanic, pro-Catholic, nationalist movements of which Peronism is the most recent example.

Alberdi's reevaluation of the gauchos and caudillos does not, however, displace his avowed purpose in the *Cartas,* namely, to explore the place of journalism in Argentine politics. Repeatedly, Alberdi accuses Sarmiento and Mitre of being "caudillos of the pen" who, like the gauchos they criticize, revel in "undiscipline, war, contradiction and adventure" (4:21). Theirs is a journalism that "incites the Argentine people against standing authority, making them believe that it is possible to terminate in one day that undefinable entity [caudillo authority], and arguing that with the mere elimination of this or that leader, it is possible to establish a representative republic from the day of his fall. It is the journalism of lies, of ignorance, of bad faith; the journalism of vandalism and mindlessness, no matter its colors or its appeals to civilization" (4:17–18).

Alberdi's insistence on a responsible press could be read as a call to censorship. Censorship, however, is not what Alberdi had in mind. Rather, he was attacking the journalism of Sarmiento and Mitre as an activity no less politically motivated than a civil war, a coup d'état, or a caudillo rebellion. It is a truism of our time that all writers bring to their writing inherited, often unconscious, political and cultural preconceptions. Freudian critics make careers of psychoanalyzing writers, readers, and reading communities, just as Marxist commentators invariably find political assumptions and class connections in seemingly apolitical texts. In the case of Sarmiento and Mitre, however, Alberdi didn't need Freudian or Marxist theory to identify them as politicians who also wrote. Both men had obvious political ambitions, and were up to their elbows in political intrigue. For both men, writing was a conscious strategy of self-promotion that included not only publishing articles and books but also founding and editing newspapers. Of Sarmiento's autobiographical *Recuerdos de provincia,* for example, Alberdi observes that "the biography about yourself is not only a work of vanity, but a means very common and well-known in politics to establish the candidacy of your name to occupy high office; although such ambition is legitimate, it nonetheless makes you a tireless agitator" (4:71). In some sense, then, Sarmiento's and Mitre's major accomplishment lay in effectively disguising their motives in texts that pretended to be historical, journalistic, objective, and disinterested. Alberdi at no point seeks to censor his

rivals; he merely wants to make known the political ambitions behind their journalism.

To further support his accusation of personalist writing, Alberdi
points out that *Campaña* is "a history without documentation" that
the reader is expected to believe merely on the basis of Sarmiento's testimony (4:41). This criticism holds true with most of
Sarmiento's "historical" works. To write *Facundo*, for example,
Sarmiento tired of waiting for documents he had requested from
friends living in Argentina, and wrote the whole thing on the basis
of personal observation, rumor, and prejudice. *Facundo* also includes frequent references to foreign thinkers, but such references usually smack of name-dropping; the important thing is not
that foreign writers contribute to Sarmiento's arguments, but that
the reader know that Sarmiento is a cultured man whose arguments should not be challenged.

Alberdi's well-honed darts in the *Cartas quillotanas* hit their
mark. Sarmiento responded in a series of open letters later gathered in a book titled *Las ciento y una*. The invective of these letters
is matched only by their intellectual vacuity. Furious beyond serious thought, Sarmiento can only call names—but this he does
extraordinarily well. The *Cartas quillotanas* in his repertoire of
epithets become "a pot of rotten stew . . . flavored with a dialectic
sauce of arsenic" (Sarmiento, *OC* 15:134). Alberdi is variously
called "a composer of minuets and a piano tuner, . . . a stupid fool
who can't even lie well, who doesn't suspect that he makes people
vomit (15:147), . . . [who] has the voice of a woman and the valor of
a rabbit" (15:181). There is little evidence that *Las ciento y una* was
widely read, a fact that probably contributed to the depression and
impotence Sarmiento felt after the whole affair was over. As he
wrote to Mitre in a letter dated October 19, 1853, "I live alone, like
a prisoner of Alberdi and his Club; I moan under their whip. They
are the powerful of the earth, they laugh in their orgies of cynicism
at my poor civic virtues" (*OC* 29:340).

After two abortive attempts to return to Argentina by getting
involved in the politics of his native San Juan, Sarmiento finally
responded to Mitre's invitation and took up residence in Buenos
Aires in late 1855. There, he renewed friendships with the porteño
leaders Valentín Alsina and Mitre. Within two weeks of his return he
was made a consultant to the provincial governor, Pastor Obligado,

and within the year, he was named head of education for the entire province. Two weeks later, Mitre, who had just been appointed minister of war, asked Sarmiento to edit his newspaper, *El Nacional*, the successor of *Los Debates*. Although Sarmiento still insisted he was a "provincial in Buenos Aires and a porteño in the provinces," by this time his sympathies clearly lay with Buenos Aires. Less clear are his reasons for not returning to Buenos Aires sooner; it has been suggested that, despite his hatred for Urquiza, Sarmiento at some level also questioned the legitimacy of the porteño government. In the meantime, Alberdi became an ambassador-at-large for the Urquiza government, visiting first the United States and later Europe. Because of events discussed in later chapters, Alberdi would not return to Argentina until 1878. Despite this mysterious, self-imposed exile, Argentina remained his passion, and he continued playing a major role in Argentine letters until his death.

Chapter Eight

Bartolomé Mitre and the
Gallery of Argentine Celebrities

The debate between Sarmiento and Alberdi would have amounted to little had it not touched on vital questions in Argentina's guiding fictions: Whose view of the past would become official? Whose history would appear in schoolbooks and popular journalism? Who would be iconized as national heroes? What tales of valor and sacrifice would be preserved and embellished to define the Argentine soul? What mention would be made of the gauchos and Argentine masses? What role in Argentine history would be assigned to the provinces and Buenos Aires? What would be said of the caudillos? Who, in short, would build the national pantheon?

The answer, as might be expected in this divided country, is that Argentine historians left competing pantheons, one liberal and porteño, the other nationalist and provincial. For most Argentines the liberal porteño histories are Official History, the version of the past that entered the schoolbooks. The chief creator of official history was Alberdi's and Urquiza's arch-rival: Bartolomé Mitre. A general, scholar, and politician, Mitre was an untiring defender of porteño privilege who approached the writing of history as one more battlefield where Buenos Aires could triumph.

Born in 1821, Mitre was some ten years younger than the Generation of '37, with which he is usually associated. Although he came to epitomize the porteño spirit, he spent much of his childhood in the remote area of southern Argentina known as the *Patago-*

nia. A bookish lad, he frustrated his father, who hoped he would become a wealthy estanciero, by whiling away the hours reading. Exiled to Uruguay with his family in 1838, Mitre showed aptitude for military leadership and fought unsuccessfully against Rosas under the Uruguayan leader Fructuoso Rivera in 1839. A year later, Rivera made the nineteen-year-old Mitre a captain; two years later, he became a major. It was at this time that Mitre published the first of his many books, a much praised manual on artillery use.

In the meantime, Mitre became involved in the Argentine exile community in Montevideo and wrote for Unitarian newspapers. Showing the same self-righteous overbearance that got so many Unitarians into trouble, Mitre eventually ran afoul of Rivera's government and was, in April 1846, forced to leave Uruguay. First in Bolivia and later in Peru, he again provoked official wrath by criticizing his host governments (Jeffrey, *Mitre and Argentina* 50–54). In mid-1849, he traveled to Chile, where he got a job working for Alberdi's anti-Rosista newspaper *El Comercio de Valparaíso.* Alberdi wrote that he hoped this professional contact "would strengthen the friendship born of our sympathy and identity with [the same] causes and ideas" (cited in Mayer, *Alberdi y su tiempo* 353). Later, however, when Alberdi decided to sell the paper, Mitre found a Chilean benefactor and became its new editor, a move Alberdi apparently resented (Jeffrey 57). With the newspaper as his mouthpiece, Mitre criticized Chile for its poor highways, insufficient schools, and corrupt elections, none of which endeared him to his Chilean hosts. As in Uruguay, Peru, and Bolivia, Mitre's criticisms, although often justified, showed little sensitivity to local susceptibilities and even less awareness of his own vulnerability as an exile. More than once his hosts pointed out that if life was so bad in Chile, Mitre could always go back to Argentina, hardly a model state what with Rosas at the helm. After Urquiza's rebellion, Mitre did in fact return to Argentina, where he led a small contingent of men in the campaign against Rosas. Like Sarmiento, however, he resented Urquiza's not giving him a more central role in the campaign.

After Urquiza's triumph and the establishment of the Confederation government in Paraná, Mitre's role in the secessionist porteño government between 1852 and 1861 proved crucial. The Province of Buenos Aires was split between two opposing ideas. Die-hard autonomists like Adolfo Alsina and his followers suggested permanent separation from the rest of the country. In contrast, the former Rosista warrior and devout Federalist, Hilario Lagos, led a pro-Urquiza rebellion in late 1852 that besieged Buenos Aires for some seven months. Lagos sought Urquiza's support, but Urquiza, still hoping for a negotiated agreement with Buenos Aires, refused to help him (Scobie, *La lucha* 79–86). Mitre, however, refused to recognize Urquiza's good intentions. As he told the provincial legislature, "Even if Urquiza never steps out of line, he will always be a despot" (cited in Scobie 44).

Mitre did not, however, spend all his time attacking Urquiza. Despite constant military and political activity, he somehow found time to expand his collection of historical documents, do research, and begin the biographies of Argentine heroes which constitute his most lasting contribution to the Patria. Mitre's passion for history early manifested itself in a newspaper article published in Montevideo on January 14, 1843, commemorating Joaquín Felipe de Vedia y Pérez, the grandfather of Mitre's father-in-law and a sometime military hero (Mitre, *Obras completas* 12:365–373). Mitre's private papers also contain notes he prepared in March 1841 on events and documents concerning Dorrego, perhaps preliminary work on a biography he never wrote (*OC* 12:340–352). Mitre's devotion to biography was further revealed two years later in an article on the most vociferous of Rosas's critics, José Rivera Indarte. This work, like many of Mitre's histories, went through several revisions, each longer than its predecessors. The first version appeared in the Montevideo newspaper *El Nacional, diario político, literario y comercial* (12 Sept. 1845, 1–4). A pamphlet containing the same article, now enlarged, was published by *El Mercurio* in the same year in Valparaíso, Chile. The third edition appeared, yet again enlarged, as a pamphlet in Buenos Aires in 1853 from which the version in the *Obras completas* is taken (*OC* 11:375–445).

Mitre launched his most ambitious history-writing projects between 1853 and 1859, some of which he would not publish in definitive form until the 1880s. The most significant of these was a lengthy entry on Manuel Belgrano in a single-volume collection of biographies titled *Galería de celebridades argentinas* (Gallery of Argentine celebrities), published in 1857. The *Historia de Belgrano* would later grow to a multivolume work that still stands as one of Argentine historiography's greatest achievements.

The book containing this first version of *Historia de Belgrano* was itself a singular event in Argentine history. Edited by Mitre with help from Sarmiento, the *Galería de celebridades argentinas* is a collection of biographies, sumptuously bound and clearly intended for a wide audience. Not surprisingly, the selection of men accorded official status in *Galería* all served the porteño cause and none was a caudillo. Some also collaborated with Rosas, but the details of that collaboration are carefully omitted. The selection also reflects a concern for finding exemplary men in different vocations; to wit, three generals, San Martín, Manuel Belgrano, and Juan Lavalle; a navy man, Guillermo Brown; a liberal priest, Gregorio Funes; two politicians, Bernardino Rivadavia and his minister, José Manuel García; a writer, Florencio Varela; and a political philosopher, Mariano Moreno.[1] In the introduction Mitre gives a quick nod toward men of other political persuasions by lamenting that three nonliberals, Dorrego, Saavedra, and Güemes, a caudillo who coincidentally was an independence hero too great to be ignored, could not be included. About the other caudillos, Mitre is more forthcoming:

But we have celebrities of another kind, who, unlike those mentioned earlier, are undeserving of a grateful posterity's blessing, and will appear to their eyes with all the sinister glory of that proud Miltonian figure who with his fall tried to drag down all the stars of the firmament with him. These men, truly distinguished in a negative sense, exercised tremendous influence over the destiny of the peoples of the River Plate. Their lives are devoid of transcendent incidents; they are the representatives of the domineering forces of barbarism, and their actions carry the seal of a primitive energy. These men can serve as a lesson for future Argentines. . . . Behold in them another series of historical portraits, terrible and threatening portraits which inspire horror, but can enhance by contrast the beautiful

1. The biography on Mariano Moreno is actually a reprint of brother Manuel's 1812 biography, which was discussed in chapter 2. At the time *Galería* was published, Manuel was near death, having only recently returned from London, where he served many years as Rosas's representative. There is then a certain irony in the inclusion of Manuel's work in *Galería:* although he was a devout Federalist and faithful Rosista, his major written work was first published in Argentina in the *Galería*, a collection of biographies specifically designed to justify Manuel's political enemies.

countenances of those who are become celebrated through their service, virtue and intellectual endeavor. (*Galería* iii)

Yet even by excluding the caudillos, the writers of the *Galería* would encounter problems. How, for example, would these propagandist-historians finesse issues like García's and Brown's association with Rosas? How would they defend democracy while condemning the caudillos' popularity? How would they account for the lack of popular appeal of their Unitarian heroes? And how would they explain away Dorrego's murder at the hands of Unitarian hero Lavalle, an act constituting the Unitarian original sin from which perhaps not even Rivadavia was unblemished?

Mitre addresses these questions by setting the premises of what would become officialist historiography. The first of these premises is a virtual refusal to see Argentina as anything other than the dreamchild of several great men, all porteños by either birth or inclination. Argentina in Mitre's view did not exist before Mayo willed it into existence, since men living in colonial Argentina "are not counted among the children of our soil" (*Galería* i). In his pamphlet on José Rivera Indarte, Mitre argues that the first great man to will Argentina's existence was Mariano Moreno, whom he calls

the Michelangelo of the May revolution, who seized . . . a magnificent block of marble and gave it form and life. Then, before the astonished eyes of the people, he unveiled a statue in which all saw concretized their aspirations for independence and liberty. Firm in his intention and strong in his means, with the work of a few months he destroyed through thought and action the ancient colonial edifice, and laid the foundations of a new society to which he bequeathed its own institutions and essentially democratic ideas. . . . Examples like [Moreno's] are not common in our history, but they have repeated themselves more than once, and they alone have impregnated with their perfume the entire road that we have travelled, and much of the road we have yet to go. The ideas Moreno sowed with the help of an enlightened minority have been subsequently cultivated by the community, struggling always against the torrent of barbarism. When everyone believed Moreno's ideas had been crushed under the horse hooves of those pampa Attillas [the caudillos], men like Rivadavia have appeared, revivifying [those ideas] with the fecund breath of civilization. (*OC* 12:380–381)

This remarkable reduction of Mayo to the work and inspiration of one man is later contradicted by Mitre himself. In the "Biografía de Manuel Belgrano" that first appeared in the *Galería* and later grew to several volumes, Mitre's own evidence shows that Mayo emerged from a complex configuration of personal alliances and rivalries, economic circumstance, and sociopolitical movements that defy easy understanding. Although too good a historian to overlook such factors entirely, Mitre nonetheless prefers to explain the past using "great-man" and "enlightened minority" theories. Writing of Manuel Belgrano, he declares that "the day a few Argentines discovered [their rights as free men], the revolution began. For this reason, the revolution was directed by an enlightened minority. . . . Although events like the French invasion of Spain contributed to their success, such events in reality only accelerated their enlightenment, giving the people's leaders . . . a full awareness of their power" (OC 11:74)[2] To bolster this view, Mitre often alludes to the reductionist distortion popularized by Sarmiento that Argentine politics was nothing more than an epic struggle between Civilization and Barbarism, with Moreno, Rivadavia, and the porteño "enlightened minority" on the one hand and the "pampa Attillas" on the other. Rivadavia and the enlightened minority, including Mitre himself, were not nearly so virtuous as this argument pretends, nor were the caudillos always so barbaric—facts Mitre surely knew. How then can Mitre, who was clearly no fool, so facilely reduce Mayo and the guardians of civilization in South America to not only a single movement but a single movement of a few enlightened men inspired by one individual?

There are several answers to this question. The most repeated and most ingenuous holds that Mitre was merely following the "great-man" historical conventions of his time. Be that as it may, Mitre himself provides a better explanation. In the introduction to the *Galería de celebridades*, he writes, "Argentine history has been rich in noteworthy men. . . . The glory of those men is the Argentine people's richest heritage; rescuing their lives and qualities from obscurity is to gather and use that heritage, for our honor and our

2. The *Obras completas* provides the complete text of several versions of what would become the *Historia de Belgrano*. I quote from the *Obras completas* because of its greater accessibility. According to the editors, the version I quote is identical to the "Biografía de Belgrano" that appeared in *Galería* (see editor's foreword, *OC* 11:13–14).

improvement. In their lives the present generation will find models
worthy of imitation. In the memorable events that those lives call to
recollection, the future historian will find themes worthy of austere
meditation" (*Galería* i–ii). Mitre, then, views history as an exemplary tale, a means for shaping the future. He consciously uses the
past to create a national mythology, a guiding fiction, whose primary
function is to justify the Argentina he envisions.

But Mitre is not only thinking of the future. Present concerns
like his own ambitions, his enmity for Urquiza and the Paraná
government, and his support for porteño hegemony form the necessary subtext for explaining his choice of material and its presentation in all his early writings. In short, his work as a historian reflects
the same concerns that prompted his political and military activity:
all were means by which he sought to legitimize both his aspirations as a national leader and Buenos Aires' grip on the country. In
describing Moreno, Belgrano, and San Martín as the basic forces in
Argentine history, Mitre justifies himself and his ambitions as a
thinker-writer-politician-soldier who aspired in his generation to
the role he projected on these carefully chosen predecessors. This
is exactly the conclusion that Juan Bautista Alberdi drew after reading the *Historia de Belgrano*. Writing from Paris, Alberdi holds
that Mitre seeks to recast Argentine history in the mold of a single
military leader, "to make an idol of military glory, which is the
plague of our [South American] republics." Alberdi further contends that "this intentional historical error, committed with the
cold, calculated selfishness of ambition" is merely another example
of Mitre's attempts to bring glory to himself as the current "great
man" of the porteño "enlightened minority" (*Grandes y pequeños
hombres del Plata* 66).

Further evidence of the role to which Mitre aspired can be found
in his odd interpretation of the short-term failures of the Mayo
revolution. As he tells the story in the "Biografía de Belgrano" in
Galería, the squabbling among different factions of Mayo was
"what always happens when there is no unity of thought, or when a
powerful personality fails to subordinate all wills to his own" (*OC*
11:89). Since political failure in Mitre's view is a failure of personality, Mitre describes Liniers, a popular independence hero and
Saavedra ally who was executed on trumped-up charges by extreme elements in the Mayo revolution, as a man "whose indecisive

character, weak albeit ardent, accepted popularity without imposing on the events the leadership of a powerful will" (*OC* 11:77). And
what does this say about Mitre and the heroic role he sought for
himself in Argentine history? Did he also seek to "impose on the
events the leadership of a powerful will" or to be "a powerful personality" who could "subordinate all wills to his own"? These statements alone should give pause regarding the role Mitre sought for
himself in Argentine politics.

Just as Mitre's praise of a single great man justifies another great
man (Mitre himself), Mitre's exaltation of an "enlightened minority"
as the force behind Mayo justifies another enlightened minority,
namely, Mitre and his porteño supporters. Similarly, his attack on
past caudillos is a veiled assault on Urquiza, whose honest attempts
at constitutional rule—with the support of every province except
Buenos Aires—Mitre had to discredit if the porteños were to maintain any sense of legitimacy. Since fact was not on his side, Mitre
resorted to condemnation by stereotype: all caudillos were barbarians; Urquiza was a caudillo like any other; therefore, Urquiza's government in Paraná represented the forces of barbarism and the
Mitrista porteños were the legitimate heirs of Moreno and Mayo,
"the enlightened minority" annointed to save the country.

The obvious elitism of such a position was politically dangerous,
however, particularly since the porteño Unitarians had long been
perceived as exclusivist and disdainful of the masses. Mitre's desire
to place an "enlightened minority" at the center of Mayo set him at
odds with another guiding fiction he wished to promote, namely,
that Mayo (and by implication the Mitrista porteños) reflected the
popular will. To reconcile these two views, Mitre seeks to endow
the porteño leaders he admires with a mystical ability to perceive
the inchoate will of the people. In the "Biografía del General
Belgrano" he writes:

Like all great revolutions, which recognize no authors, despite being
daughters of a deliberate purpose, the Argentine revolution, far from
being the result of personal inspiration, the influence of a special group or
of a surprising moment, was the spontaneous product of fecund germs
cultivated over a long period of time, and the inevitable consequence of
the energy of things in general. An active, intelligent and far-sighted
minority directed with an invisible hand the decided march of an entire
people towards unknown destinies. It was the minority which first had a

clear idea of the changes in preparation, which impressed on [the revolution] a definite direction, and gave it an organized pattern the day the revolution manifested itself in all its splendor. But not for an instant did that minority cease to represent the needs and collective aspirations of the majority, which in turn communicated to [the minority] its energy and inoculated [the minority] with its virile spirit. (*OC* 11:102–103)

Contradiction abounds in this statement. How is it that revolutions are daughters of a deliberate purpose while recognizing no authors? How does an "intelligent and far-sighted minority" direct a movement that is "the inevitable consequence of the energy of things in general"? Is Mitre suggesting, in sharp contradiction to the great-man theories he usually espouses, a Hegelian or Darwinian historicism in which humans merely serve the unperceived movement of history? Or, does his purpose, like his attacks on the caudillos, have more to do with his political ambitions than with history?

The political explanation is the more convincing: by arguing that enlightened minorities can reflect the unstated will of the people, Mitre defends his own enlightened minority against the accusations of elitism that had always plagued porteño liberals. To explain how an enlightened minority is also democratic, Mitre resorts to two much used, little studied epistemologies: truth by affirmation and truth by definition. What he cannot prove, he affirms; what he cannot demonstrate, he defines.

According to Mitre, during the conflictive days leading up to the revolutionary statement of May 25, 1810, "a new actor in the revolutionary drama was to present itself on the public stage: the people, the people of the public square who do not discuss, but always march in closed column supporting the great movements that decide their destiny" (*OC* 11:115). That is, although the historical record shows that Mitre's heroes, the Morenistas, openly opposed Saavedra's attempts to democratize the Primera Junta, Mitre by affirmation assures us that "the people" were major players in the revolutionary process. And how does he define "the people"? They are not just anyone, as it turns out. "[The people] calmly awaited the result of the deliberations among its legitimate representatives, and, mixed in with the crowded masses of native battalions, awaited the signal from their leaders to intervene with arms if necessary" (*OC* 11:115). This revealing sentence distinguishes "the people" from the "native battalions" and would thereby suggest that the people who concern Mitre are "the decent people" rather than the masses in general. This distinction becomes clearer in a later passage where he affirms that "from among that multitude alive with indignation . . . emerged a new entity, active, intelligent, audacious, which like the guerrilla fighters who clear the way for armies, was the precursor of the people soon to mobilize en masse" (*OC* 11:120). In this fashion, no sooner does Mitre affirm that the people participated fully in the revolutionary process than he again defines "the people" as an "intelligent minority" who reflected the same antipopular, pro-porteño biases of Mitre himself. To defend such positions in democratic terms, Mitre postulates a mystical bond between some of the revolution's leaders and the people, thus explaining that although the people were never consulted in any visible fashion, their will was somehow manifested in the actions of the intelligent minority. Curiously, this is exactly the same argument Sarmiento used in explaining the authority of the caudillos. Moreover, such an argument places Mitre squarely back in the position he was trying to avoid: no matter how he tries to make "the people" central participants in the revolutions, he always returns to theories of great men and intelligent minorities—and by extension to veiled defenses of himself and his porteño supporters in their fight against Urquiza's perfectly legitimate national government. In short, Mitre includes the masses only by claiming that "the people" (the decent people) reflected the mass will. That the masses also liked Rosas, were suspicious of Buenos Aires liberals, and supported several generations of caudillos are points he sidesteps altogether.

The other biographies in *Galería* are a mixed bag of varying quality, selected for reasons now unclear. Nonetheless, evident throughout is an editorial policy protecting Unitarian heroes and obscuring Federalist and Rosista connections. For example, the "Biografía de Mariano Moreno," written and published by his brother Manuel in 1812, is reproduced—but with no indication that Manuel was a faithful Federalist who had represented Rosas in England for some twenty years. Similarly, a perfunctory article on

Admiral Guillermo Brown includes no mention that Brown was also a Rosas supporter. This editorial policy of protecting Unitarian reputations is particularly evident in the treatment given Rivadavia and Lavalle.

One example of the effort to protect Rivadavia's reputation lies in the short biography on Manuel José García. Written anonymously by "A Friend of the Patria," the article appears to be the work of García's son, who is identified at the beginning only as a provider of documents, a role described as "a small token and slight tribute to filial love and respect" (*Galería* 146). García was, of course, a problematic figure. As the unlucky emissary of both Rivadavia and Dorrego in the late 1820s to the negotiations with Brazil and Great Britain that eventually made Uruguay independent, he was accused by both Unitarians and Rosistas of overstepping his authority and thereby losing Uruguay. As a work of vindication, the biography predictably defends García's role in attaining "an honorable and entirely satisfactory peace which was celebrated in 1828" (157). In point of fact, the two treaties (the first was rejected) satisfied almost no one, and were a major reason behind Rivadavia's fall and Dorrego's assassination. To make his defense credible, the anonymous biographer had to show that the unfortunate diplomat was merely following orders— and that presented the problem of how to implicate Rivadavia without mentioning Rivadavia. This the author does through five pages of euphemisms that allude obscurely to "the president," "the new president," and "the executive" without once identifying Rivadavia by name (152–157). It was almost as though the name "Rivadavia" was more sacrosanct than the man himself, that criticism was permissible by euphemism only.

The "Biografía de Bernardino Rivadavia" shows a similar concern for avoiding unpleasant details. The inclusion of the article itself amounted to something of a diplomatic gesture from Mitre since the article's author, Juan María Gutiérrez, was at the time serving as one of Urquiza's ministers. Regardless of political differences between Mitre and Gutiérrez, however, Gutiérrez fully accepted the need to create unassailable icons. Consequently, he duly praises Rivadavia's administrative vision and cultural institutions, but describes in only the most cryptic terms the controversies that forced Rivadavia to resign. Rivadavia's administrative failures are described in the following terms: "In spite of the docile willingness of the people to obey a good government, there existed a secret force which misdirected and impeded [the people's] action; it was a force formed principally by envious aspirations linked to rancid habits and concerns that a press without social doctrine had incited rather than corrected" (*Galería* 29). Exactly what this says is unclear. It would appear that Gutiérrez is somehow blaming the Rivadavians' legendary unpopularity on an unnamed force that perverted the press and beguiled the masses. Why is Gutiérrez so coy about attacking Rivadavia's enemies and discussing Rivadavia's errors and vulnerabilities? Fear of offending former Rosistas now under Urquiza's banner? Fear of discrediting Rivadavia by presenting arguments against him? Fear that any real discussion of Rivadavia's strengths and weaknesses would compromise his usefulness as a guiding fiction for future Argentines? Whatever the reason, Gutiérrez's Rivadavia is a half-figure, an icon for official history with little connection to the wily Unitarian who dominated Argentine politics between 1821 and 1827.

The respect given Rivadavia is nothing, however, compared to the propaganda blitz the *Galería* editors staged to protect Lavalle. Lavalle is a complex figure. A committed though unpredictable patriot, he fought fearlessly in the Wars of Independence, earning the respect of San Martín and Simón Bolívar, who once observed that "Commander Lavalle is a lion to be kept in a cage and loosed only on the day of battle" (cited in *Galería* 209). Born to an aristocratic porteño family in 1797, he was only a teenager when he began fighting the Spanish under San Martín and still in his twenties when hostilities between Spain and Argentina ceased. The real tragedy of Lavalle's life was that the Wars of Independence ended too soon, leaving him with the vocation of a warrior and no place to fight. He fought for the Unitarian government against Brazil, but was unable to accept the peace treaty that gave Uruguay independence. Feeling betrayed, Lavalle launched a successful coup against Manuel Dorrego's legitimate government—setting a pattern of military intervention in civilian government that still survives. To make matters worse, he executed Dorrego in late 1828, undoubtedly supported by Unitarians who feared the popular Dorrego might stage a countercoup. If these acts were not enough to compromise his reputation forever, his short foray into politics after Dorrego's death proved so disastrous that most porteños viewed with relief Rosas's advent to power. Under pressure from Rosas, Lavalle fled to Uruguay in 1829, and lived unhappily in exile until 1839, when he was convinced by other Unitarian exiles to lead a force against Rosas. This endeavor met with two years of disasters, culminating in Lavalle's death in September 1841. One of the most grisly stories in Argentine history tells how Lavalle loyalists carried the general's rotting remains in desert heat from Jujuy to Bolivia, some 250 miles, to prevent enemies from desecrating his body. A life marked by such heroism, adventure, bravura, violence, and error deserves a balanced, even sympathetic representation.

That is not, however, what the unnamed *Galería* authors of "Biografía de D. Juan Lavalle" give him. Rather, their approach is to defend Lavalle at all costs, crushing dissent with a rhetorical excess not seen since Sarmiento's *Las ciento y una.* The "Biografía de D. Juan Lavalle" may be the most representative biography in the collection since it appears to be the result of a genuine team effort of several authors, one of whom sounds a great deal like Sarmiento, not only in style but also in his propensity to cite Sarmiento. Since Lavalle was controversial even among devoted Unitarians, his biography also provides a good indication of just how far the pantheon-builders would go to support "official history."

The introduction to Lavalle's biography sets the panegyric tone of the entire piece while firmly linking it to the "truth by affirmation" epistemologies observed earlier in Mitre's "Historia de Belgrano." "General D. Juan Lavalle," we are told, "at last takes his seat at the left hand of General San Martín." This odd opener begs the question of who was to sit at the right hand of San Martín: the deceased Belgrano, perhaps, or was it reserved for some younger Argentine, maybe Mitre or Sarmiento? "Lavalle," the biographer continues, "belonged to those immortal legions destined by Providence to effect the regeneration of the world. . . . Endowed with superhuman valor and superior intelligence . . . this servant of progress will always be found struggling for the freedom of the Patria. . . . From 1828 to 1841, when he breathed his last breath, he never ceased even one day his armed protest against the bloody existence of the Hangman of the River Plate [Rosas]" (*Galería* 203–204).

Lest the reader think a being so praised needs no further defense, the biographers quickly address the central problems of Lavalle's life: his coup against Dorrego's elected government, his execution of the deposed governor, and his miserable performance as president. In handling these problems the Lavalle biography gives us as good an example of popularized, official history as we are likely to find. To defend Lavalle's illegitimate actions, the biographers must first argue that Dorrego and Federalism were so awful that they got exactly what they deserved, that Lavalle's actions were entirely warranted. This imperative leads to the following description of Buenos Aires politics toward the end of the Rivadavian years: "The situation was particularly difficult since some of the interior provinces tyrannized by Ibarra, Bustos, López and Quiroga [all provincial caudillos] refused to recognize the authority of the General Government" (226). Two problems undermine this statement: first, the provincial populations mostly supported the caudillos and profoundly distrusted Buenos Aires; nothing suggests that the provinces, even without the caudillos, would have recognized the Rivadavia government. Second, the provinces had never accepted Buenos Aires as "the General Government" and were even less disposed to do so after Rivadavia sought to impose his constitution. In short, the question at hand was not obedience but the legitimacy of Rivadavia's attempts to control the provinces. The biographers go on to lament that "in the very heart of Congress a systematic and violent opposition, headed by Colonel Dorrego, resorted to every imaginable means in order to force Bernardino Rivadavia from the presidential chair" (226). Again, the record indicates otherwise. Right or wrong, the Federalist opposition in Congress was outraged over Rivadavia's highhanded attempts to federalize the port city without Congressional approval, and expressed their dissent in their rightful function as elected officials. Moreover, there is no reason to suppose the Federalists were more underhanded than their Unitarian opponents. In short, Rivadavia's resignation resulted from political insensitivity and mismanagement rather than from the pressures of a "violent opposition."

The attacks on Dorrego get worse. Lavalle's return to Buenos Aires after the peace treaty of 1828 is described in the following terms:

On returning, he found the capital in great turmoil. The President of the Republic, too incapacitated to wage the war successfully, because of the hostility he suffered at the hands of his opponents, headed by Colonel

Dorrego, in close alliance with the interior caudillos, had sent a representative to Río de Janeiro [Manuel José García] to negotiate peace based on the independence of [Uruguay], and the envoy, overstepping the precise instructions he carried with him had signed an ignominious treaty. (231)

Again, this disjointed paragraph is more interpretive than factual. First, the writer considers Dorrego's good relations with the caudillos to be a betrayal of some sort rather than a step toward consolidation—the kind of thing Alberdi advocated in the *Cartas quillotanas.* Second, the biographers remove all blame for the first treaty from Rivadavia. In reality, little is known about how much García overstepped his instructions, partly because Rivadavia kept telling different people different things—as is amply demonstrated in H. S. Fern's account of the negotiations (Fern 179–187). It is clear, however, that no sooner did Rivadavia realize that García's handiwork was wildly unpopular than he denounced the treaty and tried to scapegoat his minister—the very thing García's son avoids saying about Rivadavia in the García biography discussed earlier. Lavalle's biographers also fail to mention that the successful treaty of 1828 that made Uruguay an independent state rather than a Brazilian or Argentine province was also negotiated by the same García, this time under Dorrego. Despite such finagling of evidence, the biographers accomplish their goals of defending Rivadavia while suggesting that Lavalle's violent response against Dorrego was somehow justified.

Nor is Dorrego allowed any merit points for his considerable popularity. "Colonel Dorrego," we are told, "rose to power pushed by the robust arm of the mob. . . . He concentrated on strengthening his power by establishing relations with the provincial caudillos and exciting more and more the savage spirit of the plebe" (229–230). What this alludes to is Dorrego's successful provincial elections by which he became governor of the Province of Buenos Aires, and his attempts to build bridges toward the provincial caudillos. The elections themselves had entailed some risk. Originally appointed by congress, Dorrego could easily have remained in power without seeking a popular mandate. Yet he felt sure enough of his popularity to schedule provincial elections, which he won handily. For Lavalle's biographers, however, winning the popular vote merely meant alliance with the mob—an epithet that recalls the ethnic and class biases found in earlier writings of the Generation of '37.[3]

Having thus set the stage for rationalizing the coup against Dorrego, Lavalle's biographers get down to the real business of the coup itself. Their first task is to show that Lavalle's takeover did not violate democratic principles since it enjoyed the support of "the people." Not surprisingly, "the people" turn out to be not just everyone but "the most select (*lo más selecto*) of Buenos Aires [who] gathered in popular assembly in the Church of San Roque, and, in a statement signed by more than 2,000 citizens, named General Lavalle Provisional Governor of the Province, charging him with the mission of annulling the power of Rosas and Dorrego. . . . [This] movement of December was nothing but the logical result of the accumulated outrages committed by Colonel Dorrego, . . . [who] because of his support from the caudillos and the brutish masses (*la masa bruta*) could be overthrown only by dint of armed civilization (*la civilización armada*)." We are told, moreover, that Dorrego's association with the caudillos was condemnation enough since these provincial leaders "were nothing other than the living representatives of barbarism . . . elevated to power by the material force of the savage masses" (*Galería* 233). But particularly chilling is the conclusion that armed overthrow of elected governments is permissible, even desirable, if done in the name of "armed civilization"—an argument used to justify virtually every coup in Argentine history.

Having thus declared that Dorrego deserved everything he got, and that the perpetrators of the coup merely sought to protect · civilization from "the brutish masses," the unnamed writers address the thorniest issue of all: Dorrego's murder. Beginning on a cautious note, they state that

The execution of the unfortunate Colonel Dorrego has been considered an errror by the best in the nation—an error that no one more than General Lavalle lamented later with all the effusion of his elevated soul. . . . Nonetheless, in our capacity as biographers, we believe it our duty to

3. Dorrego's enemies, particularly the Unitarian losers, immediately claimed that the election results were fraudulent (Mayer, *Alberdi y su tiempo* 62). Tomás de Iriarte, a generally reliable contemporary observer who criticizes Dorrego on other counts, makes no mention of fraud in his election to the governorship (Iriarte 4:80–90). But particularly significant, Mitre, in his 1841 notes on Dorrego, also takes the election results at face value (Mitre, *OC* 12:331–352).

bequeath posterity everything leading up to this fatal deed so that they [posterity] can judge and decide through a knowledge of the causes. (234)

This declared impartiality and devotion to evidence, however, quickly vanish in a cloud of apologetic rhetoric more in keeping with the rest of the biography:

Leaving aside the fact that [Dorrego] was the exclusive disruptor of the entire republic, that because of him the country was caught in a national war, that [the country] had been forced to relinquish its glory by signing a less than advantageous peace in spite of four victories [on the battlefield], that in order to reach and maintain himself in power he had humiliated the people of his birth [the upper classes] placing them under the tutelage of the chieftans from the interior, . . . the considerations that no doubt most charged the General's will in taking his mistaken resolution was the fact that Colonel Dorrego had been the first in our civil struggles to seek support from the savage tribes of the desert to fight against the Christians. (234)

The authors themselves undermine much of the foregoing. For example, their carping at the caudillos, the "brutish masses," and the Federalists contradicts their contention that Dorrego "was the exclusive disruptor of the entire republic." Moreover, the "less than advantageous peace" that granted Uruguay its independence was generally viewed as the only way to end hostilities with Brazil—and certainly better for Argentina than the terms García accepted originally under Rivadavia. Further, Dorrego's friendly contacts with the caudillos hardly came to a "tutelage," and the notion that Dorrego was stirring up the Indians to fight against "Christians" is the reddest of herrings. The biography continues:

And since Colonel Dorrego was the natural leader of the Federalist party, that is to say, the caudillo of the unbridled (*desenfrenada*) masses who from one end of the Republic to the other caused people to tremble because of their savage tumult, [Lavalle] decided that by making [Dorrego] disappear (*haciéndolo desaparecer*) he would subjugate [the unbridled masses] through one tremendous example. . . . Blinded by the smoke of fratricidal combat, with his heart lacerated by the misfortunes of his country, . . . undoubtedly hopeful that all this would end with the disappearance of Colonel Dorrego . . . he forgot that the only blood that nourishes the tree of liberty is that shed in battle. (234–235)

The biographers then insert a lengthy quotation from Sarmiento ("*El Señor Sarmiento dice así*"), which includes the following:

Lavalle did nothing more than register his confessed and proclaimed vote as a citizen. . . . By shooting Dorrego, as he intended to shoot Bustos, López, Facundo, and the other caudillos, Lavalle responded to the demands of his age and of his party. . . . What Lavalle did was cut with his sword the Gordian knot in which all Argentine sociability had become entangled; through a blood-letting, he sought to avoid a slow-growing cancer. (235)

Chilling enough in its own context, this defense of Lavalle's actions is doubly so in that it anticipates point by point arguments used in every military coup against established Argentine governments: a corrupt leader whose popularity has somehow made inoperable the checks and balances of institutional government, ignorant masses whose will must be ignored for their own good, a patriotic military man seeking to return the country to normalcy, and finally an appeal to violence, or "armed civilization," as the only solution for a situation so out of control that only extraordinary measures can work. Moreover, in the suggestion that problems can be solved through eliminating the right people, Lavalle's biographers align themselves not only with Mariano Moreno's "Revolutionary Plan" of a half-century earlier but also with the bloodiest military government in Argentine history, the junta that ruled from 1976 to 1983. Indeed, Lavalle's biographers, perhaps for the first time in Argentine history, twice describe Lavalle's murderous act with the euphemism "to make disappear," now notorious thanks to the over 10,000 Argentines "made to disappear" (*los desaparecidos*) during the infamous "dirty war" waged by the recent military government against its own people. The defense of Lavalle also underlines an unpleasant fact of Argentine history: frequently the people most vocal in supporting an institutional government are the first to support a coup when their group is out of power. Also significant is the authors' image of a cancer that needs to be cut out. Behind every coup, behind every radical economic experiment, behind every wrenching change of government lurk images of the all-knowing doctor who must perform radical surgery that, however painful, is necessary for the country's survival. The repeated use of these images in Argentine political discourse would indicate a peculiar predisposition to accept extreme solutions as necessary, even natural.

Lavalle's execution of Dorrego is covered in the same gingerly fashion in the "Biografía de Manuel José García": "The army withdrew [from Uruguay] towards the end of the year, rebelling against the authorities and executing Governor Dorrego, and civil war was engendered (*se engendró*) between Buenos Aires and the provinces" (*Galería* 157). That Lavalle initiated the whole affair in anger over the treaty is not mentioned at all; nor is there any suggestion that Unitarians, anxious to be rid of the popular Dorrego, were sympathetic with, if not actively involved in, virtually everything Lavalle did. Indeed, the convenient use of the pseudopassive, impersonal *se* in the final clause neatly deflects responsibility from anyone in particular, almost suggesting that the entire matter was somehow spontaneous and unauthored.

The "official history" of Lavalle and the Dorrego tragedy found in *Galería* is particularly interesting when compared with notes Mitre wrote on Dorrego in 1841, fifteen years earlier. Written before the exigencies of justifying an "enlightened minority" in Buenos Aires so colored his thinking, Mitre's notes present a quite different picture of the Dorrego affair. Rather than a "systematic and violent opposition in the very heart of Congress," Dorrego, in Mitre's earlier version, is "an alert, penetrating, active, elevated and sublime spirit" who contrasted Rivadavia's dreamworld with "the wounds, desires and needs of the nation" (Mitre, *OC* 12:342). In the earlier version, Dorrego is a pragmatist, constantly questioning the feasibility of Rivadavia's grand projects, asking uncomfortable questions about real costs and benefits. Moreover, Mitre recognizes in his 1841 notes that Dorrego's rise to power after Rivadavia's unlucky association with the first García treaty with Brazil was entirely understandable: "An insulting treaty, stipulated by our envoy to Río de Janeiro, an affront to our dignity and rights, divorced the Government from the people; with that treaty the faction [the Rivadavian government] fell that had until then controlled the reins of State" (*OC* 12:348). Again, this is a quite different story from the *Galería* version where "Colonel Dorrego resorted to every imaginable means in order to force Bernardino Rivadavia from the presidential chair." The early Mitre even has nice words for Dorrego's government: "Dorrego's rule is not marked by grand improvements, but it was prudent and

generous. Freedom of the press was respected, no one was persecuted or proscribed because of prior opinions, Dorrego extended
the southern borders; the Republic was organized *de facto* under a
conventional federalist formula and the Provinces gave Dorrego control over [foreign relations]." Mitre also speaks kindly of Dorrego's
treaty with Brazil, which he considers "without doubt the most
memorable moment of his government" (*OC* 12:349). Even more
striking is Mitre's condemnation of Lavalle's coup against Dorrego:
"General Lavalle, taking counsel only from his own impetuosity and
considering Dorrego the promoter of anarchy instead of the first
magistrate of the republic, decided by his order to send him to the
firing wall, casting in this fashion an indelible stain on the pages of
[Lavalle's] life" (*OC* 12:351)."[4]

What had changed between 1841, the date of the notes Mitre
wrote on Dorrego's life, and 1857, the date Mitre's group published *Galería*, to explain such radically different approaches to
Lavalle's life? The only real difference was Mitre's political situation. The notes were written in Uruguay before Mitre's political
ambitions became defined; in 1841 from the vantage point of exile
it was possible to view Dorrego with relative impartiality. Mitre
and the authors of *Galería*, however, needed to justify themselves
as the "enlightened minority" resisting barbarism which by this
time had been defined as all Federalism in general and the Federalist government of Urquiza in particular. And just as "armed civilization" incarnate in Lavalle had struggled against the "barbarism" of
Dorrego, armed civilization incarnate in the porteño Mitristas
must again prepare to subjugate the "barbarism" of the Urquicistas.
Against the different political backdrops of 1841 and 1857, each
version of the Dorrego story makes sense.

Although *Galería* may be the clearest example of the assumptions underlying Mitre's historiography, as history it is a minor
work, particularly when compared to the two monumental biogra-

4. Also included in Mitre's papers were notes he titled "Consejos y apuntes
para escribir la biografía del General Lavalle" (Recommendations and notes for
writing the biography of General Lavalle), dated August 30, 1857, slightly before
the publication of *Galería*. Devoted mostly to Lavalle's military experiences during the Wars of Independence, these notes say next to nothing about the coup and
Dorrego's execution. (See Mitre, *OC* 12:353–364.)

phies Mitre finished in the 1880s. The first of these biographies was a two-volume study titled *Historia de Belgrano y de la independencia argentina*, published in 1859, a much expanded version of the article in *Galería*, and therefore known as the "second edition." The *Historia de Belgrano* is important for many reasons. Although it had to go through four editions (the last was published in 1887), each with extensive rewriting and augmentation, before reaching its definitive form, the *Historia* remains a classic in Argentine historiography. As Rómulo D. Carbia, Argentina's best historian of historians, has noted, "Mitre gathered and studied the books of American history, he submitted them to critical testing, he classified them according to what precipitated from them, and tried to contrast the results of his personal research among unpublished sources with what was already published" (Carbia, *Historia crítica de la historiografía argentina* 166–167). In short, despite his political ambitions, Mitre brought to Argentine historiography a laudable concern for evidence and documentation. Indeed, the fourth and definitive edition of the work, published in three volumes in 1887, is a treasure trove of extensive quotations from documents Mitre collected during fifty years of archival work. Similarly admired is his three-volume work, *Historia de San Martín y de la emancipación sudamericana*, published between 1887 and 1890.

Despite the impressive bibliographical apparatus supporting his work, however, Mitre's *Historia de Belgrano* provoked an enduring polemic regarding its basic premise: that a history of Belgrano, a great man, and the enlightened minority in Buenos Aires could somehow be a history of Argentine independence. Mitre's contemporaries, Dalmacio Vélez Sarsfield and Vicente Fidel López, sustained this debate with Mitre for nearly three decades. Indeed, their criticisms of Mitre possibly led him to a much more systematic reliance on documents than might otherwise have been the case. Because of this greater bibliographical depth, each successive edition of the *Historia* improves.

The first skirmish in the debate began in a series of articles published by Dalmacio Vélez Sarsfield in the newspaper *El Nacional* in 1864. Calling Mitre's *Historia de Belgrano* "an injurious and slanderous judgement against the peoples of the interior," Vélez Sarsfield seeks to show that the masses and their caudillos played a major role in the independence movement, quite apart from porteño leadership as represented by Belgrano and San Martín (Vélez Sarsfield, "El General Belgrano," in Mitre, *Estudios históricos* 218). The focal point of Vélez Sarsfield's argument is Martín Güemes, a contemporary of José Artigas, who fought alongside both San Martín and Belgrano, leading an army of gauchos that repeatedly proved decisive in repelling royalist forces.

Güemes, however, did not always cooperate so amiably with the porteños. After the Wars of Independence, Güemes, like Artigas, resisted porteño attempts to bring Salta under porteño control. Also like Artigas, he supported policies strikingly progressive for the times. As governor of the province, he initiated progressive tax and land reform measures that got him in trouble with Salta's wealthy families—one of which was Güemes's own. Moreover, like Hidalgo, Güemes was instrumental in changing the meaning of *gaucho* from delinquent to native patriot. Modern historians generally agree that Güemes struck a good balance between loyalty to the nation and defense of his province; he is also much praised nowadays for transcending his own class roots in order to lead a popular yet progressive movement.[5]

In Mitre's view, however, popularity with the lower classes and opposition to Buenos Aires were unforgivable sins. Unable to dislodge Güemes's contribution to the independence struggle, Mitre concedes that "as a caudillo he was great in fighting for the common cause," but he also maintains that "as a caudillo he was deadly in contributing his example to the political and social disorganization [of the Patria]" (Mitre, *Estudios históricos* 69). Mitre further insists, with the now familiar condemnation by stereotype, that Güemes was a "caudillo destined to acquire a glorious yet at the same time sinister celebrity . . . [who] although educated and belonging to a prominent Salta family, always showed a tendency to flatter the passions of the multitudes in order to garner their affection and set them against the cultured classes of society" (*Historia de Belgrano* [1859] 2:202–203). As in other examples of officialist writing, what this means is that Güemes sought inclusion of the popular classes, and rejected the aspirations of Buenos Aires' enlightened minority to exclusive power over the provinces.

5. Vélez Sarsfield's clumsy defense of Güemes was actually the first of several attempts to redeem him from the degradation given all caudillos in official history. Atilio Cornejo's *Historia de Güemes* in large measure summarizes modern opinion.

Mitre's attacks on Güemes did not go unchallenged. "The fact is," writes Vélez Sarsfield, "that the *caudillo* Güemes, this man accused of having always sought to attract the masses, used those masses to save his country and to save the Revolution of May" ("El General Belgrano" 227–228). Vélez Sarsfield criticizes in particular Mitre's cavalier attitude towards the masses:

> The history of the masses cannot be separated from the history of the great men who have led them; nor can the history of those great men neglect the theater of their actions. Our historians take individual personalities, exaggerate their character, and then tell nothing about the world they lived in, the stature and valor of the peoples they led, the secondary figures who aided them. Neither do we know of the customs and opinions of the masses, nor do we know the names of the most important people who influenced them. (233)

Vélez Sarsfield further maintains that Mitre's insistence on documentary proof, rather than a virtue, merely condemns his histories to partiality since documents mostly reflect upper-class concerns. Vélez Sarsfield argues that, since the masses and their popular leaders leave few written traces, their history requires methods that include legend, hearsay, and interviews. "The problem with the *Historia de Belgrano*," Vélez Sarsfield concludes, "is that it is taken from official documents . . . in which historical truth never appears" (233). In short, Vélez Sarsfield sought inclusion in history for the masses and their caudillos just as Artigas, Hidalgo, and Alberdi had sought to include them in society.

In his response, Mitre dismisses Vélez Sarsfield's criticisms as "vague and incomplete reminiscences . . . devoid of any proof" (*Estudios históricos* 6). Always the self-righteous arbiter, Mitre insists that Güemes must be judged according to documentary evidence "with the severe impartiality of the court of history, as a lesson for everyone" (64). While Mitre's extensive documentation gives the impression of "severe impartiality," a second look reveals a careful selection of evidence that belies any claim to objectivity. For example, to document that Güemes was a caudillo as evil as any other, Mitre cites uncritically the *Memorias* of General José María Paz, a prominent Unitarian general and defender of porteño privilege whose feelings toward the caudillos were just as blindly negative as Mitre's. By citing Paz's writings as eyewitness evidence,

Mitre can dismiss Güemes as "a nasal-voiced orator, dressed in comically luxurious imitations of popular costumes; a demagogue inciting the poor to rebel against the cultured class of society [and] a caudillo idolized by the gauchos" (67). Paz's *Memorias* are in fact the major source Mitre uses against Güemes. Mitre never calls into question Paz's intentions and reliability since he needed "documentation" to support the myth of the barbarous caudillos and their savage hordes. This view of the caudillos also gave support to Mitre's refusal to negotiate in good faith with the "caudillo" Urquiza, and undergirded his view of his own role in Argentine history: as the leader of an enlightened minority called to resist "barbarism." It was precisely Mitre's selective use of evidence that led Alberdi to charge that the "*Historia de Belgrano* is documented legend, fables dressed up with documents meant . . . to be read with eyes of national vanity, that is to say with eyes closed"(Alberdi, *Grandes y pequeños hombres* 16).[6]

An irony: Mitre's own place in Argentine history has never been investigated as thoroughly as he studied Belgrano, San Martín, and the Independence period. Of all major figures in nineteenth-century Argentina—Moreno, Rivadavia, Rosas, Alberdi, Sarmiento, Urquiza—only Mitre has never been scrutinized in a rigorous, critical biography. Perhaps historians treat him gingerly because they recognize in him a fellow historian who contributed enormously to Argentine historiography. Whatever Mitre's biases, modern scholars still find useful his landmark biographies on Belgrano and San Martín. Moreover, no library of original documents on Ar-

6. The debate between Mitre and his critics entered a second round in the 1880s, a period outside the purview of this book. Vicente Fidel López, a historian just as prolific as Mitre and much under the sway of historians like Thierry and Macaulay, reiterated Vélez Sarsfield's contention that Mitre's concern for documentation blinded him to larger issues. Mitre counterattacked by calling López's histories "impressionistic" rather than factual. The debate between López and Mitre has been extensively analyzed in Carbia (*Historia* 148–172); Ricardo R. Caillet-Bois also analyzes the debate in his article "La historiografía," as does Joseph R. Barager in "The Historiography of the Río de la Plata Area Since 1830" (596–598). Moreover, as relatively recent works like Arturo Jauretche's highly entertaining and often unreliable *Los profetas del odio* (passim) and *El medio pelo en la sociedad argentina* (passim) indicate, Mitre's role in Argentine history continues to inspire debate.

gentine colonial and nineteenth-century history surpasses the one assembled by Mitre himself.

Another reason, perhaps, for the dearth of critical studies on Mitre is the complexity of the subject. Mitre, like Sarmiento, defies easy classification. A paradoxical mix of brilliance, heroism, eloquence, ambition, opportunism, and intrigue, Mitre can be viewed from many angles and combinations of angles. None of his contemporaries possessed his combined gifts as a writer, historian, politician, administrator, orator, and military leader. To be sure, Sarmiento was a better writer, Alberdi a clearer thinker, Urquiza a more selfless patriot, López a more readable historian, and almost anyone a better novelist and translator. But no one else held all these talents at once; nor did anyone else fashion his talents into a more superbly crafted vehicle for self-promotion than the one that kept Mitre in the public eye from 1852 until his death in 1906.

Yet Mitre is much more than a product of personal ambition and public relations. Once Urquiza was out of the way and Mitre became president, he busily set out to organize the country, founding schools and universities, writing civil codes and tax laws, establishing a modern banking and currency system, determining immigration policies and building ports, telegraph lines, and railroads. In all these activities he proved himself an imaginative and tireless public servant, so much so that without Mitre modern Argentina might not exist. But there was another Mitre: a man whose ambitions repeatedly disrupted national development and continue to thwart understanding of the Argentine past. When Mitre's personal ambitions coincided with the good of his country, he was a zealous, imaginative public servant; when they did not, he was a dangerous source of disruption and historical distortion.

Separating Mitre's ambitions from his patriotism is particularly daunting because of his ever-present liberal rhetoric. Whatever his actions and motives, he always said it right. His writings speak to us in the present and are heavily laden with the thick perfume of liberal eloquence, whereas his actions remain in the past, waiting to be illuminated by industrious historians. With liberal eloquence he attacked Urquiza's plans to unify the country under a government equally representative of Buenos Aires and the provinces; with liberal eloquence he named his newspaper *Los Debates*, although it served only one point of view; with liberal eloquence he named his next newspaper *La Nación*, a name that carefully disguises its heavy porteño bias; with liberal eloquence he led Argentina to the brink of a disastrous civil war that was averted only because Urquiza refused to fight; with liberal eloquence he helped wage a shameful war against Paraguay; and with liberal eloquence in 1874 he attempted a coup against a constitutional president whose only offense was defeating Mitre in his second bid for the presidency. If Mitre today is most often remembered as a liberal statesman, scholar, progressive leader, and historian, it is partly because his words still defend and promote him.

And if his words fail, his descendants quickly come to his aid. The Mitre family owns and manages *La Nación*, the country's most powerful newspaper, which in turn exerts untold influence on Argentine intellectual life simply by controlling who and what get published and reviewed in its pages. Indeed, with the collaboration of his descendants, Mitre remains almost as impregnable in death as he was in life. Given the complexity of the man and the labyrinthine ways of contemporary Argentine intellectual life, Mitre's writings remain the best window to the contradictions in the man. Through that window we see that, despite his fine words about democracy and his impressive contributions to history, he never ceases to champion great men and enlightened minorities: that is to say, himself and those who agree with him.

Chapter Nine

Roots of Argentine Nationalism, Part One

Since the beginnings of the Argentine Republic, two broad currents of thought dominated the country's guiding fictions. The first, which we have studied in detail, is a liberal, elitist position centered in Buenos Aires and the educated upper classes that advocated success through imitation of Europe and the United States while denigrating the Spanish heritage, popular traditions, and the mixed-blood masses. Articulate and prolific liberals, from Moreno to the Rivadavians to Sarmiento to Mitre, promoted their exclusivist ideologies while stereotyping their detractors as barbaric, unprogressive, and racially inferior. (It should be apparent by now that the terms *liberal* and *liberalism* in Argentina are used quite differently than in the United States and Western Europe.) The other current of thought, discussed now, is an ideologically messy, ill-defined, often contradictory tendency (or tendencies) which could be populist (caudillos like Artigas and Güemes), reactionary (conservative ecclesiastics and Rosas), nativist (Bartolomé Hidalgo's gauchesque), or genuinely federalist and progressive (Urquiza and late Alberdi). No single idea unites this opposition to liberal elitism. Indeed, certain elements of it, such as the radical democracy of Artigas and Hidalgo compared to the aristocratic paternalism of Rosas, are profoundly contradictory. Nonetheless, this inchoate, shifting, inconsistent opposition to Argentine liberalism has acquired through the years a visible if not always well-defined shape that for lack of a better term I call *nationalism.*

Two considerations prompt the choice of this term. First, many of the writers studied in this chapter referred to themselves as "nationalists" and to federalism as the "nationalist cause." For example, Olegario Andrade in *Las dos políticas,* a significant pamphlet probably published in 1866, studied in detail later in this chapter, divides Argentine political parties into two groups: "Federalists and Unitarians . . . nationalists and liberals" (54). Second, the term makes sense in light of what antiliberalism became in this century. Like Borges's Kafka who creates his own precursors, contemporary Argentine nationalism in some sense establishes its own genealogy.

What the opponents of porteño liberalism most lacked during the first fifty years of their country's existence were articulate, visible defenders of their point of view. Unlike Echeverría, Sarmiento, and Mitre, antiliberal writers worked in relative isolation, served short-lived political causes, and left no intellectual progeny to keep their work in public view. Except for Bartolomé Hidalgo's poetic denunciations of upper-class privilege and mistreatment of the gauchos, populist writings prior to Urquiza sank into oblivion. Even Artigas's pronouncements had to be resurrected by Uruguayan historians anxious to establish a separate national identity. Similarly forgotten was Father Francisco de Paula Castañeda, who waged a vigorous, often libelous, fight against Rivadavia, and later aligned himself with Estanislao López, caudillo of Entre Ríos, against the porteño liberals. Another forgotten "nationalist" is Pedro de Angelis, an Italian literato imported by Rivadavia who became Rosas's in-house intellectual; a servile flatterer of whoever happened to be in power, de Angelis left a remarkable (if probably insincere) defense of Rosas's dictatorship, compelling refutations of Unitarian arguments against Rosas, and an admirable body of serious writings on Argentine culture, language, and geography. Yet, since witers like Castañeda and de Angelis were easily discredited by their alliance to unsavory and unsuccessful political causes, they were largely forgotten and left little effect on the official guiding fictions of the country.

With Urquiza's coming to power and establishing a national government in Paraná, anti-porteño intellectuals for the first time found a sympathetic political leader and government around which a genuine school of nationalist sentiment could form. Through the Confederation, writers like Juan Bautista Alberdi (after separating from Sarmiento and Mitre), Carlos Guido y Spano, Olegario V. Andrade, and José Hernández came together in common cause against porteño domination. Yet, as is often the case in Argentine letters, even Confederation thinkers were better at explaining failure than prescribing success. As a result, the most significant examples of nationalist, populist, and proprovincial thought appear not during Urquiza's government but after his defeat in 1861 when the Mitristas and Buenos Aires again dominated the country.

This chapter and the next examine Argentine nationalist thought as it appeared between 1852 and 1880 in terms of five major impulses. The first is a restructuring of history that defines Argentina as a nation divided not by political ideologies but by economic realities with the major players being the interior against Buenos Aires, the poor against the "oligarchy"—a disapproving epithet for the porteño wealthy which during this period first enters popular usage. The second is a vindication of the caudillos as genuine popular leaders whose alleged barbarism was the only recourse available to the provinces in their struggle against Buenos Aires; this vindication of the caudillos is closely linked to the restructuring of history, and would form the basis of the historical revisionism that divides Argentine historiography even today (see Barager, "Historiography"; Kroeber, "Rosas and the Revision of Argentine History"; Navarro Gerassi, *Los nacionalistas* 131–145). The third is an expression of ideological solidarity with other Latin American countries, an attitude strikingly absent among most Argentine liberals. The fourth is a revindication of the Spanish, Latin heritage in which liberalism's enthrallment to French, English, and North American models is seen as "anti-Argentine." And the fifth is a glorification of the rural poor in which the gaucho, rather than a barbarian outcast, emerges as a prototype of authentic Argentine values and a victim of the oligarchy's selfish ambition. To a lesser degree, criticism of the Indian wars, particularly in the work of Lucio V. Mansilla, also vindicates another marginal group: the Argentine Indians, although the Indian never acquired the same symbolic value in populist thinking as the gaucho. Some of these currents were, of course, anticipated by the first populists, namely, Artigas and Hidalgo, as discussed in chapter 3. It is, however, during the 1860s and 1870s that nationalist thought enters full bloom. Here, as in earlier chapters, intellectual developments are examined alongside the sociopolitical events that inspired them.

During the mid-1850s, Urquiza's successes made it appear that Argentina's first real national government might make a go of it. Fresh from routing Rosas, Urquiza united all the provinces except Buenos Aires under a constitutional government, headquartered in Paraná, which became known as the Confederation. The Urquiza constitution was modeled after ideas found in Alberdi's *Bases,* providing for a freely elected but powerful executive and a representative congress. Elected in 1854 to be the first president of the Confederation, Urquiza implemented a truly federal system of equal political, economic, and commercial rights for all Argentine provinces, much to the horror of Buenos Aires. He also made peace with Argentina's immediate neighbors, Brazil, Uruguay, and Paraguay, resolving differences that had smoldered since Independence. In addition, he launched ambitious programs to improve transportation and education. On the diplomatic front, he signed the Treaty of Free Navigation with Great Britain which freed British traders to seek ports other than Buenos Aires, and agreed to renew payments on the loan of 1824 on which Rosas had defaulted (Ferns 291–292; Scobie, *La lucha* 166–170). His good relations with foreign governments were further enhanced by Juan Bautista Alberdi's diplomatic brilliance, which gained for Paraná the recognition of the United States, England, and France.

Relations with the Buenos Aires government, however, remained tense. Several cautious agreements were signed, but none of these came to much, mostly because Buenos Aires refused to compromise on anything substantial. The Buenos Aires constitution of 1854 makes abundantly clear the porteño attitude toward the provinces: "Buenos Aires is a state with full control of her domestic and foreign sovereignty, for as long as she does not expressly delegate that sovereignty to a federal government" (cited in Scobie, *La lucha* 127).

Not surprisingly, the porteños did not accord the same rights of self-determination to the provinces. One of their first moves was to send the aging General José María Paz, a famous Independence hero, with a war chest of 200,000 pounds sterling to woo provincial

leaders away from the Confederation. When this failed, the porteños sent two armies under Generals Manuel Hornos and Juan
Madariaga to disrupt the Santa Fe constitutional convention. Urquiza defeated them both (Ferns 296). The porteños soon realized
that Urquiza's popularity coupled with his military strength made
the Confederation impregnable—at least for the time being.

Urquiza's presidency also saw the publication of one of the most
significant documents of Argentine nationalism: Olegario Víctor
Andrade's pamphlet *Las dos políticas* (Two kinds of politics). Since
the earliest surviving copy of *Las dos políticas* mentions neither
author nor date, there is considerable disagreement concerning
the article's origins. Some attribute it to José Hernández, although its overblown, highly metaphorical style is much more
suggestive of Andrade than of Hernández. There is also disagreement as to when the pamphlet was written. Several historians
claim that it did not appear until 1866, which is in fact the date it
was first circulated widely as part of an abortive campaign to
regain the presidency for Urquiza. In contrast, José Raed, in his
convincing essay "Olegario y *Las dos políticas*," which precedes
the edition used here, argues that much of the pamphlet was
written during Urquiza's presidency, perhaps as early as 1857,
when Andrade was merely eighteen years old, and then rewritten
later to support Urquiza's possible return to the presidency. Regardless of date and authorship, however, the pamphlet is a significant statement on the politics of the Confederation, an important
key to understanding the development of proprovincial, nationalist thought, and an uncanny anticipation of guiding fictions that
still inform Argentine nationalism.

Written in a pompous style, the pamphlet affirms that "questions
of organization, forms of government and liberal institutions were
different disguises of an economic question" in which Buenos Aires
"monopolized commerce, transport of goods and the general government. . . . Instead of Madrid, the capital [after Independence]
was called Buenos Aires. Instead of monarchical and foreign colonialism, we have had since 1810 domestic and republican colonialism" (Andrade 53–54). Andrade further argues that from the first
days of independence, only one political question was important:
whether the United Provinces or Buenos Aires would control the

material bounty of the country. In Andrade's view, Buenos Aires held the upper hand in this economic struggle—a fact that accounted not only for the poverty of the provinces but also for their caudillo-based government:

The caudillos were created by the ambition of Buenos Aires. . . . [They] rose in every province as the fatal result of Buenos Aires' confiscation of their fortune. For this reason, when we see the localist party of Buenos Aires proclaim the extirpation of *caudillismo,* we lament their ignorance of history and their political myopia. What were the caudillos but the governors of provinces abandoned to their fate, spurred on by hunger and worry about the future? [They were] local governors without resources, without the limits of law, without the immediate responsibility to create order and institutions. (56–58)

In addition to seeing the caudillos as products of porteño greed, Andrade argues that the porteños, regardless of superficial political differences, behaved in remarkable union. "History," he writes, "will someday say that there has existed in Buenos Aires one localist, retrograde party which has been called Unitarian . . . and which has been called Federalist. [It is] a party of political profit-mongers without faith and without heart" (60). He also argues that within that invisible party, men as different as Rivadavia and Rosas become unknowing collaborators: "Rivadavia manufactured the tools with which Rosas forged the hard chains of dictatorship" (62). He further holds that all porteños who profit from Buenos Aires' privileged status are coconspirators, no matter their alleged political differences. "If it is unjust to attribute [Rosas's] crimes to Buenos Aires," he tells us, "it is not unjust to deny her complicity in his vain, exclusivist political pride and with his money-based aspirations for control and annexation" (72). Not surprisingly, Andrade sees Mitre and his opposition to Urquiza as only the latest episode in this ongoing conspiracy against the provinces: "[Mitre] was merely the restoration of Buenos Aires' power, the ruin and derailment of the provinces, the wealth and power of Buenos Aires. It is the same policy of the Republic's entire history. Rivadavia, Dorrego, Rosas and Mitre have been that policy's instruments" (76).

Andrade continues his essay with a resounding defense of Urquiza that portrays the Entre Ríos caudillo as the most recent and most able in a long series of caudillo heroes like Güemes,

Ramírez, López, and Quiroga, all of whom fought for the autonomy of their provinces. Urquiza, in the pamphlet's words, is the man who "raised the flag to redeem Argentine freedom [and established] a congress, a constitution and a national government" (90–91). Andrade's devotion to Urquiza had a personal basis. Born in 1839 to a poor family of country artisans and orphaned at an early age, Andrade was able to study, first in his hometown of Gualeguaychú and later in Uruguay, only through the personal generosity of Urquiza, much impressed by the young Andrade's intelligence (Tiscornia, "Vida de Andrade" x–xi, xviii–xxiv). Andrade ends *Las dos políticas* by calling on future historians to pass judgment on the conflict between Buenos Aires and the provinces: "History will tell us which side has defended local interest, ridiculous vanity and unlimited ambition. History will tell us which side has worked for peace, brotherhood and regeneration" (92). Andrade had no way of knowing it, but his call for an alternate history, for revisionist history, would become a chief rallying point of Argentine nationalism in this century.

Andrade's ideas are also heard in Alberdi. After Urquiza's triumph, Alberdi abandons the elitism of *Bases* and embraces a frankly populist view reminiscent of his *Fragmento preliminar* studied in chapter 5. Writing from Paris after Urquiza's fall, Alberdi argues that "The caudillos are the natural representatives of South American democracy. . . . Mitre and Sarmiento want to replace the caudillos in ponchos with caudillos in coattails . . . the democracy that is really democracy with the democracy that is in fact oligarchy" (*Grandes y pequeños hombres* 207–209). He continues:

If we really support republican government, we have to be logical and accept the results of that republic, which means accepting the caudillos, that is to say, the republican leaders elected by the popular majority from their own ranks, according to their own taste and trust. Asking that the uneducated segment of our people, which is just as sovereign as the educated segment, to accept as leaders men whose merit the uneducated neither understand nor recognize, is utter mindlessness. (210)

Alberdi further argues that given such tolerance the republic would eventually mature to a point where "semi-barbarous caudillos" from the provinces and "semi-educated caudillos" from the cities would merge into an inclusive nation with room for everyone, free of the civil war and bloodshed brought on by Argentine liberalism's intolerance for the popular classes and their preferred leaders (210).

Like Andrade, Alberdi is also concerned with the proper rendition of history, and like Andrade, he holds that the division between true nationalists and porteño localists had existed since the Primera Junta. "Saavedra's party," he writes, "was the truly national party, since it wanted the entire nation to participate in the government; Moreno's party was localist, since it wanted that all authority be located in the capital city rather than in the nation" (*Grandes y pequeños hombres* 99). In a very long critique of Mitre's *Historia de Belgrano* he continues this argument, maintaining that

for Buenos Aires, the May revolution meant independence from Spain and control of the provinces. . . . For the provinces, the May revolution meant separation from Spain and submission to Buenos Aires, a new configuration of colonialism rather than its abolition. This perversion of the revolution, brought on by the unthinking ambition of Buenos Aires, has created two countries, different and separate, behind the appearance of one: the metropolis state, Buenos Aires, and her servant state, the Republic. One governs, the other obeys; one enjoys the national income, the other produces it; one is fortunate, the other miserable. (107)

Here Alberdi introduces one of the most seductive and durable images of nationalist historiography: the notion of two countries, two societies, two parallel developments, two histories. One is centered in Buenos Aires, an ersatz Europe, glittering but hollow. The other is located in the provinces and the popular classes, unsophisticated but authentic. On another occasion Alberdi wrote that "Buenos Aires and the Argentine Provinces form two countries, both foreign to each other. Since this division has as its object the exploitation of one country over the other, a profound enmity divides them, making them natural enemies in the very breast of a union or federation, which exists only to facilitate that exploitation" (*OC* 6:329).

Other nationalists described Buenos Aires' relationship to the provinces as one of metropolis to colony, of potentate to peon. José Hernández in a newspaper article that appeared on October 3, 1869, in *El Río de la Plata* argues that "[Buenos Aires] still shows signs of the monstrous privileges of colonialism. There has emerged here a kind of aristocracy to which the abandoned countryside pays tribute, like vassals of feudal lords in olden times, before the formation of modern societies" (*Prosas de José Hernández* 83). In another article also in *El Río de la Plata*, Hernández identifies those feudal lords as the "oligarchy," a term still invoked by nationalists of the left and the right to condemn Argentina's upper classes. They are, Hernández writes, "Tartuffes who feign love for the liberty they violate, but think only of promoting themselves while mocking the impoverished pueblo" (*Prosas de José Hernández* 91).

The popularity in this century of Andrade, late Alberdi, and Hernández can be partially attributed to their anticipation of major currents in Marxist and third-world liberationist thought. Like Marx, they suggest that membership in the "oligarchy" (being part of or dependent on the porteño agricultural elite) is a much more important consideration in politics than the superficial debates of bourgeois democracy, that the porteño elite will always act together when their class privilege is challenged.[1] They also anticipate a basic tenet of Latin American Marxism in suggesting that the provinces were not undeveloped but "underdeveloped," that is, developed in such a way as to be permanently subservient to and dependent on the interests of Buenos Aires, much as Latin America is allegedly "underdeveloped" with regards to first-world countries today.

With Alberdi, Andrade, and Hernández, the Confederation demonstrated that, in addition to Urquiza's thoughtful leadership, an exemplary constitution, and remarkable diplomatic success, Paraná also created a paradigm of guiding fictions to challenge the liberal ideologies of Buenos Aires. Moreover, Confederation writings suggest a certain continuity of themes, if not a direct descendancy from, the gauchesque poetry of Bartolomé Hidalgo and the improvised pronouncements of José Artigas; although Artigas and Hidalgo were not the intellectual match of the Confederation intellectuals studied in this chapter, the concerns they articulated in the first decade of the Argentine Republic resonate in the Confederation thought of a half-century later.

1. Among the most coherent defenders of this point of view in recent years are Rodolfo Puiggrós and Juan José Sebreli. See Rodolfo Puiggrós, *Pueblo y oligarquía* (95–98, 123–129) and Juan José Sebreli's *Apogeo y ocaso de los Anchorena* (203–218).

Noble intentions, able leadership, and creative thinkers in the Confederation were not, however, enough to change commercial patterns that still made Buenos Aires the economic center of Argentina. In short, what the Confederation did not have was money. Even countries sympathetic to the Confederation soon tired of maintaining diplomatic relations with Paraná while trading mostly with and through Buenos Aires. As a result, toward the end of the 1850s, representatives of France and the United States presented their credentials to both governments (Scobie, *La lucha* 165–168). As if economic problems weren't enough, the Confederation also experienced increased political tension as Urquiza's six-year term as president drew to an end.

News of the Confederation's economic and political problems whetted Buenos Aires' appetite for regaining control of the provinces, so much so that in late 1859, Mitre led porteño troops against the Confederation. Urquiza met Mitre's soldiers at Cepeda in the province of Buenos Aires on October 23, and dealt them a sound beating. Despite defeat, Mitre managed to save his infantry and his artillery for future battle—a fact that Confederation forces would later regret. After Mitre's withdrawal, Urquiza was again tempted to invade Buenos Aires, but, as on other occasions, he again offered the porteños an olive branch. "At the end of my political career," he wrote, "my only ambition is to see . . . one, happy Argentine Republic. . . . I wish the children of Buenos Aires to be Argentines" (cited in Bosch 492). On November 11 the defeated porteños signed with Urquiza the Pact of San José de Flores, which stipulated that Buenos Aires would join the Confederation. To help the proud porteños save face, however, Urquiza agreed in principle to allow Buenos Aires, as the most populous province, a greater voice in the national Congress and considerable say in amending the 1853 Constitution. Urquiza also stipulated that the secessionist Alsina step down as Governor of Buenos Aires—a provision Mitre tacitly supported since it eliminated his chief political rival in the porteño province. Although superficially a victory for the Confederation, the Pact of San José in fact committed Buenos Aires to little more than continuing discussion. And Mitre was a stellar discusser.

The year 1860 marked an important transition for both Paraná and Buenos Aires. Urquiza defied a thousand porteño prophecies by retiring from office after completing his six-year term as speci-

fied by the 1853 Constitution. In national elections, he was replaced by his former minister of the interior, Santiago Derqui, a
nervous, ineffectual man whom Urquiza may have initially supported in order to maintain some voice in the national government. After Derqui's inauguration, Urquiza resumed the office of
Governor of Entre Ríos. In the meantime, with Alsina out of the
way at Urquiza's insistence, Mitre was elected Governor of the
Province of Buenos Aires. Although negotiations between Buenos
Aires and Paraná had yet to go anywhere, Mitre invited both Derqui and Urquiza to Buenos Aires for the Ninth of July celebration
commemorating the 1816 Congreso de Tucumán when Argentina
officially broke from Spain. It was a typical Mitre move: while
stubbornly protecting porteño privilege at the bargaining table
and on the battle field, he carefully projected a public image of
accommodation and unity "without surrendering a single important element of power or sovereignty to the national government"
(Scobie, *La lucha* 283–288).

After the obligatory speeches and *abrazos* at the national celebration, Mitre got down to the real business at hand: returning the
provinces to porteño control, a task in which only Rosas had ever
been successful. As Scobie notes, although Rosas and Mitre differed in many ways, "an essential attribute was common to both
regimes. The wealth and economic power of the city of Buenos
Aires participated in Argentine nationhood only when the province's security could be guaranteed by porteño leadership in the
national government" (299). As governor, Mitre immediately embarked on a three-pronged strategy to gain control of the provinces.
First, he subsidized organizations of porteño sympathizers throughout the provinces. Second, he exploited autonomist sentiment in
the interior by entering negotiations with individual provincial leaders, a move that bypassed Derqui and helped drive a wedge between Derqui and Urquiza. And third, he probably supported a
covert terrorist campaign against pro-Confederation provincial leaders that was particularly successful in the northwestern provinces
(Bosch 523–534; Scobie 304–317).

Two events in this campaign were the assassinations of Nazario
Benavídez, former caudillo of Sarmiento's native province of San
Juan, and of his Federalist successor, José Antonio Virasoro. In the
autumn of 1858, while Urquiza was still in power, Unitarian sympa-

thizers managed to take control of San Juan, replacing Sarmiento's nemesis, Benavídez, with Manuel José Gómez. Fearing that Benavídez would attempt a coup against his government, Gómez had the aging caudillo jailed. After an unsuccessful rescue attempt by Benavídez supporters, the Unitarian prison warden ordered his prisoner shot, a cowardly act that Sarmiento nonetheless managed to justify, despite his oft-avowed faith in institutions and due process (Bunkley 379–380). Partly owing to the outcry against Gómez, the newly elected Derqui replaced him with José Antonio Virasoro, a pro-Confederation governor who was in turn assassinated on November 16, 1860, in a rebellion led by Mitre supporter Antonio Aberstain, who may or may not have been acting independently of Buenos Aires.

The whole subject of porteño terrorism in the provinces, and particularly of porteño involvement in the assassinations of Benavídez and Virasoro, became a hotly debated matter. Urquiza accused Sarmiento and his porteño friends of instigating the violence, a charge Sarmiento adamantly denied. Later, when Derqui appointed a commission to investigate the murder, Urquiza objected to including Mitristas on the commission, suggesting that he may have also suspected that Mitre was involved. Urquiza's criticsm of the fact-finding commission marked the beginning of his fears that Derqui was too much under Mitre's sway. In a letter to Derqui dated December 30, 1860, Urquiza pointedly warned, "Do not let yourself be separated from your friends by ideas of the moment, accepted without sufficient meditation" (cited in Scobie 313). Whatever Mitre's involvement, he undoubtedly benefited politically from Benavídez's and Virasoro's murders since the destabilization of pro-Confederation governments in the northwestern provinces and the rift between Urquiza and Derqui were decisive in clearing the path for Mitre's eventual triumph over the interior.

Buenos Aires' successful divide-and-conquer strategy, coupled with the Confederation's increasing economic difficulties, convinced Mitre, still smarting from his 1859 defeat at Cepeda, that a second invasion of the Confederation might work. In late winter of 1861, Mitre once more marched against the Confederation. Although Urquiza agreed to lead the anti-Mitre forces against this second invasion, disloyalty from former Federalist allies, suspicions about Derqui, illness, and growing distaste for continued conflict with the ambitious and much younger Mitre gave Urquiza little enthusiasm for battle. The two forces met on September 17, 1861, at Pavón, where after a short engagement Urquiza surprisingly withdrew his troops. Without Urquiza, the Confederation resistance quickly collapsed. A treaty was eventually signed by which Urquiza agreed to return to Entre Ríos and stay out of national politics, much to the disappointment, if not outrage, of his Federalist allies. In return, Mitre promised to leave Entre Ríos alone. With Urquiza sidelined, Mitre entered independent negotiations with each provincial leader, thus undermining Derqui and showing total disregard for the Confederation. Bereft of all significant support, Derqui officially resigned the presidency in November 1861 and went into exile.

Urquiza's motives for finally yielding to Mitre are shrouded in mystery. He surely had the wherewithal and prestige to regroup and march on Buenos Aires yet another time. Instead, he returned to his beloved estancia at San José, leaving the provinces defenseless before the designs of Mitre and the porteños. Since the agreement Urquiza signed with Mitre effectively confined him to Entre Ríos, he repeatedly refused, despite frequent entreaties from former Federalist allies, to support further provincial resistance to Buenos Aires. Such behavior prompted former supporters like Hernández, Alberdi, Carlos Guido y Spano, and the caudillos Angel Peñaloza and Ricardo López Jordán to denounce him as a traitor to Federalism and to the ideals of his youth. Wrote Alberdi in 1863, "Unable to support himself against Buenos Aires, Urquiza today is supported by Buenos Aires. . . . He will probably end his public life just as he started it: by being an accomplice of Buenos Aires in plundering and dismembering the Argentine Republic." In a similar passage Alberdi writes that in allowing Mitre to win "Urquiza has restored the regime of Rosas. . . . He has destroyed the constitution he once proudly promoted, and has fatally wounded the national integrity that he formerly supported" (*Escritos póstumos* 9:327–332). As Alberdi notes, Urquiza began his public life allied to Rosas; and as Alberdi prophesied, Urquiza was still in alliance with the Buenos Aires government when murdered in 1870—by a former Federalist ally who like so many felt betrayed by Urquiza at Pavón.

What accounted for Urquiza's dramatic change of heart? Most probably, Urquiza concluded that, since Mitre and Buenos Aires would never allow peace on anything less than their own terms, the provinces had only two options: prolonged, unwinnable civil war or negotiated surrender. Ten years of futile struggle in the Confederation had convinced him that the second was the better option. A more cynical explanation holds that Urquiza yielded to the temptation of wealth. As the largest landowner in Entre Ríos, he had much to gain through peaceful relations with Buenos Aires—and in fact Urquiza died an enormously wealthy man.

With the Confederation defunct, it was Mitre's turn to organize a national government. After Derqui's resignation, Mitre became the de facto national leader; later, on October 12, 1862, a newly elected national congress made the forty-one-year-old Mitre the united country's first president. Mitre brought unprecedented administrative and diplomatic skill to the presidency. Following policies not unlike those Urquiza tried to initiate, he extended postal service, built roads and railroads, nationalized waterways and ports, regularized public finance, installed a judicial system, expanded public education, and encouraged immigration. More than 100,000 Europeans entered Argentina during Mitre's term. He also created a favorable business climate that almost doubled export-import trade between 1862 and 1868. But most important, at least on a symbolic level, Mitre retained with minor alterations the Confederation's constitution; as long as political and economic control remained in the hands of the porteños, the Federalist constitution presented no serious obstacles to his government. Mitre was particularly fortunate in that he had no enemies as capable as himself.

In the first months of Mitre's government, pro-Confederation intellectuals kept a cautious distance. Although Juan María Gutiérrez accepted the appointment of rector of the University of Buenos Aires, he avoided political involvement. Alberdi, who had resigned his diplomatic post when Derqui came to power, became a diplomat with no country to represent. Alberdi's distaste for politics kept him in Paris, but he nonetheless wrote a surprisingly conciliatory essay, *De la anarquía y sus dos causas principales del gobierno y sus dos elementos necesarios en la República Argentina, con motivo de su reorganización por Buenos Aires* in which he avoids making, for the time being at least, yet another attack against Mitre, holding that after Pavón the struggle between Buenos Aires, and the provinces was one "not of individuals" but "of special interests and institutions" (*Obras completas* 6:152). According to Alberdi, two related elements of Argentine society caused its perpetual anarchy: the selfishness of Buenos Aires, which insisted on keeping its customs earnings for herself, and the provincial caudillos, who survived because Buenos Aires offered the provinces no alternative form of self-rule. To remedy these two evils he offers two solutions: first, that Buenos Aires (and her income) be federalized, and second, that this new, genuinely federalist government be given substantial control over the provinces. In short, he advocated a strong but genuinely representative central government.

Mitre did indeed institute a strong central government, but in no way did he make it more representative. His government consisted entirely of porteños and subservient allies from the provinces. He also improved government services in the interior, but more out of a sense of paternalism and political convenience than any respect for provincial rights. In short, democracy was fine as long as its voting members were *gente decente* who accepted the dominance of Buenos Aires prior to all other debates. What this meant in practice was a protracted effort to hammer out of existence all traces of caudillo-based populism, no matter how representative it was of provincial sentiment.

The most famous caudillo to feel Mitre's fist was Angel Vicente Peñaloza, nicknamed "El Chacho," who continued to rule in La Rioja. In 1862, El Chacho began gathering arms for a popular uprising against national authorities. Sarmiento, then governor of neighboring San Juan and a Mitre appointee, reacted to the rebellion by declaring a legally irregular state of siege and sending national forces to search out and defeat the rebellious caudillo. On November 12, 1863, Peñaloza was captured and beheaded by national troops who then placed his head on a lance as a warning to his followers. Although Sarmiento denied having ordered the assassination, this act of "official barbarism" is often cited as evidence of Sarmiento's flexible standards for himself. As part of his protest of innocence he wrote yet another biography, this time dedicated to thoroughly discrediting El Chacho as the most barbarous caudillo yet and suggesting that his removal from Argentine life was worthwhile regardless of the means (*OC* 7). The controversy over Sarmiento's handling of the El Chacho affair came at a time when his utopistic promotion of unrealistic public projects, a messy love affair, and a fight with the church had already diminished his popularity in San Juan. With the additional turmoil brought by El Chacho's murder, Mitre decided, as the Chilean government had some fifteen years earlier, that Sarmiento might be less of a liability out of the country. In April 1864, Mitre appointed him ambassador to the United States, where he was less controversial (Bunkley 395–412).

Sarmiento's departure, however, did not cool the flames. El Chacho's assassination provoked immediate outrage among nationalist intellectuals. In an emotional elegy titled "Al General Angel Vicente Peñaloza," Olegario V. Andrade wrote:

> The people's martyr! Expiatory victim
> Offered up on the altar of an idea,
> You sleep now in the arms of history . . .
>
> The people's martyr! Apostle of law,
> Your blood is a nurturing rain,
> And the last breath from your breast,
> Intimately faithful to your beliefs,
> Will later fan an unquenchable flame. . . .
>
> What does it matter that the porteño
> Despot holds his knife to our throats,
> And tramples under his feet
> The patriotism of your holy banners . . .
>
> For soon, the outcasts, our brothers,
> Will go to your grave, reverently,
> To ask God, with outstretched hands,
> For the knowledge to break the tyrants,
> Or to die as brave men die.
> (*Obras poéticas* 145–147)

With the repeated use of "the people's martyr," Andrade identifies El Chacho with the rural struggle against the porteño elite, a point he makes even clearer in the last stanza where it is "the outcasts (*los proscritos*), our brothers" who will carry on the fight against porteño domination. Andrade's "people" are, like El Chacho, the oppressed rural poor. One of the most egregious examples of the high-handed ways of officialist history can be found in an 1887 edition of Andrade's poem wherein the editors recast the poem as an elegy to Lavalle rather than to El Chacho; even more remarkable, the eighty-six-page introductory essay by Benjamín Besualdo avoids all specific reference to Andrade's role as a follower of Urquiza and a devout anti-porteño intellectual.

Andrade was not the only nationalist intellectual moved by Peñaloza's assassination. On November 12, 1863, José Hernández published in *El Argentino,* a Paraná newspaper, a short biography of El Chacho wherein he declares that "the Unitarian party has one more crime to write in the page of her horrendous crimes," a crime committed by "the murderer, the barbarian Sarmiento, [representative of] the party that invokes enlightenment, decency, and progress, but terminates its enemies by butchering them with daggers. . . . Damned! Let that party poisoned with crimes that have made the Argentine Republic a theater of bloody horror be . damned, and damned a thousand times" (*Prosas de José Hernández* 50). In the same article, Hernández also uses El Chacho's murder to warn Urquiza that he may be the porteños' next victim, however much he "may avoid his personal responsibility" to the provincial cause and be seduced "by Mitre's amorous words" (50–51). Moreover, as did Andrade in *Las dos políticas,* Hernández uses his biography of El Chacho to outline an alternative history of Argentina, in which the provincial caudillos Ramírez, Quiroga, López, Urquiza (until Pavón), Benavídez, and Peñaloza are the real heroes, and the porteño liberals, Rivadavia, Sarmiento, Rosas, and Mitre, the perpetrators of poverty, disruption, and terror. In Hernández's alternative history, Peñaloza's murder is merely the most recent episode in the porteño terrorist campaign against provincial interests, a campaign that had already claimed the lives of Dorrego, Quiroga, Benavídez, Virasoro, and now Peñaloza (52–56).

Alberdi also commented on El Chacho's assassination by recognizing him as a legitimate representative of The Other Argentina. He asks rhetorically, "Who was El Chacho?" and answers that he was first of all a general surely as deserving of that title as Mitre. Alberdi goes on to say that El Chacho was "the Garibaldi of La Rioja," a reference to Peñaloza's attempts to improve the material welfare of his province. He adds that

while [Mitre and Sarmiento] were fighting against El Chacho, they had at their disposal all the income and resources of the Republic, and even then they couldn't defeat him. In contrast, to defend the cause supported by half the Nation, El Chacho had no income except the love of his *pueblo,* who followed him with neither salary nor monetary stipend. (*Escritos póstumos* 9:558)

Alberdi singles out Sarmiento for special denunciation:

With all the resources of the government of San Juan and the national government, Sarmiento could not defeat the popular hero of La Rioja, whose power consisted solely in the free and absolute devotion of his pueblo. Out of fear, Sarmiento had him murdered. . . . To justify this crime, Sarmiento has vilified El Chacho, presenting him as nothing more than a loud-mouthed ruffian. In terms of character, El Chacho was much the better man. (9:574)

Developing this final point further, Alberdi asserts that Sarmiento was the true barbarian for murdering El Chacho "as is usually done in pampa warfare, that is, without a trial, and in a savage way; not shot, but stabbed and beheaded" (9:559).

Despite such protests, Mitre continued to build support throughout the country, largely because his administration brought the promise, if not the substance, of material prosperity. Moreover, Argentina had never seen a more effective politician; his rhetoric was superb, his timing was perfect, and his newspaper faithfully reported that he was doing a great job. Indeed, given enough time Mitre might have won over even his most intractable critics except for one tragic error: his involvement in 1865 in an alliance with Brazil to wage war against Paraguay.

Like many conflicts in the River Plate, the Paraguayan war actually began in Uruguay, where a long, smoldering conflict between the Colorados, a party similar in sympathies to the Argentine Unitarians, and the Blancos, who in many ways paralleled the Argentine Federalists, erupted in open civil war. On April 19, 1864, Venancio Flores led Colorado troops against the Blanco government, attacking from Argentina, where he had received ample cooperation from the Mitre government. Dom Pedro II, emperor of Brazil, quickly gave support to Flores. Since the Blancos had close ties to Argentine Federalism, Mitre covertly provided Flores with arms and aid while publicly declaring Argentina neutral. In the meantime, Francisco Solano López, the impetuous caudillo of Paraguay, fearing that Brazil would gain control of Uruguay and close Paraguay's crucial river access to the sea, announced support for the Blancos and then—most unwisely—declared war on Brazil. In late August 1864, Solano López requested permission from Mitre to use parts of northern Argentina as a staging area for invasions into Brazil's Matto Grosso. When Mitre refused, Solano López rashly stationed troops on Argentine soil anyway and later declared war on Argentina (Kolinski, *Independence or Death!* 86–91). As a result, Mitre had no choice but to declare war on the feisty Paraguayan who had in fact invaded Argentine territory. Unfortunately, Mitre chose to do so by entering an alliance with Brazil against Paraguay—a decision that would bring tragic consequences to the region and do irreparable harm to Mitre's presidency.

To contain López the first task facing Mitre and Dom Pedro was shoring up support in Uruguay, and this meant toppling the Blanco government. To do so, Brazil sent troops to help Venancio Flores. Flores and his Brazilian allies met the Blanco forces in definitive battle on December 2, 1864, at the Uruguayan town of Paysandú. Mitre secretly supplied arms to the invaders. Despite overwhelming odds, the Blancos held out for over a month. Finally, after fifty-two hours of constant bombardment and extensive losses, the Blanco forces surrendered to Flores on January 2, 1865. It was, however, a hollow victory for Flores, who from that point on was widely and correctly perceived as a pawn of the Argentine and Brazilian governments.

Today Paysandú occupies a minor place in Argentine history. For nationalist intellectuals of the time, however, it was an enormous tragedy, not only for Uruguay but also for the Federalist ideal. Particularly affected in this regard was Carlos Guido y Spano. A gifted writer, polyglot, and expert in classical literature, Guido y Spano grew up closely associated with Federalism. His father, Tomás Guido, was a distinguished general who had fought with San Martín in the Wars of Independence and later supported Rosas. From 1840 to 1852, don Tomás served the Rosas government as ambassador to Brazil. After Rosas's fall, he joined Urquiza and was vice president of the Confederation senate. Born in 1827, Carlos spent his teenage years with his father in Río de Janeiro and thus avoided the worst years of Rosas. Much unlike his father, however, Carlos disdained politics and drew pleasure principally from classical literature, music, and art. Yet for all his attempts to live above politics, Guido y Spano found himself repeatedly forced into the fray, as becomes clear in his two-volume collection of prose writings of 1879, titled *Ráfagas*. Moreover, despite his distaste for politics, he vigorously attacked Mitre's policies and at one point tried to enlist in Uruguay's much besieged Blancos.

Guido y Spano, however, could not attack Mitre without first establishing his own integrity, and as Adolfo Prieto has pointed out, that meant explaining his father's association with Rosas (Prieto, *La literatura autobiográfica argentina* 117–124). In his autobiographical "Carta confidencial" Guido y Spano carefully expresses his disdain for dictatorship, but nonetheless argues, like Alberdi and Andrade before him, that Rosas and the caudillos were merely products of an unfortunate political reality rather than its creators, that Rosas was the result of the time and not a monster supported by lesser monsters. On similar grounds, he defends his father:

[My father], like Generals San Martín, Alvear . . . and other eminent American patricians saw dictatorship as the bitter fruit of the factionalism that brought anarchy to our country. Although their principles and beliefs made them hate dictatorship, they preferred following the logical sequence of events, in hopes of controlling or tempering their results, to opposing those events in an impotent resistance, joining their opponents who, blind with rage, actually committed the enormous error of seeking the protection of a foreign power openly hostile to the Republic. (*Ráfagas* 1:vii)

Two points in this remarkable passage deserve comment. First, Guido y Spano clearly feels that, bad as Rosas was, the liberals in their fanatical rigidity actually did more harm than good. Second, he alludes to a common current in Argentine nationalism which has repeatedly accused Argentine liberalism of being antinational, more interested in personal gain than in the good of the country even if it means entering unholy alliances with foreign powers. It is not clear, however, what power Guido y Spano is referring to. At different times during the Rosas dictatorship, liberals cultivated the goodwill of several nations; depending on the occasion, Brazil, France, or Great Britain could fit the description of "a foreign power openly hostile to the Republic." Guido y Spano concludes the defense of his father noting that "our history makes for formidable dilemmas. If these are viewed with excessive rigidity, nothing will remain afterwards but enduring bitterness and deception" (*Ráfagas* 1:vii–viii).

It was, however, Paysandú and the events leading up to the defeat of Uruguayan federalism that most incensed Guido y Spano, forcing him into the political storms he abhorred. Already suspicious of Brazil's expansionism after his years in the imperial capital, Guido y Spano immediately condemned the Brazilian invasion of Uruguay, and particularly Mitre's obvious but unacknowledged involvement. On December 20, 1864, just as the Argentine-backed Flores was joining forces with Brazilian troops for the final siege against Paysandú, Guido y Spano wrote a stinging essay titled "¡Ea, despertemos!" (Come on! Let's wake up!). Identifying himself as "a humble child of the people" he recognizes that his voice will probably be silenced or ignored by the "oligarchical factions, the arrogant fear of their spokesmen . . . the opulent patricians, the publicans who comprise the cortesans of our plundered republic . . . [and] the soldier-of-fortune press *periodismo aventurero.*" (*Periodismo aventurero* also suggests carelessness and personal ambition; it is a term frequently invoked by nationalist writers against Mitre and Sarmiento.) To explain his outrage, Guido y Spano places the anti-Blanco offensive in the context of oligarchical suppression of the masses generally, and particularly of porteño domination over the provinces. He then affirms that "the [porteño] tribunal which swears allegiance to the lie" will continue to ignore the masses unless it needs to "buy their vote or their dagger." He continues, "But if some day the masses rise in protest, Woe unto them! for their fields will be lain bare, their homes burned, their families imprisoned and their men will be pursued as wild beasts. Then the murderers will call themselves heroes and the dagger of the most vicious assassin will be transformed into the flaming sword of justice" (*Ráfagas* 1:315–316). And how will the porteño elite justify such suppression of the masses? They will claim, says Guido y Spano in a wonderful parody of liberal pretension, that:

Barbarism is with us; it is necessary to excise Barbarism, and this cannot be done without regenerating our race. FOR ARE WE NOT MORE CONNECTED TO EUROPE THAN TO AMERICA? Are we not Europeans? What have we to do with the savage pampa and its rustic inhabitants, enemies of all progress, and undutious in the passive obedience and submission that they owe us? . . . Our intelligence, our luxury, our accomplishments, our press, our pleasures, do they not bear witness of our superiority? (316)

This lush parody touches on every liberal myth. "Regenerating our race" slams the racist underpinnings of liberal immigration policy; "Are we not Europeans?" punctures liberal cultural posturing; references to the "savage pampa and its rustic inhabitants" signal liberal racism and elitism; and the last sentence undermines liberalism's claims to authority by virtue of superior culture. Guido y Spano continues his denunciation, noting that this "language of the political Sybarites" seduces those who cannot see through "the pretentions of a sham civilization" (316). He ends his essay with a strong endorsement of Paraguay's position in the war and calls on "loyal Argentines" to support the Blancos against "imperialists and traitors"—that is, against Brazil and the Mitre-backed Flores (322). Guido y Spano continued his onslaught against Mitre, either with sarcasm ("Su excelencia está enfermo" and "Le roi s'amuse") or with direct attacks on the government's alleged neutrality ("Los artículos de La Nación Argentina" and "La alianza de 1851") but to no avail (*Ráfagas* 323–338). Eventually, he was placed under house arrest by the Mitre government, but managed to escape to Uruguay. His first stop was Paysandú, which by this time had fallen. He quickly joined the Blanco forces that were supposed to defend Montevideo, but the city collapsed with little resistance since Paysandú had convinced even the bravest Blancos that theirs was a lost cause.

No less incensed by the siege of Paysandú was Olegario V. Andrade, who happened to be a few miles south on the other side of the Paraná River in Concepción, Argentina and actually witnessed the destruction of the city. He recorded the horrible sight in a long, narrative poem titled "A Paysandú" in which he invokes Paysandú as the

> Calvary of saintly democracy,
> Widow of patriotism and nobility,
> Your robes of mourning in their eternal majesty
>   are your ruins,
>   Cradle of large-souled warriors,
> Of brave-breasted women,
> Seedbed of glory and heroism:
>   Peace in your solitude.
>   (*Obras poéticas* 135–136)

Following this invocation, he describes the battle in highly symbolic terms in which the "imperial crows" and their slaves (slavery
was still legal in Brazil) defeat "the heroes of the sacred struggle"
(137–140). He ends, however, noting that although people and
cities die and fall into ruin, the ideals of liberty and true democracy
are eternal:

> Thus the martyr city had to fall,
> Just as it fell, challenging destiny;
> Thus, Andean Condor, you had to fall,
> Into the claws of the rapacious eagle;
> You were the Christ of a great idea,
> The apostle of a blessed doctrine:
> Treason has sold you just as it did Christ,
> And just as with Christ, faith will save you.
>
> Paysandú! Sacred epitaph
> Written with the blood of the free,
> Altar of supreme sacrifices,
>   To your ashes, Peace.
> Paysandú! The great day of justice
> Dawns in the American heaven,
> And like Lazarus, from the bottom of your tomb,
> You will rise again.
>
> (143–144)

Particularly interesting in Andrade's frequently overwrought imagery are the biblical allusions in which democracy becomes a sacred
cause and Paysandú, the Calvary of the democratic ideal incarnate.
Alongside the Christian imagery, however, a second set of images
invokes an American ideal in which Paysandú becomes the Andean
Condor, while slave-holding Brazil is the imperial eagle reminiscent of the Rome that killed Christ. We glimpse in Andrade's verse
a nationalist sensibility that combines religious and patriotic sentiment in ways that enlightened liberals would have found embarrassing. Andrade assumes a grand role for Argentine federalism and its
search for a genuinely American destiny, not only for Argentina,
but for all of South America.

Andrade, Alberdi, Guido y Spano, and Hernández were too
close to the events of Paysandú to reflect on their true meaning. It
was not until the Paraguayan War, or War of the Triple Alliance,

was in full swing that they could see those events in a historical perspective. This section examines important aspects of that war, and then looks at the reactions of key nationalist writers.

With Flores's triumph in Uruguay, Mitre and Dom Pedro managed to install a puppet government that José Hernández called "a fiction of sovereignty, a grotesque farce of a government" (cited in *Proyecto y construcción de una nación* 267). But the Flores regime was amenable to both Brazil and Buenos Aires and supportive of their designs on Paraguay. Mitre, Dom Pedro, and their puppet Flores signed on June 12, 1865 the Treaty of the Triple Alliance, making them allies in the war against Paraguay. The terms of the treaty indicated that once the war was over Argentina and Brazil would redraw however they pleased the borders of a defeated Paraguay (Kolinski 91–93). This provision led virtually every other South American country as well as the United States to condemn the war as a land-grab campaign in which two giants were beating up on tiny Paraguay. Indeed, much of Sarmiento's time as ambassador to the United States was spent defending Argentina's role in the war (Bunkley 424–427).

What could have been a border skirmish soon exploded into the bloodiest conflict in Latin American history. Basically a war of attrition, the struggle lasted from 1865 to 1870. When it finally ended in a victory for the Alliance, the population of Paraguay had been reduced from 525,000 in 1865 to 221,000 in 1871, of whom only 28,000 were male, a ratio of nearly one male for every eight females. Over a century later, the Paraguayan population today remains at approximately half the prewar level. Since López presented no real threat to Argentina, Buenos Aires' disproportionate response to his pretensions can best be understood in psychological terms, or as Alberdi described it, "The problem of Paraguay is nothing more than another face of the problem of Argentina's interior. The question of the provinces is the sole cause and origin of the Paraguayan War" (*Escritos póstumos* 11:395). Alberdi declares that the porteño elite viewed López as a caudillo like any other, and thereby part and parcel of Argentine caudillismo. They also viewed suspiciously López's links to real and would-be caudillos in northern Argentina. In short, at a time when Buenos Aires was struggling to rid the interior of caudillo government, the porteño elite felt that the only good caudillo was a dead one. Hence, López, a

popular caudillo who is still remembered in Paraguay as the foremost national hero, had to be killed and discredited, even if it
meant turning Paraguay into a graveyard.

In the first years of the conflict, Mitre skillfully used the war to
his advantage. Never short on oratorical talent, he assured his followers that they would return triumphant to Buenos Aires in a
matter of months. So confident was he of a quick victory that he
chose to head Argentine troops in person; as a result, he spent
much of his final three years as president in the battlefield and
neglected presidential duties at home. The war also gave Mitre an
excuse to assert even greater control over his enemies. With the
aid of the Taboada family from Santiago del Estero, he defeated and
killed Felipe Varela, the caudillo who succeeded El Chacho in La
Rioja. The war also gave him an excuse to exile troublesome opponents like José Hernández and Carlos Guido y Spano. But most
important, perhaps, it allowed him to attack the power base of the
caudillos by press-ganging gauchos to fight against the Paraguayans, a neat arrangement in which two irksome social groups killed
each other off. Another unexpected benefit of the war was economic. Porteño and Littoral landowners, including Urquiza, made
fortunes selling leather, beef, and horses to the Alliance forces as
gold flowed from Brazil to Argentina. So much did Mitre's followers benefit from the war that they became known as the *partido de
los proveedores* or "Suppliers' Party" (Rock, *Argentina* 127–129).

While the war gave the Mitristas political and economic benefits,
for the common people it became increasingly burdensome, so
much so that nationalist intellectuals were soon publishing strong
objections to the human and economic costs of the war. Of the many
documents to emerge from this published dissent, none is more
significant than Guido y Spano's lengthy article "The Government
and the Alliance" (*El gobierno y la alianza*). Published in the Buenos
Aires newspaper, *La Tribuna*, in July 1866, "The Government and
the Alliance" is Guido y Spano's most ambitious political piece and a
good indicator of nationalist sentiment as well as nationalist paradox.

Guido y Spano wrote the article with two major goals in mind.
First, he wanted to expose Mitre (and by extension Argentine liberalism generally) as a fraud, a dupe of Brazil, and an enemy to real
democracy. Second, he sought to place the Alliance in a historical
context in which the war and its destruction result inevitably from

anti-Federalist thought. These arguments are interesting in their own right, but as we shall see, Guido y Spano also exposes involuntarily a side of Argentine nationalism that does it no credit.

Guido y Spano first attacks Argentine liberalism by showing how badly Mitre practiced what he preached. He notes Mitre's promises to bring peace and union to all Argentines and writes almost admiringly of the good political sense Mitre showed in retaining with few amendments the Federalist constitution written under Urquiza. But he quickly adds that Mitre's liberalism did not include constitutional guarantees for his political opponents. Opposition newspapers were silenced, enemies were exiled, and the last Federalist caudillos were killed in terrorist campaigns:

The tumult of the civil war was followed by the silence of death in the devastated provinces. All resistance was crushed. All armed opponents [to Buenos Aires] lay fallen in the fields. Why take an enemy prisoner, and especially if the enemy is Argentine? Among the thousands of men who died because they hated living in servility, not one of them was judged in a court of law! (*Ráfagas* 1:365)

Particularly forceful in this passage is the rhetorical question indicating how little liberals valued the life of lower-class Argentines. Guido y Spano further argues that "in truth, the government, despite sermonizing about its fictitious liberalism, gave in to a reactionary Unitarianism and worked to stifle all opposition that did not spring from its own kind—opposition that would always be limited by the affinities of common origin" (1:362). In this telling sentence, Guido y Spano admits that Mitre permitted limited debate among people of similar persuasions, members of the porteño family so to speak, but only enough to protect the façade of liberalism while puting down all significant opposition. He further maintains that the Mitristas rigged elections through "fraud and violence" so that only "lawyers too mediocre to have clients, noisy newspaper hacks . . . and haughty nonentities" could win (1:363). Echoing many of these same sentiments José Hernández wrote in 1868:

Mitre has been the most malevolent entity known in these lands. . . . In bloody military campaigns, he has populated our fields with cadavers; he has trampled on the sovereignty of the provinces with illegal interventions, farcically called peaceful; he supported the barbarous persecu-

tion . . . of the Federalist party; he silenced the free press, driving into
exile those who raised their voices to ask for justice against the aggressors;
he sanctioned the Treaty of the Triple Alliance against precedent and
against national sentiment; he threw the government into a war against
Paraguay, and has remained three years at the head of the army only to
demonstrate his military incompetence and ineptitude. (*Prosas y oratoria
parlamentaria* 83)

In "The Government and the Alliance" Guido y Spano also attacks Mitre for agreeing to renew payment on a loan from Great
Britain outstanding since 1824 (*Ráfagas* 1:363). Rosas had questioned the debt's validity, and nationalists of all strains still argue
that foreign loans, rather than developing Argentina, merely enrich
international banks and compromise Argentine sovereignty. Guido
y Spano suggests that in coming to terms with England on the debt,
Mitre preferred enhancing Argentina's reputation abroad to building her welfare at home. The "to pay or not to pay" debate is, of
course, as timely today as it was then. In his denunciations of the
Mitre government, Guido y Spano repeatedly makes reference to
el pueblo, the mythical people whose rights are violated and whose
destiny is thwarted. Mitre and his recycled Unitarians then are not
just political opponents; they are enemies of the people, antipopular and anti-Argentine.

But it is in Mitre's handling of the Paraguayan War that Guido y
Spano finds his biggest target. By 1866, when "The Government
and the Alliance" was written, the war was well under way, and
Guido y Spano is able to document what he had previously just
suspected. In the articles on Paysandú we examined earlier, Guido
y Spano accused the Mitre government of doing nothing to help the
besieged Blancos and suggested that Mitre was actually supporting
Flores despite his alleged neutrality. The real extent of Mitre's
support of Brazil's invasion, however, became clear later in declarations by the Brazilian diplomat Jose Maria de Silva Paranhos and
statements by Mitre himself. In Brazil it was revealed that Mitre
not only allowed Flores to organize the invasion on Argentine territory but also that at a crucial point in Flores's campaign, Mitre
supplied him with much needed ammunition (1:391). Mitre himself
confirmed Guido y Spano's worst suspicions. In a speech to the
National Congress on May 1, 1865, the Argentine president stated
that Brazil's invasion of Uruguay was warranted by "just causes"

and "nonpartisan interests . . . which confirmed [Brazil's] profound respect for the independence of [Uruguay] of which it is was
guarantor in union with Argentina" (cited by Guido y Spano 1:389).
Even without Guido y Spano's editorial outrage, Mitre's admission
is a monument of duplicity. Only months earlier he had proclaimed
that Argentina maintained total neutrality throughout the invasion
of Uruguay and the siege of Paysandú; now he dares claim that
Argentina and Brazil's meddling in Uruguayan internal affairs, installing a puppet government under Flores, and then declaring war
on Paraguay were all motivated out of "profound respect for the
independence" of Uruguay. Again, we see the most visible spokesman of Argentine liberalism using a liberalist vocabulary to justify
actions contrary to everything good in the liberal dream.

If Guido y Spano has any forgiving words for Mitre at all, it is to
portray him as a dupe of Brazil rather than coequal perpetrator of the
invasion of Uruguay and the subsequent dismembering of Paraguay.
But it is here that Guido y Spano's argument becomes more conspira-
torial than factual. His argument rests on the questionable premise
that both Paraguay and Uruguay by nature and by birthright form
part of Argentina—a notion harking back to one of the country's
earliest guiding fictions: the need to maintain the boundaries of the
Viceroyalty of La Plata. In Guido y Spano's view, the force most
responsible for dividing that ideal Argentina was Brazil. He suggests
that Brazil's meddling permitted Dr. Francia to maintain power in
Paraguay after 1811, despite Argentina's attempts to regain the province. Similarly, he argues that Brazil kept Uruguay from rejoining
Buenos Aires during Rivadavia's time. In sum, according to Guido y
Spano's view of the world, had it not been for Brazilian interference,
Argentina's "sister provinces" of Paraguay and Uruguay would have
happily joined the Argentine union of equal provinces in a true
federation. Alberdi also described Bolivia, Paraguay, and Uruguay,
not as separate republics, but as provinces that Argentina "lost"
because of the "arrogance and incompetence" of the porteños
(*Grandes y pequeños hombres* 181–183). Alberdi also attributed the
Paraguayan war to Brazil's ambition, an ambition to which Mitre was
fast becoming an accomplice. In "El Imperio de Brasil ante la
democracia de América," he writes, "the root of the problem disguised as the Paraguayan war is nothing less than a reconstruction of
the Brazilian Empire." In the same essay he calls Mitre the man who

"pawned Argentine liberty in a Brazilian pawn shop" (*Obras completas* 6:272). In another essay of the same period, "Las dos guerras del Plata y su filiación en 1867," he wrote, "My showing of sympathy for Paraguay during the war has not been an affront to the Argentine Republic, as some have argued, but rather the painful but timely protest against an alliance that has made the Argentine peoples instruments of Brazil, in ruin of themselves" (*OC* 7:29).[2] In short, Alberdi fundamentally agrees with Guido y Spano: Brazil is the great destabilizer and Mitre is her stooge.

In this schema, Mitre and his fellow "conspirators in tailcoats" (*conspiradores en etiqueta*) betrayed the ideal of a spiritual Argentina by recognizing Uruguay as an independent member of the alliance and Paraguay as a country to be defeated and then divided with Brazil. This is, of course, much more fanciful than true. Nothing in the history of Paraguay suggests widespread desire to be under the tutelage of Buenos Aires, or for that matter, even part of a confederation of equal provinces known as Argentina.

Which brings us to a peculiar aspect of Argentine nationalist thinking: the notion of a spiritual Argentina, sometimes called *La Gran Argentina*, which is the country's true destiny—and which recalls Artigas's sense of a mythical America waiting to be realized. *La Gran Argentina* is very much the focus of a poem written by Olegario Andrade, also in 1867, titled "El porvenir" (The future). The poem tells how Andrade from a mountaintop foresaw his country's future in which a "frightful whirlpool" will engulf the enemies of Federalism the "Apostates, hangmen and tyrants / Who made of crude war their right."

> And the living word,
> The word of republican faith
>   Will announce to the spheres . . .
> [That] redeemed peoples embrace
> Before the sacred altar of ideas.
> One people leads the tumult

2. Alberdi developed these same ideas—Brazil's machinations and Mitre's complicity—in several other important essays. The most representative is perhaps "Las disensiones de las rebúblicas del Plata y las maquinaciones del Brasil" of March 1865 (*OC* 6:309–356), where Alberdi's conspiracy theories and explanations reach a complexity bordering on paranoia.

Of the audacious crusade; a great people
To whom God gave the Pampas for a carpet
   And the Andes for a dossal.

  On their head shines the prodigious seal
Of God's election . . .

   There is my Fatherland! My Fatherland! And I see her
At the vanguard of a redeemed world,
Of a world in bondage for three centuries,
Like a ship on an unknown sea,
Breaking the chains of the past
   She goes forth bravely,
Hopeful and bedecked in blue,
To the birth of holy democracy!
Hers is the flag that waves
On the age-old promontory,
The flag that brings the light of liberty
To the altar of an enslaved race.

               (Andrade, *Obras poéticas* 44–45)

The "redeemed peoples" are clearly all Spanish Americans, "in bondage for three centuries" of Spanish rule. Recalling Argentina's heroic role in the independence movements of several Spanish American countries, Andrade prophecies that Argentina will again guide the entire continent, that her flag "blue and hopeful" will lead the way to the altar of liberty. Then, as the flagship of the continent, the patria will reach her destiny as *La Gran Argentina*. This destiny lives in embryo in *el pueblo* who still await liberation, the leaderless masses, repeatedly betrayed but always deserving. Guido y Spano and his generation are among the first to use widely terms like "nationalist" and "the nationalist spirit" to refer to a populist orientation—this long before such terms became popular in the twentieth century (see, e.g., *Ráfagas* 1:361, 369). They are also among the first to bridle at the small role liberalism assigns to Argentina in the international scheme of things; the nationalist vision wants more for Argentina than being Brazil's ally, England's faithful customer, or, to use a term of a later period, the world's granary. Argentina in their view is destined to be a leader, bearer of God's prodigious seal, liberator of an entire continent, and standard to the world.

Another current in nationalist thought, apparent in Andrade's reference to "apostates, hangmen and traitors" holds that Argentina's failure to achieve that spiritual destiny derives not from the weakness of the Argentine *pueblo* but from outside meddlers and fifth-column traitors. Argentine nationalism is replete with conspiracy theories. For Guido y Spano, Brazil was the great corruptor; for later nationalists, the British, the CIA, the multinationals, the international banks, the Trilateral Commission, or whoever, would thwart *La Gran Argentina*. Yet whatever the demon's name, his henchmen were always the Europeanized, anti-Argentine elite who sold their country for personal gain, the *vendepatria* (the sellers of the Fatherland) who accepted second-rate status for Argentina as long as they cashed in on the deal.

In addition to dreams of *La Gran Argentina* and endless varieties of conspiracy theories, there is yet another current in the thought of these early nationalists that deserves comment, namely, their unabashed—and for Argentina unusual—identification with other countries of Spanish America. The tendency of Argentine liberals to see themselves as South American Europeans left them little interest in the rest of Latin America, except when they arrogated to themselves roles of mentor and example as did the Rivadavians and the Generation of '37. This attitude, which led Sarmiento to look the other way when the United States annexed half of Mexico, again surfaced during France's ill-fated attempt to install Maximilian as emperor of Mexico in 1864. Although the Mitre government maintained offical neutrality during the conflict, his newspaper, *La Nación*, published several articles defending the French invasion, arguing that "rutterless societies have throughout time been conquered or invaded because Providence always has people in reserve to occupy those lands possessed by flawed societies" (cited by Guido y Spano, *Ráfagas* 1:195). Horrified at the suggestion that Mexico, as a "rutterless, flawed society" somehow deserved to be invaded, Guido y Spano sent a long reproach titled "La cuestión de Méjico" to Mitre's newspaper—which the newspaper's editors pocketed, assuring him that it would be published as soon as space was available. After nearly a month of waiting, Guido y Spano sent his article to a rival newspaper, *El Nacional*, later to be closed by the Mitristas, which not only published the article but also Guido y Spano's blistering attack on Mitre's censorship through silence.

Mitre's reluctance to see "La cuestión de Méjico" in print is understandable. Guido y Spano first notes the irony that France, tutor and exemplar of liberal revolutions throughout America, should now be the "guilded castle of peremptory despotism. . . . The American republics have lost their natural ally, since, by attacking Mexico, France has negated her promise and been unfaithful to her history" (*Ráfagas* 1:190–191). More irritating for Guido y Spano was Argentina's official silence on the matter, particularly since the governments of Peru, Chile, and Brazil had already shown support for Mexico. More telling then his position on the French invasion, however, is his rhetoric. Guido y Spano frequently refers to Argentina as just one "American State" among many "sister republics." He also insists that his interpretation of popular attitudes is more accurate than the government's, affirming, for example, that his position on Mexico reflects "the popular instinct . . . with which superior peoples (*los pueblos superiores*) face down the greatest politicians; it is the old Spanish blood rising against the spectacle of rapacious violence and usurping force" (1:192). Again we see his belief that *el pueblo* is the real depository of Argentine virtue. But we also see a curious coupling of this idea to an exaltation of "old Spanish blood." Nowhere in Guido y Spano, or in other nationalists, for that matter, do we find the tedious denigration of Spain and the Spanish heritage that marks the work of Argentine liberals like Sarmiento and early Alberdi. It is precisely this sense of common ancestry that allows Guido y Spano to speak of "sister republics" in a way unknown in Argentine liberalism. Thus, the Mexican struggle becomes a Spanish American struggle in which "brave Mexicans, at the vanguard of a cause that profoundly affects us all, defend the rights of all these [Spanish American] peoples . . . fighting valiantly against foreigners and traitors" (1:192).

This refusal to accept the liberal view of Spain and Latin peoples is also apparent in Olegario V. Andrade. Toward the end of the 1870s, he wrote an important poem titled "Atlántida: Canto al porvenir de la raza latina en América" (Atlantis: Hymn to the future of the Latin race in America), in which he argues that race is "the raging river of history" and that God gave the Latin race the destiny "Of inaugurating history / and filling space" (*Obras poéticas* 52–53). In Andrade's reconstruction of history, the ancient Greeks were the first manifestation of Latin destiny, and from them the mantle passed to Rome. Both Greece and Rome fell, but

> Races do not perish because the peoples
> Who nourished their spirit fall,
> Without honor or glory . . .
> Races are the rivers of history,
> And the mysterious torrent of their life,
> Flows eternally.
>
> (57)

In Andrade's mind, the Latin race and its destiny as mentor and civilizer of the world continued although specific peoples, or manifestations of that race, rose and fell. Thus it was that Greece and Rome could fall, but the Latin destiny would continue to be fulfilled in the Spanish and French. As Spain and France decline, the race of destiny would again manifest itself, but this time in Latin America.

> But God reserved
> The incomplete task of renascent spirit,
> To the Latin race, leader
> Of peoples, combatant
> In the great battles of history.
> And when came the hour,
> Columbus appeared on the ship,
> That carried the destiny of the world . . .
> And brought to life [Plato's] vision of Atlantis.
>
> (64)

It is this "destiny of the world" that Andrade sees being realized in all of Latin America, in the "splendid tropics of the Antilles"; in Mexico, the "granite watchtower"; in "the oppulent Colombia / Which seemingly carries in its womb / The inexhaustible youth of the world"; in Venezuela, "cradle of Bolívar"; and so on throughout the continent. Finally, he sees Argentina,

> The blessed patria,
> Always in pursuit of sublime ideals
> A young people . . .
> That calls to its opulent feast
> All that pay homage
> To Holy Liberty, sister
> Of art, progress and knowledge.
>
> (66–69)

Andrade's view of the Latin destiny clearly distances him from the liberal thought of Sarmiento and early Alberdi, for whom Spain was a retrograde parent whose American children needed to adopt new models in northern Europe and Anglo-America. Interestingly, Andrade's *latinidad* would be transformed twenty years later into one of the most significant movements in Latin American intellectual history. In 1900 the Uruguayan essayist José Enrique Rodó would publish a short but enormously influential essay titled *Ariel* in which he argues not only that the Latin peoples are the legitimate heirs of Greek intelligence and sensibility, but also the necessary counterbalance to the utilitarian materialism of Calibán, his symbol for the United States. Rodó's debt to Andrade is seldom recognized.

Nor does Andrade appear to share the racialist preoccupations of Argentine liberalism. In his poem "La libertad y la América" he writes:

> Here, where the breasts of a mighty creation,
> Await new races to suckle their vigor . . .
>
> Here, where some day pariah races will come
> To intertwine their arms in fraternal union,
> To waken, perhaps, the solitary jungles
> With the sublime accent of mystical prayers,
> As slaves sing of their eternal redemption;
>
> Here, where a worn Europe with her emaciated hand,
> With the haughty audacity of her vile envy,
> Tries to inject her corrupt blood . . .
> In the fiery blood of a virile people.
>
> (Andrade, *Obras poéticas* 47–48)

Although supportive of immigration, these lines hardly seem consonant with Sarmiento's preference for Germanic Europe. Moreover, Andrade appears to think that Latin Americans, with all their racial crossing, are already a virile people, superior to "a worn Europe" that seeks to inject "her corrupt blood." Andrade's exaltation of Latin Americans as they are distances him from the theories that first justified immigration policy; but more important, his is clearly a populist sentiment that connects with Artigas's attempts to include "gauchos, Indians, Negroes, and zambos" in his ideal society.

As we have seen, what I have called "nationalism" in nineteenth-century Argentina was not demagoguery, nor was it merely the resentment of defeated people. Rather, it was a well-developed alternative to the guiding fictions of Argentine liberalism. At its best, it proposed a different paradigm for Argentine history in which the porteño wealthy, the "oligarchy," regardless of public ideology, were united in greed and in their hegemony over the provinces. It postulated as well a dream for Argentina, *La Gran Argentina,* which "foreigners and traitors" repeatedly frustrated. This early populism also first used the terms "nationalist" and "nationalism" to identify a political view that was proprovincial, anti-porteño, and antielitist; similarly, it branded the porteño wealthy and self-proclaimed liberals as "Europeanizers" (*europeizantes*) and "anti-Argentine"—terms that supported both a healthy national pride and a most unhealthy xenophobia. Populism also saw Argentina as part of a great Latin and Hispanic tradition, rather than a European colony surrounded by barbarians, and in that tradition affirmed solidarity with the rest of Latin America. But most important of all, perhaps, populism rejected those theories of exclusion, popular among Argentine liberals, which saw in the mixed-blood provincials an impediment to progress. In short, Argentine populism at its best offered a mythology for consensus and inclusion that, had it triumphed, might have developed the kind of all-embracing democracy to which Argentine liberalism gave only lip service.

The hypocrisy of Argentine liberalism is wryly summed up by Guido y Spano in his autobiographical letter of 1879. Guido y Spano remembers the decade of 1860 as a time when he sought refuge from politics in his books; others, he notes, "with their ignorance in tow, clawed up a tree they called liberty when in fact it was probably just a rotten ombú. . . . Up there so high, they were transformed almost by magic into governors, ministers, ephors and archons, all the while maintaining an admirable appearance, which did not prevent them from commiting acts of frightful barbarity. . . . Opposing these tinsel men, products of a mad demagoguery, there were always men of good will in Buenos Aires and in the Argentine Republic, who supported principles of liberty and order, of rights under the ample guarantees of the constitution. But their efforts could not avoid the ruin of civil war, the Paraguayan war, nor the shadowy intrigue that brought discord and ruin to Uruguay" (*Ráfagas* lvii–lviii).

Argentine liberalism, the old Unitarians, the party of the Buenos Aires intellectual elite, won the political battles of the nineteenth century and for the most part managed to impose their view of history on the minds of later generations of Argentines. As a result, Andrade, Alberdi except for *Bases,* Guido y Spano, Hernández— all could easily have been forgotten, had it not been for two exceptional literary works that continue to cast doubt on the wisdom of Argentine liberalism. The first is Lucio V. Mansilla's *Una excursión a los indios ranqueles,* which consists of a series of letters the author wrote describing his encounters with the very Indians the Sarmiento government was determined to exterminate. The second is a long gauchesque poem titled *The Gaucho Martín Fierro,* which gave populism a human face in the unforgettable image of a gaucho so persecuted by liberal governments as to become the barbarian Sarmiento most feared. These works, their context, and their enduring importance in Argentina's guiding fictions are the subject of the next chapter.

Chapter Ten

Roots of Argentine Nationalism, Part Two

Lucio V. Mansilla's *Una excursión a los indios ranqueles* and José Hernández's *Martín Fierro* did not emerge in a vacuum. Both had an intellectual tradition within Argentina, and both reflected political and social realities of their time. The Indian question that concerns Mansilla surfaces in Artigas's writings in the late 1810s and was debated extensively in the 1820s and 1830s; *rosistas* often pointed to Rosas's good relations with the Indians as proof that Federalists were better equipped than their Unitarian counterparts to solve the problems of Argentina's native populations; and one of Argentina's most loved nineteenth-century poems is "La cautiva," published in 1837 by Esteban Echeverría, which tells of a doomed love between a white woman and a noble savage who dies trying to save her. Similarly, Hernández inherited much from Bartolomé Hidalgo's populist gauchesque poetry, Confederation thought, and late Alberdi. But the most immediate context of these works was political: the war against Paraguay and the Indian Wars commonly called "The Conquest of the Desert."

The Paraguayan War seriously compromised the last three years of Mitre's six-year term. Government projects faltered as Mitre diverted resources into the war effort and personally led troops against López. Moreover, never tolerant of detractors, he forced nationalist critics into exile, and instructed his Minister of the Interior, Guillermo Rawson, to order Governor Domínguez of Entre

Ríos to close down "the newspapers *El Porvenir, El Pueblo Entre Riano, El Eco de Entre Ríos* y *El Paraná* [for] having taken a path incompatible with national order . . . using whatever means necessary" (cited in Tiscornia, "Vida de Andrade" xxxiii). The sudden death of his vice-president, Marcos Paz, in early 1868 forced Mitre, who had been heading troops in the war against Paraguay, to return to Buenos Aires after several years' absence—just in time to help select his successor. Mitre supported Rufino Elizalde, a long-time associate known for his loyalty to the president. Other contenders included Adolfo Alsina, son of Valentín Alsina, the ever-militant Buenos Aires autonomist whose separatist views tormented Urquiza and made Mitre look moderate. Although the provinces were by this time firmly in the hands of Buenos Aires centralists, latent Federalist sympathies in the interior lessened the chances of both Alsina and Elizalde. In need of a compromise candidate, the electors came up with the name of Sarmiento. One of his most vocal supporters was Lucio V. Mansilla, who, despite being Rosas's nephew and a sometime supporter of Urquiza, threw all his energies into supporting Sarmiento in hopes of being appointed Sarmiento's Minister of War. Always easier to love at a distance than at home, Sarmiento was just finishing a three-year term as Argentina's ambassador to the United States. Memory of his unfortunate governorship in San Juan had faded, and as a pro-porteño who nonetheless grew up in the provinces he seemed a choice agreeable to both provincial and porteño interests. His election was assured when Adolfo Alsina withdrew his candidacy and agreed to be Sarmiento's vice president. At the time of his election on August 16, 1868, Sarmiento was at sea, returning from New York, and had no idea of the honor (and problems) awaiting him. Informed of his new post in a stopover in Rio de Janeiro, he visited the Brazilian emperor Dom Pedro and assured him that Argentina under his presidency would not waver in the alliance against Paraguay.

Sarmiento's presidency got off to a rocky start. He offended Mansilla by assigning him to a minor military outpost in Río Cuarto instead of appointing him Minister of War, as Mansilla had hoped. If Sarmiento intended to get Mansilla out of Buenos Aires politics, he most surely failed since from Río Cuarto Mansilla began publishing the letters on which *Una excursión a los indios ranqueles* is based (more about this work later). Sarmiento then tried to woo Mitre into his government. Although surely aware of Mitre's support for Elizalde, Sarmiento hoped the former president would continue as both commander of the allied forces in Paraguay and Minister of War. Since sharing power was not his style, Mitre refused both offers and instead dedicated himself to opposing Sarmiento's policies from his Senate seat and in his newly founded newspaper, *La Nación,* which remains the country's leading daily. Mitre's opposition to Sarmiento made little ideological sense, but it underscored an essential fact of Mitre's politics: when in power he was a zealous, often effective, public servant; when not in power he opposed whoever was, regardless of ethics and ideology.

Mitre and Mansilla weren't Sarmiento's only problems. He needed to extract Argentina from the Paraguayan War, which at the time of his inauguration in 1868 was still at high pitch; to pacify the interior where provincial tensions threatened to erupt into civil war; and to protect from displaced Indians the expanding white settlements. Less than two weeks after his inauguration, support arrived from an unexpected source: Urquiza, the man Sarmiento had so misrepresented in *Campaña del ejército grande,* wrote a letter of congratulation dated October 29, 1868:

Your Excellency can count on me as the first among the servants of the nation who desires the opportunity to demonstrate his sincerity during your administration. If some resentment has put us in opposing ranks, the sole memory of having fought together for liberty beneath the shadow of the same flag and the interest that both of us have in the greatness and fortune of our homeland will unite us closely today, each in his own position, to seek what nobody has achieved, the destruction of partisanship, and the reconstruction on one basis, that of the constitution. You at the head of the nation and I as governor of a rich, strong, and moralized province are in a position to realize that aspiration. (Cited in Bunkley 453)

Sarmiento responded cautiously to Urquiza's offer, but after considerable diplomatic contact he accepted an invitation to visit Urquiza in Entre Ríos in February 1870. Although Sarmiento received a splendid reception, he continued doubting Urquiza's commitment to a unified Argentina under Buenos Aires.

A year after taking office, Sarmiento could finally claim progress in the Paraguayan War. On January 5, 1869, Alliance troops occupied Asunción, a city whose population in five years had reportedly been reduced from 500,000 inhabitants to some 80,000, mostly women and small children. López fled the city to a mountain fortress where he and most of the 500 men with him were killed on March 1, 1870. The end of the fighting, however, did not end the war's effects on Argentina. Sarmiento now had to face a war debt in excess of $50,000,000 and the needs of some 20,000 veterans. Further complicating matters were disagreements with Brazil over war indemnity and Paraguay's new—and substantially reduced—borders. In desperation Sarmiento appealed to Mitre to negotiate a settlement with the Brazilians, a task the unpredictable ex-president completed extraordinarily well. Sarmiento's presidency was also plagued (literally) by devastating outbreaks of cholera and yellow fever. To make matters worse, France's defeat in the Franco-Prussian War (1870–1872) left European markets in disarray and began a serious decline in foreign demand for Argentine goods.

Although the combined burdens of war, debt, depression, and illness left few resources for Sarmiento's grand educational and economic plans, his record in these areas is impressive. Under his administration, the number of children studying in public schools increased from 30,000 to 100,000, immigrants entering Argentina doubled, and homesteading policies were enacted. He founded normal schools and imported teachers from the United States to run them. He created the National Observatory, the School of Mining and Agronomy, the Naval Academy, and the Military Academy. He expanded the public library system, tripled the railways, established both a national and an international telegraph system, rewrote the commercial and military codes, and ordered the first census. At the same time, he was ruthless in dealing with perceived undesirables like Indians and gauchos, and autocratically intervened in provincial politics whenever things were not to his liking. Indeed, his attempts to centralize power in himself and his propensity to equate his political well-being with Argentina's, regardless of institutional procedure, led his best biographer, the sympathetic Allison Williams Bunkley, to call him "a modern caudillo" (*The Life of Sarmiento* 472).

The most dangerous political threat to Sarmiento's presidency occurred in 1870, when forces of Ricardo López Jordán, a former Confederation lieutenant much disillusioned by Urquiza's surrender at Pavón, murdered Urquiza and his two sons Justo and

Waldino, only weeks after Sarmiento had visited him in San José. A frustrated politician, López Jordán had run for the governorship of Entre Ríos in 1864, but was defeated by José M. Domínguez, who was supported by both Urquiza and Mitre. Convinced that Urquiza and Domínguez had sold out to Buenos Aires, López Jordán began organizing a gaucho army and plotting the murder of Urquiza. This grisly task accomplished, López Jordán named himself governor of Entre Ríos and began a separatist war against Buenos Aires. On being sworn in as the new governor of Entre Ríos he declared, "I regret that the patriots who decided to save our institutions could not have found another means than killing their illustrious victim, but I cannot think about a tomb when I see before my eyes the beautiful horizons of a happy and free people" (cited in Bosch 714). Sarmiento's forces chased López Jordán out of the country in a matter of months. After attempting to invade Argentine territory in 1873 and again in 1876, López Jordán finally realized that his ambitions would never enjoy sufficient popular support, and he retired to a ranch in Uruguay. In 1888 he slipped into Buenos Aires, where he was recognized and shot by the son of a military officer whom López Jordán had ordered killed fifteen years earlier. Today he is mostly remembered for plotting the assassination of Justo José de Urquiza.

With Paraguay whittled down to nothing, the caudillos either dead or exiled, and pro-porteño leaders in control of the provinces, there remained only one obstacle impeding the liberal vision of progress: the Indians who continued harassing settlements along Argentina's expanding frontiers. From the early days of the Republic, land-hungry Creoles had pushed the Indians out of their lands, although some Creole leaders, notably Rosas, enjoyed better relations with the Indians than others. Rosas effectively pitted Indians against Indians and managed to maintain Indian loyalties through annual payments to allied Pampas and Araucanian tribes, registry of which exists in government records under the rubric "Negocio pacífico con los indios." Such payments became irregular after Rosas's fall in 1852, and after Urquiza's defeat, Mitre stopped them altogether. With the stoppage in payments and the government's military force diverted to the war against Paraguay, Indian raids on white settlements picked up to such a degree that Sarmiento declared recuperation of lost lands one of his highest priorities (Jones, "Civilization and Barbarism and Sarmiento's Indian Policy" 5–7). In certain ways, the gauchos faced problems similar to those of the Indians since, although Spanish-speaking and in some sense Christian, they also lived on the margins of society, and were slowly being pushed from lands they once roamed freely. Moreover, like the Indians, the gauchos held no place in liberalism's vision of Argentina.

To resolve the Indian problem once and for all, Sarmiento fell back on his original notions of civilization and barbarism. As early as 1844 while still in Chile, Sarmiento responded to Chilean writer José Victorino Lastarria's report on Spanish cruelty during the conquest, arguing that "We must be fair with the Spaniards; by exterminating a savage people whose territory they were going to occupy, they merely did what all civilized peoples have done with savages, what colonization did consciously or unconsciously: absorb, destroy, [and] exterminate" (Sarmiento, *Obras completas* 2:219). He was further inspired by the example of the country he most admired, the United States, and at one point sent delegations to Washington to view firsthand how the United States was handling the Indian problem. Like North American leaders, Sarmiento and many other Argentines spoke grandly of civilizing the Indians, but the program Sarmiento actually followed came to little more than a policy of deliberate dislocation and extermination. No doubt the ideologies reflected in *Facundo,* which saw the Indians as a race unfit for true democracy, comforted him in this endeavor.

Since the Argentine press was filled with reports of Indian attacks, or *malones,* in which white settlers were killed or carried away, never to be seen again, it is not surprising that most Argentine intellectuals, liberal and nationalist, supported the Indian wars, tacitly or overtly. An interesting and partial exception to this dictum, however, is Lucio V. Mansilla, a complex figure who with less psychological baggage might have been one of Latin America's best writers. Born in 1831, he was the son of Lucio Norberto Mansilla, a distinguished Independence hero and politician who became prominent in the Rosas government, and Augustina Ortiz de Rosas—sister of the dictator. Educated in Buenos Aires, young Lucio showed little interest in the family meat-salting business and took to reading dangerous Frenchmen. His father once caught him reading Rousseau and promptly informed him that "when you are a nephew of Juan Manuel de Rosas, you don't read the *Social Contract* if you plan to remain in the country" (cited in Caillet-Bois, "Prólogo" ix). Shortly thereafter, Lucio Norberto arranged for his son to travel to India to purchase jute.

The young Lucio remained abroad for nearly three years, and traveled overland from India to London. These travels provided the basis for his first publications, gathered later in two short volumes titled *De Edén a Suez* and *Recuerdos de Egipto*. Still in London in 1851, when Urquiza began his campaign against Rosas, Lucio returned to Buenos Aires only weeks before Rosas's fall in 1852. Rather than face the hostility of the anti-Rosas victors, he fled with his family to France, where the good-looking young Argentine was well received. But Lucio grew bored with life in exile, and two years later returned to Mitre's Buenos Aires. He remained in the capital city long enough to get embroiled in a fight with José Mármol over some passage in Mármol's novel, *Amalia*, which cast doubt on his family's honor. He then fled to Paraná, where he worked as a journalist, associated with other Federalists and children of Federalists who feared remaining in Buenos Aires. Mansilla remained faithful to the Confederation throughout Urquiza's presidency, and helped repel Mitre's attack at Cepeda in 1859. But once Derqui succeeded Urquiza, Mansilla's faith in the Confederation faltered; in 1861, when Mitre fought Urquiza at Pavón, Lucio switched sides and fought for Buenos Aires.

This equivocation in his loyalties would characterize much of his political life. At some level, the burden of being a nephew of the most reviled man in Argentina took a daily toll; like Guido y Spano, Mansilla never quite outlived his family's association with *rosismo*. Repeatedly he tried to find a political patron, first in Urquiza, and later in Mitre and Sarmiento, but each time he was rejected. To further ingratiate himself to Mitre after Pavón, he fought for Buenos Aires in Paraguay, thus distancing himself even further from former Federalist friends like Olegario Andrade and Carlos Guido y Spano, who vehemently opposed the war. In Paraguay, he befriended Sarmiento's son, Dominguito, and was present when he was killed. Sarmiento greatly appreciated Mansilla's kindness to Dominguito—but not enough to offer him a significant post in his government.

Thus it was that Mansilla, after supporting Sarmiento for president and hoping to be named Minister of War, ended up in late 1868 in Río Cuarto in the Province of Córdoba—hardly a plum appointment. Unhappy with Sarmiento's perceived ingratitude, Mansilla nonetheless did his work well, and very shortly letters appeared in the porteño daily, *La Tribuna,* praising his accomplishments in pacifying the Indians and safeguarding settlers and railways. Edited by Mansilla's friend, Héctor Varela, the newspaper may have planted the letters to irritate Sarmiento and keep Mansilla's name in the public eye. In February 1870, Mansilla and a representative of the Indian chief, Mariano Rosas, agreed on a peace treaty that Mansilla sent to Sarmiento for final approval. When Sarmiento suggested changes in the treaty, Mansilla wrote an angry letter charging that the president never took him seriously. In the meantime, the Indians began doubting the good faith of the government and backed away from the treaty. Partly to reassure them and partly to relieve his own boredom, Mansilla embarked on a journey into Indian territory, recording his experiences and observations in a series of letters addressed to an old friend, Santiago Arce. The letters were published in the Varela newspaper between May 20 and September 7, 1870. Later collected by Héctor Varela, these letters became the singular work of Argentine literature now known as *Una excursión a los indios ranqueles* (Caillet-Bois vii–xxii).

Three main currents permeate Mansilla's text. First, he sought to describe the Ranquel Indians—their attitudes, customs, beliefs, and principal spokesmen—to enter their world as completely as possible, or as he puts it "to eat an ostrich omelette in Nagüel Mapo" (*Una excursión* 11). Critic Julio Ramos perceptively calls Mansilla's trip "a deliberate journey to barbarism," the inverse of his travels to Egypt and Europe as well as of the obligatory trip to Europe that was on the agenda of every upper-class Argentine youth (Ramos, "Entre Otros" 144). A second current in the work is Mansilla's effort to vindicate himself, to prove that, although Rosas's nephew, he deserved better than Río Cuarto. And third, he attacks Sarmiento's Indian policies, sometimes directly but more frequently through abstract discussions regarding the notions of civilization that supposedly justified the government's campaign against the Indians. Unfortunately, although a prolific writer, Mansilla is not a rigorous thinker. As a result, he frequently brushes on fascinating questions that, with more attention, would have led him to embrace a kind of cultural relativism very unlike liberalism's facile exaltation of "civilization" and the brash self-confidence of the Sarmiento government.

Despite this tendency to drop important questions in midflight, Mansilla's attacks on Sarmiento often connect with guiding fictions of land, class, and race traceable at least back to Artigas and his view of a preexisting Argentine character, invisible to the Europeanized porteño and extant only in the pampas and their inhabitants who were somewhow the "real" *pueblo.* "Those who have portrayed the pampa, supposing it to be in all its immensity a vast plain," he writes, "all are mistaken. The idealized landscape of the pampa, or pampas in plural as I would call them, and the real landscape are two completely different perspectives. We live in ignorance even of the the physiognomy of our patria" (1:92). Mansilla repeatedly derides Buenos Aires for miscomprehending the country. Like Guido y Spano, he attacks the Eurocentric focus of Argentine liberalism that blinds the country's leaders to Argentina's autocthonous nature and virtues. He also praises the "national type" who turns out to be none other than the gaucho as "a generous sort, whom our politicians have persecuted and stigmatized" and, in a reference to the "blackface" gauchesque, "whom our poets have not had the valor to praise, but to caricature (2:49–50). In a similar passage, Mansilla speaks of the gaucho as "our race," again distancing himself and his own class from the true national soul (1:96). In a particularly revealing passage he describes a gaucho, Manuel Alfonso, nicknamed Chañalao, who moved easily in Creole country society as well as among the Indians, as "the truly native plant of Argentine soil." Yet he laments that Chañalao repeatedly had difficulties with the law of the cities, the legalities of Sarmiento's civilization, and concludes that "Such is our land: like our politics, it usually consists in making enemies of our friends, pariahs of the children of the nation, and secretaries, ministers, and ambassadors of those who fight against us" (2:262). Thus it is that Mansilla identifies—occasionally—with the populist notion that liberalism abandons the real children of Argentina, preferring to promote as "secretaries, ministers, and ambassadors" those who fight against the authentic Argentina. Of course, Mansilla's concern for the downtrodden might have remained unexpressed had he been appointed Minister of War instead of Comandante of Río Cuarto.

In other parts of *Una excursión,* Mansilla argues that liberalism's inability to include the nation's true children accounts for the artificial, deracinated, imitative society of trendy Buenos Aires:

> This narrow obsession [*monomanía*] for imitation seeks to strip us of everything: our national appearance, our customs, our tradition.
>
> We are being turned into a people for an operetta. We have to play all roles, except the one we know how to play. We are besieged by foreign institutions, laws and accomplishments. And without doubt we are progressing.
>
> But would we not have progressed more had we viewed our process of organization from a different perspective, drawing inspiration from the real needs of the land?
>
> We are better at inspired outbursts than cold and reflective meditations. Where are we headed in our present course?
>
> Somewhere for sure.
>
> We cannot remain still when there is a social dynamic that makes the world march and humanity progress.
>
> But those currents that mold us like soft wax, leaving us made against ourselves [*contrahechos*], will they carry us any faster or more surely than our own turbulent, confused impulses to abundance, wealth, leisure, and liberty under law?
>
> I'm nothing but a modest chronicler. Gratefully!
>
> (2:48–49)

No passage reveals better than this one Mansilla's multiple ambiguities. First is the uncertain referent of "we" and "our." On the one hand, like Artigas, Hidalgo, and others in the populist tradition, he assumes that Argentina already has an identity, referred to as "our national appearance, our customs, our tradition" and that that identity somehow lies in the gauchos, Indians, and country-dwellers. Yet in the following paragraphs he distances himself from that identity by saying that he and his group (clearly the porteño upper class rather than the gauchos and Indians) are being forced to play a Europeanized role, incongruent with the country's nature.[1] Just as ambivalent is his attitude toward progress. While he admits the

---

1. Julio Ramos's "Entre otros" describes with brilliant insight the many dimensions of Mansilla's "I," "we," and "our." Similarly insightful in its exploration of Mansilla's shifting autobiographical persona is Sylvia Molloy's "Imagen de Mansilla."

material progress Argentine liberalism was bringing to the country, he suggests that such progress is in some sense against the land and its people, that it would have been better to listen to the inspired outbursts of less educated people [the caudillos?] than to the cold reasoning of Europeanized intellectuals. His fear is that European thought and its kind of progress will leave the country *contrahecho*, made against itself, developed contrary to its nature. These are fascinating suggestions, but, as is typical in Mansilla, they penetrate no farther than the surface. More a friend of chatty comment and flippant witticism than of rigorous thought, Mansilla quickly abdicates intellectual responsibility to probe deeper by calling himself "nothing but a modest chronicler" and proceeds to the next anecdote.

No clear voice emerges in Mansilla. Mansilla could not take a strong, consistent position precisely because he didn't know where to place himself. Was he the educated, Frenchified dandy who is also the nephew of Rosas? Or was he the sometime supporter of both Urquiza and Mitre, who fought in the Paraguayan War that he later condemned (1:86)? Or was he the man who, while contemplating his own bad luck in landing a ministership from Sarmiento, claims that liberalism abandons Argentina's own children, yet never ceases to view the Indians and gauchos as "them" against the "us" of Buenos Aires? Or was he the dilettante *causeur*, flitting from one topic to another, with amusing pointlessness? While speculating that true national identity lies in the lower-class gauchos and Indians whom he and his class oppress, he ultimately recommends nothing to replace Sarmiento's program of forced assimilation, displacement, and annihilation. Mansilla's best alternative is "to civilize [the gauchos and Indians], make them Christians, and use their muscle for industry, work, and the common defense" (1:87). In sum, despite his rapturous accounts of Indians and gauchos as the "true" children of the country, in the final analysis, Mansilla proposes assimilation and exploitation in terms only slightly more humane than those of the liberalism he attacks. At best, as Julio Ramos notes, Mansilla criticizes Argentine liberalism, but always from a liberal perspective; Sarmiento's policies are not bad because they are liberal, but because they are bad liberalism (Ramos 165). Yet Mansilla's many poignant descriptions of the Indians and gauchos he met during his famous *excursión* gave human faces to the Other Argentina and still serve to undermine Official History's view of Sarmiento as defender of civilization. Mansilla also provides a sad portrait of the intellectual who looked at everything, but never quite found a cause deserving of his energy. His literary persona as a result is the one he carefully sculpted: that of the dandy, the raconteur, the witty observer, the sprightly conversationalist, paralyzed by too much sophistication and too aware of the world to ever commit to it.

The Indian wars that framed Mansilla's famous account of his "journey to barbarism" also form the backdrop of Hernández's *El gaucho Martín Fierro*, but in quite a different fashion. While Mansilla is concerned mostly about the Indians and the gauchos living among them, Hernández rises to defend the gauchos still left on the frontier, particularly those whom Sarmiento press-ganged to fight against the Indians. José Hernández wrote *The Gaucho Martín Fierro*, which appeared in 1872, during the fourth year of Sarmiento's presidency, two years after Mansilla's *Una excursión*. Its sequel, titled *The Return of Martín Fierro*, was published in 1879 during a period of relative harmony. As we will see below, the two texts respond to dissimilar historical contexts and as a result differ markedly from each other.

José Hernández is an anomaly among Argentine writers for many reasons, the least not being his evident distaste for writing about himself. As a result, his life before he became a nationally famous writer is often difficult to trace, so much so that even his most dedicated biographers (of whom there are many) disagree on essential details of his early development. Born on November 10, 1834, Hernández spent much of his early life with his mother's sister, owing to his parents' frequent trips to the pampas to buy cattle for Buenos Aires traders. Although a precocious reader, he completed only four years of primary school. After his mother died in 1843, Hernández continued living with his aunt until 1846, when his father took him and his brother Rafael to live on an estancia in the pampas south of Buenos Aires where, in the words of his brother, "he became a gaucho" (Hernández, [Rafael], *Pehaujó* 81). The adolescent Hernández not only acquired the rustic skills of riding, bulldogging, and throwing *bolas* (leather-wrapped stones connected by thongs that gauchos used to entangle an animal's legs) but also learned the metaphorically rich dialect of the gaucho and developed a profound appreciation for the human worth of Argentina's rural poor.

As for his political formation, his mother, a Pueyrredón, came from staunch Unitarian stock, whereas his father was a Federalist. While living with his mother's sister in 1840, his Pueyrredón relatives, with the six-year-old Hernández in tow, were forced to flee the *mazorca*, Rosas's secret police force. Hernández was eighteen years old when Urquiza defeated Rosas. Later, he witnessed first-hand the struggles between Mitre's centralist forces and the remnants of Federalism in the Province of Buenos Aires. After an initial ambivalence, he sided with the autonomist forces of Federalism, largely out of his sympathy for the gauchos. These twin concerns—defense of the gaucho and opposition to porteño centralism—marked his work as a journalist, politican, and poet.

Hernández began his journalistic career in 1856, working for *La Reforma Pacífica,* a pro-Confederation newspaper published in Buenos Aires by Nicolás Antonio Calvo. Calvo, Hernández, and their allies were also active in the Federalist Reform Party, which had as its principal goals Buenos Aires' union with the Confederation and the defeat of the Liberal Party headed by Valentín Alsina and Mitre. The Reformists lost to the liberals in the 1857 elections, which even Sarmiento admitted were fraudulent; in a letter to Domingo de Oro, dated June 17, 1857, Sarmiento affirms that "The gauchos who resisted voting for the government candidates were jailed, placed in stocks, or sent with the army to serve on the borders with the Indians; many of them lost their lands, their limited possessions and even their wives" (cited in Chávez, *José Hernández: Periodista* 16). Following their "victory," the Liberals, in most unliberal fashion, began harassing opposition newspapers by levying ridiculous fines for "libel" that eventually drove them out of business. *La Reforma Pacífica* suffered eight such fines, one of which reached 10,000 pesos (Chávez 26). As a result of the persecution, in 1858 Hernández moved to Paraná, headquarters of the Urquiza government, where he worked variously as a journalist, teacher, and scribe. Like many Federalists, he was quietly disillusioned by Urquiza's refusal to continue fighting for the Federalist cause after the Battle of Pavón in 1861. Further, Hernández showed early sympathy for Ricardo López Jordán, the man who would plot Urquiza's murder and lead an abortive revolution against Buenos Aires. Nonetheless, as a journalist Hernández claimed loyalty to Urquiza, perhaps because his job depended on it. As Tulio Halperín Donghi wryly puts it, Hernández was always "sensitive to the dominant tendencies of his surroundings" (*José Hernández y sus mundos* 41). During the decade 1858–1868, Hernández wrote for several interior newspapers; his most significant piece was *Vida del Chacho* of 1863, discussed earlier. Much moved by the fall of Paysandú in 1864, Hernández joined fellow Federalists Guido y Spano and Olegario Andrade in their futile defense of the Uruguayan Blancos. Later, he worked for several provincial newspapers, until finally, in 1869, ten months after Sarmiento assumed the presidency, he returned to Buenos Aires, where he founded *El Río de la Plata*, one of the most important newspapers in Argentine history.

   Although *El Río de la Plata* lasted scarcely eight months, it represents the culmination of Hernández's political thought and forms the ideological frame for the first part of *Martín Fierro*. Moreover, except for his famous poem, the newspaper embodies Hernández's most noble effort on behalf of the disenfranchised. In sober, unembellished prose, Hernández's editorials in *El Río de la Plata* advocate greater autonomy for the Interior, popular elections for local authorities, and equitable land distribution for immigrants and the rural poor—a program not unlike that recommended by Artigas fifty years earlier. He also takes a hard line against press-ganging ill-equipped gauchos to fight against Indians, and questions the prudence of the Paraguayan War. But more important perhaps is the rhetorical framework of his writing—a framework that clearly unites him with Alberdi, Andrade, and Guido y Spano in denouncing the "cultured barbarism" of Argentine liberals, the exclusion of the poor from the political process, and the antinational oligarchy.

   The good sense of his journalism, however, did not always carry over to his politics. After Urquiza's murder on April 11, 1870, most Argentines, even those who resented the fallen general for abandoning the Federalist cause, closed ranks behind Sarmiento in condemning López Jordán. Not so Hernández. In a letter to Urquiza's assassin, Hernández wrote of his former employer:

Urquiza was the Tyrant Governor of Entre Ríos, but even worse he was the Traitorous Head of the Great Federalist Party, and his death, a thousand times deserved, is a great and exemplary act of justice from the party he so often sacrificed and sold out. . . . For ten years you [López Jordán] have been the hope of the masses, and today, postrate, beaten and shackled, they see in you a savior! (Cited in Chávez 79)

Virtually nothing in Hernández's work in *El Río de la Plata* anticipates his support for the violence unleashed by the ill-fated López Jordán. Although critical of the Sarmiento government, *El Río de la Plata* strikes a tone of loyal opposition, in favor of free debate, opposed to noninstitutional solutions, supportive of new immigration, and anxious to work within a truly liberal system. López Jordán represented none of these, nor was there any objective reason to think he could withstand the inevitable military retaliation of Buenos Aires. In short, Hernández for bad reasons bet on the wrong man. On April 22, 1870, he closed *El Río de la Plata*, partly as a result of rising pressure from the Sarmiento government, and fled north, where he eventually joined the Jordanistas.

Although his support of López Jordán was a wrong political decision, in some sense it began the process that culminated in *The Gaucho Martín Fierro*. Hernández joined López Jordán just in time to see him beaten by government forces and driven into exile. In the meantime, however, contact with gaucho soldiers and other members of the rural poor revitalized Hernández's interest in their problems and their language. It was probably at this time that he conceived his character Martín Fierro, who on a personal level reflects the problems Hernández had previously addressed only in the abstract.[2] After López Jordán's defeat, Hernández lived in exile

2. He may also have been inspired by another gauchesque work "Los tres gauchos orientales" by the Uruguayan poet Antonio Lussich which was published only months earlier. Although literarily inferior to many other gauchesque works, Lussich's poem has the distinction of restoring to gauchesque poetry its element of protest on behalf of the gauchos themselves, which, as we have seen, was lost after Bartolomé Hidalgo's work. In "Los tres gauchos orientales," three former supporters of the Blanco cause lament their lost place in Uruguayan society in the aftermath of Flores's triumph and the Paraguayan War. On June 20, 1872 Hernández wrote a letter to Lussich praising him for portraying so vividly "the distress and suffering of the gaucho forced to be a soldier, his heroism, the devastation brought by a fratricidal war and the sterility of a peace that does not safeguard the rights of diverse political groups" (cited in *Antología de la poesía gauchesca* 1133). But he makes no mention of *Martín Fierro*, which by this time must have been well along.

for a time, first in Brazil and later in Montevideo. In 1872 he secretly returned to Buenos Aires, where he took up residence in the Hotel Argentino. There, partially in hiding since the government had no tolerance for *jordanistas*, he wrote the first part of *El gaucho Martín Fierro*, which he published on November 28, 1872 in a cheap edition.

No description of Hernández's motives for writing the poem is better than his own. In a letter written in December 1872 to the poem's first publisher, Hernández indicated his desire to expose "the abuses and denigrations endured by this disinherited class . . . the hardship, misfortune, and haphazardness of gaucho life" (letter transcribed in *Antología de la literatura gauchesca* 1375–1376). But he also sought to paint a picture that would win not only political sympathy for gauchos, but also understanding of their peculiar culture and language. In this endeavor, Hernández occasionally patronizes his subject—but only occasionally. As he writes in the same letter:

I have tried . . . to present a type who personifies the character of our gauchos, concentrating in his way of being, feeling, thinking and expressing all that is peculiar to them; giving him the array of images and color that fills his imagination; the impetuousness of his pride, excessive to the point of crime; and all the drive and tumult found in children of nature who remain unpolished and unrefined by education. (1375–1376)

Yet the poem is ultimately much more than a political pamphlet and social portrait. As in many great works of literature, it appears that at some point the subject took possession of the author, compelling him to go beyond his intentions, often in verses of great beauty. As a result, *Martín Fierro* portrays a man who is at once individual and prototypical, a compelling literary persona and also a representative victim of Argentine liberalism. In this interweaving of the individual, the psychological, the sociopolitical, and the artistic lies the poem's greatness.

At the beginning of the poem, Martín Fierro identifies himself as a *payador,* a kind of gaucho troubador known for his ability to improvise verses and tell stories in song. With echoes of Hidalgo clearly apparent, Fierro states that his is a story of suffering and hardship, that in some sense liberal society has deprived him of everything but his story:

Here I come to sing
to the beat of my guitar:
because a man who is kept from sleep
by an uncommon sorrow
comforts himself with singing
like a solitary bird.

(Hernández [José], *El gaucho Martín Fierro*, trans. C. E. Ward 3)

Fierro further notes that his suffering results not from what he has
done but from what he is, a gaucho:

I am a gaucho . . .

I was born as a fish is born
at the bottom of the sea;
no one can take from me
what I was given by God—
what I brought into the world
I shall take from the world with me.

It is my glory to live as free
as a bird in the sky:
I make no nest on this ground
where there's so much to be suffered,
and no one will follow me
when I take to flight again.

Let whoever may be listening
to the tale of my sorrows—
know that I never fight nor kill
except when it has to be done,
and that only injustice threw me
into so much adversity.

And listen to the story told
by a gaucho who's hunted by the law;
who's been a father and husband
hard-working and willing—
and in spite of that, people take him
to be a criminal.

(9–11)

Fierro makes clear, however, that his is the story of all gauchos,
that his task is not only identifying himself but speaking for a peo-

ple. In this endeavor, his voice assumes a peculiarly epic tone, of prenational unity, in which the gaucho story begins in a lost paradise, an uncertain past when gauchos lived lives of dignity, fulfillment, and self-determination:

> I have known this land
> when the working-man lived in it
> and had his little cabin
> and his children and his wife. . . .
> It was a delight to see
> the way he spent his days,
>
> Then . . . when the morning star
> was shining in the blessed sky,
> and the crowing of the cocks
> told us that day was near,
> a gaucho would make his way
> to the kitchen . . . it was a joy.
>
> And sitting beside the fire
> waiting for day to come,
> he'd suck at the bitter maté
> till he was glowing warm,
> while his girl was sleeping
> tucked up in his poncho.
>
> And as soon as the dawn started to turn red
> and the birds to sing
> and the hens came down off their perch,
> it was time to get going
> each man to his work.
>
> (13)

Like all myths of lost paradise, this one cannot be situated in history. If the gaucho ever enjoyed, however approximately, such an idyllic existence, it would have been during colonial times when gauchos roamed the plains uninhibited, living off the bounty of an untamed land. Yet, Hernández's allusions to the "working man" in his "little cabin" surrounded by "his children and his wife" with each man preparing for "his own work" suggest a way of life and division of labor found only on large *estancias* where gauchos were peons, treated more or less well according to the whims of the *estancieros*. Consequently, Hernández's nostalgic evocation of a past where gauchos lived contentedly, at one with their environment and their work, has been seen as a defense of the *estanciero* system in which gauchos were supposedly happy peons. Tulio Halperín Donghi, one of Hernández's most informed detractors, argues persuasively that many of Hernández's ideas in *El Río de la Plata* and in his later *Instrucción del estanciero* do indeed point in this direction (*José Hernández y sus mundos* 224–277). Leftist writers like Melcíades Peña (*De Mitre a Roca* 40–50) and José Pablo Feinmann (*Filosofía y nación* 71–189), who would like to claim Hernández as a precursor, have reluctantly come to similar conclusions.

Three points must be taken into account, however, lest we fall too easily into this condemnation of Hernández. First, whatever the evidence that in other contexts Hernández supported positions held by the landowning oligarchy, his poem at most gives only an oblique nod in that direction—so much so that the rural poor never read the poem as anything other than their own vindication. Whatever Hernández's intentions as reconstructed in light of his other writings, this mass-reader response to the poem remains valid; in short, by authority of many readers, *El gaucho Martín Fierro* continues to be a populist and even revolutionary defense of the gaucho even if in other contexts Hernández showed ambivalence regarding the place the rural poor might occupy in an ideal society. Second, in view of the poem's own rhetorical framework, the lost-paradise theme functions effectively in counterpoint to the lamentable present, thus deepening Fierro's tragedy and by extension its condemnation of government policy. Third, in Hernández's nostalgia for a lost past, he suggests like Mansilla that Argentina in its infatuation with foreign models lost its way, that a return to the past was somehow the country's best hope. This nostalgia is a constant of Argentine populism, found in the country's folklore, tango lyrics, revisionist histories, and antiliberal ideologies. Concerning the poem's contribution to Argentine guiding fictions, these three points far outweigh clever carping about what Hernández "really" meant to say.

Following Fierro's evocation of former gaucho life, he begins his tale of misfortune. While Fierro and other country people, including immigrants and an Englishman, were at a country dance, government officials arrived on the scene and pressed the unfortunate revelers into the armed forces to fight Indians on the frontier:

As they sent us off, they made us
more promises than at an altar.
The Judge came and made us speeches
and told us again and again:
"In six months' time, boys,
they'll be going out to relieve you."

(29)

With a naive, patriotic willingness to fight the marauding Indians,
Fierro took his best horse along with "halter, tether, leading-rein,
lasso, bolas, and hobbles" (29). He was early surprised, however,
that the government was not forthcoming with equipment of similar quality. The recruits received mostly "pikes and old swords"
(35) instead of guns, and what firearms were available proved use-
less since the government did not provide ammunition. Nor were
firearms the only thing lacking:

I won't tell you anything about our pay,
because it kept well out of sight.
At times we'd reach the state
of howling from poverty—
the money never came
that we were waiting for.

And we went around so filthy
it was horrible to look at us.
I swear to you, it hurt you
to see those men, by Christ!
In my bitch of a life I've never seen
poverty worse than that.

(49)[3]

To survive, Fierro had to sell his beloved horse to the
Comandante who "wanted to teach him to eat grain" (51). He
further indebted himself to a frontier trader who gave credit
against future earnings. As a result, when payday came he, like
most of his comrades, wasn't "on the list." When several gauchos
complained, the Comandante launched a phony investigation "to
get things straightened out—[to show] that this wasn't Rosas's

3. The miserable conditions under which the gauchos were forced to fight
were also documented in reports sent to London from England's representative in
Buenos Aires (Ferns 324).

time." The Comandante speaks with the rhetoric of Argentine liberalism—that justice will be done, that the government is a reliable investigator of itself, that one must only trust the law. But this show of institutional rule "was all a lot of fuss about nothing, and play-acting." In this incident, Hernández effectively reveals the underpinnings of liberal corruption, a corruption that not only lines the pockets of the powerful and excludes the lower classes, but also perverts the very language of liberalism. Despite the rhetoric of institutional, representative rule, Fierro discerns that no one speaks for him. As with all rural poor, his needs and point of view are excluded from offical Argentina:

> But what could I do against them,
> I was like an ostrich-chick in the wilds!
> All I could do was give up for dead
> So as not to be worse off still. . . .
> So I acted sleepy in front of them,
> though I'm pretty wide awake.
>
> (61)

Moreover, he suggests that liberal Argentina as seen through the military was interested only in maintaining a comfortable façade behind which corruption and "barbarism" flourish:

> You couldn't call that service
> nor defending the frontier,
> it was more like a nest of rats
> where the strongest one plays the cat—
> it was like gambling
> with a loaded dice.
>
> In this merry-go-round, I've seen
> many officers who owned land,
> with plenty of work-hands
> and herds of cattle and sheep—
> I may not be educated
> but I've seen some ugly deals.
>
> (63)

After the mock investigation, the Major takes revenge on Fierro for complaining about loss of pay. Fierro's punishment for seeking justice through institutional means is fittingly barbaric:

They stretched me on the ground
between four bayonets.
The Major came along, fairly stinking,
and started screaming out,
"I'll teach you, you devil,
to go around claiming pay!"

They tied four girth straps
to my hands and my heels;
I put up with their hauling
without letting out a squeak,
and all through the night I cursed
that gringo, till I wore him out.

(69)

After this humiliation, Fierro deems desertion his only option, and "like an armadillo I headed straight for my den." He finds, however, that his cabin is gone, his wife in order to survive has taken up with another man, and his boys, although "like young pigeons not yet finished feathering," now work as peons. Contemplating the pitiless fate of his wife and children, Fierro laments:

Maybe I'll not see you again,
love of my heart!
God give you his protection
since he didn't give it to me—
and, from this place, I send out
my blessing to my sons.

They'll be wandering motherless
like babes from the orphanage—
already left without a father—
that's how fate has abandoned them,
with no one to protect them,
not even a dog to bark at them.

(80–81)

Denied a place in Argentine society, Fierro turns to a life of crime "like a wildcat after they've stolen its young." Crime is the only path left for the outcast to show "there's blood left in his veins" (85). It is as a criminal that Fierro acts out the most vivid scene of the poem. In a rural dance, he insults a black woman for no apparent reason, calling her a cow and then suggesting she would make a good mattress. To deepen the insult, he sings:

> God made the white men,
> Saint Peter made the brown,
> and the Devil made the black ones for coal
> to keep the hell-fires goin'.
>
> (89)

When the woman's black boyfriend rises to her defense, Fierro calls him "fuzzy in the head," thereby provoking a duel. After a brief but brutal knife fight, Fierro kills the black man:

> He kicked a few times
> and then he gave his last gasp. . . .
> The death throes of that Negro
> is something I'll never forget.
>
> At this point, up came the negress
> with her eyes red as chili—
> and, poor thing, there she started
> howling like a she-wolf.
> I'd have liked to give her a whack
> to see if it would make her shut up—
> but on second thought I realized
> it wouldn't do just then,
> and I decided not to beat her
> out of respect for the deceased.
>
> I cleaned my knife on the grass,
> I untied my colt,
> I mounted slowly, and went off
> at a jog trot, towards the lowlands.
>
> (95)

Later, Fierro hears that the Negro was not given a proper burial and that his soul still wanders the earth in search of rest. The episode ends with Fierro saying:

> And sometimes I think what I'll do
> so that he won't suffer so long,
> is take his bones out from that place
> and stick them into the burying-ground.
>
> (97)

Three items make this episode particularly striking. First, to prove that he is not entirely impotent, Fierro must insult and kill, choosing as his victims people he views as his racial inferiors. So reduced are his pride and circumstances that only in violence can he affirm himself. Second, Fierro shows little, if any, remorse. Statements that he will never forget the agony of the Negro or that he may eventually give him a proper burial possibly suggest regret but not necessarily; they could just as easily indicate superstition. Nor can the lack of remorse be attributed to Fierro's reluctance to show emotion since in other parts of the poem his emotions are evident to the point of undermining his credibility. Third, the grief of the black woman does not move Fierro. His initial reaction is to beat her so she will stop crying, but he decides against it with the stock phrase "out of respect for the deceased."

This remarkable episode lends itself to several interpretations. If we confine ourselves to the political, the scene suggests how much society's mistreatment of Fierro has brutalized and alienated him, making him a criminal of the most vile sort. The scene thus could allow Hernández to repeat a commonplace of his journalism that gauchos would become good citizens only through education and political inclusion—and perhaps this was his intention. Such an argument, however, does not account entirely for Hernández's willingness to risk the reader's sympathy for Fierro. Before the fight, Fierro is an innocent victim, guilty only of being a gaucho in a society that allows him no room. Yet in killing the Negro and wanting to beat his grieving girlfriend rather than hear her sorrow, Fierro becomes a brutal, unpitying aggressor and thereby endangers the sympathy we have felt for him up to this point. Borges suggests that in this scene Fierro takes over Hernández, that the internal logic of the fictional character forced the writer beyond his conscious intentions, that Hernández did not endanger the reader's goodwill knowingly (*Obras completas* 195–197). Whether so intended or not, the scene reveals extraordinary psychological perception into Fierro's need for violence as a means of denying his inability to control his own destiny. Although the fight and murder lend uncertainty to Hernández's political agenda while risking loss of the reader's sympathy, this scene more than any other makes Fierro believable.

After another murder, this time provoked by a bully, Fierro

becomes a hunted man. Sleeping in abandoned shacks, he lives on the run, philosophizing on the plight of gauchos, whose "only use . . . in this land is to vote" (105), an allusion to the corrupt election practices Hernández deplored in *El Río de la Plata.* Trapped eventually by a posse, Fierro decides to fight to the death rather than give up. Despite his remarkable resistance, he is eventually overpowered by superior numbers. But suddenly, unexpectedly, one of the policemen, a gaucho recruit named Sargento Cruz, joins Fierro, saying, "I'll have no part in the crime / of killing a brave man this way" (125). Together they fight off the remaining troopers, share a bottle, and ride off to tell each other their respective stories.

Although Hernández offers little reason for Sargento Cruz's defection to help Fierro, the episode suggests that the bonds of shared hardship and *hombría,* the cult of manliness, triumphed over Cruz's loyalty to his uniform. Cruz affirms that "It's at times like these you show you are a man of strength—until death comes and grabs you and knocks you in the head." He later says "It's no discredit to me / going around so poorly dressed. / I may not be a saint, / but I can feel for someone else's troubles" (131). Like Fierro when he kills the Negro, Cruz echoes the creed of manly bravura in which it is strength that counts, not institutions and associations. He reinforces the point by ironically calling attention to his trooper's garb as something that does not detract from his worth as a man sympathetic to the hardship of others. Some complain that in this episode Hernández elevates friendship over the law, personalism over institutionalism—that Hernández glorifies on a small scale the personalism that Sarmiento deplored in his criticism of *rosismo.* In the minds of Hernández's popular readers, however, Cruz's collaboration with Fierro was apparently the only means to dignity when the cards were stacked against the little guy.

Cruz's story in large measure parallels Fierro's in that he is the victim of corrupted power. Once happily mated to a beautiful woman, Cruz tells how a Comandante from the militia took an interest in his companion. To get time alone with Cruz's spouse, the Comandante sends Cruz on make-work errands. Cruz eventually discovers the Comandante in an amorous embrace with his wife, fights with him—but then runs, knowing that the law will eventually favor his rival, and that among his peers, he has become a cuckold. Despite years of roaming "like an orphan calf / that's lost after a storm" (149), Cruz cannot flee his disgrace and eventually gets into a brawl where he murders a *payador* who has insulted him. Finally, a friend intervenes to "put [him] right with the judge" (157), who in turn assigns Cruz to the rural police force through which he meets Fierro. The two gauchos conclude their tales swearing eternal friendship—outside of the law:

> We'll live like outlaws
> as we have to, to save our lives—
> we never need to go short of
> a good horse to get away on,
> nor a stretch of high grass to sleep in,
> nor good meat to put on the spit.
>
> (161)

Hernández returns to the political intentions of the poem by having Cruz conclude his tale with:

> and I let the ball roll on,
> because one day it'll stop.
> A gaucho has to put up with it
> until he's swallowed by the grave. . . .
> Or else til there comes a real *criollo*
> to take charge of things in this land.
>
> (161)

The phrase "a real *criollo*" anticipates what would become a major theme in the nationalist/nativist credo. Rather than an *europeizante* liberal, what Argentina needed was a real Argentine, someone in tune with the authentic Argentina that liberalism repeatedly betrayed to the latest ideological fad from Europe and the United States. This real *criollo* would by definition represent rural, provincial, and gaucho interests, and be a real man, someone who could "take charge" (*mandar*). Hernández rightly identifies the gaucho's craving for a trustworthy strongman, a powerful friend to speak for the people and set things straight. In a word, a caudillo. How much this passage represents Hernández's feelings, and not just those of Cruz, is unclear. Although Hernández was an acerbic critic of Rosas, the "real *criollo*" Cruz/Hernández longs for would in some sense be another Rosas. Moreover, in his personal political life, Hernández easily fell sway to López Jordán, a would-be caudillo

who aspired to "real *criollo*" status. In this century, Perón successfully packaged himself as a friend of the masses, an authentic Argentine not afraid to challenge the "anti-Argentine" liberal elite. Even
today, this longing for a real Argentine who will miraculously set
things straight remains a durable guiding fiction—and a powerful
threat to institutional democratic government.

Finding friendship in their common past, Cruz and Fierro resolve to leave Argentina forever and live among the Indians where
"the powers of the government don't reach" (169). Fierro symboli-
cally smashes his guitar "because no one else is going to sing / once
this gaucho here has sung" (175). Hernández then takes up the
narration, relating how Fierro and Cruz cross the border and look
back sadly on the last Argentine settlements while "two big tears
went rolling / down Martín Fierro's face" (177). The poet finishes
his story by returning to the political concerns that motivated him
in the first place:

> And now with this report
> I've come to the end of my story.
> All the sad things you've heard about
> I've told because they are true—
> the life of every gaucho you see
> is woven thick with misfortunes.
>
> But he must fix his hope
> in the God who created him.
> And with that I'll take my leave.
> I've related in my own way
> EVILS THAT EVERYONE KNOWS ABOUT
> BUT NO ONE TOLD BEFORE.
>
> (177)

With the phrase "every gaucho you see," Hernández makes Fierro
a representative of the rural poor generally who most suffered
under Mitre and Sarmiento. Moreover, with the ending in capital
letters, he insists that Argentine liberalism, when it wasn't persecuting the gauchos, damned them through neglect and mar-
ginalization. The gauchos simply did not figure in the liberal dream
of Europeanization and progress. They were ignored, outcast, and
marginal; necessary only for rigging elections and fighting wars. In
short, Hernández sees his primary mission as that of giving voice to

the voiceless, of making a place for the excluded, of inscribing the gaucho into Argentina's guiding fictions.

The first edition of *El gaucho Martín Fierro*, published on November 28, 1872, received little critical notice in Buenos Aires, but in the countryside it was a different story. The first printing sold out in two months, and in less than two years the poem had gone through seven editions. Sections of the poem were also published in newspapers throughout Argentina and Uruguay. But most interesting of all, for the first time in the history of the gauchesque, a gauchesque work actually became popular among the gauchos themselves, some of whom, although illiterate, reportedly learned the poem from memory. The early success of *Martín Fierro* among the popular classes no doubt derives from its political message. For the first time, the gauchos heard recounted in their own language the alienation, hardship, and frustration that were constants of their existence.

Despite the poem's popularity, educated critics virtually ignored it until the early 1900s. Key works in the critical revision of attitudes toward *Martín Fierro* are Leopoldo Lugones's *El payador* of 1916 and Ricardo Rojas's muiltivolume work, *La literatura argentina*, published between 1917 and 1922. Both Rojas and Lugones consider *Martín Fierro* a national epic, the first witness of an autochthonous Argentine soul, incarnate in the gauchos and their archetypal representative, Martín Fierro. Peronist populists made of Martín Fierro a battlecry against the abuses of Argentine liberalism. Typical is the following statement from Raúl Scalabrini Ortiz, taken from a lecture titled "The Enemies of the Argentine People," delivered on July 3, 1948, when Peronism was at its apex: "the oligarchy governed the country with no concern beyond the ambition and selfishness of their own. . . . *Martín Fierro* is the tragedy of the entire pueblo" (*Yrigoyen y Perón* 14–15). Peronist writers like Pedro de Paoli in *Los motivos del Martín Fierro en la vida de José Hernández* (1968) and Fermín Chávez in *José Hernández* (1973) continue to use Martín Fierro as a nationalist banner and symbol of populist protest.

As would be expected in this divided country, liberal critics have produced alternate views of Martín Fierro. Writers like Ezequiel Martínez Estrada in *Muerte y transfiguración de Martín Fierro* (1948) and Jorge Luis Borges in *Aspectos de la literatura gauchesca*

(1950) prefer praising the work's "universalism," thus dismissing the poem's obvious political emphasis. A recent work of "anti-Hernández" criticism is Tulio Halperín Donghi's *José Hernández y sus mundos* (1985), which suggests that Hernández's concern for the gaucho was paternalistic at best and exploitative at worst. Indeed, Halperín's study, although extensively documented and highly informative, seems primarily aimed toward destroying a favorite nationalist icon. In sum, *El gaucho Martín Fierro* grew out of a profoundly divided society; discussion of the poem continues to reflect that essential division.

In 1879 José Hernández published a sequel to *El gaucho Martín Fierro* titled *La vuelta de Martín Fierro* (The return of Martín Fierro). Not only is the sequel literarily inferior to the earlier poem; it reflects a fundamentally different view of the gaucho—a view prompted by changes in Argentina and changes in Hernández's circumstances. Before discussing the sequel, I will look at its political and social context as well as an important debate on free trade versus protectionism that arose in the mid-1870s. I will then discuss *The Return of Martín Fierro.*

In early 1873, López Jordán again invaded Argentine territory. Sarmiento immediately ordered the arrest of López Jordán sympathizers, thus compelling Hernández to flee Buenos Aires for Montevideo. On June 28, 1873, government soldiers trounced López Jordán's irregular troops, forcing the would-be caudillo to return to Uruguay. Barred from Buenos Aires, Hernández took a job with *La Patria*, an Argentine newspaper in exile, from which he fulminated against the Buenos Aires government. He also joined a movement to get Brazilian support for *jordanismo*, which not only failed but also undermined his criticism of Mitre for getting entangled with Brazil during the War of the Triple Alliance (Chávez, *José Hernández* 95).

In the meantime, new political winds were blowing in Buenos Aires which would eventually cause a remarkable transformation in Hernández's political attitudes. With Sarmiento's term drawing to a close, Mitre tried to regain the presidency. Despite Mitre's political maneuvering, Sarmiento's Minister of Education, Nicolás Avellaneda, won the elections. Mitre immediately cried fraud, perhaps with justification, although the elections of 1874 were probably no more dishonest than others of the period. A month after losing,

Mitre organized a militia and tried to overthrow the government. Government forces quickly defeated the would-be coup, court-martialed Mitre, and condemned him to death. Hernández quickly denounced Mitre's hypocrisy. In the October 24, 1874, edition of *La Patria*, Hernández wrote: "Mitre again seeks to aggrandize himself, satisy his insatiable ambitions, and secure his rule of [Argentina], submitting her to his will and whim. A mediocre general, clumsy revolutionary, inept politician, and lousy writer, he lives and has always lived in a mysterious dream world. . . . Always a bad influence, he brings blood, fire and devastation everywhere" (*Artículos periodístics de José Hernández* 69). Although the pragmatic Avellaneda quickly pardoned Mitre, the incident ended . Mitre's chances of ever regaining the presidency.

Mitre's fall from political grace signaled that power had finally passed to a new generation. Of that generation, Avellaneda was prototypical, favoring economic progress to the ideological and personal rivalry of his predecessors. Avellaneda expanded the liberal economic policies begun under Mitre which offered liberal tax exemptions, land, and subsidies of public funds, much of them borrowed, to attract foreign investment, mostly British. The Argentine economy became even more tied to Great Britain, which provided a market for Argentine exports, investment (and control) in transporation and communications, and credit for both public and private sectors (Ferns 323–373). Avellaneda also continued the unfortunate practice, begun by Mitre, of servicing existing debt with new loans, a policy that worked reasonably well during periods of rapid growth but led to disaster during economic contractions (Rock, *Argentina* 147). With the Paraguayan War behind him, Avellaneda intensified the wars of displacement and extermination against the Indians, thereby making available large tracts of new lands. These lands were intended for immigrants who would fill Alberdi's dictum *gobernar es poblar*, "to rule is to settle." Yet, although immigrants arrived in large numbers and Argentina enacted laws similar to the United States Homestead Act, many newcomers failed to obtain land.

Several reasons explain the failure of Argentine homesteading. First, much of the new land offered limited agricultural potential because it was too infertile or too far from transportation. The best lands in Argentina were those near the waterways, along the northern edge of the Province of Buenos Aires and the Littoral, and these for the most part already belonged to the oligarchy. Second, Argentine banks made no attempt to extend credit to small landowners; indeed, the banks often required land as collateral, a policy that allowed credit only to the already rich (Díaz Alejandro, *Essays on the Economic History of the Argentine Republic* 35–40, 151–159). The result was change without change. As historian David Rock notes, "Although the country was undergoing profound change and development, and a new [immigrant] population was forming, no concomitant change occurred in the distribution of wealth nor in the power structure. In different parts of the country landowning and mercantile groups had slowly patched up their earlier differences, but the outcome of this accommodation was a society heavily biased toward the oligarchy" (Rock, *Argentina* 141–142).

Saying that wealth and power remained in the same hands, however, does not mean a lack of economic activity. During the 1870s, land speculation in the Province of Buenos Aires and along the Littoral drove prices up by as much as 1,000 percent. Federal and provincial governments as well as individuals contracted heavy debts from foreign creditors, often using overvalued land as collateral. By the mid-1870s, bust became inevitable, and Argentina entered its first nationwide depression. The depression prompted a lengthy congressional debate on the future of the Argentine economy, and identified what might be called a populist position in economic matters.

The great themes of the debate, protectionism versus free trade, were of course far from new. The mercantalist economy of the Spanish Empire based itself on protectionist practices by which Spain sought to safeguard its colonial markets from outsiders. As discussed in chapter 2, Mariano Moreno in his *Respresentación de los hacendados* of 1809 was one of the first to argue against mercantilism and in favor of free trade, a position he later reversed in his famous Plan. Artigas writing in 1816 opposed open economic borders. Alberdi favored protectionism in his *Fragmento preliminar*, argued in favor of free trade in *Las bases*, and later reverted to his previous position. These, however, remained largely theoretical questions until President Mitre in 1862 opened the Argentine economy to foreign investors and creditors, mostly British. The outcome was a kind of development by which Argentina supplied raw goods and a ready market for British manufactures while its own industrial potential went unrealized. In such an economy, Argentine landowners and middlemen acquired great wealth to the exclusion of the mass of workers confined to menial jobs as peons, packers, and stevedores. It was precisely this state of affairs that provoked the debates of the 1870s.[4]

Arguments in support of free trade as cited by the Mitre and Sarmiento governments derived from Adam Smith and David Ricardo, both useful although perhaps unwitting servants of British expansionism. Free-trade theories dominated instruction on economics in Buenos Aires universities where the standard textbook was a Spanish translation of Joseph Garnier's 1858 manual *Abrégé des éléments de l'économie politique*, which drew heavily from the free-trade theories of Smith, Quesnay, Malthus, and Ricardo (Chiaramonte, *Nacionalismo y liberalismo* 126). President Avellaneda was a principal supporter of free trade. To defend his new tax program, Avellaneda wrote that his administration governed on "the broad base of international free trade . . . [since] free trade is what most behooves all new countries and the special conditions of [Argentina]" (cited in Chiaramonte 113).

As the crisis in the mid-1870s deepened, attacks on free trade came from several sources, most under the tutelage of historian Vicente Fidel López, who, as mentioned in chapter 7, was a major critic of Mitre's historiography. López argued that Argentina's error was its blind faith in European economic theories that did not take into account that "every economic theory will produce different results according to the nature and situation of the country where it is applied" (Chiaramonte 129). Carlos Pellegrini, an ally of López's who would become president in 1890, continued the argument saying that "although free trade can develop an industry that has already acquired a certain vigor . . . it kills new industry" just as "too much air kills the young shoots of a plant" (cited in Chiaramonte 129). But without question the most remarkable statement of the protectionist position belongs to Emilio de Alvear, who, in three famous letters to *La Revista de Buenos Aires*, attacks Fed-

4. For a detailed description of the economic context of the debate and the debate itself, see José Carlos Chiaramonte's *Nacionalismo y liberalismo económicos en Argentina, 1860–1880*. Also helpful is Chiaramonte's essay "La crisis de 1866 y el proteccionismo argentino en la década del 70."

"the improvisatory and excessively liberal nature" of Argentine trade policy. He further protests that "Free trade makes no sense for [Argentina]" and argues that Argentina should follow the protectionist example of the United States, where in fact industry was heavily protected against foreign, and especially British, competition until the 1930s. But more important, Alvear finds a tacit admission of inferiority in liberalism's willingness to make Argentina nothing but a big farm. "Why," he asks, "do [liberals] doubt and minimize the ability of Argentina? Do they perhaps believe in privileged races?" (cited in Chiaramonte, "La crisis de 1866" 214–215). And once again we see how populist thinking attacks Argentine liberalism for failing to believe in Argentina and the Argentine people. In essence, Alvear, like Guido y Spano and Andrade, maintains that a deep sense of inferiority underlies liberalism's obsession for imported culture and technology and its willingness to consign Argentina to the role of "big farm."

The congressional debate on free trade lasted several years but produced little in new legislation and no change in Argentina's concept of its role in the world. In 1877, a new tariff law was passed which granted protection to three products, sugar, wine, and wheat. But as these were agricultural products, the new law did not alter liberalism's basic view of Argentina's role in the world division of labor. The big farm merely became bigger. This particular dispute surrounding free trade died as Argentina in the 1880s entered another cycle of boom, but with the economic crisis of 1890 a powerful current favoring protectionism surfaced again (Rock, *Argentina* 149–152). Protectionist sentiment would smolder well into this century, heating up during moments of economic hardship, and eventually contribute to an ill-advised economic policy under Perón. But I get ahead of my story.

Avellaneda's nonpartisan devotion to "progress" also cooled the personalist passions of his predecessors and created an atmosphere in which disagreements could be resolved without war. Favoring the limited, upper-class pluralism that always defined Argentine democracy, he appointed porteños and provincials, ex-Rosistas and Unitarians to important posts. Moreover, by naming autonomist Adolfo Alsina Minister of Defense, he allayed, temporarily at least, porteño fears of provincial domination. At the same time, he strengthened his support in the interior by helping form a league of provincial governors who could count on special favors in return for supporting Buenos Aires, even if it meant stuffing ballot boxes.

The relative peace of Avellaneda's presidency was also served by the fact that the political antagonists of the past were growing old. Sarmiento continued in public life for a time, first as a senator and later in an abortive campaign to regain the presidency, but eventually, much saddened by the corruption that appeared endemic in the new republic, he retired to write his *Memorias* and the racialist *Conflicto y armonías de las razas en América*, both pessimistic reflections on what he saw as Argentina's political failure. Alberdi returned to Buenos Aires in 1878 after being named senator from his home province of Tucumán. A tired, frightened, sentimental old man, he was devastated by the daily criticism and confrontation of political life and eventually returned to Paris, where he died in 1884. Mitre remained in public life as a senator from the Province of Buenos Aires and a highly visible historian and journalist, but despite his flirations with different political groups, his political power diminished with age. Of the populist writers, Olegario Andrade died in 1882, and Guido y Spano became an avuncular senior poet, ceremoniously admired but generally ignored.

The spirit of accommodation that characterized Avellaneda's presidency also provides the necessary backdrop for *The Return of Martín Fierro* and the extraordinary transformation of José Hernández from provincial rebel to respected public servant, prosperous businessman, and moral preceptor of untutored gauchos. In January 1875, weeks after Avellaneda took office, Hernández returned to Buenos Aires. Writing for *La Libertad*, he immediately showed his old spirit in a newspaper debate with Sarmiento over the relative merits of his *Vida del Chacho*, which had recently been republished (Chávez, *José Hernández* 105–114). But Hernández was tired of being an itinerant journalist with a cause. He now had a family and wanted a calmer life. Besides, there was money to be made. Working first as a land agent and later on the board of directors of a mortgage bank, he acquired a small fortune and in the process contributed to the very concentration of property he once condemned. He continued dabbling in politics but had trouble identifying with any party in Buenos Aires. He rightly viewed the Autonomists' concern for states' rights as a legitimate descendant of

eralism, but was put off by their separatist tendencies. Hernández's political contacts eventually paid off. In March 1879 he was
elected representative and later senator to the legislature of the
Province of Buenos Aires where he served until his death in 1886.

In this life of relative comfort, Hernández elaborated a different
view of the gaucho, or better said, he focused on themes that in his
earlier work were more implied than explicit. The change in Hernández's life and the change in Argentina are well reflected in the two
parts of Martín Fierro. *El gaucho Martín Fierro* of 1872, is primarily
a poem of protest. Except for allusions to a lost paradise which
suggest life on a large estancia, it prescribes little to improve the
gaucho's existence. As such it cohered well with the circumstances of
Hernández's own life in 1872; like Fierro, Hernández was a wanted
man with an uncertain future, living on the run and fighting for a lost
cause. In contrast, *The Return of Martín Fierro* was written seven
years later during a period of relative calm when Hernández had
gained a stake in the new Argentina of pragmatism, wealth, and
progress. As a successful businessman with a political future, he lost
his taste for violent rebellion. Moreover, with the conclusion of
Roca's successful "Conquest of the Desert," the specific injustice—
mistreatment of gauchos in the border wars—addressed in Part I
(Hernández's *The Gaucho Martín Fierro*) became a thing of the past,
although gauchos still remained on the margin of political life generally. In this new world, Hernández decided the gaucho most needed
instruction toward finding a place in, rather than against, the system. He also concluded that since Argentina is after all an agricultural nation, the gauchos and their knowledge of the countryside
constitute a national resource that should be protected, included,
and developed for the good of the entire country. As José Pablo
Feinmann points out, Hernández's ideas in this regard owe much to
Alberdi's argument that Argentina's civilization could not be separated from her wealth—and that her wealth was in the countryside.
Hernández takes Alberdi's argument one step further, maintaining
that Argentina's agricultural potential cannot be realized apart from
the well-being of her agricultural laborers (Feinmann 176–179). As a
result, *The Return of Martín Fierro* is both a justification for the new
Argentina and an advice manual written for gauchos on how to become good, productive, acquiescent citizens.

To meet this agenda, Hernández adopted for *The Return* a structure that is part narrative, part framing tale for interpolated stories, part philosophical debate, and part lecture on moral and civic virtues. In addition, unlike the earlier poem, *The Return* is targeted specifically toward the gauchos. *El gaucho Martín Fierro* was written to rouse the indignation of educated readers against excesses of the liberal governments. As it turned out, it was scarcely noticed by educated readers but acquired extraordinary popularity among the gauchos themselves, a fact that surprised even Hernández. In *The Return* gauchos become the target audience as well as the subject of the text. They are, however, an audience Hernández repeatedly patronizes. As he explains in the foreword to *The Return*, the sequel is "destined to awaken the intelligence and love of reading among a nearly primitive people." Hernández further declares that the gauchos will find *The Return* "entertaining, interesting and useful." But he is most intent on imparting moral values: "Teaching them that honest work is the principal source of all improvement and welfare. Instilling in [them] a sense of reverence towards their Creator and disposing them towards good works. Making unattractive and ridiculous widely held superstitions born in [their] state of deplorable ignorance." Hernández further wishes to inculcate in the primitive masses praiseworthy virtues like respect for parents, due reverence for marriage and the family, charity for the unfortunate, and love of truth. Particularly striking is Hernández's insistence that his readers be law-abiding citizens, "lovers of liberty who do not forget to pay proper respect to superiors and magistrates." All this he must do in a book "that does not reveal its intention," using the colloquial language of the gauchos so that they don't realize they are being instructed (*Antología de poesía gauchesca* 1437–1438).

How well does Hernández accomplish this ambitious if seemingly tedious task? Not well at all if we compare Part II with Part I. Except for flashes of humor, sporadic indictments of injustice, and many well-turned aphorisms, *The Return* cannot bear comparison to Part I. The clumsiness of the structure, the forced episodes, the incessant moralizing, and the digressions into dimestore philosophy strain the narrative to the breaking point. Particularly damaging is the virtual disappearance of Martín Fierro as a possible man of flesh and blood; so intent is Hernández on proclaiming moral values that he preempts his character, forcing him to say what

Hernández wants to say and not what would render him convincing. Nonetheless, as an indicator of values in the new Argentina
and of Hernández's betrayal of the populist ideal, it is a text that
demands consideration.

The degree to which Hernández has accepted the values of the
new Argentina is readily apparent in the lengthy, extraordinarily
negative portrait of the Indians presented in the first pages of *The
Return.* The government wants to kill Indians and open their lands
to white settlers; Hernández makes it sound like a moral duty to do
so. The wretchedness of the Indians in Hernández's description
knows no bounds:

> The Indians spend their life
> stealing or lying on their bellies.
> The law of the spear's point
> is the only one they'll respect—
> and what they're lacking in knowledge
> they make up with suspicion.
>
> (*The Return* 205)

> they're savage born and bred—
> there's no beat of compassion
> within a heathen's breast.
>
> (217)

> They leave all their heavy work
> to be done by the women:
> an Indian's an Indian
> and doesn't care to change his state—
> he's born an Indian robber
> and stays a robber till his death.
>
> (219)

Lest anyone remember the extraordinary accomplishments of pre-
Columbian civilizations, Fierro (Hernández) assures us that Argentine Indians were a different lot:

> But I think the pampa tribes
> must be the stupidest of all:
> they're going around half naked,
> but can't even see what's good for them—
> for any one cow that they sell
> they kill five hundred uselessly.
>
> (225)

These verses served one purpose only: to justify the brutal extermination of Argentine Indians currently in progress under General Roca and President Avellaneda. To rationalize genocide, its victims must be viewed as subhuman, beastial, inferior by nature, unopen to improvement. Further, their inability to see profit in cattle gives them no place in The Big Farm that Argentine liberals saw as their national destiny. Hernández concludes with a hymn of praise to their genocide:

> Things like these and others worse
> I saw for many years—
> but if I'm not mistaken
> these crimes are at an end,
> and the savage heathens
> can do no harm any more.
>
> The tribes have been disbanded—
> the proudest of the chiefs
> are dead or taken captive
> with no hope to rise again,
> and of all the braves and their followers
> there are very few now left alive.
>
> (225)

In short, the Indians deserved to die. Alive, they were unfit; dead, they could offend no more. Can we forgive or at least understand Hernández's attitude as a product of the times? As a land agent, Hernández benefited from the wars. Moreover, like his entire generation, he was blinded by a vision of progress that had no place for the Indian. Is it fair then to expect him to comprehend the horror of the genocide? Perhaps not. At the same time, it is disappointing to see the champion of the rural poor use the same racialist arguments against the Indians that his enemies often deployed against the mixed-blood gaucho. Would that he had at least adopted the distant but sympathetic stance of Mansilla's *Una excursión.*

Following this assault on the Indians, Hernández gets on with his story. Cruz dies, victim of "the plague," and Fierro, after saving a white woman captive from the Indians, makes his way back to the pampas "where now / the savage no longer treads" (279). An old friend tells him that the current government no longer persecutes people and that his murder of the Negro is forgotten. Fierro then quite miraculously finds his two sons, the son of Cruz and the son of

the Negro he killed. Each grabs a guitar and sings his tale. Their
interpolated stories return to familiar themes—injustice, hardship,
persecution, corruption—and in their lament we occasionally hear
echoes of moving passages in Part I. The first son spent most of his
life in prison, victim of arbitrary laws and judges. Rather than
counsel rebellion, however, Fierro tells his son to "take notice of
my words [and] there will be no dungeons full. Keep on the right
side of the law" (311). In Hernández's view, the law has changed so
the gaucho should now become a good citizen. The second son
ended up with an unsavory old drunkard named Don Viscacha who
stole for a living but hated seeing animals die. Although of questionable morals, Viscacha is an unlimited source of advice, most it
practical, some of it humorous and ironic. But even in Viscacha's
antimoralisms, we hear a didactic Hernández striving to make the
gaucho a better citizen. Picardía, Cruz's son, narrates a tale filled
with imprecations against the government, management of the frontier wars, fraudulent elections, corrupt judges, and the like. Yet,
although his is the longest, most vivid, and most negative of the
tales, even Picardía suggests that new times are ahead:

> I won't go on repeating the complaints
> of what you suffer there—
> they're things that have been said often before,
> and even forgotten, they're so old.
>
> (419)

Following is a long debate between Fierro and the Negro's son.
Framed as a *payada*, a traditional verbal duel in which each singer
tries to outsmart, out-riddle, or out-improvise the other, the discussion between Fierro and the Negro takes on philosophical dimensions. Yet, when the Negro finally confronts Fierro regarding the
death of his father, Fierro insults him:

> I've never been able to get along
> with any man of low color;
> they generally turn vicious
> when they get their temper up—
> they become like spiders,
> always ready to bite.
>
> (483)

Fierro gives a partial explanation of his crime as the result of his own suffering. But at the crucial moment when he might express regret, he essentially tells the Negro to live with his problems: "Each of us has to pull / in the yoke he finds himself in." Following this final insult, the listeners prevent Fierro and the Negro from fighting. Fierro and his sons then leave the *payada*—slowly so as not to indicate fear.

Up to this point, Hernández has tried to conceal his moralism behind the mask of his characters. But toward the end, realizing, perhaps, that Part II is already too long, he throws caution to the wind, and has Fierro preach a farewell sermon to his children, and by extension to all gauchos. But lest his gaucho readers think they are being preached at by someone who deems himself their superior (e.g., Hernández in the Foreword), Hernández claims authority in popular knowledge: "A life of misfortunes / is the only school I ever had. . . . Better than learning a lot of things / is learning a few things that are good" (489). By rooting himself in popular knowledge and common sense, Hernández also gives a left-handed compliment to the gauchos. In reality, Fierro's proverbs, as ex-president Avellaneda pointed out in a little-known commentary, are drawn from "the Koran, the Old Testament, the Gospels, [and mostly in] Confucious and Epictetus" (cited in Halperín Donghi, *José Hernández* 316). Hernández merely gave them a gaucho vocabulary. Be that as it will, Hernández (Fierro) shows a special preference for sayings that emphasize self-reliance and hard work:

> A man must work
> in order to earn his bread;
> because Poverty's always eager
> to get you in a thousand ways:
> she knocks at everybody's door,
> and if it's a lazy man's, she goes in.
>
> If a man's a good worker
> he'll make the most of the right occasion . . .
> the right occasion is like iron,
> you have to strike while it's hot.
>
> (491)

Similarly, Hernández emphasizes being a submissive citizen and employee:

> No one whose job is to obey
> has an easy time of it,
> but if he's proud he only increases
> the hardship he has to bear—
> if you're the one to obey, then obey,
> and the one who gives orders will behave well.
>
> (495)

Fierro ends his comments and departs with his sons. As they go, Hernández finally emerges as himself to make two recommendations concerning the gauchos:

> He's a poor orphan, and he's the one
> who gets crushed by fortune;
> because no one takes the responsibility
> of standing up for his kind—
> but the gauchos ought to have houses
> and a school and a church and their rights.
>
> (501)

If given these things, Hernández assures us, "The gauchos are the lean leather / that gives the best thongs to make rope" (503). In short, they are the necessary foundation for an agricultural society. Without their labor and knowledge about the land and cattle-raising, The Big Farm cannot grow. Feed, clothe, and include the gaucho, and Argentina can assume its place among nations.

Although Hernández's role as defender of the new Argentina and moral preceptor of the gauchos comes through on virtually every page of Part II, its meandering narrative and interpolated tales make it difficult to classify. José Pablo Feinmann's contention that "the end of *The Return* is nothing more than an expression of the fraternal union of Buenos Aires, the Littoral and the liberal groups in the mediterranean Interior" (181) seems facile and reductive. Yet without taking into account Hernández's vision of the new Argentina and the gaucho's role in it, Part II would appear an impossible hodgepodge with no unifying element at all.

More interesting is what *The Return* says about Hernández's sometime populism. Hernández's dramatic shift from dissident to preceptor is particularly graphic when compared to Sarmiento's views on the gaucho. Nationalist and revisionist criticism in this century has made much over Martín Fierro as the "anti-*Facundo*," the archetypal gaucho who defends Argentine identity against *europeizante* usurpers. Sarmiento claims the gaucho must be changed or eliminated; in contrast, Hernández in Part I gives the gaucho dignity with few recommendations to change him. *The Return*, however, is a different story. As mentioned in chapter 4, although Sarmiento had a clear plan on how to deal with the gaucho—death or forced assimilation through education and intermarriage with superior races—a fundamental ambivalence underlies much of his thinking. Like Hernández, he, too, was charmed by the gauchos' picturesque ways, their poetry, their rustic skills.

The portrait of Fierro in *The Return* is remarkably similar. Fierro is a singer, a repository of popular wisdom, an uneducated savant who possesses skills the country needs. Hernández therefore tells the government to give gauchos "a school and a church and their rights" while advising gauchos to be docile, productive members of the new order. In short, his solution for the gaucho in *The Return*, like Mansilla's recommendations on the Indian question, differs from Sarmiento's in degree, not substance. Moreover, like Mansilla, whatever radical position he may have embraced as a young man disappeared as he became one with the easy prosperity of the 1870s.

Having studied several nationalist writers associated with the Confederation, I now address the question asked at the beginning of our discussion: Did the nationalism of the 1860s and 1870s really offer an alternative to liberal mythologies of nationhood? Nationalism, as noted earlier, has no clear-cut agenda, no single spokesperson, no particular party, no unequivocal leftist or rightist bias, and no consistent repertoire of ideas. What it does have is a tradition of similar attitudes, emphases, and rhetorical gestures stretching back at least to Saavedra, Artigas, and Hidalgo. An important current in Argentine nationalism is populism, although nationalism also includes populism's opposite in Rosista-style paternalism. The populist current in nationalism is seen in the support Alberdi, Guido y Spano, Andrade, and Hernández give to inclusive democracy, and in their recognition of the caudillos as authentic folk leaders of an inchoate democracy, preferable to the high-handed ways of Buenos Aires; it is also seen in Mansilla's insistence that the gauchos and Indians are the true children of the patria. Yet none of these writers could be called populist in a folksy sense. Alberdi writes in terse prose, Guido y Spano loves irony and classical references, Andrade recalls the neoclassical verse of the early Independence period, and Mansilla affects the style of the French *causeur*. Only Hernández cultivates a deliberately populist style in the folksy language of the gauchesque, but this only in his poetry; his prose imitates the clear, largely unemphatic style of Alberdi, whom he much admired. Moreover, Hernández's attitudes toward the gaucho are ultimately more paternalistic than fraternal.

Yet, although none of these writers can be called populist without qualification, their emphasis on authenticity, respect for autochnous values, and concern for inclusive democracy certainly have a populist flavor that would resurface in contemporary Argentine nationalism, particularly in Peronism. No single person speaks for nationalism. Nationalism and its populist handmaiden can best be described as a kind of *Volksgeist*—the unarticulated attitudes of a group, the vague underpinnings of class identity, the partially spoken premises of peoplehood. Despite nationalism's inexactness, however, from our discussion thus far we can outline the general shape of Argentine nationalism as it begins in the nineteenth century. To this task, we turn our attention now.

Argentine nationalism is first and foremost nativistic, proud of the country's Hispanic heritage and its mixed ethnicity. In affirming "who we are as we are," nationalist populism repudiates the "enlightened" racism of Argentine liberalism; Guido y Spano mocks elitist immigration plans to "regenerate our race," Andrade praises El Chacho and the "pariah races" newly arrived to Argentine shores, Mansilla calls the Indians "the true children of the patria," and Hernández turns an outlaw gaucho into a national archetype. Nationalism rejects as well liberalism's negative attitudes toward Argentina's Spanish heritage. Guido y Spano claims that "old Spanish blood" unites decent Spanish Americans everywhere in their refusal to see Mexico dominated by France. The same sentiment led him to sympathize with Paraguay in her war against the unholy trinity of imperial Brazil, the Mitre regime, and their puppet government in Uruguay. Andrade anticipates Rodó's *arielismo* in claiming that the Latin peoples are the legitimate heirs of the Greeks, thus rebuking liberalism's enthrallment to the United States and northern Europe.

The primary enemy of Argentine nationalism is a nebulous group of wealthy Argentines variously called the *oligarchy*, the antinational liberals, or the anti-Argentine *europeizantes*. While the radical democracy of populism is the logical conclusion of much liberal political theory, nationalist intellectuals accuse Argentine liberals of corrupting the language of freedom, of giving lip service to republican democracy while excluding the very people in whose name they would rule. Moreover, nationalists hold that, despite their rhetoric, Argentine liberals are just as quick to resort to violence and corruption as the worst of the caudillos; they are in Alberdi's memorable phrase "caudillos in coattails." In the nationalist view, liberalism is antinational—more interested in cultivating the goodwill of foreign powers than serving the interests of Argentina. Liberal merchants are the greedy servants of foreign bankers and traders, willing to sell out Argentina in order to make a fast buck for themselves and their foreign masters. Nationalism also postulates that the *europeizantes* lack faith in Argentina, that their enthrallment to foreign interests and ideas is motivated primarily by a sense of inferiority. In the nationalist view, the elite are not real Argentines but glittering, hollow imitations of Europeans.

Argentine nationalism also postulates an alternative view of history in which there are two Argentinas inhabiting the same geographic area but never the same arena of power. One is in Buenos Aires and the other, in the Interior. One is articulate and wealthy while the other is inchoate and impoverished. Nationalism sees the caudillos as the authentic, albeit noninstitutional, voice of the Other Argentina. In line with the idea of two countries, nationalism postulates two parallel developments in which the economic interests of Buenos Aires united all porteños, despite their avowed political differences, in a single party, the Oligarchy, while the rural poor had no recourse but the caudillos. In the nationalist view the civil wars that besieged Argentina from the first days of her independence were perpetrated by the porteño appetite for control and wealth. Rather than wars pitting one leader against another, or one idea against another, they were the struggle of one nation against another. Alberdi was particularly influential in focusing attention on the economic aspects of the struggle rather than the ideological differences emphasized by Sarmiento and Mitre.

Historical revisionism as first articulated by Andrade, Alberdi, and Hernández became one of Argentina's most important intellectual currents in this century. In the 1930s Carlos Ibarguren, Ernesto Palacio, Rodolfo and Julio Irazusta, and Raúl Scalabrini Ortiz wrote damning indictments against the "traitorous liberals" who betrayed their country to English capitalism and in so doing enriched mercantile Buenos Aires at the expense of the interior. Later writers like Juan José Hernández Arregui, Rodolfo Puiggrós, Juan José Sebreli, and David Viñas, who became popular between 1955 and 1970, continued beating the same drum. Perhaps the man most responsible for popularizing revisionist sentiment in recent years is Arturo Jaureteche, who in 1968 published a hilarious—and mischievous—book titled *Manual de zonceras argentinas (Guide to Argentine Stupidity)* in which he deflates every liberal pretense, attacks every liberal spokesman, belittles every liberal idea, and defiles every liberal icon that 150 years of Official History had managed to erect.[5]

Also significant in Argentine nationalism is its fascination with strong leaders. No phrase in this regard is more telling than Martín Fierro's lament that Argentina needed "a real *criollo* to set things straight," someone in tune with the nation, a spokesman of the people, an authentic Argentine rather than an ersatz European; in a word, a caudillo. Perhaps Hernández's ill-fated allegiance to López Jordán sprang from a belief that the rebel leader was such a real criollo. Perhaps the rehabilitation of Rosas that reached near-fever pitch in the 1930s originated in such a longing. Perhaps the mystifying success of Perón and Peronism emanated from wanting "a real *criollo.*" Argentine nationalism is impatient. It wants powerful leaders with quick fixes and fast cures.

Argentine nationalism also has a strong isolationist and protectionist current. Reflecting attitudes articulated by Artigas in 1816, Carlos Guido y Spano, Vicente Fidel López, Carlos Pellegrini, and Emilio de Alvear argued against free trade and foreign indebtedness in the 1870s. Those arguments, little modified, still inform Argentine nationalism and are powerful currents in Peronism.

5. Important studies on historical revisionism include Marysa Navarro Gerassi's *Los nacionalistas*, particularly chapters 6, 7, and 8. See also Joseph Barager's "The Historiography of the Río de la Plata Area Since 1830"; Clifton Kroeber's "Rosas and the Revision of Argentine History, 1880–1955"; and Tulio Halperín Donghi's highly critical but well-argued *El revisionismo histórico argentino*.

Nationalism accuses Argentine liberalism of sacrificing Argentine industry and industrial potential to benefit British merchants and manufacturers along with their "anti-Argentine" intermediaries. Nationalism also questions policies by which key services such as transportation and communication were turned over to British developers. Nationalism holds liberalism responsible for limiting Argentina's economic role in the world to that of "big farm," in accordance with Great Britain's economic plan for the world. In addition, nationalism argues that foreign indebtedness compromises national sovereignty, that creditor nations inevitably end up dictating policy to an indebted Argentina. Indeed, nationalism would avoid all foreign entanglements, whether the Paraguayan War of 1865–1870 or World War II, when Argentina was the only Latin American nation to maintain official neutrality up until the very last months of the war.

Nationalism is protectionist and isolationist in intellectual and artistic matters as well. Nationalism charges that the *europeizante* liberals are always too quick to import the latest idea or artistic trend from abroad rather than seek policies and artistic forms that reflect the Argentine spirit. Nationalism, to use Mansilla's phrase, holds that liberalism's "narrow obsession for imitation" (*monomanía de la imitación*) is making Argentines "people for an operetta." Liberal economic and governance policies, imported artistic trends, economic and historical theories developed by "foreign-trained" intellectuals are in short "anti-Argentine." They were made for other countries and have little to do with Argentina. In modern Argentina, Juan José Hernández Arregui has been particularly articulate in attacking "*europeizantes*" and "anti-Argentines" in books significantly titled *La formación de la conciencia nacional* and *La cultura colonizada.* The previously mentioned Arturo Jaureteche is another important critic of the *monomanía de la imitación*. In 1957 he published *Los profetas del odio* (The prophets of hate), a damning indictment of "colonialized pedagogy" accusing Argentine schools of teaching foreign methods, theories, and ideas that lead Argentine youth to misinterpret and undervalue their country. Another of his books, *El medio pelo en la sociedad argentina* of 1966 (very roughly translated as Pretense and social climbing in Argentine society) holds that what passes for high culture in Argentina is all sham, mannerism, affectation,

posturing, and insecure arrogance—attitudes that recall Guido y
Spano's caricature of Argentine liberalism in "¡Ea, despertemos!"

Parallel to nationalism's sense of Argentina's uniqueness is the
notion of *La Gran Argentina,* the country destined to play a major
role in the world. Andrade captures this spirit particularly well in
his poem "El porvenir" (The future), where he suggests that Argentina's role as continental leader in the independence struggle was
merely the first step toward her destiny as a leader among nations.
He further suggests that Argentina is nothing less than the legitimate grandchild of the Greeks, thereby destined to be an intellectual and spiritual leader among nations. By framing his argument in
religious imagery, he confers divine approbation on the nationalist
dream to make real his vison of *La Gran Argentina.*

The dark side of this nationalist vision of greatness is its obsession with conspiracy theories. Nationalism readily admits Argentina's ongoing failure to realize its destiny, but only by blaming
"anti-national" Argentines and their foreign masters who repeatedly thwart Argentina in realizing her spiritual destiny. The nationalist thinkers we have examined demonized Brazil for Argentina's
participation in the Paraguayan War. Later nationalists would de-
monize the British, the Yankees, the CIA, the Vatican, the multinationals, and the Tri-lateral Commission for all that ails Argentina.
Conspiracy theories would emerge in nationalism of both the left
and right as easy explanations of failure. They are heard in the
right-wing fantasies of Federico Ibarguren as well as in the neo-
facist ravings of contemporary Argentina's most visible maker of
coups, Colonel Aldo Rico.

Since nationalism has no stated doctrine, no creed, no program
or platform, it is unlikely that any single person or any single
movement will reflect all the attitudes described above. Yet certain
political movements and intellectuals are, according to the description given above, nationalist in orientation if not totality. In sum,
the shape of Argentine nationalism is large but vague, omnipresent
but indefinite. Although contemporary nationalism differs from
nineteenth-century nationalism in important ways, the nationalism
of Andrade, Alberdi, Guido y Spano, and Hernández still echo in
contemporary politics and remain a potent force, occasionally creative and often disruptive, that has yet to be merged into the
productive life of the nation.

Epilogue

Perhaps the ideal epilogue to this book would be another book, at least as detailed as the present volume, tracing intellectual developments in Argentina since 1880 up to the present. Ideal, perhaps, but not practical. Rather, I will end as I began: with an anecdote.

A naive graduate student intent on interviewing Borges for my doctoral thesis, I first visited Argentina thanks to an OAS grant in 1975. Perón had died scarcely a year before, and his widow, the stunningly incompetent Isabel, was president. My first contacts were friends of Argentine residents in the United States. Without exception these early contacts were unmercifully dismissive in criticizing Peronism, Isabel's political and economic chaos, and the "nazi-onalistas." They were also models of cosmopolitanism, urbanity, and style, conversant with opera, art, literature, Chomskian linguistics, Lacanian psychoanalysis, European cinema, and other subjects required to render one *culto*. The Rivadavians would have undoubtedly recognized them as kindred spirits, and I must say I thoroughly enjoyed their company. I fondly remember endless conversations on every subject imaginable, often in *confiterías*, splendid institutions found on almost every Buenos Aires street corner that exist primarily for practicing the art of conversation. These Argentines were also extraordinarily hospitable toward me as well as indulgent of the "cultural primitivism" educated Argentines frequently find in North Americans.

With time I met Argentines who reflected quite different perspectives. One of these was the woman hired to clean my apartment who after several conversations told me I would never understand Argen-

tina if I spent too much time with Borges. (The limited encounters I
had with Borges convinced her I was spending time with the wrong
people.) Although critical of Isabel, she was loyal to the memory of
Perón: the man who stood up for common people, who put the anti-
Argentine oligarchy in its place, who defended national sovereignty
against foreign capitalism, who made workers feel good about themselves, who safeguarded the country's Catholic traditions, and protected the family. I was later invited to meet her mother, who lov-
ingly showed me her scrapbook replete with newspaper clippings
and pictures of Eva Perón. I also met other Peronists: leftists who
insisted Perón was a revolutionary with a different vocabulary; intellectuals who readily admitted Perón's defects, but still insisted that
Peronism was the only alternative to the liberal *vendepatria*, or
sellers of the Fatherland; Peronist historians who first introduced me
to terms like *Official History* and *historia falsificada;* nationalists
who identified themselves as *rosistas* and called their enemies
sarmientistas, although Rosas and Sarmiento were long dead; a
frightening anti-Semitic zealot who saw Argentina as the last stronghold of true Christianity and argued that only by eliminating anti-
Argentine subversives (including liberationist priests) could Argentina reclaim its destiny as a leader among nations.

The divisions I was observing, with limited comprehension, to
be sure, became particularly visible to me in one of the most
uncomfortable experiences of my life. Just before returning to the
United States, I gave a large party to which I invited people who
had helped me. I naively failed to consider political persuasion in
writing the guest list, and ended by inviting liberals and nationalists, cosmopolitans and populists, *sarmientistas* and *rosistas.* No
sooner had the party begun than several of my guests got into a
heated, unpleasant argument. The liberals talked of national decline as measured in rates of economic growth, inflation, real
wages, productivity, gross national product, social problems, and
the like—all of which made perfect sense to me, a liberally educated person. The nationalists, in contrast, spoke an unfamiliar
language of "being authentically Argentine" and "thinking national." They argued that Argentina's greatest need was a real Argentine president who could resist foreign influences and intuit the
authentic will of the people beyond the bourgeois conventions of
the ballot box. For the life of me I could not make out what they

were talking about—a fact they attributed to my being non-Argentine, a rubric nationalists regularly assign to anyone questioning their assumptions, not just foreigners. But what most impressed me was their rhetoric. My guests were speaking different languages that appealed to radically different guiding fictions. Consensus, or even an appreciation of different points of view, was impossible.

Since that first visit I have returned to Argentina many times and devoted much of my professional life to studying Argentine history and literature. While real changes in Argentine rhetoric are undeniable, I am often struck by how much modern Argentina remains in dialogue with its past, how echoes of nineteenth-century debates still resonate in virtually every discussion Argentines have about themselves and their country, how the rhetorical ghosts of Moreno, Hidalgo, Rivadavia, Sarmiento, Alberdi, Mitre, Andrade, and Hernández continue to haunt the land. These ghosts survive perhaps because Argentina never agreed on its guiding fictions. Argentina is a house divided against itself and has been at least since Moreno tangled with Saavedra. Sarmiento codified the split in his unyielding polarities of civilization and barbarism, and in this century liberals and nationalists, elitists and populists—albeit with many new nuances—continue the debate, often using inherited arguments and images. At best, Argentina's divisions lead to a lethargic impasse in which no one suffers too much; at worst, the rivalry, suspicion, and hatred of one group for another, each with different notions of history, identity, and destiny, lead to bloodlettings like the civil wars of the 1800s and even "the dirty war" of the late 1970s which saw the "disappearance" of thousands of Argentines. While Argentina's recurrent crises obviously have many causes and explanations, I can't help sensing that the competing myths of nationhood bequeathed by the men who first invented Argentina remain a factor in the country's frustrated quest for national realization.

Bibliography

Alberdi, Juan Bautista. *Escritos póstumos.* 16 vols. Buenos Aires: Imprenta Europea, 1895–1901.

———. *Grandes y pequeños hombres del Plata.* Paris: Editorial Garnier Hermanos, 1912. This is a collection of Alberdi's essays.

———. *Las "Bases" de Alberdi.* Ed. Jorge M. Mayer. [1852] Buenos Aires: Editorial Sudamericana, 1969. This book contains Alberdi's entire text of *Bases y puntos de partida para la organización política de la República Argentina.* The title *Las "Bases" de Alberdi* suggests a critical study rather than the critical edition that it actually is.

———. *Obras completas.* 8 vols. Buenos Aires: La Tribuna Nacional, 1886.

Alonso, Carlos. "Facundo y la sabiduría del poder." *Cuadernos americanos* 5 (1979): 116–130.

Andrade, Olegario Víctor. *Las dos políticas.* Ed. José Carlos Maube and José Raed. [1866?] Buenos Aires: Editorial Devenir, 1957.

———. *Obras poéticas.* Ed. Benjamín Besualdo. Buenos Aires, 1887.

———. *Obras poéticas.* Ed. Eleutorio F. Tiscornia. Buenos Aires: Academia Argentina de Letras, 1943.

Angelis, Pedro de. *Acusación y defensa de Rosas.* Ed. Rodolfo Trostiné. Buenos Aires: Editorial "La Facultad," 1945.

Antología de la poesía gauchesca. Ed. Horacio Jorge Becco. Madrid: Aguilar, 1972.

Artigas, José. *Archivo Artigas.* 20 vols. Montevideo: Comisión Nacional Archivo Artigas, 1950–1981.

———. *Citas a Artigas.* Montevideo: Ediciones Grito de Ascencio, 1979.

———. *José Artigas, Documentos: Compilación y prólogo.* Ed. Oscar H. Bruschera. Havana: Casa de las Américas, 1971.

Assunçao, Fernando O. *El gaucho.* Montevideo: Imprenta Nacional, 1963.

Azcuy Ameghino, Eduardo. *Artigas en la historia argentina.* Buenos Aires: Corregidor, 1986.

Barager, Joseph R. "The Historiography of the Río de la Plata Area Since 1830." *The Hispanic American Historical Review* 39 (Nov. 1959): 588–642.

Barba, Fernando E. *Los autonomistas del 70.* Buenos Aires: Editorial Pleamar, 1976.

Belgrano, Manuel. *Autobiografía.* [1814] Buenos Aires: Editorial Universitaria de Buenos Aires, 1966.

Bercovitch, Sacvan. *The American Jeremiad.* Madison: The University of Wisconsin Press, 1978.

———. *The Puritan Origins of the American Self.* New Haven: Yale University Press, 1975.

Besualdo, Benjamin, ed. "Prólogo. In Olegario Victor Andrade, *Obras poéticas.* Buenos Aires, 1887.

Bolívar, Simón. *Obras completas.* 3 vols. Ed. Vincente Lecuna. Havana: Editorial Lex, 1950.

Borges, Jorge Luis. *El idioma de los argentinos.* Buenos Aires: Peña Del Guidice, 1928.

———. *Obras completas.* Buenos Aires: Emecé Editores, 1974.

Borges, Jorge Luis et al. *Obras completas en colaboración.* Buenos Aires: Emecé Editores, 1979.

Bosch, Beatriz. *Urquiza y su tiempo.* Buenos Aires: Editorial Universitaria de Buenos Aires, 1971.

Bruschera, Oscar H., ed. "Prólogo." In José Artigas, *José Artigas, Documentos: Compilación y prólogo* 9–56. Havana: Casa de las Américas, 1971.

Bunkley, Allison Williams. *The Life of Sarmiento.* Princeton: Princeton University Press, 1952.

Busaniche, José Luis. *Historia argentina.* Buenos Aires: Ediciones Solar, 1965.

Caillet-Bois, Julio. "Introducción a la poesía gauchesca." In Rafael Alberto Arrieta, ed., *Historia de la literatura argentina* 3:51–89. Buenos Aires: Ediciones Peuser, 1959.

———, ed. "Prólogo." In Lucio V. Mansilla, *Una excursión a los indios ranqueles* i–xlii. Mexico City: Fondo de Cultura Económica, 1947.

Caillet-Bois, Ricardo R. "La historiografía." In Rafael Alberto Arrieta, ed., *Historia de la literatura argentina* 34–80. Buenos Aires: Ediciones Peuser, 1960.

Carbia, Rómulo D. *Historia crítica de la historiografía argentina.* La Plata: Facultad de Humanidades de la Universidad de La Plata, 1939.

————. *La Revolución de Mayo y la Iglesia*. Buenos Aires: Editorial Huartes, 1945.

Chávez, Fermín. *José Hernández*. 2d ed. Buenos Aires: Plus Ultra, 1973.

————. *José Hernández: Periodista, político y poeta*. [1959] Buenos Aires: Plus Ultra, 1973.

Chiaramonte, José Carlos. "La crisis de 1866 y el proteccionismo argentino en la década del 70." In Torcuato S. Di Tella and Tulio Halperín Donghi, eds., *Los fragmentos del poder* 171–215. Buenos Aires: Editorial Jorge Alvarez, 1969.

————. *Nacionalismo y liberalismo económicos en Argentina, 1860–1880*. Buenos Aires: Solar/Hachette, 1971.

Concolorcorvo (Carrió de la Vandera, Alonso). "An Unflattering Glimpse of the Gauchos," trans. Irving A. Leonard. In Emir Rodríguez Monegal, ed., *The Borzoi Anthology of Latin American Literature*. New York: Alfred A. Knopf, 1977.

Coni, Emilio A. *El Gaucho: Argentina, Brasil, Uruguay*. [1945] Buenos Aires: Solar/Hachette, 1969.

Cornejo, Atilio. *Historia de Güemes*. Buenos Aires: Academia Nacional de la Historia, 1946.

Díaz Alejandro, Carlos. *Essays on the Economic History of the Argentine Republic*. New Haven: Yale University Press, 1970.

Echeverría, Esteban. *Dogma socialista*. [1837] Buenos Aires: El Ateneo, 1947.

————. *Obras completas*. [1951] Buenos Aires: Ediciones Antonio Zamora, 1972.

————. *Ojeada retrospectiva sobre el movimiento intelectual en el Plata desde el año '37*. Included in *Dogma socialista*. [1846] Buenos Aires: El Ateneo, 1947.

————. "The Slaughterhouse," trans. Angel Flores. In Emir Rodríguez Monegal, ed., *The Borzoi Anthology of Latin American Literature* 210–222. New York: Alfred A. Knopf, 1977.

El Argos de Buenos Aires. 5 vols. Facsimile ed. Buenos Aires: Academia Nacional de la Historia, 1937–1942.

Feinmann, José Pablo, *Filosofía y nación*. Buenos Aires: Editorial Legasa, 1982.

Ferns, H. S. *Britain and Argentina in the Nineteenth Century*. London: Clarendon Press, 1960.

Forbes, John Murray. *Once años en Buenos Aires:* Ed., trans. Felipe A. Espil. Buenos Aires: Emecé Editores, 1956.

Frizzi de Longoni, Haydee E. *Rivadavia y la reforma eclesiástica*. Buenos Aires: La Prensa Médica Argentina, 1947.

Galasso, Norberto. *Vida de Scalabrini Ortiz*. Buenos Aires, 1970.

Gálvez, Manuel. *La vida de Sarmiento*. Buenos Aires: Emecé Editores, 1945.

Gandía, Enrique de, ed. "Estudio preliminar." In Lucio V. Mansilla, *Rozas: Ensayo histórico-psicológico*. [1913] Buenos Aires: Edición Argentina, 1946.

———. *Historia de las ideas políticas en la Argentina*. 6 vols. Buenos Aires: R. Depalma, 1960–1074.

———. "Las ideas políticas de Pedro de Angelis." Included in *Acusación y defensa de Rosas* 93–170. Ed. Rodolfo Trostiné. Buenos Aires: Editorial "La Facultad," 1945.

Ghiano, Juan Carlos, ed. "Prólogo." In José Mármol, *Amalia*. Mexico City: Editorial Porrúa, 1971.

Gibson, Charles. *Spain in America*. New York: Harper and Row, 1967.

González Echevarría, Roberto. "The Dictatorship of Rhetoric/The Rhetoric of Dictatorship: Carpentier, García Márquez, and Roa Bastos." *Latin American Research Review* 15 (1980): 205–228.

Griffin, Charles C. "The Enlightenment and Latin American Independence." In R. A. Humphreys and John Lynch, eds., *The Origins of the Latin American Revolutions, 1808–1826*. New York: Knopf, 1965.

Groussac, Paul. "El Plan de Moreno." *La Biblioteca* 1 (1896).

Guevara, Ernesto "Che." *El socialismo y el hombre en Cuba*. [1960] Mexico City: Siglo Veinte, 1971.

Guido, Tomás. *Autobiografía*. In *Memorias y Autobiografías*. 3 vols. [1855] Buenos Aires: M. A. Rosas, 1910.

Guido y Spano, Carlos. *Ráfagas*. 2 vols. Buenos Aires: Igon Hermanos Editores, 1879.

Gutiérrez, Juan María, ed. "Noticias biográficas sobre Don Esteban Echeverría." In Esteban Echeverría, *Dogma socialista*. [1837] Buenos Aires: El Ateneo, 1947.

———. *Origen y desarrollo de la enseñanza pública superior en Buenos Aires*. [1868] Buenos Aires: La Cultura Argentina, 1915.

———. "Vida de Esteban Echeverría." In Esteban Echeverría, *Obras completas* 9–52. [1951] Buenos Aires: Ediciones Antonio Zamora, 1972.

Halperín Donghi, Tulio. *José Hernández y sus mundos*. Buenos Aires: Editorial Sudamericana, 1985.

———. *El pensamiento de Echeverría*. Buenos Aires: Editorial Sudamericana, 1951.

———. *Politics, Economics and Society in Argentina in the Revolutionary Period*. Trans. Richard Southern. Cambridge: Cambridge University Press, 1975.

————. *El revisionismo historico.* Mexico City: Siglo Veintinino Editores, 1971.

Hegel, G. W. F. *The Philosophy of History.* Ed. C. J. Friedrich. New York: Dover Publications, 1956.

Henríquez Unreña, Pedro. *Las corrientes literarias en la América Hispana.* Mexico City: Fondo de Cultura Económica, 1949.

Hernández, José. *Artículos periodísticos de José Hernández.* Ed. Walter Rela. Montevideo: Editorial El Libro Argentino, 1967.

————. *The Gaucho Martín Fierro.* (Bilingual edition; English version by C. E. Ward). Ed. Frank G. Carrino and Albert J. Carlos. [1872] Albany: State University of New York Press, 1967. Also includes *The Return of Martín Fierro* [1879].

————. *Personalidad parlamentaria de José Hernández.* La Plata: Cámara de Diputados de la Provincia de Buenos Aires, 1947.

————. *Prosas de José Hernández.* Ed. Enrique Herrero. Buenos Aires: Editorial Futuro, 1944.

————. *Prosas y oratoria parlamentaria.* Ed. Rafael Oscar Ielpi et al. Buenos Aires: Editorial Biblioteca, 1974.

Hernández, Pablo. *Conversaciones con el Teniente Coronel Aldo Rico* and *De Malvinas a la Operación Dignidad.* Buenos Aires: Editorial Fortaleza, 1989.

Hernández, Rafael. *Pehaujó: Nomenclatura de las calles.* Buenos Aires, 1896.

Hernández Arregui, Juan José. *La formación de le conciencia nacional.* Buenos Aires: Ediciones Hachea, 1960.

————. *Imperialismo y cultura: La politica de la inteligencia argentina.* Buenos Aires: Editorial Amerinda, 1957.

Herring, Herbert. *A History of Latin America from the Beginnings to the Present.* 2d ed. New York: Alfred A. Knopf, 1965.

Ibarguren, Carlos. *Juan Manuel de Rosas, su vida, su tiempo, su drama.* [1930] Buenos Aires: Librería "La Facultad" de Juan Roldán y Cia, 1933.

————. *Las sociedades literarias y la revolución argentina.* Buenos Aires: Espasa Calpe Argentina, 1937.

Ibarguren, Federico. *Nuestra tradición histórica.* Buenos Aires: Ediciones Dictio, 1978.

Ingenieros, José. *La evolución de las ideas argentinas.* 2 vols. [1918] Buenos Aires: Editorial Futuro, 1961.

————. *Los iniciadores de la sociología argentina: Sarmiento, Alberdi y Echeverría.* Buenos Aires: P. Ingenieros, 1928.

Irazusta, Julio. *Breve historia de la Argentina.* 2d ed. Buenos Aires: Editorial Independencia, 1981.

————. *Ensayos históricos.* [1952] Buenos Aires: Editorial Universidad de Buenos Aires, 1968.

————. *Tomás Manuel de Anchorena.* [1950] Buenos Aires: Editorial Huemul, 1962.

Irazusta, Julio, and Rodolfo Irazusta. *La Argentina y el imperialismo británico: Los eslabones de una cadena 1806–1933.* Buenos Aires: Editorial Tor, 1934.

Iriarte, Tomás de. *Memorias.* 12 vols. Buenos Aires: Ediciones Argentinas, 1945.

Jaureteche, Arturo. *El medio pelo en la sociedad argentina.* Buenos Aires: A Peña Lillo, 1966.

————. *Los profetas del odio.* Buenos Aires: Ediciones Trafac, 1957.

Jeffrey, William H. *Mitre and Argentina.* New York: Library Publishers, 1952.

Jitrik, Noé. *Muerte y resurrección de Facundo.* Buenos Aires: Centro Editor de América, 1968.

Jones, Kristine. "Civilization and Barbarism and Sarmiento's Indian Policy" 1–16. Unpublished paper presented at Symposium on D. F. Sarmiento, Harvard University, October 15, 1988.

King, John. *Sur: A Study of the Argentine Literary Journal and Its Role in the Development of a Culture, 1931–1979.* Cambridge: Cambridge University Press, 1986.

Kolinski, Charles J. *Independence or Death! The Story of the Paraguayan War.* Gainesville: University of Florida Press, 1965.

Korn, Alejandro. *Influencias filosóficas en la evolución nacional.* Buenos Aires: Editorial Claridad, 1936.

Kroeber, Clifton B. "Rosas and the Revision of Argentine History, 1880–1955." *Interamerican Review of Bibliography* 10 (1960): 3–25.

La Lira Argentina, o colección de piezas poéticas dadas a luz en Buenos Aires durante la guerra de independencia. Ed. Pedro Luis Barcia. [1824] Buenos Aires: Academia Argentina de Letras, 1982.

La Moda. Facsimile ed. Buenos Aires: Academia Nacional de la Historia, 1938.

Leonard, Irving A. *Baroque Times in Old Mexico.* Ann Arbor: University of Michigan Press, 1959.

————. *Books of the Brave.* Cambridge, Mass.: Harvard University Press, 1949.

Levene, Ricardo. *Fundación de escuelas públicas en la provincia de Buenos Aires durante el gobierno escolar de Sarmiento. 1856–61, 1875–1881.* La Plata: Taller de Impresiones Oficiales, 1939.

————. *Ensayo histórico sobre la Revolución de Mayo y Marianó Moreno.* 3 vols. Buenos Aires: Editorial Peuser, 1960.

Lewis, Wyndam. "De Toqueville and Democracy." *The Sewanee Review* 54 (1946): 557–575.

Lichtblau, Myron I. *The Argentine Novel in the Nineteenth Century.* New York: Hispanic Institute in the United States, 1959.

López, Vicente Fidel. *Historia de la República Argentina: su origen, su revolución su desarrollo político.* 10 vols. [1883–1893] Buenos Aires: Kraft, 1913.

Ludmer, Josefina. *El género gauchesco: Un tratado sobre la patria.* Buenos Aires: Editorial Sudamericana, 1988.

Luna, Félix. *Los caudillos.* Buenos Aires: Editorial Jorge Alvarez, 1976.

Lynch, John. *Argentine Dictator: Juan Manuel de Rosas, 1829–1852.* Oxford: Clarendon Press, 1981.

Mansilla, Lucio V. *Rozas: Ensayo histórico-psicológico.* [1913] Buenos Aires: Edición Argentina, 1946.

———. *Una excursión a los indios ranqueles.* Ed. Mariano de Vedia y Mitre. [1870] Buenos Aires: Biblioteca de Clásicos Argentinos, Ediciones Estrada, 1959.

Mármol, José. *Amalia.* Ed. Juan Carlos Ghiano. [1855] Mexico City: Editorial Porrúa, 1971.

———. *Asesinato del Señor Dr. D. Florencio Varela y Manuela Rosas.* Ed. Juan Carlos Ghiano. [1848] Buenos Aires: Casa Pardo, 1972.

Martínez Estrada, Ezequiel. *Muerte y transfiguración de Martín Fierro.* Mexico City: Fondo de Cultura Económica, 1948.

———. *Radiografía de la pampa.* [1933] Buenos Aires: Editorial Losada, 1961.

Maube, José Carlos, and José Raed, eds. "Prólogo." In Olegario Víctor Andrade, *Las dos políticas.* Buenos Aires: Editorial Devenir, 1957.

Mayer, Jorge M. *Alberdi y su tiempo.* Buenos Aires: Editorial Universitaria de Buenos Aires, 1963.

———, ed. "Prólogo." In Juan Bautista Alberdi, *Las "Bases" de Alberdi.* Buenos Aires: Editorial Sudamericana, 1969.

Mitre, Bartolomé. *Estudios históricos sobre la revolución argentina: Belgrano y Güemes.* Buenos Aires: Imprenta del Comerico del Plata, 1864.

———. *Historia de Belgrano y de la independencia argentina.* 2d ed. 2 vols. Buenos Aires, 1859.

———. *Obras completas.* 18 vols. Buenos Aires: El Congreso de la Nación Argentina, 1938.

Mitre, Bartolomé, and others. *Galería de celebridades argentinas: Biografías de los personajes más notables del Río de la Plata.* Buenos Aires, 1857.

Molloy, Sylvia. "Imagen de Mansilla." In Gustavo Ferrari and Ezequiel

Gallo, eds., *La Argentina del ochenta al centenenario* 745–749. Buenos Aires: Editorial Sudamericana, 1980.

Moreno, Manuel. *Vida y Memorias del Doctor Mariano Moreno.* Reprinted in *Memorias y Autobiografías.* [1812] Buenos Aires: Imprenta M. A. Rosas, 1910.

Moreno, Mariano. *Escritos de Mariano Moreno.* Ed. Norberto Piñero. Buenos Aires: Biblioteca del Ateneo, 1896.

Morgan, Edmund S. *Inventing the People.* New York: Norton, 1988.

Navarro Gerassi, Marysa. *Los nacionalistas.* Buenos Aires: Editorial Jorge Alvarez, 1968.

Pagés Larraya, Antonio. *Prosas del Martín Fierro: Con una selección de los escritos de José Hernández.* Buenos Aires: Editorial Raigal, 1952.

Palacio, Ernesto. *La historia falsificada.* Buenos Aires: Editorial Difusión, 1939.

Palacios, Alfredo L. *Esteban Echeverría.* Buenos Aires: La Tribuna Nacional, 1951.

Palcos, Alberto. *Sarmiento, la vida la obra, las ideas, el genio.* Buenos Aires: El Ateneo, 1938.

Paoli, Pedro de. *Los motivos del Martín Fierro en la vida de José Hernández.* Buenos Aires: Libería Huemul, 1968.

———. *Sarmiento: Su gravitación en el desarrollo nacional.* Buenos Aires: Ediciones Theoría, 1964.

Paz, José María. *Memorias póstumas del brigadier general José María Paz.* 4 vols. Buenos Aires: Imprenta de la Revista, 1855.

Pelliza, Mariano A. *Dorrego en la historia de los partidos unitario y federal.* Buenos Aires: C. Casavalle, 1878.

Peña, Melcíades. *De Mitre a Roca. Consolidación de la oligarquía anglo-criolla.* Buenos Aires: Fichas, 1968.

Perón, Eva. *Discursos completos, 1949–1952.* 2 vols. Ed. Carlos E. Hurst and José María Roch. Buenos Aires: Editorial Megafón, 1986.

Perry, Ralph Barton. *Puritanism and Democracy.* New York: The Vanguard Press, 1944.

Piccirrilli, Ricardo. *Rivadavia y su tiempo.* 3 vols. [1943] Buenos Aires: Ediciones Peuser, 1960.

Prieto, Adolfo. *La literatura autobiográfica argentina.* Rosario: Facultad de filosofía y letras, 1962.

Proyecto y construccíon de una nación. Ed. Tulio Halperín Donghi. Caracas: Biblioteca Ayacucho, 1980.

Puig, Juan de la C., ed. *Antología de poetas argentinos* 10 vols. Buenos Aires: M. Biedma e Hijo, 1910.

Puiggrós, Rodolfo. *Los caudillos de la Revolución de Mayo.* 2d ed. Buenos Aires: Ediciones Corregidor, 1971.

———. *Pueblo y oligarquía.* Buenos Aires: Editorial Jorge Alvarez, 1965.

Ramos, Julio. "Entre Otros: Una excursión a los indios ranqueles." *Filología* (Buenos Aires) 21 (1986): 143–171.

Ramos Mejía, José. *Rosas y su tiempo.* 2 vols. Buenos Aires, 1907.

Ravignani, Emilio. *Antonio Sáenz, fundador y organizador de la Universidad de Buenos Aires.* Buenos Aires, 1925.

Rivera, Jorge B. *La primitiva literatura gauchesca.* Buenos Aires: Editorial Jorge Alvarez, 1968.

Rivera Indarte, José. *Rosas y sus opositores.* Montevideo: Imprenta de El Nacional, 1843.

Rojas, Ricardo. *Sarmiento: El profeta de la pampa.* Buenos Aires: Editorial Losada, 1945.

Rock, David. *Argentina 1516–1982: From Spanish Colonization to the Falklands War.* Berkeley, Los Angeles, London: University of California Press, 1985.

———. *Politics in Argentina 1890–1930: The Rise and Fall of Radicalism.* Cambridge: Cambridge University Press, 1975.

Rodríguez Molas, Ricardo E. *Historia social del gaucho.* Buenos Aires: Ediciones Marú, 1968.

Romero, José Luis. *Las ideas políticas en Argentina.* [1946] Buenos Aires: Fondo de Cultura Económica, 1983.

Rojas, Ricardo, ed. "Noticia preliminar." In Juan Cruz Valera, *Tragedias.* Buenos Aires: J. Roldán, 1915.

———. *El radicalismo de mañana.* [1932] Buenos Aires: Editorial Losada, 1946.

———. *La restauración nacionalista.* Buenos Aires: Ministerio de Justicia e Instrucción Pública, 1909.

Rosenblat, Angel. *Argentina, historia de un nombre.* Buenos Aires: Editorial Nova, 1949.

Rosenkrantz, Eduardo S. *La bandera de la patria.* Buenos Aires: Editorial "Grito Sagrado," 1988.

Ruiz-Guiñazú, Enrique. *El Presidente Saavedra y el pueblo soberano de 1810.* Buenos Aires: Angel Estrada, Editores, 1960.

———. *Epifanía de la libertad: Documentos secretos de la Revolución de Mayo.* Buenos Aires: Editorial Nova, 1952.

Saavedra, Cornelio. *Autobiografía.* In *Memorias y Autobiografías.* 3 vols. [1824] Buenos Aires: M. A. Rosas, 1910.

Sala de Touron, Lucía, Nelson de la Torre, and Julio C. Rodríguez. *Artigas y su revolución agraria, 1811–1820.* Mexico City: Siglo Veintiuno, 1978.

Salessi, Jorge. "La intuición del rumbo: El andrógino y su sexualidad en la narrativa de Eugenio Cambaceres." Dissertation, Yale University, New Haven, Conn., 1989.

Sánchez, Luis. *El pensamiento político del despotismo ilustrado.* Madrid: Instituto de Estudios Políticos, 1953.

Sánchez Reulet, Aníbal. "La 'Poesía Gauchesca' como Fenómeno Literario." *Revista Iberoamericana* 52 (1961): 281–299.

Sarmiento, Domingo Faustino. *Civilización y barbarie: Vida de Juan Facundo Quiroga.* Ed. Raimundo Lazo [1845] Mexico City: Editorial Porrúa, 1977.

———. *Obras de D.F. Sarmiento.* 39 vols. Buenos Aires: Imprenta Mariano Moreno, 1900. Cited as *Obras completas (OC).*

———. *Viajes por Europa, Africa y Estados Unidos.* 3 vols. Ed. Julio Noé. [1849–1851] Buenos Aires: La Cultura Argentina, 1922.

Scalabrini Ortiz, Raúl. *El hombre que está solo y espera.* [1931] Buenos Aires: Editorial Plus Ultra, 1976.

———. *Historia de los ferrocarriles argentinos.* [1939] Buenos Aires: Editorial Devenir, 1958.

———. *Política Británica en el Río de la Plata.* [1939] Buenos Aires: Fernández Blanco Libros Argentinos, 1957.

———. *Tierra sin nada: Tierra de profetas.* [1945] Buenos Aires: Editorial Plus Ultra, 1973.

———. *Yrigoyen y Perón.* Buenos Aires: Editorial Plus Ultra, 1972.

Scobie, James R. *Argentina: A City and a Nation.* 2d ed. New York: Oxford University Press, 1971.

———. *La lucha por la consolidación de la nacionalidad argentina, 1852–1862.* Trans. Gabriela de Civiny. Buenos Aires: Hachette, 1964. (Although this book was translated from a manuscript titled *The Struggle for Nationhood: Argentina, 1952–1862,* apparently it was never published in English.)

Sebreli, Juan José. *Apogeo y ocaso de los Anchorena.* 2d ed. Buenos Aires: Siglo Veinte, 1974.

Stepan, Nancy. *The Idea of Race in Science.* Hamden, Conn.: Archon Books, 1982.

Tiscornia, Eleutorio F., ed. "Vida de Andrade." In Olegario Víctor Andrade, *Obras poéticas* vii–lxxv. Buenos Aires: Academia Argentina de Letras, 1943.

Tjarks, Germán, and Alicia Vidaurret de Tjarks. *El comerico inglés y el contrabando: Nuevos aspectos en el estudio de la política económica del Río de la Plata, 1807–1810.* La Plata: J. Héctor Matera, 1962.

Varela, Juan Cruz. *Poesías.* Ed. Vicente D. Sierra. Buenos Aires: La Cultura Argentina, 1916.

———. *Tragedias.* Ed. Ricardo Rojas. Buenos Aires: J. Roldán, 1915.

Vélez Sarsfield, Dalmacio. "El General Belgrano." In Bartolomé Mitre,

Estudios históricos sobre la revolución argentina: Belgrano y Güemes. Buenos Aires, 1864.

Viñas, David. *De Sarmiento a Cortázar.* Buenos Aires: Ediciones Siglo XXI, 1971.

———. *Literatura argentina y realidad política.* Buenos Aires: J. Alvarez, 1964.

Weddell, Alexander W. "A Comparison of the Executive and Judicial Powers under the Constitutions of Argentina and the United States." *Bulletin of the College of William and Mary* 31 (1937): 37–84.

Weiss, John. *The Fascist Tradition.* New York: Harper and Row, 1967.

Wright Ione S., and Lisa M. Nekhon. *Historical Dictionary of Argentina.* Metuchen: The Scarecrow Press, 1978.

Index

280; Generation of 1837 on, 133–136, 148, 165; immigration and, 279, 280; redistributed, 59–60, 100, 121; Rivadavia's policy on, 100–101, 110, 117; Rosas's policy on, 100, 117, 121; speculation, 280
La Patria, 278, 279
La Reforma Pacífica, 262
Larra, Mariano José de, 128, 139
Larreta, Enrique, 139
Las Heras, Juan Gregorio de, 82, 87, 106
Lastarria, José Victorino, 255
Latifundia, 59
Latins, 245–247, 292, 296
La Tribuna, 238
Lavalle, Gen. Juan Galo, 47, 115; coup/ assassination of Dorrego by, 116, 192, 198, 199, 200–206, 207, 230; v. Federalists, 116–117; Mitre protects, 191, 198, 199–207, 229; v. Rosas, 200; Sarmiento on, 205
Lavardén, Manuel José de, 16
League of Free Peoples of the Littoral, 58
Leonard, Irving A., 14
Lerminier, Jean Louis, 123, 138–139 n. 1
Levene, Ricardo, 41
Liberalism, 45, 215, 262, 298; Alberdi on, 182–183, 293; Andrade on, 245, 247, 282; as antinational, 233, 234–235, 293; as antipopular, 143–144 n. 2; as barbaric, 263, 270–271; as caudillismo in coattails, 293; as corrupt, 269–270, 293; as enlightened racism, 292; as Eurocentric, 258, 295; exclusivist democracy of, 51, 150–151, 293; on gaucho, 11–12, 276; guiding fictions of, 214, 248; Guido y Spano on, 233, 234, 235, 239, 248, 258, 282, 296; Hernández on, 263, 269–271, 276, 277; as hypocritical, 248; in independence movement, 16, 19–20; lacks faith in Argentina, 282, 293; official history of, 188, 190–211, 249, 291, 299; opposition to, 105, 182 (*see also* Nationalism); on Spain, 245, 247, 292
Lima, Peru, 8, 9, 10
Liniers, Santiago, 17, 19–20, 26, 27, 30, 31, 44, 194–195
Literary Society of Buenos Aires, 87–88, 96. See also *El Argos de Buenos Aires*
Littoral, 10, 48, 58, 169, 280
Localism, 45, 46, 221; in Buenos Aires, 22, 88; of *cabildo* system, 10–11; of caudillismo, 5–6, 11; colonial policies affect, 10; isolation encourages, 10

López, Estanislao, 52, 64, 65, 66, 83, 116, 215, 220
López, Vicente Fidel, 85, 129, 164, 173, 208, 211 n. 6; on Buenos Aires, 86–87; on free trade, 281, 294
López Jordán, Ricardo, 226, 253–254, 263–264, 278, 294
López y Plano, Vicente, 7
Los Debates, 172
Luca, Don Tomás de, 86
Ludmer, Josefina, 67
Lugones, Leopoldo, 277
Luján, 11, 101, 109
Luna, Félix, 56
Lussich, Antonio, 264 n. 2

Mackinnon, Alexander, 31
Madariaga, Gen. Juan, 217
Mansilla, Lucio Norberto, 255
Mansilla, Lucio V., 216, 249, 252, 268; as anti-European, 258, 259, 260; as antiliberal, 258–259, 260; on Argentine identity, 258, 259, 260; on Buenos Aires, 258; early writings of, 256; equivocates, 256; on gaucho, 258, 291; guiding fiction of, 258; on Indians, 216, 255–261, 291, 292; v. Mármol, 256; on Mitre, 256; on pampas, 258; on progress, 259–260; on Sarmiento, 251, 255–261; *Una excursión a los indios ranqueles* of, 250, 251, 257–261; writing style of, 292
Mármol, José, 129–130, 140, 141, 256
Martínez Estrada, Ezequiel, 135, 167, 277
Marxism, 222
Mate, 72, 73
Maximilian, 244
Mayo. See Independence movement
Mazorca, 120, 262
Men of Mayo, 22. *See also* Independence movement
Men of '37. *See* Generation of 1837
Mercantilism, 8–9, 15–16, 99, 280
Mexico, 4, 10, 159, 244–245
Mitre, Bartolomé, xiii, 28, 174, 188–213, 219, 223, 262, 283; and Alberdi, 182, 185–186, 189, 194, 211, 221, 227–228, 241–242; on Argentine heroes, 193–194; aspirations/ambitions of, 194–195, 196, 207, 212; on barbarism, 193, 195, 203, 207; on Belgrano, 190–191, 193, 208, 211; biographies/historiography of (*Galería de celebridades argentinas*), 164, 188, 190–211, 221; and British

loan, 240; on caudillismo, 191–192, 193, 195, 203, 209–211, 220, 228–231, 238; censorship by, 251; in Chile, 189; on civilization, 193; on civil wars, 293; coup by, 213, 279; on democracy, 26, 47; on Dorrego, 199, 201–207; on election of 1874, 278; as elitist, 195, 196, 214; in exile, 189, 190; exiles his enemies, 238; Flores supported by, 231, 232, 240; on France in Mexico, 244–245; on García, 191, 198; and Generation of 1837, 188; government of, 212, 213, 224, 227–228, 231, 239, 250–251; on Güemes, 209–211; guiding fictions of, 172, 194, 195; v. Guido y Spano, 233, 234, 235, 238, 239, 240–241, 242, 244–245; v. Hernández, 238, 239–240, 278, 279; on immigration, 227; on Lavalle, 191, 198, 199–207, 229; Mansilla on, 256; on Mayo revolution, 192–193, 194–196; military writings of, 189; on Moreno, 24–25, 191, 192, 193; newspapers of, 172, 173, 187, 212–213, 252; opposition to, 208, 211 n. 6, 238, 239–240, 256, 278, 279; v. Peñaloza, 230–231; defines "the people," 195, 196–197; as porteño apologist, 172, 173, 182, 188, 194, 195–196, 197; on provinces, 224–226; v. Rosas, 189, 197–198; Rosas compared to, 224; and Sarmiento, 229, 237, 252; terrorism by, 224–225, 238, 239; on trade with Britain, 280–281; in Triple Alliance, 231, 232, 234, 237, 238, 240–241, 250–251, 253, 292; v. Urquiza, 172–173, 177, 189, 190, 194, 195, 197, 207, 212, 219, 224–227, 256

Montesquieu, Charles de, 133
Morenistas (Morenista Patriotic Society), 87; on doctrinaire democracy, 47; as elitist, 44–45, 46, 47, 74, 214; on independence, 74; on rule of law, 76; v. Saavedrists, 43–45; found Unitarian party, 43, 44, 47, 51
Moreno, Manuel, 20, 91, 114; on brother Mariano, 25, 26, 32, 191 n. 1, 197; on education, 14–15; on independence, 18, 24–25; as localist, 22, 221
Moreno, Mariano, xiii, 22, 24–46; Alberdi on, 34, 45, 221; authoritarianism of, 28, 29, 30, 46, 95; Catholicism of, 36; compared to Echeverría, 132; compared to Robespierre, 36; death of, 27; on democracy, 26; on economy, 37–38; education of, 102; on education, 30; as

elitist, 28–29, 43; on evil, 39–40; followers of (*see* Morenistas); foreign policy of, 38–39; on free trade, 30–31, 32–34, 38, 44–45, 58–59, 280; guiding fictions of, 23, 39–40, 42, 43, 47; in independence movement/as *mayo*, 18, 24–25, 34, 38, 39, 74, 192; influence of, 42–43; influences on, 25–26, 27–28, 29, 33; Jacobinism of, 36; v. Liniers, 30; Mitre on, 24–25, 191, 192, 193; Manuel Moreno on, 25, 26, 32, 191 n. 1, 197; newspaper of, 26–27, 29; Plan of, 34–42, 205, 280; on pluralism, 29–30; political activities of, 26–27, 30; and Primera Junta, 27, 34, 35, 39; on public opinion, 28; on redistribution, 37–38; *Representación* of, 30–31, 32–34, 37, 135, 280; on repression of dissidents, 35–36, 39–40; v. Saavedra, 27, 36, 44; on secret police, 36–37; on Spanish colonial policy, 26; on state, 37, 40; translated Rousseau, 27, 30; on truth, 28–29; writings of, 27–43
Morgan, Edmund S., xi
Mythology, national, 1–2. *See also* Guiding fictions

Narváez, General, 137
Nationalism, 214–296; Alberdi's, 182, 183, 214, 215–216, 221, 263, 291, 292, 296; alternative history of, 135, 186, 188, 220, 221, 229–230, 291, 293–294; Andrade's, 218–220, 244, 263, 296; as anti-elite, 248, 293; as anti-Europe, 248, 293, 295–296; on authentic Argentine, 216, 275–276; on caudillos, 216, 291, 293; conspiracy theories of, 244, 295, 296; emphathizes with other Latin American countries, 216, 244–246, 292; as federalism, 215; on foreign debt, 295; on gaucho, 11–12, 216; guiding fictions of, 248; of Guido y Spano, 238, 239, 243, 263, 291, 293, 296; of Hernández, 263, 291, 292, 296; on inclusive democracy, 291; as isolationist, 294, 295; on *La Gran Argentina*, 242–243, 244, 248, 296; as opposition to liberalism, 214, 215, 233, 234–235, 248, 292, 293, 295–296, 298–299; Peronism as, 294; as populism, 248, 291–292; on porteños, 248, 293; as protectionist, 294–295; revindicates Spanish heritage, 216, 292; of Saavedrists, 221; on strong leaders, 294; today, 298; writers of, 215–216, 291

Designer: U.C. Press Staff
Compositor: Huron Valley Graphics, Inc.
Text: 11/13 Baskerville
Display: Baskerville
Printer: Princeton University Press Printing
Binder: Princeton University Press Printing